Commercial
Liability
Risk Management
and
Insurance

Volume I

Commercial Liability Risk Management and Insurance

Volume I

DONALD S. MALECKI, CPCU
Insurance and Risk Management Consultant
Donald S. Malecki & Associates, Inc.

RONALD C. HORN, Ph.D., CPCU, CLU
Ben H. Williams Professor of Insurance Studies
Baylor University

ERIC A. WIENING, M.S., CPCU, ARM, AU
Director of Curriculum Development
American Institute for Property and Liability Underwriters

JAMES H. DONALDSON, LL.B., LL.M.
of the New York and New Jersey Bars

Second Edition • 1986

AMERICAN INSTITUTE FOR
PROPERTY AND LIABILITY UNDERWRITERS
720 Providence Road, Malvern, Pennsylvania 19355-0770

©1986
AMERICAN INSTITUTE FOR
PROPERTY AND LIABILITY UNDERWRITERS, INC.

Second Printing • October 1987

Library of Congress Catalog Number   86-72708
International Standard Book Number   0-89463-049-0

Printed in the United States of America

The revision of this text has been made possible through a generous donation to the American Institute by the Florida Gold Coast Chapter of the Society of Chartered Property and Casualty Underwriters in memory of Susanne DiDonna Moore, CPCU, ARM, CPIW.

Susanne Moore was dedicated to the professionalization of the insurance business through continuing education. One sign of this dedication was her pursuit of the CPCU professional designation. She had successfully completed all of the examinations and had met all of the requirements for the designation prior to her untimely death in an airplane crash on August 2, 1985.

The members and officers of the Florida Gold Coast Chapter of the Society of CPCU felt that support for a CPCU text revision would be a way for them to recognize the achievements of Susanne Moore and make a fitting tribute to her memory.

Foreword

Over the years, the American Institute for Property and Liability Underwriters and the Insurance Institute of America have responded to the educational needs of the property-liability insurance industry by developing new programs.

The American Institute maintains and administers the program leading to the Chartered Property Casualty Underwriter (CPCU) professional designation.

The Insurance Institute of America offers programs leading to the Certificate in General Insurance, the Associate in Claims (AIC) designation, the Associate in Management (AIM) designation, the Associate in Risk Management (ARM) designation, the Associate in Underwriting (AU) designation, the Associate in Loss Control Management (ALCM) designation, the Associate in Premium Auditing (APA) designation, the Accredited Adviser in Insurance (AAI) designation, the Associate in Insurance Accounting and Finance (AIAF) designation, the Introduction to Property and Liability Insurance (INTRO) certificate, and the Supervisory Management (SM) certificate.

This is one of the texts developed by the Institute for use in the CPCU program. Throughout the development of this series of texts it has been—and will continue to be—necessary to draw on the knowledge and skills of Institute staff members. These individuals will receive no royalties on texts sold, and their writing responsibilities are seen as an integral part of their professional duties. We have proceeded in this way to avoid any possibility of conflicts of interests.

We invite and welcome any and all criticisms of our publications. It is only with such comments that we can hope to provide high quality texts, materials, and programs. Comments should be directed to the curriculum department of the Institutes.

Edwin S. Overman, Ph.D., CPCU
President

Preface

This text was designed for one of the ten courses in the curriculum leading to the Chartered Property Casualty Underwriter (CPCU®) professional designation. Study aids are provided in a companion volume—the *CPCU 4 Course Guide,* revised annually. The Course Guide contains educational objectives, outlines of study material, terms and concepts, review and discussion questions, and, where appropriate, updated or supplementary reading material. The Course Guide also contains administrative information about the CPCU program and registration forms for the CPCU 4 national examination. Policies and forms are not included in this text, but are available in a *Policy Kit,* revised annually. Both the *Course Guide* and the *Policy Kit* may be purchased from the American Institute.

This text is devoted primarily to the identification, analysis, and treatment of the *liability* exposures faced by modern business firms, professional persons, governmental bodies, educational institutions, and charitable organizations. Additionally, in keeping with the overall goals of the CPCU curriculum, the text includes sections on surety, aircraft physical damage, and auto physical damage exposures and their treatment.

Like the original 1978 edition, this second edition stresses the legal nature of the loss exposures and the corresponding insurance coverages or bonds, supplemented by a description of noninsurance techniques that may be efficacious. In other noteworthy respects, the second edition bears little resemblance to the first.

In recent years, the nature and scope of liability loss exposures have been substantially altered by landmark court decisions and the enactment or revision of applicable statutes. New exposures have emerged. Previously existing exposures have been expanded to formidable proportions. The insurance business has responded, in part, with major changes in the language of most widely used liability insurance forms. And the risk management community has responded, in part, with the use of increasingly sophisticated methods of financing liability losses. As a result of such developments, virtually all of this second edition consists of newly written or extensively revised material. A mere updating would not suffice.

After briefly reviewing the risk management framework and emphasizing the distinguishing characteristics of liability risk management, the first two chapters of Volume I set forth the fundamental legal concepts that govern the liability loss exposures of "commercial entities," broadly defined. Methods of identifying, measuring, and controlling these exposures are elaborated upon in a subsequent chapter, while another chapter is devoted to explaining the basic structure and content of modern liability insurance forms. In the remaining chapters of Volume I, the basics of tort law and liability insurance are applied specifically to the loss exposures and coverages associated with premises, operations, products, completed operations, contractual, environmental impairment, directors and officers, employee benefits, municipal, and railroad protective liability.

Volume II of the text continues to examine specific loss exposures and relevant insurance coverages, including those that may be classified under the headings of motor vehicle, aviation, employers liability and workers compensation, and professional liability. One full chapter is devoted to suretyship exposures and their treatment. Another chapter considers the various methods of financing liability losses. Then, in the concluding chapter, the student is provided with several comprehensive case studies and illustrative risk management programs. These survey cases address both property and liability exposures, based on text material in both this text and the CPCU 3 text, *Commercial Property Risk Management and Insurance.* Their purpose is to give the student the simulated experience of applying both property and liability risk management and insurance principles in a variety of situations.

Completion of this second edition would not have been possible without the teamwork and willing assistance of a great many dedicated professionals. It can truly be said that every single page of the text bears the touch of several authors, editors, and reviewers.

We are especially grateful to the contributing authors, listed separately following this Preface, for writing, rewriting, or revising manuscripts upon which a number of the chapters are based. Their specialized knowledge, writing and research skills, and cooperative attitudes significantly enhanced the overall quality of the text. Ellen L. Klimon, J.D., CPCU ably applied considerable legal knowledge, experience in both risk management and technical writing, and talent in updating, revising, and rewriting much of the material that appears in Chapters 1, 2, and 12 of this second edition. Dr. C. Arthur Williams, Jr., is widely recognized as a highly competent insurance professor and authority and the author of many texts and articles in the field of risk management and insurance—including the text, *Principles of Risk Management and Insurance* used in CPCU 1. Art's expertise shines through in Chapters 3 and 4. Samuel L. Rosenthal, CPCU, ARM, an active insurance consultant, has previously handled many smaller writing and editing projects. However, his most challenging project to date was the manuscript for Chapter 7—a chapter involving several different subtopics in areas of rapid change. Trudy Tappan Rosenthal, B.S.N., M.S., M.A., Sam's wife, has published many articles in the nursing field, and assisted Sam in writing and revising his manuscript. These contributing authors also reviewed some of the chapters drafted by others. Dr. Alexander T. Wells, currently in the aviation department of Broward Community College, formerly worked in the field of aviation production and underwriting, and has previously published books and articles on aviation and aviation insurance. His understanding, experience, and ability to communicate are apparent in the aviation portion of Chapter 9.

Two chapters of this text are adapted, in part, from other sources. Jack P. Gibson, M.B.A., CPCU, CLU, ARM drafted Chapter 14 based on materials previously published by the International Risk Management Institute, Inc. as recognized in that chapter. He also reviewed several other chapters. The garage and truckers portions of Chapter 9 were adapted from an Insurance Institute of America text written for the Accredited Adviser in Insurance (AAI) program, as recognized in that chapter.

Many chapters of this text deal with coverages and copyrighted forms developed by Insurance Services Office, Inc. (ISO). Excerpts from ISO policies are used with permission.

The following persons reviewed major portions of the text and provided constructive suggestions, comments, and edits that significantly improved the completeness, accuracy, and clarity of the presentation: John D. Horton, CPCU, ARM, AIM, Senior Analyst/Auditor, Technical Operations, St. Paul Fire and Marine Insurance Company; Daniel P. Hussey, Jr., CPCU, ARM, AAI, Vice President, Joseph A. Rigg Insurance Agency, Inc.; Larry L. Klein, CPCU, Director of Professional Development, Reliance Insurance Companies; Erin A. Oberly, CPCU, ARM, President, Warren, McVeigh, & Griffin, Inc.; and David C. Sterling, CPCU, CLU, ChFC, CIC, AIM, ARM, AU, ALCM, APA, AAI, ARP, AIC, Secretary, Commercial Insurance Division, Hartford Insurance Group.

Reviewers who provided special expertise in more limited subject areas include Dick McGreal, United States Aviation Underwriters; Carl T. Ernstrom, CPCU, CLU, President, Ernstrom and Hefferon Associates, Inc.; Donald G. Farr, CPCU, Insurance Consultant; Lloyd Provost, President and Dennis E. Wine, Vice President, The Surety Association of America; Bruce T. Wallace, Executive Vice President, National Association of Surety Bond Producers; Michael P. Holm, CPCU, Assistant Vice President—Field Services, Tim Niehoff, CPCU, Assistant Vice President—Bond Department, and Sally Kelsall, Editing—Field Services, Great American Insurance Company.

During an especially busy year, Domenick J. Yezzi, CPCU, Assistant Manager, Insurance Services Office (ISO) coordinated the reviews of many chapters dealing with ISO forms. We are grateful to the following ISO personnel for the special insights provided in their reviews: Michael L. Averill, CPCU, Gary Grasmann, and Lawrence P. Kenny.

Others who provided valuable reviews of portions of the text include Eliot Daniels, CPCU, CLU, ARM, Vice President—Casualty Department, Johnson & Higgins; Michael C. Dowling, M.B.A., CPCU, AAI, Vice President, Fireman's Fund Insurance Company; Homer W. Hilst, CPCU, Bryce Insurance; Robert J. Prahl, CPCU, Assistant Vice President, State Auto Insurance Company; and Colin J. Rose, CPCU, Product Consultant, Royal Insurance.

Despite the extent of the revision in this second edition, the text continues to benefit from the work of the following who served as contributing authors to the first edition: John R. F. Baer, J.D., and Douglass F. Rohrman, J.D., Keck, Cushman, Mahin & Cate; Martin R. Cohen, J.D., Attorney at Law; Clement J. DeMichelis, LL.B., McCaslin, Imbus & McCaslin; Donald J. Hirsch, J.D., Research Director, Defense Research Institute; Anthony M. Lanzone, LL. B. and Alan M. Kramer, J.D., Lanzone & Kramer; Edward S. Silber, J.D., General Counsel, Nelsen Steel Company; Bernard L. Webb, CPCU, FCAS, Professor of Actuarial Science and Insurance, Georgia State University; and George I. Whitehead, Jr., LL.B., former Corporate Counsel, Piper Aircraft.

We are also grateful to all the American Institute staff members who patiently coordinated our efforts, provided us with encouragement and counsel, and assisted in every phase of the project.

Except as noted above, Don Malecki was the primary author of the chapters and chapter sections dealing with insurance coverage. His task was made especially difficult by the extensive policy and forms changes that were implemented by the Insurance Services Office during the time this text was being written. Ron Horn served as the primary author for most of the legal sections that were rewritten, expanded, or added during the text revision process. He also reviewed the entire manuscript and provided detailed suggestions for improvement. Eric

Wiening, as the American Institute staff member responsible for the CPCU 4 curriculum, developed the outlines and objectives for the entire text, coordinated all writing and reviewing activities, edited all chapters, and made the final decisions on all substantive and organizational issues. His work, too, involved a significant amount of drafting, revising, and rewriting. While the late Jim Donaldson was not involved in this revision, his pioneering work as a primary author of the first edition helped to lay the foundation, and portions of his work have survived the extensive rewriting found in this second edition.

Donald S. Malecki
Ronald C. Horn
Eric A. Wiening

Contributing Authors

Ellen L. Klimon, J.D., CPCU
Director, Department of Risk Management
University of Pennsylvania

Dr. C. Arthur Williams, Jr.
Professor of Economics and Insurance
Curtis L. Carlson School of Management
University of Minnesota

Samuel L. Rosenthal, CPCU, ARM
Insurance Consultant
Industrial Insurance Management Corp.

Jack P. Gibson, M.B.A., CPCU, CLU, ARM
President
International Risk Management Institute, Inc.

Dr. Alexander T. Wells
Formerly with Rollins-Burdick-Hunter Co.

Table of Contents

Controlling Other General Liability Loss Exposures ~ *"Pure" Premises-Operations Liability Loss Exposures; Contractual Liability Loss Exposures*

Controlling Motor Vehicle Liability Exposures ~ *Avoidance; Loss Control; Transfers*

Conclusion

General Content ~ *Declarations; Insuring Agreements; Exclusions; Conditions; Definitions; Miscellaneous Provisions; Where These Provisions May Be Found*

Policy Construction ~ *Preprinted or Manuscript; Self-contained or Assembled*

A Policy Analysis Framework

Who Is Insured? ~ *Insurable Interests; What Interests Are Insured?*

What Events Are Covered? ~ *Covered Activities; Covered Causes; Covered Loss Consequences; Locations at Which Coverage Is Provided; Covered Time Periods*

How Much Will the Insurer Pay ~ *Policy Limit or Limits; Defense Costs and Supplementary Benefits; No Limits; Deductibles; Other Insurance; Subrogation*

Insured's Duties Following a Loss ~ *Prohibition of Certain Acts; Notice of the Occurrence; Notice of Claim or Suit; Cooperation with the Insurer*

Background ~ *Early Policies; The Comprehensive General Liability Policy; Owners', Landlords', and Tenants' (OL&T) Policy; Manufacturers' and Contractors' (M&C) Policy; 1966 Revision; 1973 Revision; Broad Form CGL Endorsement; 1986 Revision—Commercial General Liability; The Coverage Trigger—Evolution*

CHAPTER 1

Commercial Liability
Loss Exposures

This chapter is devoted to "commercial liability loss exposures" and their relationship to general principles of risk management. As used here and throughout the CPCU curriculum, the term *commercial* is intended to include all governmental bodies and nonprofit private organizations, as well as all profit-seeking business firms. A *loss exposure* is a set of circumstances that presents a *possibility* of loss, whether or not a loss actually takes place. A *liability loss* is an expenditure of time and money for the investigation, negotiation, settlement, defense, and/or payment of a claim or suit that arises out of a real or alleged failure to fulfill an obligation or duty. Whenever a claim or suit for money damages is brought against an uninsured entity, the entity invariably suffers a liability loss; it must at least investigate the claim and/or defend a suit, even if it does not pay anything to settle the claim and it is not later held liable for damages per se. Accordingly, a *commercial liability loss exposure* is essentially the exposure of a commercial entity to the possibility that a claim for money damages will be brought against that entity.

Subsequent chapters of the text deal mainly with the various liability insurance coverages that are available for specific kinds of commercial liability loss exposures. The bulk of this first chapter is an attempt to explain the fundamental legal characteristics of various liability losses to which a commercial entity may be exposed. To understand the scope and rationale of the coverages and exclusions under modern commercial liability insurance policies, it is first essential to understand the underlying sources and characteristics of the loss exposures that are explicitly or implicitly referred to in such policies. A knowledge of the distinguishing features of a liability loss exposure is also a prerequisite to its effective management, whether or not insurance is available, desirable, or utilized as a technique for handling that particular exposure.

Before exploring the legal foundations of liability loss exposures, the chapter briefly examines the typical objectives of commercial liability risk management, the important respects in which liability loss exposures are unique, and the types of commercial entities that are exposed to the possibilities of sustaining the various kinds of liability losses.

ROLE OF LIABILITY LOSS EXPOSURES IN RISK MANAGEMENT

Typical Objectives of Commercial Liability Risk Management

A commercial entity should formulate its own explicit set of risk management objectives. Yet, with respect to the management of liability risks, there are some common objectives shared by most commercial entities. These typical risk management objectives have been divided into two categories, *pre-loss* objectives and *post-loss* objectives.[1]

Pre-Loss Objectives Though liability loss exposures may or may not result in actual losses, it is important to anticipate the *possibility* of loss. Thus, pre-loss objectives should be accomplished, regardless of whether a loss takes place. Typical pre-loss objectives include the following desired achievements:

- *Economy*—The relative cost of various alternatives should be considered.
- *Reduction in Anxiety*—Loss exposures involve uncertainty, and uncertainty raises anxiety levels. When liability loss exposures have been properly treated, there should be less uncertainty concerning loss.
- *Meeting Externally Imposed Obligations*—Many risk management obligations are imposed by statute or regulation. For example, a variety of regulations require that a workplace be kept free of certain hazards, and the purchase of liability insurance is mandatory in some situations.
- *Social Responsibility*—Society is threatened by actual and potential liability losses. Some risk management measures attempt to reduce the likelihood of liability losses, while others ensure that injured parties can be paid damages in situations where the losses have not been prevented.

Post-Loss Objectives   Once a liability loss takes place, most commercial entities wish to accomplish one or more of the following post-loss objectives.

- _Survival_—This objective means being able to preserve the entity's existence and eventually resume normal operations, at least to some degree. Although this is an important objective, it is not always attained, because liability loss potential is virtually unlimited (as explained later in this chapter).
- _Continuity of Operations_—A somewhat more ambitious objective than mere survival, this objective means continuing operations after a loss with only minimal interruption or impairment. In the context of liability losses, this means having sufficient financial resources to make any payments that might be necessary. It also requires, of organizations engaged in competitive activities or operations, the ability to preserve the reputation of the organization and maintain a flow of customers, patients, clients, donors, or students, as the case may be. It can be difficult for a business to retain former customers or attract new customers, for instance, if the business has suffered a loss of reputation in the wake of a liability claim and its attendant publicity.
- _Earnings Stability_—Even though this may be a lower priority than survival and continuity of operations, earnings stability is still an important goal of organizations that normally have earnings, and revenue stability is likewise important to such organizations as nonprofit hospitals and universities. A large liability loss can create substantial disruptions in the earnings of a business or the revenue of a nonprofit organization. On the other hand, proper planning (such as the sound use of insurance) can help to stabilize loss costs, earnings, and revenues from year-to-year.
- _Continued Growth_—Perhaps the most ambitious objective of all is the desire to continue growing, without noticeable disruption, despite any liability losses.
- _Social Responsibility_—Social responsibility is both a pre-loss and a post-loss objective. Before and after a loss occurs, proper risk management can protect investors, suppliers, employees, customers, taxpayers, and others against losses or inconvenience.

Conflicts Among Objectives   As is true of many other objectives, risk management objectives are not always achieved. Also, some risk management objectives inherently conflict with others. For example, a decision not to buy insurance may seem to achieve the pre-loss

Exhibit 1-1
Techniques for Treating Loss Exposures

CONTROL TECHNIQUES	FINANCING TECHNIQUES
Avoidance	Some Noninsurance Transfers
Loss Control	Insurance Transfers
Loss Prevention	Retention
Loss Reduction	
Separation	
Combination	
Some Noninsurance Transfers	

objective of economy, but it may conflict with the post-loss objective of survival. Or, a drug manufacturer's desire to preserve earnings stability may conflict with its social responsibility objective when it decides whether to recall all products that possibly could be contaminated with poison. A sound risk management program uses a systematic approach to meeting as many of these objectives as possible, with no unacceptable trade-offs. This requires the entity to prioritize its risk management objectives.

The Risk Management Process

Once goals have been set, the risk management process involves:

1. identifying and analyzing loss exposures
   - hazards
   - potential loss frequency or severity
2. selecting the technique or techniques to be used to handle each exposure (see Exhibit 1-1)
   - techniques for controlling loss exposures
   - techniques for financing loss exposures
3. implementing the techniques chosen
4. monitoring the decisions made and implementing changes when appropriate

DISTINGUISHING CHARACTERISTICS OF LIABILITY RISK MANAGEMENT

There is an important sense in which the management of liability loss exposures is unique and problematical. The management of liability loss exposures differs from the management of property loss exposures in a number of ways. Some of these differences are merely differences in degree, yet, taken together, the differences constitute a group or collective of characteristics that is unique. These differences, which may be thought of as the distinguishing characteristics of liability risk management, are as follows:

- the involvement of a third party in insured claims,
- the difficulty of measuring loss potential,
- the effects of changing rules of tort law,
- the so-called "long tail," and,
- the widespread use of contractual transfers.

Each of these characteristics will be explained briefly, in turn.

Involvement of Third Party in Insured Claims

Insured property losses normally involve only two parties—an insured (customarily called the *"first" party*) and the insurer (the *"second" party*). Insured property claims, as those for windstorm damage to a building, are referred to as *first-party* claims, because they are made by the "first" party to the insurance contract. The relationship between these two parties is governed by *contract* law.

In contrast, insured liability claims always involve a so-called *third party*—the claimant. Though not a legal party to the insurance contract, the claimant is obviously an interested party who has various legal rights and remedies. And, in relation to the two legal parties to the insurance contract, the claimant stands as a third "party." This is one reason why insured liability claims are referred to as *third-party claims.* They are *initially* made by a claimant who is not one of the two parties to the insurance contract.

With insured liability claims, the compensatory damages are normally payable, if at all, to the third-party claimant (or the claimant's legal representative) as a matter of *tort law.* Two minor variations exist:

- Under most liability insurance policies, the *insurer* pays compensatory damages directly to the claimant, on behalf of an insured.
- Under the so-called "indemnity" type of liability insurance, the *named insured* pays the compensatory damages directly to the claimant. The named insured is then indemnified or reimbursed by its liability insurer.

Under either type of liability insurance, the claim for compensatory damages is initially made by—and is ultimately payable to—a third party whose entitlement to the damages is governed by the law of torts.

There are some subtleties in the foregoing paragraphs that should not pass unnoticed. In the resolution of the usual *property* insurance claim, the insured is also the claimant; the claimant is dealing directly with an insurer to which it pays premiums; the claimant has a contractual relationship with the insurer; the claimant-insured or its representative has normally chosen the insurer from a number of available alternatives; the claimant-insured can cancel the policy, if it is not satisfied with the insurer's denial or settlement of the claim; the claimant is not an adversary, in the absence of a dispute; and, while the loss payment may be made payable jointly to the insured and another entity, such as a mortgagee, the payments are in essence made to the insured. If there is a dispute that cannot be resolved without litigation between insurer and insured, the court will determine any amount payable under the terms of the policy by applying the law of *contracts*. (Extra contractual tort claims for punitive damages are discussed later.)

In the resolution of the usual *liability* insurance claim, on the other hand,

- the initial claimant is not the insured;
- the initial claimant has no contractual relationship with the liability insurer of the alleged tortfeasor;
- the claimant has not chosen the liability insurer with which it must negotiate;
- the claimant cannot cancel the policy, if it is dissatisfied with the insurer's denial or settlement offer;
- from the outset the claimant is likely to view both the insured and the liability insurer as adversaries, even if the claim is settled without animosity or dispute; and,
- any compensatory damages are payable to the third-party claimant, not to the insured.

Two types of disputes may arise that cannot be resolved without litigation. As with property insurance, if the dispute is between insurer and insured as to whether or to what extent the insurance contract provides coverage for a given claim, the courts will resolve the dispute by applying the law of *contracts*. However, if the issue in question is whether the insured is liable to the third-party claimant for damages, the court will resolve the dispute by applying the law of *torts*. Disputes of both types can arise from the same claim, requiring two separate decisions to determine (1) whether, or to what extent, the insured is *liable* and (2) whether, or to what extent, the insured is *covered*.

Both property insurers and liability insurers have contractual and extra-contractual duties to their insureds. But the duty to defend its insureds against third-party tort claims is a duty that is unique to liability insurers. Moreover, as will be elaborated upon later, the liability insurer frequently must defend its insured, even if the court does not require the insurer to pay damages to the third-party claimant. In this sense, the liability insurer has duties to its insured that the insurer does not have to the claimant. The duties that a property insurer has to its insured are the same as the duties the property insurer has to the claimant, since the insured and the claimant are one and the same.

A partial exception to the foregoing generalizations can be found in the uninsured and underinsured motorists coverages of auto insurance policies. ("UM" coverage is explained in Chapter 8.) What is noteworthy here is that UM coverage is rather difficult to classify. Since UM coverage is provided under a contract between the insurer and its own insured, UM insurance claims are first-party claims, and they are similar to property insurance claims in most respects. Nonetheless, the UM claim is similar to a liability claim in the sense that the damage payments for both types of claims are conditioned upon a finding of negligence, whether the "finding" is a formal court decision or an informal determination by the insurer. (In the case of a hit-and-run motorist, negligence is presumed.) A UM claim made only for bodily injury damages is also similar to a liability claim in another sense; namely, both claimants are entitled to receive from the insurer, up to the applicable policy limits, whatever kinds and amounts of compensatory damages are allowed by law. However, the damages payable for a UM insurance claim are conditioned upon the actual or presumed negligence of the *third party* (the uninsured motorist), whereas the damages payable under a liability insurance claim are conditioned upon the negligence of the insured. Finally, a UM claim for *property* damage differs from both a property damage *liability* claim and a first-party property insurance claim. (Only in a few states is property damage included in the UM coverage, and even in these few states property damage portion of the UM coverage is subject to a mandatory deductible and it frequently has a lower maximum limit than the limit that applies to property damage liability coverage.) To the extent that UM coverage and limits do apply to property damage, the UM insurer's damage payments are conditioned upon a finding that the uninsured motorist was negligent. And there would be no such condition under the insured's own collision insurance.

Despite the partial exception of UM claims, the involvement of a third party in *insured* liability claims is one of the distinguishing characteristics of liability risk management. If a commercial entity has no liability insurance to cover a particular liability exposure, or if the entity has coverage subject to a deductible larger than the alleged damages and its liability insurer does not share the handling or attendant expenses of the claim, there are not literally three parties involved in the claim. Nevertheless, it is conventional to refer to an outsider as a third party. The claim brought against the entity that is not insured is still referred to as a third-party claim. And the claimant has all the same rights and remedies against an uninsured entity that the claimant would have had against this entity if it had been insured for the alleged damages.

Maximum Loss Difficult or Impossible to Measure

The potential consequences of property losses are relatively easy to project. Generally speaking, the maximum possible loss is equal to the total of the replacement cost of the property exposed plus the business income or revenue that would otherwise be derived from the use and/or rental of that property for a period equal to the time required to repair or replace the property and resume the normal level of gross earnings from its use or rental. At any given point in time, a qualified person can estimate maximum potential property losses with a degree of confidence and accuracy that is quite satisfactory for insurance and other risk management purposes. Such loss estimates can become obsolete quickly in periods of rising construction costs and earnings, but sophisticated means of updating the estimates periodically are readily available and comparatively inexpensive.

Liability losses are another matter entirely. Ultimately, there is no upper dollar limit on the amount a court of law may award in a tort lawsuit. In theory, judges are said to be the "conscience of the court," and they have the power to reduce a jury award or set it aside. Judgment amounts may also be reduced in retrials or upon appeals to higher courts. And there are still a few statutory constraints that impose dollar limits on certain types of damage and/or in a limited number of situations. Even so, multi-million dollar tort judgments and defense costs have become quite commonplace. Tomorrow's trials continue to break the records set by yesterday's judgment and defense-cost amounts, and the maximum liability loss potential of the future is beyond the forecasting abilities of even the most competent actuaries.

Effects of Changing Rules of Law

Later portions of this chapter deal more specifically with legal issues. For now, it is sufficient to note that the rules of law governing various kinds of tort liability claims have been changed rapidly and sometimes drastically. Such changes have had the general effects of creating new liability exposures for some commercial entities, increasing the difficulty of successfully defending lawsuits arising from previously existing exposures, and subjecting all entities to the likelihood of larger and larger claims. Most property loss exposures are not as extensively affected by changes in the applicable law.

The "Long Tail"

Property losses are generally settled within a relatively short period of time after they happen. When property suffers damage, it is usually obvious almost immediately. Repairs commence, repair or replacement bills are paid, and the property is put back into use. Only rarely do property losses drag out for several years.

With liability losses—especially those involving bodily injury— delays are common. A long period of time may elapse between the time when an accidental injury takes place or an illness-producing condition begins to exist on the one hand, and the time when a claim is made, on the other. A further delay may occur while the claim is litigated. Even after a final judgment has been entered, the payment of damages may take place over a period of many years.

Take, for example, the situation facing many pharmaceutical firms. Drugs developed over the last decade and manufactured today may be consumed over the next several years. Latent problems in the medication may not become apparent until ten or twenty years later— perhaps when children of the drug-takers are born with birth defects. If the drug manufacturer is found to be responsible for these birth defects, payments for damages may have to be made over the entire lifetimes of the affected children. Although this may seem like an extreme example, many cases have already occurred in which liability claims have involved events and/or payments over three or four decades.

A graph depicting the pattern of liability loss payments, with amounts paid on the vertical axis of the graph and years on the horizontal axis, would contain a long line extending to the right, over a period of years. On such a line graph, a long line of this type is often termed a "tail." In the jargon of risk management and insurance, the potential time lag relating to liability losses is termed the "long tail"— even when no graph has been drawn. The "long-tail problem" is that an event today—even one that seems insignificant—could possibly lead to a large liability payment years later. The difficulty is compounded when a variety of liability insurance policies were in force during the many years in question and there is some basis for arguing which policy or policies should respond. The primary ramifications of this problem will be treated in detail in subsequent chapters.

The Widespread Use of Noninsurance Contract Provisions to Transfer Liability Loss Exposures

From the viewpoint of insurance buyers, the purchase of insurance contracts involves the transfer of loss exposures to professional risk bearers (insurers). However, there are countless other types of contracts entered into daily in the modern world of commerce, and many if not most of them contain provisions that seek to transfer loss exposures to other contracting parties. Such contracts are widely referred to as *noninsurance contracts*, because they are not insurance contracts (and the transferees are not otherwise acting as insurers of the loss exposures they have contractually assumed). Construction contracts, lease-of-premises agreements, easements, equipment leases, purchase order and sales agreements, elevator maintenance agreements and contracts for services are among the noninsurance contracts that commonly involve the transfer of loss exposures.

While attempts to transfer *property* loss exposures may be found in the provisions of leases and certain other types of contracts, attempts to transfer *liability* loss exposures are so widely used in so many different types of contracts that such attempts may be referred to accurately as a distinguishing characteristic of liability risk management. The word "attempts" is deliberate and precise, in this context. The mere fact that a contract contains a loss-transfer provision does not necessarily mean it will be enforced by a court of law.

Among the various contract provisions seeking to transfer *liability* losses, some have been declared illegal and void by virtually all courts, whereas others have been enforced by some or most of the courts that have been called on to resolve the numerous disputes about their meaning and enforceability. In a particular case, the outcome will depend upon a combination of factors, including (1) the type of noninsurance transfer provision involved, (2) the language of the provision(s) in question, and (3) public policy considerations. After each of these factors is reviewed, the risk management implications will be summarized.

(1) **Types of Noninsurance Transfer Provisions** Literally hundreds of different types of non-insurance transfer provisions may be found in the several dozen different types of contracts that are entered into each year by a countless number of commercial entities. Some are provisions that have been drafted "from scratch," so to speak. Other are verbatim or modified versions of clauses or provisions contained in books of specimen legal forms and/or in actual contracts already in use. The transfer provisions so drafted, modified, or selected are rarely the entire contract between the parties. Instead, the loss transfer

provisions are usually just part of an overall agreement that is executed by the parties for the primary purpose of selling goods or services, constructing a building, leasing a truck, or some other common business purpose.

The transfer provisions, as well as various other provisions in the overall agreement, are frequently referred to by practicing attorneys and judges as "boilerplate." Sometimes they mean that the language of a particular provision has been standardized in contracts of that kind. More often, they mean that the inclusion of a loss transfer provision *of some sort* is standard or common practice in the drafting of all contracts of the same generic class (e.g., all construction contracts). In given geographical areas, many contracts of the same general kind are also standardized—such as in areas where members of state or local apartment owners associations use the same printed lease forms. Standard construction contract provisions have likewise been developed and recommended for use by such national organizations as the American Institute of Architects. Nevertheless, both the language of loss-transfer provisions and their interpretation by the courts continue to vary significantly among different general kinds of contracts, and even among contracts of the same general kind that have been executed within the same geographical area. These variations make it extremely difficult to classify loss-transfer provisions into meaningful categories.

Further compounding the classification difficulty is that many attorneys, judges, authors, risk managers, and insurance practitioners do not agree on the meaning or proper use of such terms as "exculpatory," "hold harmless," "save harmless," "indemnity," "general release," "limited release," "contractual liability," "mutual waiver of rights," and "unilateral waiver of rights." While some of these terms may reasonably be used interchangeably, they are not equally meritorious as general categories or sub-categories of loss-transfer provisions.

As used in this text, an *exculpatory provision* is any kind of contract provision that by nature or purpose seeks to absolve, relieve, or excuse one or more contracting parties from the defense and/or consequences of an alleged fault, blame, or guilt the defense and/or consequences of which the party(ies) would otherwise bear by the operation of the law. In other words, the adjective "exculpatory" refers to a generic or broad *class* of contract provisions. All provisions in this broad class seek to transfer loss exposures from at least one contracting party to another, whether or not the intended transfer(s) will be enforced by the appropriate court(s).

A *hold-harmless provision* is merely a type of exculpatory provision under which at least one of the contracting parties agrees to "hold harmless" another contracting party for specified kinds of losses.

For example, in a lease between a tenant of a building and the building owner, the tenant might agree to hold the owner harmless for any negligence liability the owner might otherwise have for the injury of a third party. Suppose an injured visitor to the premises successfully sues the tenant for damages. Assuming the court enforces the provision, the tenant would not be allowed to recover from the owner any portion of the damages the tenant paid to the injured third party since the tenant had agreed to hold the owner harmless for such damages. However, in the absence of any such language in the lease, the owner might well have had to pay all or a portion of the damages. Since the owner has no contractual standing with the injured third party, the third party could have been successful in a negligence suit naming the owner as the sole defendant or as a co-defendant with the tenant. This is exactly why virtually all hold harmless agreements also contain an *indemnity provision* under which at least one of the contracting parties agrees to "indemnify" another party, as well as hold that party harmless. Thus, the tenant in the above example normally would have been contractually bound to indemnify the owner for any damages the owner was required to pay to the injured third party.

Many if not most hold harmless and indemnity agreements also apply to all costs of investigating, negotiating, and settling or defending the kind of claims specified in the agreements, as well as to damages. The party that assumes a contractual obligation to indemnify is called the *indemnitor*, while the party that imposes the obligation is called the *indemnitee*. This is a precise use of terms in the context of true indemnity provisions, strictly defined, because the party assuming the obligation (the indemnitor) has agreed to indemnify or reimburse the other party only *after* the other party has first paid the loss. But some exculpatory provisions do not seek indemnity as such. They instead seek to require one party to pay damages and defense costs *on behalf of* the other party, without the precondition of their prior payment by the other party. The parties to this latter kind of exculpatory agreement are "payors" and "payees"—or "transferors" and "transferees," to the extent that the assuming party honors the agreement. Still, if the assuming party refuses to provide a defense or pay any damages, the other party may be forced to do so and then to seek indemnity from the assuming party in a breach-of-contract action.

From the viewpoint of the transferor, a hold-harmless provision is one kind of exculpatory agreement. From the viewpoint of the transferee, a hold-harmless provision is one kind of *waiver agreement*—that is, it is an agreement in which at least one contracting party has expressly waived its rights and remedies against another. If only one party waives its rights and remedies, it is said to be a *unilateral waiver.* If each of two parties waives its rights and remedies against the other, it is said to be a *mutual waiver,* and each party becomes both a transferor and a transferee. Since a transferee has waived its rights and remedies against the transferor, the agreement is also one kind of *release.* The transferee has expressly released the transferor from various legal obligations or duties the transferor would otherwise have to the transferee. Indeed, whether a particular contract provision uses the words "release," "waiver," and/or "hold harmless," it usually has the same basic intention of transferring losses of some sort from one party to another (and vice versa, in a mutual transfer).

Under some contracts, the intention is to transfer to another party virtually all kinds of liability losses, whether from civil or criminal wrongs or acts of nature—and regardless of who may have committed the wrong. Other contractual transfers are expressly limited to torts, while still others are limited to the tort of negligence. It is also common practice to supplement the transfer provisions with additional provisions setting forth the specific types and amounts of insurance that each party is required to purchase and maintain. In fact, some transfer provisions are intended to apply only to the extent that the transferor is uninsured or underinsured.

Effect of the Language of Noninsurance Transfer Provisions Putting aside, for the moment, the question of the extent to which noninsurance transfer provisions are enforceable by the courts, it is first worth repeating that the language of transfer provisions varies considerably—even when the focus is on contracts of the same general kind, such as construction contracts. Furthermore, the terminology, punctuation, and overall syntax of transfer provisions often make it very difficult for the courts to interpret the provisions and give them legal effect. Many of the provisions have been drafted by only one of the contracting parties and "adhered to" by the other. Hence, they are *contracts of adhesion,* and the courts will normally interpret any ambiguities strictly against the drafter of the provision and liberally in favor of the other party. In any event, the courts must first decide what the provisions mean before they decide whether to enforce them in whole or in part.

Public Policy Considerations Once the meaning of a particular transfer provision is clear to the court, the court must then decide the legality of the transfer. The courts will not allow alleged or convicted criminals to transfer their responsibilities for the commission of crimes. The courts in all jurisdictions will also consider whether the transfer of responsibility for a civil wrong is contrary to public policy. But the courts have great latitude in interpreting the phrase "contrary to public policy," and they must take account of any statutes and prior court decisions that are applicable to their own jurisdictions. As a result, a transfer provision may be deemed illegal and void by a court in one jurisdiction; an identical provision may be enforced by a court in another jurisdiction.

Many courts will consider carefully the relative bargaining strength of the parties. If one party drafted the instrument and clearly has much greater bargaining strength than the other party, the courts are reluctant to permit a transfer of loss to the inferior party. In contrast, if the parties have approximately the same bargaining strength and both parties participated in the drafting of the instrument, the courts are more likely to uphold the validity of unilateral or mutual transfers between the parties.

Even if the parties have about the same bargaining strength, many courts will not permit persons who commit willful and malicious acts to transfer their legal or financial responsibility for such acts to another contracting party. Some courts are also reluctant to permit indemnity for a person's own negligence. Additionally, statutes in some states specifically prohibit certain kinds of contractual loss transfers.

Liability Risk Management Implications Noninsurance transfers of liability loss exposures have risk management implications of enormous import. Most of these implications are discussed in subsequent sections and chapters of this text. At this point, only the following generalizations are offered:

- Because attempts to effect noninsurance transfers of liability exposures are not always upheld by the courts, most transferors use such attempts as a supplement to their own liability insurance, not as a substitute for its purchase.
- Because some kinds of noninsurance transfers of liability exposures are regularly enforced by the courts of one or more jurisdictions, most transferees should consider carefully the merits of contractual liability insurance.
- It can be a mistake to think of noninsurance transfers as a cost-free or economical method of handling the liability loss exposures of an entity with superior bargaining strength. Such strength may tempt a court to void an attempted transfer to a party with inferior bargaining strength. Even if the court upholds such a transfer, many transferors continue to maintain their own liability insurance. And, transferees either purchase contractual liability insurance or retain additional loss exposures; either approach increases the transferee's cost of doing business, which is likely to be reflected in its charges to the transferor. Unless the transferor can exact sufficient conces-

sions from its liability insurer—and/or from the transferee—
the attempted transfer, combined with liability insurance, may
be more expensive than liability insurance alone.

TYPES OF COMMERCIAL ENTITIES EXPOSED TO LIABILITY LOSS

The types of commercial entities facing liability loss exposures are
those that may be charged with responsibility for some wrongdoing
against a third-party claimant. These entities include all entities the law
recognizes as "persons," such as proprietors and proprietorships,
partners and partnerships, joint venturers, corporations and their
stockholders, stockholders who also render professional services,
associations and their members, and all employers and their employees
and legal agents.

Individual Proprietorship

An *individual proprietorship* is a form of business organization
in which one individual is the sole owner and manager of the entire
operation. The business and its owner are legally a single being. The
individual proprietor is *personally* liable for the debts of the business,
including any settlements or court-imposed judgments in a tort claim or
suit.

Partnership

A *partnership* is a type of business organization formed by a
contract between two or more individuals. The partners agree to use
their capital and labor in operating the partnership business, as well as
to share in the profits and losses of the partnership. All partners are
jointly and severally liable for the debts of the partnership. Therefore,
any or all partners may be held personally responsible for a tort
judgment against the partnership.

A *limited partnership* involves both *general partners* and
limited partners. The general partners, who are jointly and severally
liable as ordinary partners, conduct the business. The limited partners
contribute a specific amount of capital, but they are not liable for the
debts of the partnership, beyond the amount they have contributed. The
limited partners participate in the profits on an agreed basis. Since they
have no voice in the management of the business, they may be regarded
as nothing more than financial backers. A partnership is dissolved

whenever any partner ceases to be associated in carrying out the business.

Joint Venture

A *joint venture* is similar to a partnership, but it is formed to accomplish one specific mission (such as a single construction project). All persons engaged in the joint venture, sometimes called a *joint enterprise* or *joint adventure*, must have a voice in its management. As is true of general partners, all joint ventures are jointly and severally liable to third persons. The negligence of one venturer, if related to the venture, may be imputed to the other venturers.

Corporation

A corporation is an artificial "person" or entity that is created by or under the authority of the laws of a state or nation, has a capacity for perpetual existence, and is able to act only through agents. A corporation has a separate existence. Though its individual directors, officers, and/or shareholders may change due to death, disability, retirement, resignation, or discharge, such changes do not affect the corporation's continuing existence.

The owners of a corporation—the shareholders—are partially shielded from any personal liability for acts of the corporation. Shareholders are usually not required to spend personal funds to pay a judgment or other debt of the corporation they serve. Yet, directors and officers may be held personally liable for negligent management of the corporation (as detailed in Chapter 7).

A *private corporation* is one that is founded by private individuals for private purposes. A *public corporation* is one created by a state legislature or by Congress to act as an agency in the administration of government. Many public corporations operate within a particular territory or subdivision of a state, and they are usually invested with limited legislative power at the local level. Some such corporations administer an entire county, city, town, or school district, whereas others are created for a single purpose, such as a turnpike authority, a transit authority, or a port authority. The principal distinction between public and private corporations is that public corporations are organized for some governmental purpose.

Public corporations may also be shielded from liability in situations and jurisdictions where the *doctrine of sovereign immunity* applies, as discussed later in the chapter.

Professional Corporation   Over the years, a majority of states have enacted legislation that permits specified classes of professionals to do business as professional corporations (PCs) or professional associations (PAs) in which all the stockholders must be professionals of the same type (e.g., all physicians). In the absence of such a statute, physicians, attorneys, and public accountants are limited to practicing either as sole proprietors or as a partner in a partnership.

As noted earlier, a stockholder of a traditional corporation is usually not liable for *corporate* obligations. Likewise, under all professional corporation statutes, the shareholder of a professional corporation can lose no more from corporate debts than the shareholder's interest in the corporation—*except for professional torts committed by the shareholder-professional or for which the professional is vicariously liable.* Some professional corporation statutes also impute the negligence of one professional to other professionals who, having participated in a professional capacity in the rendering of the professional service, are jointly and severally liable (e.g. one negligent surgeon and two other surgeons assisting in the same surgery).

Association

An association is formed when a number of persons unite for some special purpose or business. An association is similar to a partnership in its fundamental nature. It differs from the usual partnership in that it is not bound by the acts of the individual members, but only by the acts of its manager(s) or trustee(s). Unlike a partnership, the shares in an association are transferable, and the association is not dissolved by the retirement, death, or bankruptcy of its individual members.

A *condominium association* is formed by the owners of condominium units to manage the business of the condominium. The condominium association owns the real property and may be held liable for any claims arising from this ownership. Individual unit owners may be assessed in order to provide funding for any claim(s) that exceed(s) the assets of the association. The directors of a condominium association also face the possibility of liability claims by unit owners who feel they have suffered damages because the directors have mismanaged the association.

Membership of a particular condominium association changes as units are bought or sold. Similar associations may be formed by homeowners in a particular development who might, for example, own a clubhouse or other property used by members.

Agency Relationships

Agency may be defined as every relationship in which one party acts for or represents another according to the latter's orders and directions. An agency relationship may be created either by an express or implied contract or by law. It is a relationship between an agent and a "principal."

One general rule in agency law is that if the agent is negligent in performing an act and the negligence results in injury or property damage to another, the principal is liable as if he or she had done the act personally. The agent's negligence is "imputed" to the principal, and the principal is jointly and severally liable for damages sustained by the injured person. In legal terms, the principal has *vicarious liability* for the acts of the agent.

The principal's vicarious liability is limited to situations in which the agent is acting within the scope of the authority granted to the agent by the principal. If the agent is acting for his or her own purposes, the principal is not liable for the conduct of the agent, but there are some exceptions to this general rule.

Generally, an employee is an agent of the employer while the employee is in the course of employment and doing the assigned job. Likewise, each partner is an agent of the partnership, representing all of the individual partners. It follows that each partner is both a principal and an agent in all acts.

Independent contractors are not considered common-law employees if they are not subject to the right of the employer to control or direct the contractors, in terms of *how* the work is to be performed. It is not uncommon for a court to rule that an alleged "independent contractor" was, in fact, an employee, as a result of which the employer is held vicariously liable for the contractor's commission of a tort in the performance of the work for which the contractor was hired.

For the purpose of determining whether an insurer (as a principal) is vicariously liable for the torts of an *insurance* agent, an insurance agent may be deemed an agent or a common-law employee of the insurer, in some situations, and an independent contractor in other situations. A "broker" also may be deemed an agent of the insurer, for tort law purposes. The courts normally will not relieve the insurer from vicarious liability merely because a statute says that a broker is an agent of the insurance buyer. Nor will the insurer be automatically relieved merely because its contract with the agent calls the agent an independent contractor. In either case, the issues are (1) whether the person committed the tort while acting as an agent of the insurer and (2) whether the insurer had the *right* to control or direct *how* the work in question was to be performed. If the answers to both questions are yes, the insurer may become jointly and severally liable with the agent (or broker) for the tort the agent (or broker) committed in the course of the work.

GENERAL NATURE OF THE LIABILITY EXPOSURES OF COMMERCIAL ENTERPRISES

Businesses, hospitals, municipalities, and various other commercial, industrial, or educational enterprises all face the possibility of losing their financial assets due to claims that may be brought by a third party. Such loss may arise out of injury caused by the products a company sells, by the failure of a city to maintain its roads and sidewalks in a safe manner, or by the failure of a hospital to provide appropriate medical care and treatment. The basis for assigning responsibility for such loss is the body of law governing the legal rights and duties of all members of society. Recognition and understanding of its obligations allows a commercial operation to manage its exposures to loss.

Nature of Legal Rights and Duties

Rights The English common law, which was adopted by virtually all American courts, recognized that each individual was endowed with certain rights the law was bound to protect. These legally protected rights included the right to security of person, property, and reputation. Over the years, as a result of the judicial modification of the common law and by the enactment of statutes, other rights of individuals have been established such as the right of privacy and the right to vote.

Like an individual, a business organization has certain legally protected rights such as the right to the security of its property and its good reputation, and the right to be free from malicious interference. Any wrongful invasion of such legally protected rights entitles the business organization to bring an action against the wrongdoer for damages or other relief that the court may deem appropriate. The general rule is that where there is a right which has been invaded, there is a remedy.

Duties In a legal sense, a *duty* is the correlative of a right. Where there is a right, there is a duty on the part of others to respect that right and to refrain from any action or omission that will impair or damage that right. In the case of any wrongful act or omission that deprives an individual of a right, the injured party may bring an action at law to recover money damages for the loss that has been sustained.

In certain cases, other forms of recovery, such as injunctive relief, are possible.

With respect to the rights of others, duties are likewise imposed upon commercial entities. For example, businesses are under a duty to maintain their premises in a reasonably safe condition, to exercise care in their operations, both on and off their premises, to exercise care in the manufacture of any product, and to operate their motor vehicles in a reasonably safe manner. If a business is guilty of a wrongful act or omission that causes damages, the business may be held legally liable to the injured party. However, the nature of a commercial entity's liability exposure depends partly on the type of business organization or public body involved, as explained earlier.

Broad Sources of Legal Liability

Legal liability, whether criminal, civil, or both, is imposed by (1) common law and/or (2) statute.

Common Law The common law consists of a body of principles and rules of conduct that derive their authority mainly from custom and precedent. These principles and rules can be found only by referring to court decisions and formal published compilations called "restatements."

Originally, most American courts applied English common law as the rule of decision in all cases, both civil and criminal. With the Declaration of Independence, the courts were freed from any continuing obligation to follow English rules. However, since the new nation had no legal rules of its own, most American courts continued to apply English common law as it existed at that time. This formed the basis for the development of American common law, which has also been influenced by French law (in Louisiana) and by Spanish law (in several southwestern and western states).

Since common law reflects the customs and usages of society, the law changes with the customs or attitudes of society. Where the reason for a rule no longer exists, the courts generally will abandon it. Where a new rule seems necessary, the courts will provide one. For example, the original common-law rule with regard to the ownership of land was that the owner owned not only the land on the surface but also the airspace to the heavens above. With the advent of aircraft, the courts abandoned the old rule and fabricated a legal concept that established three zones above the land:

- The first zone consists of that part of the airspace that had been reduced to possession by the owner's buildings. Thus, regardless of the size of the building, whether it be a 2-story house or a 100-story office building, the owner is entitled to sole and exclusive possession of the airspace occupied by the building.

● The second zone consists of the space above the buildings that the owner requires for the peaceful enjoyment of his or her property. To this zone also the owner is entitled to sole and exclusive possession.

● The third zone is above the other two. The third zone is in the public domain and may be used by private, public, or commercial aircraft (subject to licensing restrictions, federal regulations, and treaties with other countries).

Any intrusion into either of the first two zones is an actionable trespass.

Statutes A statute is a written enactment of a legislative body. A statute is thus an expression of the will of the people through their elected representatives. Statutes can alter or amend the common law, or they can create liabilities that never existed at common law:

● The enactment of workers' compensation laws created an entirely new basis of liability for the employer.

● "No-fault" auto statutes partially changed the common-law concept of recovery based on fault.

● Comparative negligence laws changed the common-law rule that contributory negligence is a complete defense to a negligence action.

● Wrongful death statutes replaced the common-law rule that a dead person had no legal rights, creating instead a cause of action that could be brought by dependents of the deceased whose death had been caused by a wrongful act. All states have passed such wrongful death statutes.

Nature of Criminal Liability

Early in the development of common law, the courts decided that certain acts and/or omissions were offensive to the peace and dignity of the community as a whole. Such acts and/or omissions were designated as crimes. The federal government and all states have codified criminal law by enacting penal statutes. These statutes set forth the elements of each crime and prescribe the punishments that should be imposed. The criminal statutes also set forth the procedures to be followed from the time of arrest to the time the accused is either found innocent and set free or found guilty and punished.

A crime is often classified as a "felony," a "misdemeanor," or a "summary offense." The meanings of these terms vary from one jurisdiction to the next; however, the more serious crimes, such as murder, armed robbery, and rape, are considered felonies in every jurisdiction.

Criminal Liability of Commercial Entities   When an agent commits a crime, even though it is in the course and scope of the agency, the principal usually is not criminally liable—unless the principal aids, abets, conspires in, or compels the commission of the crime, in which case the principal is just as guilty as the agent.

While the corporation itself cannot be guilty of a crime for which the sole penalty is imprisonment or capital punishment, it can be fined, enjoined from committing illegal acts, and/or stripped of its license to do business. However, a corporate officer, director, or employee can be held guilty of any crime an individual can commit. And officers of corporations can be sentenced to prison for crimes they did not personally commit, when they are held criminally liable because of their positions.

Insurance and Crime   It is obviously not in the public interest to encourage or reward the commission of crimes. Therefore, any type of insurance that would cover a criminal for the commission of a crime is void, because it is contrary to public policy.

On the other hand, a business that has committed no crime may be subject to civil liability as a consequence of the criminal acts *of another* for whom it is responsible. To protect against such situations, the business may obtain liability insurance for its own protection. Such policies may cover the firm's legal liability to the injured victim of a crime. However, liability policies generally do not cover the business in the case of an assault committed by or at its own direction.

Criminal and Civil Liability

The same act can have both public and private consequences. It can be an offense against the peace and dignity of the community and also invade the rights of an individual. Hence, the offender can be subject to both criminal and civil liability. An example is a person who steals an auto owned by another. Such a thief is answerable to the public for violation of his or her public duty, and is also answerable to the injured person for wrongful invasion of the latter's private right. A criminal action may be brought by the state and tried in a criminal proceeding. An action for compensatory damages may be brought by the auto owner and tried in a civil proceeding. For a second example, assume that a man drives an auto in a wantonly careless manner and causes the death of another. He may be indicted for vehicular homicide and brought to trial in a criminal court. A civil action for wrongful death may also be brought against him.

The accused may be found innocent by the criminal court and lose the case in the civil court. The opposite is also possible—or, the offender could win or lose both cases. It is especially commonplace for a damaged plaintiff to win a case against a tortfeasor who is found innocent of criminal charges or had them dismissed. These different outcomes are sometimes partly due to the fact that two separate actions and two separate juries are normally involved. More often, they are due to the dismissal of criminal charges on procedural grounds or the significantly different standards of proof required in tort suits and criminal suits, respectively. The plaintiff is said to have the burden of proof in both types of actions, as a general rule. However, in a criminal action, the state has the burden of convincing the jury that the accused is guilty "beyond any reasonable shadow of a doubt." If the jury has a lingering doubt about the guilt or innocence of the accused, the accused *Criminal* must be found innocent of the criminal charge(s) involved. In a tort action, the plaintiff has the burden of convincing the jury of the defendant's tort liability, but the proof needed by the plaintiff is a "preponderance of evidence." A mere "preponderance" of evidence is *Civil* ordinarily much easier to provide than the amount and types of indisputable evidence that will remove all shadows of doubt.

Nature of Civil Liability

Civil liability arises out of a breach of some private duty owed by one legal "person" to another. Such duties are imposed by the common law, prescribed by civil statutes, and/or voluntarily assumed by contract. A person or business that breaches such a duty is subject to an action for damages.

Common Law and Statutes

At common law a party is under a duty to exercise reasonable care for the safety of others. Thus, a business must exercise such care in the operation and maintenance of its premises, in the manufacture and design of its products, in the use of dangerous chemicals or explosives, and in the operation and use of its motor vehicles.

Since statutes modify and define the extent of the duty to be undertaken, a violation of a statute will be considered a breach of the duty. For example, a local ordinance may apply to the use and storage of dangerous or inflammable material. A violation of the requirements of a statute would constitute a breach of the duty of care.

Contracts

If one party to a contract fails to perform contractual obligations and the failure results in injury damage to the other party, the aggrieved party may bring a *breach-of-contract action* against the defaulting party to recover the resulting damages. Most insurers are not willing to provide liability insurance that would cover a breach of contract. However, a single act or omission often gives rise to causes of action in both contract and tort. If the plaintiff alleges a covered tort, as well as a breach of contract, the liability insurer has a duty to defend its insured. But damages awarded solely due to a breach of contract would not be covered by the standard forms of "contractual liability insurance." As explained in a later chapter, contractual liability insurance is intended to cover only an insured's contractual assumption of the *tort* liability that the other contracting party may have to an injured third party.

The "preponderance of evidence" standard applies in breach-of-contract actions. As noted earlier, the standard in a criminal action is "beyond any reasonable shadow of a doubt." As one noteworthy result of this distinction, crime insurers are frequently obliged to pay theft, burglary, robbery, embezzlement, fraud, or dishonesty losses—even if an accused person is found innocent of all criminal charges, or the accused is dismissed on procedural grounds, or the criminal is not known or is known but not caught. The insurer is obligated to make payment under its contract of insurance if the insured can prove, *with a preponderance of evidence*, that it incurred a covered loss of a provable amount. If this were not the case, crime insurance would not be worth much. Indeed, if an insurer withheld payment of an otherwise covered loss until after a criminal was caught and convicted, the insurer might be held liable for punitive damages for the tort of breaching its implied contract of good faith and fair dealing. (Bad faith, as a type of intentional tort, is discussed later in the chapter.)

Legal Actions

Whether the duties arise in contract, statute, or common law, if there is a breach of a private duty, the injured party may initiate a civil action against the allegedly responsible party. Legal actions may consist of (1) an *action at law* for money damages, or (2) a *suit in equity* for one of the many forms of equitable relief (e.g., an injunction). The party bringing the suit is called the *plaintiff* and the party against whom action is taken is called the *defendant*. Action is begun by the service of two legal documents respectively called a summons and a complaint. A *summons* is a document or writ issued by the clerk of the appropriate court and directed to the sheriff or other proper officer. It requires the officer to notify each person named as a defendant in the action by serving a copy of the summons on him or her personally. The _complaint_ is essentially a statement of the plaintiff's claim and a demand for damages. Since the complaint must also be served on each defendant, it is almost always served along with the writ of summons.

After service of the summons and the complaint, the defendant is required to answer the complaint within the period of time prescribed by the procedural rules of the particular jurisdiction involved. Failure to answer will result in a "default judgment" (an automatic judgment in favor of the plaintiff for the relief demanded in the complaint). After a defendant has properly answered, a substantial period of time invariably is required for the filing and disposition of pre-trial motions and the implementation of "discovery." The term _discovery_ refers to the process by which one party "discovers" or obtains, from an opposing party to the lawsuit, the facts, documents, and information that are needed by the party seeking discovery in order to prepare for trial. The phrase _discovery procedures_ refers to the devices and formal procedures that may be used by a party to discover such facts, documents, and information. Two widely used discovery devices are the discovery deposition and the interrogatories.

A _discovery deposition_ is a pre-trial device by which one party's attorney questions the person being deposed (called the "deponent") under oath and in the presence of a court reporter. The questions and answers are recorded and transcribed into a word-for-word account called the "transcript." Each party may elect to depose one or more of the persons who are likely to testify in the trial on behalf of the opposing party, such as an expert witness, an eyewitness, a person who has knowledge of pertinent facts, and/or the opposing party(ies) in the suit. Most of the costs of taking a deposition are normally borne by the party demanding the deposition. These costs include attorney's fees, the court reporter's fee, the fees and travel expenses of expert witnesses, and the cost of transcribing the record, a copy of which must be served on the other party and also made a part of the court record. Depending upon the length of a deposition and the location where it is held, these costs can be considerable.

Interrogatories are written questions set forth in a formal document that is prepared by one party's attorney and submitted to the other party's attorney or to a witness. Written _answers_ to the interrogatories must be provided within a time period specified by the judge and/or by the applicable rules of civil procedure. In the usual tort lawsuit, both interrogatories and depositions are used by both parties to obtain information prior to trial.

Assuming the judge has not disposed of the case by a pre-trial ruling of some sort, and after the discovery process has been completed, the case will be scheduled for trial. Still, a case may be settled by agreement at any time before or during the trial, right up to the moment the jury returns with a verdict.

Litigation Exposures

It has been said that one way to avoid a lawsuit is not to deserve one. Unfortunately, this is not entirely true. Many suits are frivolous, fraudulent, or groundless. Since the failure to defend a suit will result in a default judgment, all suits must be defended regardless of their merit. In the absence of liability insurance, the defendant must engage an attorney and pay whatever attorney and filing fees are required. If the case goes to trial, the defendant must pay for subpoena fees, witness fees and, if a jury is demanded by the plaintiff, the jury fee. Defendants who win are entitled to reimbursement for statutory costs. *Statutory costs* usually include only the filing fees incurred, statutory witness fees, public notary fees, and subpoena fees. Unfortunately, the statutory costs that are reimbursed are relatively small, and the defendant will not be reimbursed for the defense attorney's fees or the other expenses incurred (though the defendant can sometimes recover such outlays in a counter-claim or subsequent claim based upon the "malicious prosecution" doctrine). This is one reason why many suits are compromised in advance of the trial, usually for an amount approximating the cost of trial, even though liability is specifically denied.

On the other hand, in bodily injury claims the plaintiff may be able to employ an attorney on a *contingent fee basis* under which the attorney charges as a fee a percentage of the verdict or settlement. In the event of no recovery, the attorney receives nothing. If there is a recovery, the plaintiff's attorney will ordinarily charge a fee equal to from 25 percent to 50 percent of the amount recovered depending upon such matters as whether an appeal is required or whether a statute or a judge restricts the fee percentage.

The mere fact that a suit has been filed does not necessarily mean that the defendant is liable. As noted earlier, the burden of proof is ordinarily on the shoulders of the plaintiff. If the plaintiff does not sustain this burden, there will be a verdict for the defendant.

Regardless of the outcome of the suit, the defendant may incur other indirect losses as a result. These will include:

- any uninsured costs of bonds to release attachments,

- the impairment of business operations caused by injunctions and the like,
- the loss of executive time,
- the cost of answering interrogatories,
- the possible impairment of the firm's credit standing, and
- the loss of customers (particularly in products cases) from the adverse publicity surrounding a lawsuit.

Contractual Liability Exposures

For the purposes of this brief summary, an *enforceable contract* may be defined as a promise, the performance of which the law in some way recognizes as a duty and for the breach of which the law provides a remedy to the innocent party.

A contract may be discharged by the full performance of both parties. A contract is "breached" when one party has performed and the other party has not performed within the time limit in the contract (or, if no time is expressed, within a reasonable time). The party who has performed then has a cause of action for damages for breach of contract. The damages that may be claimed are such amounts as the aggrieved party would have received had the contract been fully performed by the other, sometimes referred to as the "benefit of the bargain."

When a contract has been breached, the innocent party may consider the contract at an end. Should an action be begun by the offending party, the innocent party may interpose the nonperformance of the other as a complete defense. On the other hand, the performing party may seek *specific performance*—that is, an order from a court of equity that directs the delinquent party to perform the contract.

If there has been no breach of contract but one party discovers that it has been induced to enter the contract through fraud or duress or some form of mistake, that party may pursue the remedy of *rescission* (annulling the contract) or *reformation* (reforming the contract to express the real agreement of the parties).

In a breach-of-contract action, the size of the potential losses are determined largely by the nature of the contract and the original terms. However, the breach of a contract may also give rise to an action in tort. For example, assume that an employee has a contract of employment which, among other things, provides that the employee will not engage in the same trade or business within 500 miles of the employer's place of business at the termination of employment. The employee breaches the contract and is hired by the employer's competitor, who operates in the same city. The former employer might have a cause of action against the former employee, for breach of the covenant not to compete. The former employer might also bring a tort action against the new employer, for wrongful interference with an advantageous business relationship. Note that there is no contractual relationship between the former employer and the new employer.

Tort Liability Exposures

Tort Defined A tort may be defined as a "wrongful act or omission, independent of contract, for which the law provides a remedy in the form of an action for damages."

The person committing a tort is called a wrongdoer or a *tortfeasor*. When two or more persons unite in causing the tort, they are called *joint tortfeasors*. However, to be joint tortfeasors, they must act together in committing the wrong; or, their acts, if independent of each other, must unite in causing a single injury. For example, a motorist negligently injures a pedestrian. While the pedestrian is still lying on the road he is run over by another negligent motorist. The motorists are joint tortfeasors, even though the act of the second motorist was not concurrent with the act of the first motorist. In another situation, motorist A collides with the car of motorist B, driving his car onto the sidewalk where he strikes C, a pedestrian. A and B are *concurrent joint tortfeasors*, since their negligent acts together resulted in the single injury to C.

Regardless of the legal grounds for the imposition of civil liability, the only damages recoverable are those that are proximately caused by the wrongful act or omission. Damages are said to be "proximately" caused only when there is an unbroken chain of causation from the wrongful act or omission to the resulting damages. Damages that are not proximately caused by the wrongful act or omission are not recoverable.

Grounds for the Imposition of Tort Liability Assuming that all procedural and substantive preconditions have been met satisfactorily, a court may impose liability upon the defendant(s) for any act or omission that the law recognizes as a tort. The numerous torts currently recognized by law may be classified into three broad types:

1. intentional torts,
2. negligence (the most prevalent kind of unintentional tort), and
3. torts for which strict (or absolute) liability may be imposed, regardless of negligence or intent.

The modern tort lawsuit is rarely as neat and tidy as the use of these three categories might imply, even in a suit limited to tort causes of action. The plaintiff's complaint often alleges that several torts were committed by one or more of the defendants, and neither the alleged torts of any one defendant nor the combination of torts allegedly committed by the collective of all defendants will necessarily fall within one of the broad categories listed above. Furthermore, a single act or omission can be sufficient grounds for the imposition of strict or absolute liability, whether it was intentional, negligent, or otherwise unintentional in nature. As long as such realities are kept in mind, the three broad categories have merit as a framework for conveying the general nature of more specific kinds of torts.

LIABILITY FOR INTENTIONAL TORTS

The intentional interference with the person or property of another is a tort, whenever such interference is an invasion of a legally protected right of the natural person or entity whose right is invaded. To secure such a right, the law provides its holder with a remedy in the form of an action for money damages. The alleged tortfeasor becomes a defendant in an action brought by the holder of the right (the plaintiff). If it can be proved that the plaintiff sustained damages as the proximate result of the defendant's wrongful invasion of a legally protected right, the defendant will be held liable for the damages sustained. This is another way of saying that a defendant will be held liable for whatever allowable damages were the direct result of the defendant's wrongful breach of a legal duty the defendant owed to the plaintiff. One person's legally protected right imposes upon other persons the legal duty to refrain from interfering with or invading that right.

Though torts of intentional interference are commonly called "intentional torts," this useful convenience of language should not be taken too literally. A tortfeasor can be held liable without really intending to cause bodily injury, property damage, or any other recognized form of personal injury (such as injury to a person's reputation).

The imposition of liability for many torts in the intentional interference category requires a showing of "intent" only in the sense that:

- the *act or omission* complained of must have been voluntary— that is, it was not done at gunpoint or under some other form of duress, coercion, or intimidation to which the act or omission was the defendant's only viable or reasonable response;
- the *damages* complained of either were or should have been *reasonably foreseen by the defendant as the natural and*

predictable consequences of the defendant's act or omission; and

- the tortfeasor has no valid defense that would relieve the tortfeasor from liability.

In other words, suppose a male defendant testifies that he did not intend to do a particular act, and he did not intend to harm the plaintiff. If the plaintiff can prove that the act was not done under any duress, intent to do the act may be inferred from the voluntary nature of the act; if the plaintiff can also prove that the defendant actually foresaw the consequences of his act, or that a reasonable and prudent person would have been able to foresee the natural consequences of such an act, the defendant may be held liable for many specific torts in the intentional interference category. But this assumes the defendant has no valid defense to defeat the claim. As a general rule, for instance, a police officer with a proper warrant is not liable in tort for arresting a suspected criminal. Nor is a homeowner liable to an injured adult trespasser in situations where the court finds that the homeowner used no more than reasonable force to expel the trespasser from the premises.

To recover damages for some kinds of torts, the plaintiff must prove not only that the defendant's conduct was voluntary or intentional; the plaintiff must also establish that the conduct was engaged in with actual or constructive malice, in a legal sense of these terms. Generally, an act is done with *actual malice* when it is done with the intent to do harm or with wanton, willful, or reckless disregard of the rights of another person or entity. An act is done with *constructive malice* when malice can be inferred from the facts and circumstances and imputed to the actor.

An example of a tort requiring the proof or inference of malice is the tort of malicious prosecution. Additionally, actual malice usually must be proved in libel and slander actions brought by so-called "public figures," while malice usually may be inferred or presumed when the plaintiff in a libel or slander action is not a well-known politician, entertainer, professional athlete, or other person who is in the public eye. However, the issue of malice, like the broader issue of intent, is a moot point whenever the defendant has a good and complete defense against the claim (e.g., truth is said to be a viable defense in libel or slander actions).

Assuming the defendant does not have a defense that would completely bar recovery by the plaintiff, the proof or allowable presumption of malice can serve to increase the total amount of damages awarded for the commission of virtually any specific kind of tort in the intentional interference category (and in the strict or absolute liability category). In jurisdictions recognizing the concept of punitive damages, an award of punitive damages is usually conditioned upon a finding of actual or constructive malice. Based upon a preponderance of evidence concerning the facts and circumstances surrounding the defendant's conduct, a jury is normally permitted to infer malice from conduct that demonstrates an indifference to, or a reckless disregard of, the legally protected rights of the plaintiff. And punitive damages may be awarded, whether or not actual malice can be proved.

Specific Types of Intentional Torts

Defamation—Libel and Slander Persons have a right to maintain the reputations they have established. An untrue published statement that damages a person's reputation may be actionable, the wrongdoer having committed an intentional tort referred to as defamation (or defamation of character).

Defamation may take one of two forms, libel or slander. Originally *libel* consisted of anything of a defamatory nature that was written or printed, whereas *slander* consisted of defamation of an oral nature, conveyed by speech alone. Libel now includes pictures, cartoons, moving pictures, signs, and statues. In today's world of sophisticated devices for rapid and widespread communications, either libel or slander is capable of inflicting great damages. Yet before the defendant may be held liable for the damages, the following elements of defamation must be established by the plaintiff:

1. a false statement about the plaintiff that is injurious to the reputation of the plaintiff,
2. publication of the false statement, and
3. damages.

Even if these three elements are proved conclusively, there still may be a defense that would prevent any recovery of damages by the plaintiff.

A False Statement. A true statement may be injurious to the reputation of a person about whom the statement is made, but a true statement will not result in liability for defamation. Instead, the statement must be a *false statement* that impairs the reputation of the plaintiff in a manner serious enough to result in actual or presumed damages. Such statements include false statements that degrade or disgrace a person, expose the person to ridicule or contempt, or otherwise demean the person's character. The false statement must also be a so-called "public utterance."

(2) *Publication.* The statement must be published or brought to the attention of one or more persons, other than the person defamed. Merely to call a person a crook, a shyster, or a "dead-beat" is not defamatory when no other person is present. However, to dictate a letter containing defamatory statements to a secretary amounts to publication, even though no other person sees it.

(3) *Damages.* Generally, damages must be alleged and proved by the plaintiff. Even though the words were offensive and did result in injured feelings or insult, unless some actual damage came about as a result, the most that the plaintiff would be able to recover would be nominal damages. In some aggravated cases (defamation per se) damages are presumed, and the jury can return a verdict without any specific proof of monetary damages. Such cases include:

1. imputation of serious crimes;
2. imputation of a loathsome disease, such as leprosy or syphilis; and
3. imputations adversely affecting the plaintiff in his or her business, trade, or profession, such as calling a surgeon a butcher, or a lawyer a shyster or a crook.

If the plaintiff is not a public figure, it is also *presumed* that the defendant acted with malice. However, if the plaintiff is a public figure—such as a well-known politician or entertainer—actual malice must be proved in order for the plaintiff to recover.

Defenses to Libel and Slander. The defenses to actions for libel or slander are (1) truth and (2) privilege.

1) Truth. It is frequently said that truth is a complete or absolute defense in a defamation action. Since one of the elements to be established is the falsity of the published statement(s) in question, proof that the statement(s) is(are) true would relieve the defendant of liability. However, the courts have not been in agreement on the issue of whether (1) the plaintiff has the burden of proving the falsity of the statement or (2) the defendant has the burden of proving the truth of the statement. Recently, the U. S. Supreme Court partially resolved the matter by ruling that when a newspaper publishes statements of public concern about a private figure, the private-figure plaintiff cannot recover damages without showing that the statements at issue are false.

2) Privilege. Privilege may be a complete or a partial defense to actions for libel and slander, depending upon whether the privilege is (1) absolute or (2) qualified.

An *absolute privilege* grants a person complete immunity from liability the person might otherwise have for a defamatory, false public statement, even if the statement is made maliciously. Examples of absolute privilege include: the statements made by judges, attorneys, witnesses, and jurors in a legal proceeding; statements made by members of Congress during official legislative proceedings; communications made by high-ranking executive officers in the performance of their official duties in federal, state, and local government; and, statements made by one spouse to another while they are alone.

A *qualified privilege* is a conditional privilege that grants a person immunity from liability the person might otherwise have for a defamatory, false public statement, *if* the following conditions are met: the statement must not be made with actual malice; the statement must not be knowingly false; the statement must not be made with the intention of injuring another; and, with respect to the news media's privilege of "fair comment" on matters of public concern, the statement must be fair and without malice. In addition to the news media, the doctrine of qualified privilege has also been applied to such situations as those involving published reports of the proceedings of political subdivisions, communications between political subdivision executives and state legislatures, statements made by commercial credit agencies to persons having a legitimate interest in receiving such information, and communications to members of a religious organization.

Invasion of the Right of Privacy Federal and state statutes regarding the right of privacy are beyond the scope of this text. At common law, the right of privacy is the right of an individual to be let alone and to be free from unauthorized publicity of essentially private matters. A wrongful invasion of this right will give rise to a tort action for damages.

Actionable invasions of the right of privacy can take the form of the unauthorized release of confidential information, the illegal use of hidden microphones or other surveillance equipment, an unauthorized search, or the public disclosure of private facts. However, in respect to the public disclosure of private facts, entertainers, politicians and others who have attained public prominence are generally entitled to a lesser degree of privacy than ordinary citizens who do not seek publicity.

Assault and Battery *Assault* consists of an intentional, unlawful *threat* of bodily harm to another under circumstances creating a well-founded fear of imminent harm. *Battery* consists of any unlawful and unprivileged *touching* of another person. Battery and assault often happen together at approximately the same time, but either offense can happen without the other. In any event, an individual is entitled to the legally protected right of safety of person. Therefore, an assault and/or battery is an invasion of that right.

Defenses to Assault and Battery. The defenses that may be interposed to an action for damages for assault and battery include (1) consent, (2) self-defense, (3) defense of property, (4) defense of others, and (5) discipline.

1) Consent. If consent to do a particular act of touching is given by a person with the legal capacity to give consent, the doing of the act cannot be battery, as long as it was done within the scope of the consent that was given. The consent provides the privilege to perform the act agreed upon. Though mere silence is not usually a valid basis for an inference of consent, a participant in a contact sport impliedly consents to the kind and intensity of physical contact that is normal to the sport.

2) Self-defense. All persons are entitled to use reasonable force to prevent injury to themselves. They may use whatever force is reasonably necessary under the circumstances, even to the extent of taking the life of the attacker. The amount of force reasonably necessary will differ with the circumstances. The individual does not necessarily have to wait until the first blow is struck. If the individual has good reason to believe that he or she is about to be attacked, the individual may take whatever measures may be necessary for self-protection. However, since the question of whether or not the person acted reasonably under the circumstances will be a question of fact for the jury to decide, whether self-defense will be an effective defense against a claim or battery will depend largely on how the jury defines the phrase "reasonable force."

3) Defense of Property. The owner of real property, be it an individual or a corporation, is entitled to the sole and peaceful possession of the property without the intrusion of others. When a trespasser is on the property, the owner has the right to exercise reasonable force to eject the trespasser. The owner may not, however, erect spring guns, traps, or other devices to injure the trespasser. The owner may employ a guard to eject unwanted visitors, but the guard likewise must use only reasonable force.

Many businesses maintain a watchdog on the premises to discourage any unwelcome visitors. This effort to protect property may be an effective defense to a battery claim. Yet, such firms cannot maintain a vicious dog on the premises solely for the purpose of intentionally injuring known trespassers. Posting notice of the presence of a dog and bringing it to the attention of potential trespassers does not remove this duty.

4) Defense of Others. There is no duty to come to the aid of a person who is being attacked. However, an individual may do so, in which case the same rules that apply to self-defense are applicable. In

going to the defense of another, the individual may mistakenly believe that he or she is aiding the attached person when, in fact, the individual is aiding the attacker. The majority of the courts hold that intermeddlers take their own chances. Persons who mistakenly defend attackers are guilty of assault and battery, since there is no privilege of self-defense.

5) Discipline. Historically, parents, military officers, prison guards, and others in positions with similar responsibilities have had the legal privilege to use the milder forms of corporal punishment as disciplinary methods. As long as they used reasonable force and acted in good faith in the performance of their employment or parental responsibilities, discipline could be used as an effective defense against a battery claim. This is still generally true today. Even so, changing values and the widespread publicity given to such phenomena as child abuse and police brutality seem to have changed the views of many people on what constitutes "reasonable force" in situations where physical forms of discipline are no longer as common as they used to be.

False Arrest and Wrongful Detention Every individual has the legally protected right of liberty of movement. Any wrongful act that deprives a person of that right is an actionable tort. Placing a person against his or her will into a locked room amounts to false imprisonment or wrongful detention. In addition, a person on crutches may be wrongfully detained when the tortfeasor takes away the crutches. If a store or other type of commercial enterprise tries to keep a suspected shoplifter confined, this likewise may be deemed an act of wrongful detention.

Malicious Prosecution Malicious prosecution involves the legally protected right of safety of reputation. When a criminal proceeding is brought against a person, it is published to all that the person has been accused of a certain crime. The damage to that person's reputation and business and credit rating can be considerable.

The elements of an action for malicious prosecution are the following:

1. The plaintiff in the malicious prosecution action shows that a criminal proceeding was instituted or continued against the plaintiff by the party who is now a defendant in the malicious prosecution action.
2. The criminal proceeding was terminated in favor of the accused party.
3. Probable cause for the criminal proceeding was absent.
4. The defendant had "malice" or some other primary purpose other than bringing an offender to justice.

Criminal Prosecution. The actual criminal prosecution must be commenced. The fact that the defendant has sworn out a warrant or has testified before a grand jury is not enough. The criminal prosecution must actually have been instituted and the resultant publicity must have been damaging to the plaintiff's reputation.

Termination in Favor of the Accused. The accused must be found not guilty. If he or she is found guilty, such a verdict is a bar to an action for malicious prosecution.

Absence of Probable Cause. The plaintiff must show that the facts and circumstances were such that no reasonable person would have concluded that the plaintiff was guilty of a crime. The law generally encourages citizens to come forward where a crime has been committed about which the citizen has knowledge. Therefore, the burden of proof on this issue is on the plaintiff. Also, the fact that the defendant has instigated the criminal proceedings on advice of counsel is some evidence of probable cause. It should be repeated that a conviction in a criminal proceeding must be supported by evidence beyond a reasonable doubt. In civil cases the plaintiff ordinarily must sustain the burden of proof, and the plaintiff must do so with a preponderance of evidence. Therefore, despite the criminal acquittal, the defendant of the civil case can show, by a preponderance of evidence, that the plaintiff was in fact guilty of the crime. Again, the quality of evidence needed to establish a preponderance of the evidence is much less than that which would be required to establish the crime beyond a reasonable doubt.

Malice. In the context of a malicious prosecution action, malice may be thought of as a form of ill will, hostility or harassment. If the primary purpose in bringing the proceeding was to give vent to motives of ill will, malice will be established. Another means of establishing malice is by providing evidence to show that the defendant initiated the criminal proceedings to extort money, to collect a debt, or to recover property. However, even though the defendant felt hatred, resentment, or indignation toward the plaintiff, if the proceeding was otherwise a proper one, the feelings of the defendant would not themselves establish malice.

Trespass The owner or occupier (renter) of land has the legally protected right to the exclusive possession and use of the land. A trespasser is a person who is on the premises without the legal right to be on the premises. The trespass may be on the surface of the land, beneath it, or over it within the airspace required by the owner for the peaceful enjoyment of the property. Though he or she may not physically be on the land itself, a person who dumps garbage on the land is a trespasser, even if the garbage is dumped in an area that the owners use for their own garbage. A person likewise may not encroach by building a structure that is partly on another's land; that person has trespassed by such a positioning of the structure. A person who constructs on his or her own land a dam that backs up water on another's land is also guilty of a trespass, even if the dam owner was never physically on the other's land.

Trespass is an intentional tort. The trespasser is liable for any damage that the wrongful intrusion may cause. The amounts of such damage may be slight and call only for an award of nominal damages, or they may be substantial, such as for a building encroachment, in which case the owner of the building would be required to relocate the building onto his or her own land.

Conversion Conversion is an intentional tort that occurs when one person commits the act of appropriating the property of another to his or her own beneficial use and enjoyment, and/or of destroying it or altering its nature.

A classic example illustrates the problem of distinguishing conversion from incidents that do not involve conversion. An auto owner entrusts her auto to a dealer for the purpose of sale, and the dealer uses the car for a ten-mile trip on his own business. This is not a conversion. The use is minimal and does not cause any harm to the auto. On the other hand, if the dealer uses the car on his own business for a trip exceeding, say, 2,000 miles, it would be a conversion. The owner would be deprived of the use of the car, and driving 2,000 miles would reduce its value to some extent.

Similarly, suppose A, on leaving a restaurant, takes B's hat from the rack, believing it to be his own. When he reaches the sidewalk, A puts the hat on and discovers the error. He immediately reenters the restaurant and returns the hat to the rack. This is not a conversion. There was no intent to deprive B of the ownership of the hat. A's good faith is evidenced by the fact that he immediately returns the hat.

The relationship of bailor and bailee offers opportunities for unauthorized use of the bailed property. For example, a woman takes a dress to a dry cleaner for cleaning. The dry cleaner's wife wears the dress to a dance and the dress is damaged beyond repair. This is a conversion. The dry cleaner is liable for the value of the dress.

A car is parked in a garage for storage. The garage owner uses the car for the illegal transportation of narcotics. He is arrested and the car is confiscated by the federal government. This is a conversion and the garage owner is liable for the value of the car.

Nuisance The owner or occupier of real property is entitled to the undisturbed enjoyment of the premises. Neighboring landowners or occupiers have a duty to make reasonable use of their premises so as not to invade the other's rights of enjoyment. Activity of neighbors that impairs the right of the landowner or occupier is a private nuisance that may be abated by an action for damages, an injunction, or both.

There is a fine distinction between trespass and nuisance; in some cases the difference is almost indiscernible. Trespass is the wrongful intrusion onto the lands of another by an individual or by things under the individual's control, such as water or cattle. Thus, trespass invades the right of exclusive and peaceful possession of the land. On the other hand, nuisance invades the owner's right to enjoy the property owned.

What constitutes a nuisance will in many cases be governed by the area in which the activity is being carried on. For example, the operation of a factory, a dog boarding kennel, or a slaughterhouse in a residential area would constitute a nuisance. However, since it is socially advantageous to have such things, they are not nuisances when conducted in an area set aside for that purpose.

Remedies Available. As with any other tort, the remedy for a private nuisance is an action for damages. The elements of the damages that may be claimed include the value of the use and enjoyment of the property of which the owner has been deprived; the rental loss, if any, caused by the nuisance; and the future reduction in value that will occur if the nuisance is continued. Where the property involved has a business use, the loss of business caused by the nuisance will be an additional element. If the nuisance is such that it causes injury to the health of the owner or family members, any injury that may have proximately resulted from the nuisance may also be claimed as damages. A suit for an injunction restraining the defendant from continuing the nuisance may also be brought, together with a plea for the damages that have been incurred up to the time of the granting of the injunction.

Defenses. The only complete defense to an action based on nuisance is that the defendant's actions did not amount to a nuisance but represented only a reasonable use of the premises. As a partial defense, it could be shown that the plaintiff could have avoided some of the consequences of the nuisance and, thus, was not entitled to recover for the full damages claimed. For example, the plaintiff is under a duty to prevent cattle from drinking water that he or she knows is contaminated by the defendant's activity. Likewise, the plaintiff cannot hold the defendant liable for the stench from an unburied dead animal, where the plaintiff could have buried the animal so as to prevent further damage to the enjoyment of the property. The defendant would, however, be liable for any inconvenience that occurred before the plaintiff was made aware of the cause of the difficulty. Thus, the defendant is not liable for the avoidable consequences of maintaining a nuisance when some action on the part of the plaintiff would have reduced the amount of damages.

Wrongful Interference with a Business Relationship Congress and the fifty state legislatures have expressly granted monopolistic powers to public utilities and various other public enterprises. Under federal and state statutes, labor unions also have been given specific rights to engage in anti-competitive behavior, such as the right to strike and the right to form collective bargaining units. Otherwise, the statutes governing business conduct are devoted largely to the protection of the general public and the preservation of fair competition.

In addition to the penalties that may be prescribed for statutory violations, a business firm may be held liable in tort for damages it causes by means of an *unlawful interference with a business relationship*. Many specific types of torts fall within this broad category.

For example, a business firm may be held liable for the tortious act of *malicious interference* with another firm. This can happen whenever one firm interferes maliciously (without justification or excuse) for the purpose of injuring another firm, such as by means of boycott, intimidation, or the circulation of false reports about another firm's honesty or solvency. It can also take the form of *unfair competition through deception,* such as when a firm deceives the public into buying its goods by use of labels, wrappers, or other fraudulent imitations leading buyers to believe, mistakenly, that they are buying the goods of a better-known competitor. Business firms or individuals may be held liable for *unlawful interferences with copyrights, patents, or trademarks.* Once governed entirely by the common law and now set forth in statutes that are beyond the scope of this text, violations of the rights and remedies associated with copyrights, patents, and trademarks have otherwise retained their basic nature as torts.

A *copyright* is essentially an exclusive right, granted by federal statute for a limited period of time, to reproduce, publish, and sell an original work of a literary, musical or artistic nature. Though copyright protection is available only for *original* works of authorship, such "works" are not restricted to printed books or articles, and the holder of the copyright does not necessarily have to be the author of the work. The work can be any original work that is capable of being reproduced or otherwise communicated, either directly or through the aid of a machine or device. Thus, a photograph, a book manuscript, a dramatic play, or the words and notes of a musical composition can be copyrighted. A mere idea, concept, process, or system cannot. If the copyright holder is the author, the right is good for 50 years beyond the lifetime of the author; for a corporation (such as a publisher), it is good for 100 years.

A _patent_ is generally an exclusive right, granted by federal statute for a limited period of time, to make, use, and sell an original invention. Usually (though not always) the patent is held by the inventor. A patent can apply to a "first" invention—or an improvement upon a prior invention—as long as it is a discovery of a new product, process, chemical composition, machine, or other device that embodies a new idea or principle not previously known. In a way, a patent is a nonrenewable monopoly granted for a period of seventeen years.

A _trademark_ is a distinctive mark, word, name, motto, device, or combination of the foregoing that is stamped, printed, or affixed to the goods of a manufacturer or a merchant to distinguish them from the goods of other manufacturers and merchants. Anyone who resells a trademarked àrticle can leave the mark affixed to the article. It is also possible for a firm to use another's trademark in an unrelated business, if there is no chance that the public will be deceived or the original owner of the trademark will be harmed. However, by adopting, using, and registering a distinctive trademark, the original owner of the trademark acquires a valuable proprietary right. If another party knowingly affixes the same trademark (or a confusingly similar trademark) to its own products of an identical or substantially similar nature, this fraudulent act can deceive buyers of the product and decrease the sales of the original trademark owner. Therefore, the trademark owner can bring a tort action against the other seller, because the improper use of another firm's trademark is one of several forms of unfair competition.

Bad Faith   If an insurer refuses to honor its express contractual obligations under an insurance policy, the insured may sue for damages in a breach-of-contract action. Furthermore, virtually all courts now recognize that insurers have various obligations of a so-called _extracontractual_ nature. All of these obligations are in some way related to the provisions of insurance contracts. They are "extracontractual," in the sense that the breach of such obligations will make the insurer liable for _tort_ damages, in addition to or beyond the insurer's liability under the express obligations of the insurance contract.

For example, with respect to _liability_ insurance, nearly all courts now recognize that an insurer may be negligent in defending a claim or suit against the insured. Suppose the claimant makes a pre-trial offer to settle the claim for a dollar amount that is less than the applicable policy limit, and the insurer refuses this offer of settlement. The case then goes to trial and the court enters a judgment for an amount well in excess of the policy limit. Owing to its negligence, the insurer would probably be held liable for the full amount of the judgment, despite the fact that it exceeds the dollar limit expressly stipulated in the insurance contract.

In recent years, a growing number of courts have also recognized a new kind of intentional interference tort, the *tort of bad faith.* They have applied it only to insurers, and they have extended it to all types of insurance.

Every insurer is said to have an "implied covenant or duty to act fairly and in good faith" in discharging its express duties under the insurance contract. The breach of the implied covenant of good faith and fair dealing is a tort. And the essence of this tort lies in the reasonableness of the insurer's conduct. Thus, suppose an insurer delays or refuses the payment of an otherwise covered fire loss, for good reason, such as the insured's failure to file a sworn proof of loss or the insured's misrepresentation of a material fact. The insurer would not be guilty of bad faith. But if a liability insurer refuses to defend an insured against a suit for which the complaint alleges a tort that might be covered by the policy—or, if a crime insurer withholds for two years the payment of an otherwise covered embezzlement loss merely because no suspect has yet been caught and convicted in a criminal trial—the insurer has acted unreasonably, without justification, and in bad faith, and the insured can recover its compensatory damages. If the conduct of the insurer is malicious, or if the court can infer malice because of the insurer's indifference to, or reckless or conscious disregard of, the rights of the policyholder, the insurer may also be held liable for punitive damages.

TORT LIABILITY FOR NEGLIGENCE

In a conceptual or definitional sense, *negligence* is an unintentional tort involving the failure of a natural person to exercise the degree of care that a reasonably prudent person would have exercised, under similar circumstances, to avoid harming another natural person or a legally recognized entity. If a person does something that a reasonably prudent person would not have done under similar circumstances, the person's conduct is referred to as a negligent *act* (or act of *commission).* If a person fails to do something that a reasonably prudent person would have done under similar circumstances, the person's conduct is referred to as a negligent *omission* (or act of *omission*).

A person may be guilty of a negligent act or omission without having any tort liability to another. In some instances, no claim or suit is brought against a person who was actually negligent. When a suit is brought against an allegedly negligent person (a defendant), tort *liability* will be imposed upon the defendant only if four essential elements can be established to the satisfaction of a court of competent jurisdiction. These same elements are used by liability insurers to resolve claims brought against their insureds.

Essential Elements of Negligence Liability

Ordinarily, a defendant will be held *liable* for negligence only if the plaintiff can sustain the burden of proving that:

1. a defendant owed a legal duty to the plaintiff,
2. the defendant breached the legal duty it owed to the plaintiff,
3. the plaintiff suffered actual damages, and
4. there was a "proximate" or close causal connection between the defendant's negligent act or omission and the resulting damages to the plaintiff.

A Legal Duty Owed In the context of negligence law, a legal duty is a mandatory obligation to exercise reasonable care for the safety of others. Such legal duties are created by statutes, by contracts, and by court decisions that together constitute the so-called common law. One who violates or "breaches" such a duty may be held liable for any resulting damages suffered by the person to whom the duty was owed.

For example, employers have both statutory and common-law duties to their employees for job-connected injuries and diseases. The operator of an auto has a general common-law duty to drive at a speed that is safe for existing conditions, even if it is a slower speed than the posted maximum limit. A landowner usually has statutory, contractual, and common-law duties to tenants and others who legally are on the premises. And, a construction firm may enter into an enforceable contract under which the firm assumes the tort liability that the building owner may have to injured third parties.

Breach of the Legal Duty Owed Regardless of the source of a duty or to whom it is owed, the person who has the duty must exercise reasonable care to observe that duty (or face the consequences of a failure to do so). Since the degree of care required to protect others will vary with the circumstances, the courts have adopted the *reasonably prudent person test* to evaluate the conduct of the defendant. The factual issue is whether the trier of fact believes that the defendant behaved the way a reasonable person of ordinary prudence would have behaved under like circumstances. Stated another way, the jury (or the judge, in the few cases where a jury has been waived) must answer the hypothetical question of whether a reasonable person of ordinary prudence, if faced with circumstances similar to those faced by the defendant, would have foreseen the natural consequences of the kind of act or omission committed by the defendant. If a reasonable and prudent person would not have indulged in such an act or omission, because of its foreseeable consequences to others, the defendant failed to observe the standard of care that was required by the particular circumstances involved. Hence, the defendant was negligent, having failed to observe the required standard of care.

In other words, the failure to observe the required standard of care is a breach of a legal duty owed by a natural person to another person or entity. This breach is also the essence of "negligence," in its definitional sense.

As a general rule, adult persons are always responsible for the consequences of their own negligence. But there are also numerous situations in which one person or entity may be held liable for the negligence of another. For example, because a corporation is an artificial entity that cannot act or fail to act except through a natural person, a corporation cannot be negligent. Yet, as noted earlier in this chapter, a corporation can indeed be held *liable* for the negligence of employees who are acting within the scope of their employment. The liability for an employee's negligence is imputed to the corporation, while the employee is *also* liable for his or her negligent act or omission. Accordingly, the liability of the corporation and the employee is said to be *"joint and several."* An injured third party may recover damages from the employee, the corporation, or both. When the liability of a negligent person is imputed to another person or entity, the liability of the negligent person is direct; the liability of the other person or entity is said to be indirect or "vicarious." The mere fact of negligence is not enough to establish liability in tort. There must also be actual damages as a direct result of the negligence.

Damages   In contrast to the liability that may attach to some types of civil wrongs, liability for negligence cannot be based either upon assumed or nominal damages. The plaintiff must establish actual damages of a type recognized by law and measurable in pecuniary terms. In tort law, the following types of damage are recognized and expressible in monetary terms, but only one of the types serves as a precondition to negligence liability:

1. compensatory damages—special or specific, and general
2. punitive damages

Compensatory damages represent the combined total of monetary losses actually sustained by the plaintiff and any additional monetary losses that can be inferred from the facts and circumstances of the case. While the plaintiff seldom if ever gets an itemized breakdown of the total compensatory damages awarded in a particular case, for the purpose of analysis compensatory damages are customarily divided into two categories, "special" damages and "general" damages.

Special damages are compensatory damages of a specific nature that have resulted—or will result—in measurable dollar amounts of actual loss to the plaintiff. Special damages must be established by the plaintiff as a precondition of recovering any damages from the defendant. Assuming they are the direct result of the defendant's negligence, special damages could include any of the following:

- any reasonable *medical expenses* incurred by the plaintiff (here, as elsewhere, what is "reasonable" is a question of fact that ultimately must be decided by the trier of fact);
- any *direct damage to property* owned by the plaintiff, as measured by the lesser of the cost to repair the damage or the cost to replace the damaged property with undamaged property of like kind and quality;
- any indirect damages from *the loss of use of damaged property*, such as the loss of earnings of a business firm or the loss of rental income of a landlord;
- if the plaintiff dies or is physically disabled by the negligence of the defendant, any *loss of earnings from personal services* up to the date of the trial; and,
- if the plaintiff dies or is physically disabled by the negligence of the defendant, the so-called *"present value" or lump-sum equivalent of potential future earnings* from personal services, from the date of trial to the date of the anticipated retirement or life expectancy of the plaintiff.

Once the plaintiff has established special damages, an additional amount may also be awarded for general damages. *General damages* are compensatory damages for intangible losses that may be *inferred* from the special damages and the other facts and circumstances of the case, such as the intangible losses from physical "pain and suffering," "mental anguish," "bereavement" from the death of a loved one, and the loss by one spouse of the "consortium" of a deceased or disabled spouse. Though any general damages awarded are theoretically to compensate the plaintiff with the monetary equivalent of such intangibles, the total amount of general damages is essentially an arbitrary amount determined by the trier of fact.

In almost all jurisdictions, punitive damages also may be awarded to the plaintiffs in certain types of tort actions, but they are not common in ordinary negligence actions, and they are not compensatory in nature. *Punitive damages* are imposed upon the defendant to punish the defendant, to teach the defendant a lesson, to deter others from engaging in the same kind of conduct, and otherwise to serve as an example to others. For the latter reason, punitive damages are often referred to as "exemplary" damages.

Historically, punitive damages were very seldom awarded in ordinary negligence lawsuits. They were imposed upon defendants only in "gross" negligence or intentional interference suits when the conduct of the defendant was "wanton and willful," "malicious," and/or "outrageous." While this is still the general rule, the frequency and severity of punitive damage awards have increased noticeably in recent years, especially in medical malpractice and products liability suits. Moreover, in many types of tort actions, the trier of fact may *infer* malice (and therefore justify punitive damages) when the conduct of the defendant indicates a reckless disregard of the rights of others, or even an indifference to such rights.

When punitive damages are awarded, they are awarded as an additional amount, over and above what is awarded to the plaintiff for compensatory damages. And the insurability of punitive damages continues to be a controversial issue.

Traditional liability insurance forms made no mention whatever of punitive damages. As punitive damage awards became more commonplace, insurers tried to exclude their payment from the various forms, but some of the key state insurance departments would not approve such exclusions—and insurance agents, brokers, and buyers also complained; as a result the exclusions were temporarily withdrawn. Some foreign insurers and reinsurers have announced, at this writing, that they will no longer pay punitive damages. In the meantime, some courts have required liability insurers to pay punitive damages on behalf of their insureds. Other courts have prohibited liability insurers from paying punitive damages on behalf of insureds, even when the relevant form does not exclude such damages. Punitive damages are designed to *punish* a defendant, it is reasoned, and to allow their payment by the defendant's liability insurer would defeat this basic purpose. In any event, the future of punitive damages remains to be seen.

Defenses to Negligence Actions

Contributory Negligence "Contributory negligence" refers to a situation in which the negligence of one person in a lawsuit is a contributing cause of the person's own damages. At common law, contributory negligence was a complete defense against a negligence claim or suit. Thus, if the plaintiff's own negligence was a contributing *cause* of the plaintiff's bodily injury and/or property damage, the plaintiff was not entitled to recover any damages from the defendant. All persons were expected to exercise care to protect themselves from injury and damage. Persons who fell below the required standard could not expect to recover from others, even if their own negligence was slight. The common law did not recognize comparative degrees of negligence.

The contributory negligence defense often produced such harsh results that juries gradually began to interpret slight negligence as though it were no negligence. Eventually, the contributory negligence defense was replaced by the enactment of comparative negligence statutes in about three dozen states.

Comparative Negligence The typical comparative negligence statute provides that when the plaintiff and the defendant are both negligent, damages are to be apportioned between them according to their comparative degrees of negligence, as measured by percentages. The degree or percentage of negligence assigned to each party is ultimately a question of fact for a jury to decide. Though it is assumed here that two persons are involved, for the sake of simplicity, it should be obvious that there could be three or more persons whose negligence served as causes of a particular loss. Regardless of the number of persons involved, the percentages of negligence assigned to each should add up to a total of 100 percent.

There are three broad kinds of comparative negligence statutes:

1. The *"pure" type* represents the maximum departure from the contributory negligence rule. It provides that a party may recover damages, but the amount otherwise recoverable must first be reduced or diminished by his or her proportion of the total negligence. Thus, a plaintiff who is 99 percent negligent can still recover 1 percent of his or her damages.

2. The *"50 percent" type* permits a plaintiff to recover reduced damages only if his or her negligence is *not greater than* that of the other party. If the plaintiff is up to 50 percent negligent, he or she can still recover up to 50 percent of the damages. However, if the plaintiff is 51 percent negligent, no recovery by that particular plaintiff is permitted.

3. The *"49 percent" type* allows a plaintiff to recover reduced damages only if his or her negligence is *"less than"* or *"not as great as"* that of the other party. Therefore, a plaintiff whose negligence was 49 percent or less could recover the corresponding percentage of his or her damages, while a plaintiff who was 50 percent or more negligent could not recover at all. When three or more persons are negligent, the percentages would

differ from those used in the illustrations, but the basic principles would be the same.

Assumption of Risk At common law, persons who knowingly and voluntarily expose themselves to the danger of injury are said to have assumed the risks involved. A plaintiff who has assumed the risks involved in a particular activity cannot later recover damages from a negligent defendant. However, the assumption-of-risk defense is available to a negligent defendant only under the following circumstances:

1. The jurisdiction in question must not have abolished the assumption-of-risk defense by statute. To the extent that workers compensation statutes are applicable to job-connected injuries and diseases, all fifty states have abolished the defense. And some have at least partially done so under comparative negligence and no-fault auto statutes.
2. The plaintiff must understand the extent of the danger involved in the particular activity in question, if the defendant is to make good the defense that the plaintiff knowingly assumed the risks that lead to his or her injury. For example, a professional boxer or a race car driver understands that such activities can result in serious bodily injury or death. On the other hand, a passenger of an auto who is not aware of its defective brakes does not assume the risks involved.
3. The injury-producing exposure to the danger must have been voluntary on the party of the plaintiff. The exposure cannot be voluntary if the insured had no other viable alternative (e.g., a plaintiff does not voluntarily assume the risks of a fall caused by a loose handrail while escaping from a burning hotel on the stairway to the only exit). However, if the plaintiff fails to establish any objections to well-known dangers, prior to injury, it can often be inferred that the plaintiff's exposure to those dangers was voluntary. For this reason, professional football players would be hard put to convince a jury that they did not voluntarily assume the risks of suffering a bone fracture during a Super Bowl game.

   Nonetheless, some courts have held that professional athletes voluntarily assume only the usual risks of their particular sports. For instance, a professional basketball player knows that the game involves a lot of injuries and a considerable amount of bodily contact. But another player who attacks him during a game is not allowed to plead the assumption of risk defense. The attack is the intentional tort of battery, not negligence, and even if the resulting injury was unintentional or negligent, a pro basketball player does not voluntarily assume the risk of having his jaw fractured by repeated blows from another player's clinched fist. Similarly, a professional hockey player was allowed to recover damages from a player on the opposing team. The court did not stretch a point when it concluded that a hockey player does not voluntarily assume the risks of having his face rearranged by a hockey stick while pinned down helplessly on the floor of a spectator section of the arena.

Statute of Limitations The legislatures of all states long ago concluded that there should be some point in time when the threat of litigation must cease. State statutes set forth the periods of time within which various types of actions must be brought. Such statutes are called *statutes of limitation*. Failure to bring the action within the time set forth in the statute terminates the plaintiff's right to enforce a claim.

Note that the running of the time period of the statute does not nullify or void the cause of action. It merely makes the action unenforceable. In many states, the defense of the statute of limitations must be pleaded by the defendant. If it is not pleaded, the trial will proceed just as if the suit were brought within the time limitation.

The statutes also provide that the time limitation is automatically extended for certain classes of persons. Generally, it does not run against a minor during the period of minority. After attaining the age of majority, the former minor is usually granted an additional period within which a tort action may be initiated. In the case of insane persons, the time limit does not run during the period of insanity or during the period in which the insane person is not represented by a guardian.

The time periods in statutes of limitations differ state by state. Within a given state, the time periods also vary for different kinds of torts.

Minority As a general rule, a minor may be held liable for negligence long before reaching the common law age of majority (age twenty-one). Some courts have taken the expedient positions that:

- A minor under the age of seven is incapable of negligence or contributory negligence.
- Between seven and fourteen the minor is presumed to be incapable of negligence, but the contrary may be proved.
- Between the age of fourteen and the common law age of majority, a minor is presumed to be capable of negligence, but evidence to the contrary may be asserted.

Other courts have taken the position that whether or not a minor is capable of negligence is a matter of proving capacity. It would seem, however, that a child under the age of seven would not have much capacity for negligence.

A minor who engages in an adult activity, such as driving a car or flying an airplane, usually is treated as an adult and is liable for negligent acts, regardless of age or capability. The reasoning is that responsibility for the injury or damage should fall on the minor rather than the innocent victim.

Contrary to popular belief, parents are not always responsible for torts committed by their children, unless the child or children are clearly acting as agents for the parent at the time or such responsibility is defined by statute. The agency could come about where the parents instruct the child to do a certain act, and the child obeys. A parent also may be liable for negligently leaving a loaded revolver where it is accessible to a child. If the child uses the gun to injure another person, the parent would be liable for negligently making the gun available to the child. Parents are under a duty to adequately supervise the activities of their children.

Some state statutes change the common law and make the parents liable, within certain dollar limits, for the torts of the child. Most statutes cover only property damage. Such statutes have generally been enacted at the request of highway departments, to cover the cost of replacing street and traffic signs that are common targets of vandals, including no small number of minors.

Immunities

Throughout history in the United States, immunities from tort liability have been granted to various kinds of entities under certain circumstances. These immunities were originally legacies from the legal systems of the regal monarchies to which the colonies and territories had been attached. Some courts that have continued to recognize tort immunities have done so on the political or constitutional grounds that any drastic changes in the law should be made by elected members of legislative bodies, while other courts have explained their continued recognition of tort immunities with the public policy argument that it is better for an individual to go without a remedy than to divert public or charitable funds to the liquidation of private damages.

In jurisdictions that continue to recognize them, tort immunities are in the nature of legal "defenses" against tort actions—at least in the sense that they are effective bars to the tort suits of plaintiffs until a court or a legislature abolishes them. Until then, immunities do not prevent tort suits from being brought against the entities that claim entitlement to some sort of tort immunity.

In recent years, there has been a readily observable trend towards restricting or eliminating immunities from many kinds of civil liability, either by judicial fiat or by legislation. In the meantime, the three major classifications of immunities that affect the liability exposures of commercial entities are: (1) governmental, (2) public official, and (3) charitable.

(1) *Governmental Immunity*   The rule of immunity that protects the federal government from civil suits applies to all types of actions—from condemnation proceedings to personal injury, contract, and injunctive actions against the federal government. Sovereign immunity can thus protect the United States from liability exposures in a variety of ways. In the last fifty years, however, the immunity has been appreciably restricted by congressional enactments that authorize suits of many kinds against the United States. Congress has the discretionary power to give or withhold such consent on whatever terms and conditions it deems appropriate.

Federal Tort Claims Acts (FTCA).   Perhaps the most important legislation waiving immunity is known as the Federal Tort Claims Act (FTCA). The FTCA provides that the United States shall be liable for injuries resulting from the negligence or other tortious conduct of any of its officers, agents, or servants, if committed in the performance of their duties, to the same extent and in the same manner as a private individual under like circumstances. While this act would appear to open the door to myriad claims against the government, certain procedural requirements and substantive exclusions significantly narrow the tort liability exposure of the United States under the act.

For example, the United States can be held liable only for compensatory damages. Punitive damages are expressly prohibited under the act. Nonetheless, the FTCA potentially subjects the United States to liability for an enormous amount of compensatory damages.

Federal Employees' Compensation Act (FECA).   The Federal Employees' Compensation Act (FECA) entitles federal employees or their heirs to receive compensation for disability or death resulting from injury sustained while in the performance of their duties. Like most state workers' compensation laws, the FECA holds the United States liable for such compensation even when the employee's injury did not result from any fault on the government's part. As with the Federal Tort Claims Act, a claimant under the FECA must comply with a series of procedural requirements in order to recover.

Other Federal Acts.   The right to recover disability compensation from the United States is also extended to dockworkers and longshoremen by the Longshore and Harborworkers' Compensation Act, as well as to military support personnel by the Military Claims Act. Recovery against the United States is likewise possible in many property damage cases.

State Governments, School Boards, and Counties. Like the federal government, a state legislature may waive sovereign immunity on whatever terms and conditions it sees fit. Some states confine waivers of governmental immunity to particular state departments or agencies. In other states, statutes waive immunity from liability with respect to any and all private claims arising from the negligence of state officers, agents, and employees.

The courts in a few states have abolished the doctrine. In this small minority of jurisdictions, the courts reason that the doctrine is unnecessary to preserve any public interest and, indeed, is subversive to that interest, in view of the hardship the rule may impose on private parties injured by the state. A few other jurisdictions determine a state's liability by applying a distinction used in municipal law for determining the liability of municipal corporations. In these states, private persons may sue the state when their injuries result from acts committed in the exercise of the government's purely "private" or "proprietary," as opposed to its "public" or "governmental," functions.

Finally, a small but growing number of state courts hold that a state waives its immunity to the extent that it obtains insurance coverage for the activity that allegedly caused the plaintiff's injury. From the standpoint of the insurer, the effect is the same as if no immunity existed.

Even in jurisdictions still recognizing absolute governmental immunity, a state may be held liable for its breach of a contract entered into with a private party. This exception is based on the rationale that the state implicitly waives its immunity by entering into the contract.

In addition, the doctrine of governmental immunity does not apply where the injury complained of is the taking or damaging of private property for public use without compensation, or in cases involving damage to property without an actual taking. This exception stems from federal and state constitutional prohibitions against the taking of private property without just compensation.

For the purposes of determining liability for civil damages, school boards and counties come within the same protection from liability as the particular state of which they form a part.

Municipal Corporations. Most of the rules that determine the civil immunity or nonimmunity of a state or state agency apply also in the case of municipal corporations, such as an incorporated city government. However, municipalities in most states are more vulnerable to private civil suits, by reason of a long recognized exception to governmental immunity for claims arising out of municipal acts committed in a private or proprietary capacity (rather than in a governmental or public capacity). A few states still recognize the common-law rule of absolute immunity, even for municipal corporations.

Proprietary Versus Governmental Functions. Tremendous variation exists among jurisdictions in the classification of governmental versus proprietary functions. In general, the courts use certain tests to determine whether an act falls within either category. However, the general rule is that a function that could be performed by a private entity is proprietary; a function that only can be performed by a government is governmental.

Even in the absence of statutes waiving their immunity to suit, municipalities are exposed to liability from a wide range of activities. This exposure has been steadily increasing as the courts have narrowed the range of activities characterized as public and therefore immune from suit. Some states and municipalities have even enacted legislation imposing liability on local governments for negligently inflicted damages occurring during the execution of purely public functions. For instance, cities in many states are subject to the requirements of workers compensation acts and similar legislation intended to compensate employees injured in the course of their employment.

2) *Public Official Immunity* Under prescribed circumstances, absolute or qualified governmental immunity also applies to federal, state, and municipal officials. Judges and legislators are granted absolute immunity for acts done in their official capacity. Other officials are given only a qualified immunity. The extent of the immunity depends on whether the acts were administrative or ministerial.

- An *administrative* act is one that the official has discretion to perform or not perform. A public official has full immunity in carrying out a discretionary act, but only so long as the act is within the scope of his or her authority and there is no malice or bad faith.
- A *ministerial* act is one that is specified or directed by law or other authority, giving the official no discretion as to whether or not the act is proper. Since the official has no choice in the matter, the official is immune from liability.

Under most tort claim acts, immunity is granted to public officials to the same extent as the governmental body, although the laws frequently exclude certain acts such as operation of autos, assault and battery, and malicious or fraudulent acts.

③ *Charitable Immunity* The common law extended immunity from liability to charitable institutions. Such institutions include nonprofit hospitals, religious, educational, and other eleemosynary or not-for-profit institutions. This extension was grounded on several theories:

- *The trust fund theory* holds that the funds used to operate such enterprises come mainly from others and are basically held "in trust" by the charitable institution to be used only for its stated purpose. To subject such funds to the payment of liability claims would divert the funds from their original purpose.
- A second theory is that the "owners" of a charity derive no benefit or gain from their operation. To subject such entities to liability would diminish their ability to use funds for the benefit of society.
- Another theory is that since many charitable institutions assumed some of the responsibilities of government (i.e., health care, education), they should receive some of the benefits (i.e., governmental immunity).

As with governmental immunity, the trend has been to abolish or severely limit immunity by judicial decisions or by statute. The rationale for such decisions includes the fact that many charitable institutions purchased insurance. To this extent, any liability judgments would not deplete or divert funds from the charity's purpose. Jurisdictions that continue to apply some form of immunity will often distinguish between charitable and noncharitable activities (just as with governmental immunity a distinction is made between governmental and proprietary functions). Thus, if a charity engages in a commercial enterprise, it uniformly can be held responsible for any liability arising out of such activity.

A clear majority of states has rejected the theory of charitable immunity as it applies to nonprofit institutions. Thus, it is evident that schools, churches, universities, and hospitals now face the same liability exposures as other commercial or for-profit enterprises.

STRICT LIABILITY

As noted earlier in this chapter, the numerous torts currently recognized by law may be classified into three broad types:

1. intentional torts,
2. negligence, and
3. strict liability torts.

Having examined the primary kinds of intentional torts and the unintentional tort of negligence, the focus of attention now turns to strict liability torts and the various other ways in which strict liability may be imposed upon commercial entities.

General Nature of Strict Liability

As noted earlier, experts do not agree on the best ways to define and classify torts. This is particularly true of the general class of torts discussed under this heading. The differences in usage need to be acknowledged. Yet it is also necessary for a writer to select a usage that can serve the reader's objectives.

Some experts view the term "absolute" liability as a synonym for "strict" liability. Others view strict liability as a form of absolute liability that is unique to modern products liability law, while still others view absolute liability as one form of strict liability.

Likewise, there is a difference of opinion about the nature of a statutory obligation, such as a covered employer's statutory obligation to pay the medical expenses of a covered employee who has been injured on the job. Some argue that this kind of obligation is not really a tort, presumably on the grounds that the loss payment *is* a statutory duty of the employer and not damages for the breach of a legal duty. Others insist that both employers liability and workers compensation exposures are properly viewed as tort liability exposures, because: Employers liability exposures are still based on negligence law; workers compensation exposures are based on statutes that did not entirely replace negligence law; and, from the viewpoint of employers, applications of workers compensation statutes are not fundamentally different from other situations in which an entity may be held strictly liable without proof of negligence or intent.

Each of the foregoing positions has a relative merit of its own. The widely used phrase "liability without fault" does not. Regardless of how torts are classified, all torts and breaches of contracts are among the civil wrongs for which legal "fault" may be assigned. Thus, it is essentially correct to speak of "tort liability without regard to negligence or intent," or "negligence liability without proof of negligence," or even "liability for intentional interference without proof of intent to do harm." It is *not* correct to say "liability without fault," since this is a contradiction in terms, and it does not by itself reveal the source of the liability.

For the purposes of this text, the phrase *strict liability torts* refers to a generic class of torts that includes *all* torts for which liability may be imposed upon a commercial entity, apart from the issues of negligence or intent. The breadth of this definition makes it unnecessary to reserve a separate category for what some call "absolute" liability. With all due respect to those who feel otherwise, there is a sense in which the distinction between strict and absolute liability is a distinction without a difference. Both are imposed without regard to negligence or intent; both are imposed only in prescribed circumstances and subject to at least some conditions; both notions may involve common law, statutes, and/or contracts; and it is not unusual for both notions to be included in a plaintiff's complaint.

To achieve its objectives without prolonging the classification arguments, this chapter hereafter drops the word "torts" from the phrase "strict liability torts" and uses the remaining phrase *strict liability* as a concept broad enough to include *all* types of civil liabilities that may be imposed upon commercial entities, apart from the issues of negligence or intent, as a result of recognized torts, contractual assumptions of tort liability, or statutory obligations that are intended as partial or complete substitutes for common-law determinations of tort liability and damages.

Types of Strict Liability

Defined broadly, *strict liability* may be imposed upon commercial entities as a result of:

1. abnormally dangerous instrumentalities,
2. ultrahazardous activities,
3. the sale of dangerously defective products,
4. workers' compensation statutes,
5. disability benefit statutes,
6. aviation law,
7. dram shop acts, and
8. contractual assumptions of strict liability.

(1) *Abnormally Dangerous Instrumentalities* Any person who owns, possesses, maintains, or stores an "abnormally dangerous instrumentality" can be held strictly liable to anyone who is injured by the instrumentality. Examples of instrumentalities the courts might regard as abnormally dangerous include dynamite, gasoline, noxious chemicals, explosives, or any type of firearm. Liability is imposed because the safe use of the instrumentality is too beneficial to prohibit, but its unsafe use exposes the community to an unreasonable risk of harm. Citizens of the community who are not public officials are under no legal duty to discover an abnormally dangerous instrumentality or anticipate its unsafe use. Therefore, such citizens are ordinarily under no duty to guard against the possible results of the dangerous

instrumentality, by boarding up their windows, by evacuating the area, or by similar means.

An abnormally dangerous instrumentality can also include an animal owned by a public zoo, a private business firm, or an individual. The animal could be wild or domestic.

Wild Animals. As a general rule, all wild animals that have been removed from their natural habitats are considered abnormally dangerous instrumentalities. If the animal causes bodily injury or damage, the animal's owner may be held strictly liable to the injured party. The mere fact that the owner exercised great care in confining the animal will not necessarily insulate the owner from liability. However, if a wild animal (such as a rattlesnake) escapes and returns to its normal habitat, the former owner is not responsible for any injury subsequently caused by the animal.

Domestic Animals. Unless there is persuasive evidence to the contrary, animals such as horses, cows, dogs, cats, songbirds, and chickens are presumed to be domesticated and relatively harmless. If such an animal causes injury or damage to a third party, the owner of the animal ordinarily would not be held strictly liable (though the owner could be held liable for negligence).

On the other hand, an animal such as a Brahman bull is known to be abnormally dangerous by nature, and its owner is subject to the doctrine of strict liability. The same can be said of a dog that has previously bitten someone or otherwise exhibited "wild and vicious propensities." Such animals are treated by tort law as wild animals, even if they are used for domestic purposes. They are abnormally dangerous instrumentalities to which the doctrine of strict liability may be applied.

(2) **Ultrahazardous Activities** An abnormally dangerous instrumentality can result in injury or damage to others even when no *active* role is played by the owner of the instrumentality. A dangerous instrumentality can be utilized while engaging in an otherwise harmless activity. In any event, any person or entity can be held strictly liable for engaging in an activity that is unreasonably dangerous and produces injury to others. Such activities are called "ultrahazardous activities," and they may include blasting, oil well drilling, mining, the production of dangerous chemicals, the handling of propane gas, and similar activities.

(3) **Dangerously Defective Products** As will be discussed more fully in the next chapter, the rule of strict liability in tort is generally applied to the sale of products that are defective and unreasonably dangerous to the person or property of users or consumers. Under such circumstances, the seller is subject to strict liability. Mere proof of the

defect and the consequent damages will be sufficient to support a cause of action against the seller. This rule may be imposed even though the seller has exercised all possible care in the preparation of the product.

(4) **Workers Compensation Statutes** These statutes are described in some detail in Chapter 10. Briefly the state statutes sought to abolish the negligence remedy for most job-connected injuries and diseases and substituted a system whereby the injured employee and/or the employee's survivors receive specified benefits for a work-related injury or disease. These benefits include weekly compensation benefits and the payment of medical, surgical, and hospital expenses.

The state statutes impose strict liability on the employer for the payment of benefits set forth in the statute. The employer is also required to purchase workers' compensation insurance or otherwise provide proof of financial responsibility in a form acceptable to the jurisdiction involved.

(5) **Disability Benefit Statutes** Several states have statutes that require the employer to provide insurance covering nonoccupational injuries sustained by employees. The insurance is a form of accident insurance under which benefit payments are not conditioned upon a finding of negligence or intent, and its purchase by employers is compulsory. Therefore, some employers view the obligations under the laws as a type of strict liability.

(6) **Aviation Law** Aviation exposures are discussed in Chapter 9. Here, it only needs to be noted that the ownership or operation of private or commercial aircraft can give rise to strict liability, whether by statute, common law, or treaty.

(7) **Dram Shop Acts** A number of states have passed "dram shop acts" that impose strict liability on the seller of intoxicating beverages to a person who becomes intoxicated and, in turn, causes injury to the person or property of another. A sale could be tortious, for example, if made to an obviously intoxicated person.

(8) **Contractual Assumptions** Just as a commercial entity may contractually assume the *negligence* liability that another party may have to a third person, a commercial entity may also contractually assume the *strict liability* that another party may have to a third person. The latter presupposes that the relevant contract provision is enforceable in the applicable jurisdiction. If so, the assumption may be thought of as a form or source of strict liability.

VICARIOUS LIABILITY

As explained earlier, "vicarious" liability is liability that is imputed to one party for the tortious act or omission of another. Since a corporation cannot act or fail to act except through a natural person, the tort liability of a corporation is always vicarious. The corporation may be held jointly and severally liable for the torts of an employee that are committed in the course of employment, and for the torts of any other agent that are committed within the scope of the agency. The same is generally true of a partnership entity (though each partner is an agent of the partnership). Also, a sole proprietor may be vicariously liable for the torts of his or her employees or agents.

Either a natural person or commercial entity can be held vicariously liable for the *negligence* of another—or for an *intentional tort* of another. In either case, the vicarious liability can be viewed as a form of strict liability. It can be imposed upon an entity, regardless of whether the entity itself was guilty of negligence or intentional interference. In like manner, vicarious liability may be imposed upon the owner of an auto or aircraft that is driven or flown by another.

Under some circumstances, the agent may exceed the scope of the authority granted, yet the agent's acts may be for the benefit of the principal. If the principal accepts the beneficial results of unauthorized acts, the legal effect is known as a ratification. Having ratified the acts, the principal may be held vicariously liable for any consequences of the acts.

Chapter Note

---

1. Discussion here is based on Williams, Head, Horn, and Glendenning, *Principles of Risk Management and Insurance*, 2nd ed. (Malvern, PA: American Institute for Property and Liability Underwriters, 1981), Chapter 1. Williams et al. base their discussion of pre-loss and post-loss objectives on suggestions made by Professors Robert I. Mehr and Bob A. Hedges.

CHAPTER 2

Premises, Operations, Products, and Contractual Exposures

Chapter 2 continues the analysis of liability exposures begun in Chapter 1 by focusing on specific exposure types. Addressed in this chapter are tort liability exposures associated with premises, operations in progress, completed operations, products, and contractual assumptions. These exposures correspond to major coverage areas of the commercial general liability insurance policy, which will be examined in Chapters 5 and 6. Other specific liability exposures will be examined in subsequent chapters, where they will be related to other categories of liability insurance.

PREMISES LIABILITY EXPOSURES

General Nature of Premises Liability Exposures

Premises liability exposures are exposures to the *tort* liabilities that may be imposed upon owners and other "possessors of land" for the breach of legal duties they owe to one another and/or to third parties. These exposures are occasionally referred to in insurance circles as owners', landlords', and tenants', or "OL&T" exposures.

The legal notion of *land* is broad enough to include not only the earth and the airspace above it, but also the permanent things affixed to the earth, growing from the earth, or beneath its surface, such as buildings, trees, plants, water, and mineral deposits. Taken together, these things constitute the "land," realty, real property, or "premises" in question.

Premises liability exposures arise from the legal duties associated with the ownership, use, occupancy, and/or possession and control of land. These include the duties an owner owes to a tenant, the duties a tenant owes to an owner, the duties one tenant owes to other tenants, and the duties a possessor owes to a "third person"—that is, a person who is not a party to the lease and who is on the premises (or in the vicinity thereof) for a reason other than to work as an employee of the possessor. The discussion immediately following is devoted to the duties and tort liabilities that any possessor of land may have to such third persons, apart from any duties arising out of a contract.

Liability of Possessors of Land to Third Persons Generally

When a third person suffers bodily injury or property damage on or near the premises of another and the entire premises is clearly in the sole possession and control of its owner, any subsequent tort action by the injured third party is normally brought against the owner. However, in the familiar situation involving the occupancy of the premises by its owner *and/or* a mere tenant, the tort action of an injured third party is normally brought against both the owner and the tenant. Either or both may be held liable to the injured party, depending upon the resolution of such questions as who committed the tort, who may be held responsible for the tort, the applicability of a statute, the common-law duties owed to the injured party, and who is deemed to have possession and control of the premises at the time of injury.

Of the legal duties a possessor of land owes to third persons, comparatively few are unique to owners or unique to tenants. As a general rule, they are duties owed by all possessors of land. And their breach may give rise to tort liability based on any of the usual grounds—intentional interference, strict liability, or negligence. *Per Inj*

For example, an owner or tenant who *intentionally interferes* with the person or property of a third party who is on or near the premises may be held liable for such specific torts as assault and battery, wrongful detention, or malicious prosecution. Such torts are insured only to the extent that they are included as so-called "personal injury" coverages in the possessor's general liability insurance. In most respects, the intentional interference portion of premises liability exposures does not differ from the intentional interference portion of other tort exposures.

Similarly, a possessor of land may be held *strictly liable* to third parties who are injured on or near the premises if the injury was the proximate result of "abnormally dangerous instrumentalities" or "ultrahazardous activities" used or engaged in by the possessor. These particular strict liability exposures may be insured under standard liability insurance forms, but the exposures themselves are not confined to a premises possessed and controlled by the entity exposed, nor are other kinds of strict liability exposures.

The distinctive nature of premises liability exposures emerges primarily from the application of common-law *negligence* principles to the possessor of land. Thus, to understand premises liability exposures, one must first understand the common-law duties a possessor of land owes to third parties *in its capacity as a possessor* of land. As a possessor of land, the possessor has common-law duties to third persons outside the premises as well as to third persons on the premises.

Duties to Persons Outside the Premises

At common law, the possessor of land is under a duty to exercise reasonable care for the protection of third persons who are outside the premises but in the vicinity of the premises. Such persons include neighbors, passersby, and others who may be near the premises.

Signs Many business organizations erect signs for advertising, or other purposes. Some signs are flat against a building while others are free-standing or suspended over public sidewalks. In erecting a sign, the owner or occupier of the property must exercise reasonable care for the safety of others. The failure to do so constitutes negligence.

Some municipalities regulate the placement of signs by city ordinances. If the owner of a sign fails to erect or maintain it in accordance with such a city ordinance, the owner may be held liable for any resulting injury to another person.

A question often raised is whether a sign must be strong enough to withstand the effects of all kinds and degrees of weather. Generally, if a sign withstands (or would have withstood) the storms and winds that normally are to be expected in the geographical area of its location, the owner is deemed to have met the required duty of care.

Streets and Sidewalks As a general rule, a possessor of land has no common-law duty to maintain or repair public streets or sidewalks that are adjacent to the possessor's premises. However, virtually any person who creates an unsafe condition on a street or sidewalk may be held liable to a party injured as a proximate result of that condition. If the street or sidewalk has been damaged by the possessor of a nearby premises, the possessor is under a legal duty to correct the defect. Either the failure to repair the defect or repairing it in a negligent manner will subject the possessor to liability for any resulting accidents.

When damage to public streets or sidewalks is not caused by the possessor of a nearby premises, a state or political subdivision that does not have immunity from tort liability may be held liable for injury resulting from such defects, provided that the state, county, township, or municipality has notice of the defect and fails to repair it or erect barricades.

Snow and Ice The same general rules that apply to defects in public streets and sidewalks also apply to the accumulation of snow and ice. Unless modified by statute or ordinance, the state or municipality is responsible for the maintenance of the streets and sidewalks; accordingly, the possessor of nearby land has no responsibility to remove snow or ice. As a matter of business practice, many businesses do remove snow and ice from public sidewalks that provide customers and suppliers access to the business premises. If so, having voluntarily assumed the task, the business is under a duty to exercise reasonable care in the process. If the snow removal makes the condition worse, the business may be liable for any consequences of the worsened condition.

Some municipal ordinances require the possessor of abutting land to remove snow and ice from public sidewalks within twenty-four hours after the snow has stopped. (If the owner or occupier fails to remove snow and ice, the municipality usually may remove it at the expense of the owner and impose a fine.) Such ordinances do not create a tort liability where none existed before. But violation of such an ordinance may be accepted by a court as evidence of negligence.

However, if a possessor of a nearby premises creates an unsafe condition by placing an abnormal amount of water on the street or sidewalk (e.g., by means of a poorly located downspout or the operation of a car wash), the possessor may be liable for damages should the unsafe condition result in injury.

Parking Lots A business in possession and control of a parking lot for the convenience of customers is under a duty to maintain both the parking lot and all passageways from the lot to its building(s). Liability may be imposed when a customer is injured due to the failure of the business to maintain the lot or the passageways in reasonably safe condition.

Pollution A possessor of land who pollutes the air or an adjoining waterway may do so negligently or intentionally. In either case, the person(s) affected may bring a tort action for damages, as well as an action for injunctive relief. Pollution liability is examined more specifically in Chapter 7.

Natural Conditions of the Land Generally, a possessor of land has no legal duty to correct a natural defect or condition of the land even if the defective condition is bothersome or injurious to neighbors or passersby. For example, a possessor is not obliged to fill or drain a natural swamp that emits foul odors and facilitates the breeding of mosquitoes. Nor does the possessor have a duty to remove or spray dandelions and crabgrass to prevent their spread to a neighbor's lawn. Likewise, the possessor has no legal duty to divert or impede the natural flow and drainage of surface water on the land, even if the natural water flow damages the property of a neighbor or prevents the use of public sidewalks or streets adjoining the land.

The early common-law rule regarded trees as natural conditions of the land. Whether or not they were planted by the possessor, no liability was imposed upon the possessor for any damage the trees might cause. However, this original common-law rule has been modified with respect to dangerous trees located in cities. Now, if a dead or diseased tree is near a public street, a public sidewalk, or a neighbor's land, the possessor is under a common-law duty to remove the tree or take other steps to avoid injury or property damage to persons in the vicinity of the premises.

Some municipalities also have local ordinances under which possessors are required to remove dangerous trees that are close enough to public streets or highways to threaten the public safety. If the possessor fails to do so, the municipality is empowered to remove the dangerous trees at the expense of the possessor, and the failure can be used as evidence of the possessor's negligence.

A somewhat lesser standard of care is owed by possessors of trees in rural areas. Unless the possessors have actual knowledge of the dangerous condition of trees abutting public roads or highways, they are usually not liable for any injury or property damage the trees may cause to persons outside the premises. Even so, there are exceptions to virtually every general rule. A court may hold the possessor liable in situations where the possessor's awareness of a dangerous tree may reasonably be inferred—or where it would be reasonable to impose on the possessor a duty to make periodic inspections of the premises for the purpose of discovering any hazardous conditions.

Duties to Persons on the Premises

A possessor of land owes identifiable common-law duties to each of the various classes of persons who may enter the premises for purposes other than to work as employees of the possessor. The "degree of care" a possessor owes to a particular class of persons may be slight, moderate, or considerable, depending upon the number and types of duties the law recognizes as obligations to that class.

Subject to the partial exceptions noted later under a separate heading, persons who may enter the premises of another have been classified according to their legal status as "trespassers," "licensees," or "invitees." However, most, if not all, courts have held that "children of tender years" are owed a higher degree of care than adults, in *each* of the three major classifications, and some courts have also made distinctions among business invitees, public invitees, and social guests.

In order to focus on the loss exposures of commercial entities and provide a rough ranking of the relative degree of care owed to each class of persons who may enter the premises of a commercial entity, the following categories will be used as a framework for discussion: (1) adult trespassers, (2) adult licensees, (3) adult business invitees, and (4) children. Some partial exceptions to the general rules will then be described.

Adult Trespassers A *trespasser* is a person who is on the premises of another without first having a legal right or privilege to do so. A person who does not have a prior invitation from the possessor is not necessarily a trespasser. If the person has requested and obtained the consent of a possessor with authority to give consent, the person is said to have the privilege or "legal license" to enter the premises and use it within the scope of the permission granted. Also, a person may have the legal right or authority to enter the premises of another, even in the absence of invitation or consent. Examples include a police officer with a properly issued search warrant, a sheriff with authority to serve a summons, a person entrusted with the power to enforce an eviction notice, and a federal income tax official authorized to conduct a mandatory audit of a business firm's book of account. Thus, a trespasser is a person who enters the premises of another without invitation, consent, legal privilege, lawful authority, or legal right to enter the premises (or one who enters lawfully but *uses* the premises for a purpose that is without legal sanction).

To an *adult* trespasser, the possessor of land owes a relatively low degree of care. For example, as a general rule, the possessor has no legal duty to make the premises safe for adult trespassers. To this extent, the possessor does not have a legal duty to remove or correct a hazardous condition on the premises, even if it is not a natural condition of the land. Nor does the possessor have a legal duty to discover the presence of a trespasser on the premises. Nonetheless, once a trespasser's presence is known to the possessor, the possessor owes the trespasser a notably higher degree of care than many people seem to believe.

The possessor of land may use *reasonable force* to expel a known trespasser from the premises. Even so, because the issue of "reasonable force" is ultimately a question of fact for a jury to decide, there is always the realistic possibility that a jury might regard the expulsion

efforts of the possessor as excessive force in relation to the circumstances. Indeed, most courts have deemed the force to be automatically
unreasonable and excessive when it has involved the use of traps,
snares, or other devices that are actually or inferably intended to harm
trespassers. Though the *criminal* law recognizes the concepts of "self-
defense" and "justifiable homicide" in a limited number of narrowly
defined situations, the criminal guilt or innocence of the trespasser or
the possessor does not necessarily bar a *tort* action against the
possessor for intentional interference with the person of another. There
have been well-publicized cases in which a convicted and jailed criminal
(or the familial heir of a deceased criminal) has successfully recovered
money damages for an intentional tort of the possessor of land.

A few courts have gone one step further and held that, once the
possessor is aware of the presence of a trespasser, the possessor has a
duty to forewarn the trespasser of any hazardous conditions on the
premises that are known to the possessor but not readily apparent to
others. The failure to provide such a forewarning may constitute
actionable negligence or intentional interference by the possessor. On
the other hand, the mere posting of "no trespassing" signs does not in
itself relieve the possessor of legal duties it would otherwise have for
several reasons:

● Whether or not such signs are posted, the possessor has no
  legal duty to make the property safe for the trespass of an
  adult.
● A court might not regard such signs as a sufficient forewarning
  of impending danger to an adult trespasser whose presence is
  known, especially if the signs are illegible or spaced too far
  apart—or if the adult trespasser is illiterate or understands
  only a foreign language.
● The posting of signs does not diminish the special care the
  possessor owes to child trespassers (discussed later).

In short, possessors of land generally owe adult trespassers a
lower degree of care than they owe to other classes of persons who
may enter the premises. But possessors who "take the law into their
own hands," so to speak, are not free of the risks it involves.

Adult Licensees   For tort law purposes, a *licensee* is a person
who is (1) on the premises of another with the *legal privilege* to be on
the premises and (2) on the premises for the *personal benefit* of the
licensee. Persons who meet both tests are deemed to be licensees.

The term "licensees" is not used here to refer to persons who have
been issued tangible documents as evidence of their licenses to drive an
auto, fish or hunt, or solicit business on premises they do not own.

Instead, "licensees" is used in the broader sense to refer to persons who have the legal privilege or "license" to be on the premises in question.

It is frequently said that this kind of license is obtained by acquiring the *consent* of the possessor. While it is true that the possessor's consent grants a legal privilege, a person may have a recognized privilege to be on the premises without obtaining the *express* consent of the possessor. For example, a firefighter who volunteers to extinguish a fire that is beyond the control of the possessor is usually treated as a licensee. The consent of the possessor is at least *implied* (e.g., when the possessor does not object to the firefighter's conduct or the possessor is not present at the time), and the consent may be expressed (e.g., when the possessor telephones the fire department for help). In addition, a police officer who lawfully enters the premises on official business may not have express or implied permission; yet, such a police officer is usually treated as a licensee for tort law purposes. The police officer has the legal privilege of entering the premises for a lawful purpose, apart from any consent by the possessor.

According to the second test or precondition of licensee status, the persons in question must be on the premises for their own personal benefit. (Their presence may also be of benefit to the possessor, but this is not a precondition of licensee status.) The benefit to the licensee may take the form of actual or desired convenience or pleasure, as well as monetary reward. And, in the case of firefighters and police officers, the notion of personal benefit is stretched a bit to include the benefit of doing one's job.

In addition to firefighters and police officers, courts have also classified as licensees those persons who enter the premises of another as door-to-door salespersons, solicitors of charitable contributions, visitors touring a business at their own request, persons seeking refuge from inclement weather without objection by the possessor, and persons on the premises to borrow property from neighbors who are not close friends.

To the adult licensee, the possessor of land owes two basic legal duties. First, the possessor is obliged to forewarn the licensee of any hazardous conditions on the premises that are known to the possessor but may not be readily apparent to licensees. Second, the possessor is expected to exercise reasonable care to avoid bodily injury or property damage to the licensee. Otherwise, licensees are said to "take the premises as they find it" and expose themselves to whatever conditions the possessor is also exposed to. The possessor has no duty to inspect the premises periodically to discover hazards unknown to the possessor. Nor is the possessor required to correct any natural or unnatural conditions of the land, whether or not they are known by the possessor to be hazardous.

In the jurisdictions that obligate a possessor to forewarn a trespasser of concealed hazards once the possessor is aware of the presence of a trespasser on the premises, the degree of care owed to licensees is about the same as it is to trespassers whose presence is known. However, since some jurisdictions have not recognized a duty to forewarn persons of impending danger when they are known to be trespassing, and since the recognized duties to potential trespassers are not much more than to avoid the use of excessive force to expel and otherwise to avoid intentional injury, the degree of care owed to adult licensees is generally greater than the degree of care owed to adult trespassers.

Adult Business Invitees A *business invitee* is a person who (1) has an express or implied *invitation* to be on a premises possessed and controlled by a business entity and (2) is invited to be on the premises in the hopes of achieving a present or future *business benefit for the possessor*. Persons who meet both preconditions are deemed to be invitees, apart from whether or not their presence on the premises may also benefit themselves.

In terms of the very large number of persons involved, actual and prospective customers of retail stores constitute the most common type of business invitee. Supermarkets and other familiar retail stores are continually advertising. Their doors are unlocked and their lights are on during posted business hours. They are expressly and impliedly inviting members of the public to enter the premises and either purchase something or browse (hoping that the browser will buy something next time and/or tell friends about the merchandise available at the store). Thus, all such persons are clearly business invitees.

In addition to actual and potential customers of retail stores, the courts of at least several jurisdictions have also treated the following classes of persons as business invitees when they are on the premises in question:

- people delivering raw materials, finished products or supplies to manufacturers, wholesalers, or retailers;
- pick-up and delivery persons working for express and parcel service firms;
- meter readers of utility companies;
- trash and garbage collectors;
- persons doing repair or alteration work; and
- persons who visit tenants in apartment houses while they are in the portion of the premises under the landlord's control.

The courts often disagree on the question of whether persons in a particular role qualify as business invitees. But many courts have defined the phrase "business invitee" broadly enough to include persons whose presence on the premises could conceivably be in the nature of a business advantage to the possessor.

To adult invitees, a business firm owes all the legal duties it owes to adult licensees, plus an additional duty of considerable significance. Specifically, a business firm has the duties that follow:

1. to *forewarn* business invitees of any hazardous conditions on the premises that are known to the business but may not be readily apparent to invitees;
2. to exercise *reasonable care* to avoid bodily injury or property damage to invitees, including the duty to establish and maintain appropriate safeguards for the prevention of accidents on the premises; and
3. to *inspect the premises*, at reasonably necessary intervals, *to discover—and eliminate or safeguard the public against*—any hazardous conditions of the type that periodic inspections by a prudent business person would normally reveal.

Whether a particular combination of forewarning, exercise of care, and inspection was "adequate," in relation to the undisputed facts and relevant circumstances of the case, is a question of fact to be decided by the trier of fact (normally a jury). If any one of the duties is deemed to have been breached by an employee or any other legal agent of the business entity, the entity may be held vicariously liable for negligence.

With respect to governmental bodies, private educational institutions, charitable organizations, and other "commercial" entities that are not business firms as such, persons who are on their premises may still be classified by courts as trespassers or licensees. They may even be classified as "business" invitees, especially in connection with any *proprietary* function or activity of the entity involved. However, as explained in the first chapter, some of these entities might be entitled to use absolute or conditional immunity as a defense against a negligence action. Some of the individuals involved may also be entitled to tort immunities in particular situations.

The issue of how to classify *social guests* has posed some rather unique problems for all courts that have attempted to distinguish between licensees and invitees, as a result of which the decisions of courts have not been entirely consistent. When an unwanted social guest unexpectedly appears at a private residence owned or occupied by a casual acquaintance and the possessor reluctantly acquiesces to the visit, it would seem logical to treat such a guest as a "licensee" during the period of the visit. In contrast, when a social guest is expressly invited to a private residence and the visit is devoted largely or entirely to business or professional matters, it would seem logical to treat such a guest as a "business invitee" of the possessor during the period of the visit. Yet, a number of courts have treated virtually all social guests as licensees, without making distinctions of the type just illustrated. Other courts have imposed on possessors, in at least some social guest situations, the same duties that are owed to business invitees. Since the degree of care owed to business invitees is higher than the degree of care owed to licensees, the effect is to make it easier for a social guest to prevail as the plaintiff in a negligence action against the possessor of the premises on which the guest was injured.

The social guest issue has practical significance to the hundreds of commercial entities that conduct business or quasi-business activities in a number of different legal jurisdictions. Though it is frequently said that social guests virtually always have been treated as licensees, the unqualified assumption that this will continue to be true does not justify a relaxation of sound risk management practices in business entertainment situations. The safest objective for a business is to observe persistently the highest degree of care that is owed to any class of persons who might be deemed to be a part of its premises liability exposure (and/or some other liability exposure, regardless of what it may be called). In connection with the premises exposure, the highest degree of care is owed to an invitee who is also a child of tender years.

Children For the particular purpose of determining the degree of care owed by a possessor of land, there is no fixed age that distinguishes an "adult" from a "child of tender years." Rather, the trier of fact must decide, on a case-by-case basis, whether the person in question has enough maturity, intelligence, and life experience to have the capacity to understand the existence and degree of danger that a particular condition or activity inherently involves. If so, the person is deemed to have the status of an adult. If not, the person is deemed to have the status of a child of tender years.

To children of tender years, the possessor of land owes a higher degree of care than the possessor owes to an adult in the same general category. In other words, more care is owed to a child invitee than to an adult invitee; more care is owed to a child licensee than to an adult licensee; and more care is owed to a child trespasser than to an adult trespasser.

The greater care owed to children in all categories is justified in general terms by the argument that the "reasonable care" standard requires a bit of extra care to avoid harm to children. More specifically, it is justified by the need to recognize and anticipate the "meddling propensities" of children. That is to say, it is not unnatural for children to be inquisitive and unafraid. They like to explore that which is new and unusual to them. Without hesitation, they will tamper and experiment with tangible objects. They tend to meddle. Therefore, a possessor of land has the general duty to anticipate and guard against the meddling propensities of children. This may obligate the pharmacist to keep poisons and other dangerous products out of the reach of children—or the supermarket to provide shopping carts suitable for carrying children—or the auto mechanic to avoid allowing children in work areas near hoists or dangerous machinery or tools.

In addition, with respect to the duties a possessor of land owes to trespassing children, the majority of courts have applied the *attractive nuisance doctrine* (sometimes called the doctrine of attractive "allurement") to prescribed sets of facts and circumstances. As a theoretical concept, the notion of an attractive nuisance is general enough to include nearly any tangible and visible "thing" that is attractive or alluring to members of the public and yet potentially harmful to them. In practice, the doctrine has been applied only to trespassing children of tender years, in rather narrowly defined situations as a partial but far-reaching exception to the usual rules applicable to adult trespassers. The attractive nuisance doctrine is normally applied only under the following circumstances:

1. The premises in question must be in the possession and control of the defendant (hereafter called the possessor).
2. The possessor must have created, maintained, or otherwise permitted to exist on the premises an artificial condition or a tangible and visible object that is reasonably known to be both attractive to children and unreasonably dangerous to them.
3. The dangerous condition or object must be located in a place where children are likely to trespass if permitted to do so.
4. The possessor must have failed to exercise reasonable care (given the well-known meddling propensities of children) to eliminate, remove, or protect children from the dangerous condition or object.
5. A child of tender years must have suffered bodily injury as the proximate result of the possessor's breach of the duty to exercise reasonable care.

The doctrine of attractive nuisance has often been applied in situations where small children have drowned in privately owned swimming pools. Many local communities have ordinances requiring pool owners to have fences of a minimum height surrounding the pool. Nevertheless, compliance with such an ordinance does not in itself absolve the owner or possessor of the pool from tort liability for a child's injury or death. The trier of fact may give some weight to evidence of fences and locks in deciding whether a possessor was negligent, but if a small child has drowned in the pool, it is difficult to convince a jury that the safeguards used were adequate.

In addition to privately owned swimming pools, the doctrine of attractive nuisance has also been applied in situations involving man-made lakes or ponds, dangerous machines and equipment, dangerous animals in unlocked cages, and various other conditions or instrumentalities that are especially attractive and dangerous to children of tender years. Seldom (if ever) is the doctrine applied to a situation involving a *natural* condition of the land.

Partial Exceptions to the General Rules   Either expressly or by jury interpretation, all jurisdictions have continued to recognize the extra degree of care that is reasonably owed to children of tender years. However, a number of jurisdictions no longer attempt to distinguish between licensees and invitees, and a few jurisdictions have abolished all three of the traditional classifications of persons who may be on the premises of another—or, they have ruled that a person's status as a trespasser, licensee, or invitee is no longer the decisive factor; it is merely a factor that may properly be considered in deciding whether a possessor has exercised the degree of care that a "reasonable and prudent" possessor would have exercised under like circumstances.

Landlords and Tenants

"Premises liability exposures" include all exposures to *tort* liabilities arising from the ownership, use, occupancy, and/or possession and control of real property or "land." Thus far, the discussion has focused on tort liabilities that *any* possessor of land may have to third persons. The discussion now turns to the similarities and differences between the third-person liability exposures of landlords and tenants, respectively, and the tort liabilities that landlords and tenants may have to one another.

Liability of Landlords and Tenants to Third Persons   In the absence of a statute, the third-person premises liability exposures of a tenant are identical or quite similar, in most important respects, to the third-person premises liability exposures of a landlord. These similarities are as follows:

1. *In their capacity as possessors, both the landlord and the tenant have essentially the same common-law duties to third*

persons who are on or near the premises. Since either a landlord or a tenant can have possession and control of all or a portion of the premises, either can be a possessor of land. Whether a tort suit is brought against the landlord, the tenant, or both, the applicable law is the law of the jurisdiction in which the tortious act or omission occurred, and this is also the jurisdiction in which the premises are located, in a tort suit based on possession and control of the *premises* (in contrast, say, to a products or auto suit in which the applicable jurisdiction can differ from the location of a particular premises). If the courts of the applicable jurisdiction distinguish between business invitees and various nonbusiness invitees, the duties of a tenant to third persons would differ slightly from those of a landlord when one is a business and the other is not. Otherwise, to the extent that a tenant and a landlord are both possessors, they have essentially the same premises-related duties to third persons who are on or near the premises in question.

2. *As a possessor, the landlord and/or the tenant may be held liable to an injured third person on any of the usual tort grounds—intentional interference, negligence, or strict liability.*

3. *There is an important sense in which a landlord has no more of a need to have premises liability insurance than a tenant of the same premises.* Either may be held liable for damages that are unlimited in amount. Furthermore, the third-person plaintiff frequently names both the landlord and the tenant as co-defendants in the action, in which event they must at least defend themselves, in the absence of liability insurance coverage. They may also be held jointly and severally liable for damages in some situations. There may be unilateral or mutual loss-transfer provisions in the lease between the tenant and the landlord. However, as explained in Chapter 1, such lease provisions are not complete substitutes for premises liability insurance. Mutual loss-transfer provisions do not alter the third-party premises liability exposure of either party to the lease. And unilateral loss-transfer provisions do not relieve the transferor from its own tort liability; they merely give the transferor a contractual remedy by which to hold the transferee financially responsible for loss, to the extent that the contractual provisions are legally enforceable.

In the context of premises-related liability exposures, there are also a few noteworthy differences between a landlord's duties and liabilities to third persons and a tenant's duties and liabilities to third persons. These differences are:

1. *Landlords are normally liable for any violation of applicable statutes and ordinances in the nature of building safety laws.* Numerous state statutes and municipal ordinances pertain to the safety of buildings for their use and occupancy by human beings. These laws include the electrical wiring and sanitation requirements under building codes, provisions requiring the maintenance of adequate lighting of stairs and hallways, and provisions requiring the installation and maintenance of automatic sprinkler systems in hotels and dormitories. Some kinds of safety laws also apply to tenants, but the statutory obligations regarding the construction and maintenance of the building itself are usually imposed on the building owner.

   Despite what the lease may say about such matters, statutory violations by the building owner might be given weight as evidence of negligence in a tort suit brought directly against the owner by an injured third person.

2. *Landlords normally retain their common-law liabilities with respect to any public portions of the premises.* In the familiar situation where a portion of the building is leased to each of several tenants, the landlord invariably retains possession and control of elevators, entranceways, hallways, stairways, and privately owned sidewalks, pools, parking lots, and other "public" or common areas that are used by all the tenants, their guests, delivery and repair persons, and other members of the general public (including trespassing children). Having retained possession and control of such public areas, the landlord also retains the common-law duties and liabilities of a possessor of such areas.

   In the smaller number of instances where the landlord leases the *entire* premises to one tenant, the tenant is said to acquire the attributes of ownership during the period of the lease. But a court may hold that the landlord *also* retained a degree of possession and control over elevators, stairways, hallways, and other areas customarily used by third persons, especially if the plaintiff's injury was at least partly caused by the landlord's violation of a safety statute and/or the landlord's breach of the common-law standard of reasonable care. This potential outcome and the obligation of the landlord to defend against allegations of such tortious conduct are not rendered impossible or unlikely by a contrary lease provision.

While the landlord may have statutory duties under safety laws and does have common-law duties with respect to areas over which the landlord has possession and control, apart from any lease provisions, the same can also be said of tenants. One should not make too much of the differences between their premises exposures to third-person liabilities. They both need adequate premises liability insurance (or other suitable loss-financing and judgment), and they also may need contractual liability coverage—to be discussed later.

Liability of Tenants to Tenants   There is nothing truly unusual or unique about the legal duties that one tenant owes to other tenants of the same building. When one tenant is inside the portion of the building that is in the possession and control of another tenant, the visiting tenant could be an invitee, a licensee, or a trespasser (the significance of which would depend on the jurisdiction involved). When a tenant is inside his or her own portion of the building, or in a hallway or other common area, that tenant is entitled to receive from another tenant the same degree of care that would be owed to any member of the public who is outside the premises of a possessor but in a nearby area.

In view of the foregoing, it should be obvious that one tenant may be held liable in tort to another tenant on the grounds of intentional interference, negligence, or strict liability. With regard to the negligence exposure, the general duty one tenant owes to another, in all jurisdictions, is the duty to exercise reasonable care. A breach of this duty can result in tort liability to a tenant injured as a proximate result of the breach, just as it can to any injured member of the general public.

Liability of Landlords to Tenants   Despite any loss-transfer provisions in the lease, the landlord still has the extra-contractual duty to exercise reasonable care for the protection of the tenant. Generally, the landlord has the duty to maintain the common areas of the premises and the building itself in safe condition, either by common law, by the terms of the lease, and/or by provisions in any applicable safety statute or ordinance. In the absence of a statutory violation by the landlord, the landlord's duty of reasonable care to the tenant might not require the landlord (or the landlord's managing agent) to repair or eliminate a hazardous condition on the premises, especially if the tenant is aware of the condition and has not given prior notice to the landlord of the existence of the condition. But reasonable care might well require the landlord to make inspections, at reasonable intervals, to discover any hazardous conditions that might not be readily apparent to tenants.

Moreover, for the breach of a specific duty recognized in the jurisdiction involved, a landlord may be held liable to the tenant on the grounds of intentional interference, strict liability, or negligence. The extent to which a landlord might be able to transfer the consequences of such torts to the tenant was discussed in Chapter 1.

Liability of Tenants to Landlords In addition to any contractual obligations specified in the lease, the tenant also has the extra-contractual duty to exercise reasonable care for the protection of the landlord. Just as the landlord may be held liable to the tenant, the tenant may be held liable to the landlord on any one of the three general grounds for imposing tort liability. However, tort claims brought by landlords against tenants are predominantly claims for *property* damage that was allegedly caused by the tenant's negligence.

Most commercial buildings are owned by business corporations, governmental bodies, educational institutions, foundations, or individuals who are not tenants of the building. Therefore, it is comparatively rare for the legal owner of a commercial building to suffer *bodily* injury as a proximate result of tortious conduct by the tenant. Property damage liability is another matter entirely.

As an inherent part of the landlord-tenant relationship, the tenant has possession and control of property owned by the landlord. The negligence of the tenant or the tenant's employees can easily damage or destroy both (1) the property under the possession and control of the tenant and (2) other nearby property owned by the landlord. Serious damage or destruction of property owned by the landlord is often the result of negligently caused fires and explosions.

General liability insurance forms typically provide property damage liability coverage for an insured tenant with respect to nearby property that is not in the possession or control of the tenant (including any such property owned by the landlord). However, by virtue of an exclusion, property damage liability coverage usually does *not* apply to *real or personal property the insured tenant owns, rents, or occupies.* An adequate amount of fire legal liability coverage is a reliable way to plug this coverage gap. Fire legal liability coverage is provided in the commercial general liability policy by virtue of a separate policy provision, as explained in Chapter 5. Coverage is also available on a commercial property form. Other approaches to the problem have been used extensively—such as hold-harmless provisions as well as other contractual arrangements that are beyond the scope of this text—but these approaches are most often used as supplements to fire legal liability insurance, because the noninsurance approaches are not always reliable (and they are frequently not enforced until after a lengthy process of litigation).

LIABILITY ARISING OUT OF OPERATIONS IN PROGRESS AND COMPLETED OPERATIONS

A business firm is exposed to liability for the tortious conduct of its operations whether the operations are conducted on or away from its own premises. In addition to direct liability, the business entity may be held vicariously liable for torts committed by its employees during the course of the work or operations. Liability may result from (1) operations in progress or (2) completed operations.

In the conduct of business operations, as well as in other roles, employers and employees have the general duty to exercise reasonable care to avoid bodily injury or property damage to others. They also have specific legal duties that vary according to the circumstances and the type of operations involved.

The term "operations" has a narrow and specialized meaning in the language of insurance and risk management. It refers to a kind of miscellaneous or catch-all category that includes all activities of a commercial entity (except) those for which separate, insurable categories have been reserved—such as insurable operations involving tort liability for: the sale of products; the ownership and operation of autos, aircraft, or watercraft; the job-connected injuries and diseases of employees; the ownership, occupancy, possession, and control of premises; the rendering of professional services; and so on. Activities at the insured's own business premises are operations, but the activity-related exposures cannot clearly be distinguished from the premises exposures previously described. As a result, on-premises activity-related exposures are usually lumped together with premises exposures under the more inclusive category, "premises and operations."

Since most insurable business operations of retailers, wholesalers, manufacturers, governmental bodies, and institutional entities are in one or more of the above categories, *what remain as distinctly "operations" liability exposures are essentially those involving construction, alteration, maintenance, and/or repair operations that are conducted away from the business's own premises.* Thus, the so-called "operations liability exposures" emphasize third-person liability exposures faced by contractors or repair personnel as a result of work they are performing or have already performed for another party who employed them.

Independent Contractors

As noted in Chapter 1, "independent contractors" are not common-law employees of those who employ their services. An *independent contractor* is a party to a contract in which the contractor agrees to undertake and complete a task for another party, the employee of the contractor, under the condition that the contractor will have the exclusive right to determine and *control* the means of completing the task. Unlike the employer of a common-law employee, the employer of an independent contractor does not have the right to direct or control *how* the task or work is to be completed, but only the right to enforce the contractual provisions regarding such matters as the date the work is to be completed, the design and materials specifications that define the work, and the employer's right to reject or approve the completed work, depending upon whether it satisfies the relevant requirements of the contract.

An independent contractor can be a *general contractor* employed under the terms of a contract with an *owner of land*. Or, an independent contractor can be a *subcontractor* employed under the terms of a contract with a general contractor. In either case, the duties that the contracting parties have to third persons are based on the same broad principles and concepts. To simplify the rest of the discussion of operations exposures, therefore, the terms "employer" and "contractor" are used. This helps in avoiding unnecessary repetition. But it requires the reader to remember that it is the general contractor or subcontractor who faces the *operations* exposure as such, even though the general contractor is an employer in relation to a subcontractor.

As a general rule, the employer of an independent contractor is *not* vicariously liable for the torts committed by the independent contractor in the performance of delegable duties. The employer may be held vicariously liable for torts of the independent contractor involving duties that the law will not allow the employer to avoid by delegating the performance of work to another party. These are called "nondelegable" duties. In addition to its vicarious liability for the breach of nondelegable duties, the employer always may be held directly liable for its own torts and vicariously liable for the torts of its common-law employees. Thus, either an *owner of land* (as an employer of a general contractor) or a *general contractor* (as an employer of a subcontractor) may be held liable to third persons for any of the following:

1. Direct liability of the employer for negligently selecting an incompetent independent contractor.
2. Vicarious liability of the employer for the breach of nondelegable duties created by common law or statute. Examples of vicarious liability based on nondelegable duties include:
   - strict liability for injuries resulting from the contractor's involvement in ultrahazardous activities and/or abnormally dangerous instrumentalities,

- liability for the contractor's negligence in the performance of work close to public highways, and
- liability for delegating the performance of an act requiring a license to an unlicensed person.

3. Vicarious liability of the employer for torts committed by its common-law employees in the course of their employment.

The other party who may face "operations" exposures is the subcontractor. If the subcontractor happens to employ another independent contractor to perform some of the work (and is permitted to do so by the general contractor), the subcontractor would be exposed to the above-listed liabilities of an employer. Otherwise, the subcontractor is liable for its own torts and such torts of its common-law employees as are committed in the course of their employment.

Clearly, a contractor can become liable in tort for bodily injury or property damage when both the tort and the resulting harm become manifest *during operations in progress*, whether the harm is suffered by the employer of the contractor or by a third person. A contractor's exposures to liability *after the operations have been completed* may not be as obvious. One first needs to know the underlying legal rationale of completed operations exposures.

Completed Operations Exposures

In general, *completed* operations exposures arise out of work performed by a firm, and after the performance of such work has been completed. These exposures are based on such common-law notions as the original "accepted work doctrine" and its subsequent modifications over the years.

Accepted Work Doctrine The original concept adopted by the courts was that once the work was completed and accepted by the owner, the liability of the contractor was at an end, whether or not the work had been performed negligently. This rule was based on the theory that, in the absence of privity of contract (a direct contractual relationship), the contractor owed no duty to anyone other than the contractee.

The rationale behind the accepted work doctrine was that the acceptance and subsequent control of the owner was tantamount to the owner having adopted the completed work as its own work. Thereafter, the owner was liable to any third person who might be injured or suffer property damage due to the negligence of the owner in owning or maintaining an unsafe condition.

In the absence of an express or implied agreement to the contrary, the contractor had no duty to inspect the work after it was completed and accepted by the owner—unless, in the exercise of reasonable care, there was or should have been knowledge that a defect was likely to develop and make the project imminently dangerous.

A contractor could have been held liable if the work was accepted by someone other than the owner or employer. For example, a contractor was not relieved of liability by his argument that the work was accepted by an *employee* of the user of the property on which the work had been performed.

Thus, according to the early common-law rule, if there was a valid acceptance of the contractor's work, the third party liability exposure of the contractor ceased at the time of acceptance. The duties associated with the maintenance and use of the property shifted to the property owner the moment the work was accepted.

Departures from the Accepted Work Doctrine About half of the jurisdictions eventually replaced the accepted work doctrine with a new rule (discussed later). The other half retained the general rule, but numerous exceptions to the rule have evolved. Under various exceptions now recognized in a number of jurisdictions, a contractor may be held liable after the work has been completed and/or accepted in the following situations:

- *Completed operation that is inherently dangerous if the work is negligently performed.* Liability may be imposed when a third party is injured as a direct result of an inherently dangerous act, or when the act results in a dangerous situation, the natural and probable consequence of which would be injury to a third party.
- *The thing dealt with is imminently dangerous in kind.* Explosives and poisonous gases are examples of imminently dangerous things. This exception to the accepted work doctrine was applied in one case where a contractor negligently constructed a chimney that allowed carbon monoxide gas to escape into living quarters, creating an imminently dangerous condition.
- *The contractor has knowledge of the danger.* This exception applied in a case where a general contractor was sued when the ductwork in a supermarket fell, striking the plaintiff (a shopper) three years after completion of construction. The contractor raised the defense that it could not and did not know of or discover the improper installation. The defense was rejected because the defendants designed the building and supervised construction, and thus had the opportunity to know of the danger.[1]

- *The subject matter is to be used for a purpose requiring security for the protection of life and limb.* This exception was applied when a contractor who had improperly attached an attic stairway was held liable for injuries. The plaintiff was using the stairway when it became detached, causing the plaintiff to be injured.[2]

- *The contractor knows about a defect but deceitfully or deliberately conceals it.* The contractor may be held liable in such circumstances, provided the defect causes an accident when the thing is used for the purpose for which it was constructed.[3]

- *The completed work constitutes a nuisance.* A contractor has been held liable to third parties who came into contact with the nuisance and were injured by it.

The end result of each of the above exceptions was the same—the contractor was held liable to third parties injured by the contractor's negligence even after acceptance of the work by the owner.

Abandonment of Accepted Work Doctrine The numerous exceptions to the accepted work doctrine eventually led to abandonment of it by about one half the jurisdictions. The modern view adopts the doctrine of *MacPherson v. Buick Motor Co.* (discussed later in connection with products liability exposures), applying it to independent contractors.[4] The duty owed to third parties after completion of work is the same as that owed by manufacturers to users and consumers of their products, despite the absence of privity.

The rationale for this view is that there is no reason to distinguish between the negligence of a manufacturer and that of a contractor. The emphasis under the modern view is on the probability of injury, which gives rise to a duty, rather than the fact of completion and acceptance.

Representative of the cases rejecting the doctrine of nonliability is a case in which a minor plaintiff was burned by exposed hot pipes leading to the radiator in her room.[5] The defendants in the case included the heating contractor, the architects, and the builder. The court was ready to abandon the accepted work doctrine and did not even consider the patency (or openness) of the defect as defense. The court could see no reason why the principles of negligence should not apply to all builders and contractors involved in mass housing developments.

Thus, the modern view is that liability may be imposed on the architects and engineers on the basis of negligent design and on the contractors for defective materials and workmanship. The lack of privity is no longer an issue. Thus, a general contractor was liable for injuries caused to a longshoreman due to the collapse of a boom, rigging, and mast the defendants had remodeled for the longshore-man's employer.[6]

Owner Aware of Condition. Where the owner maintains the work in an unsafe condition, and knows (or should have known) of the dangerous condition, the owner is not insulated from liability because the work has been negligently performed by the contractor. The owner is liable as a joint tortfeasor, and the injured person may maintain an action against the owner, against the contractors, or both. A question of intervening and superseding cause arises in this context in the defendant's effort to avoid joint liability. An owner's negligence may supersede the contractor's or repairer's negligence if the owner knew of the defect when the owner accepted the work or if, by reasonable care, the owner should have discovered it and avoided the accident. Acceptance of completed work is not automatically an intervening cause. Failure of the owner to inspect adequately may not be foreseeable, and the contractor may be found not liable if his or her negligence as the cause of the accident cannot be established.

Owner Could Not Have Discovered Condition. Where the owner is not aware of the unsafe condition and could not have discovered it by inspection, he or she clearly is not subject to liability. For example, the unsafe condition might be concealed in such a way that it could not be discovered by reasonable inspection. The owner is not required to dismantle the work in order to ascertain whether or not the contractor has used safe and satisfactory materials.

The rule that has been adopted in several states is that liability is imposed on the contractor for injuries to a third person occurring after the completion of the work and its acceptance by the contractee, where the work is reasonably certain to endanger third persons if it has been negligently performed. A sun deck constructed by an independent contractor collapsed and injured a social guest on the owner's premises. The work had been completed and accepted by the owner. In an action against the contractor, the defense of the accepted work doctrine was rejected, and the contractor was held liable for injuries to third persons proximately caused by his negligence.[7]

A contractor is held liable in some cases despite the fact that a subcontractor is responsible for the negligent act. In one such case, the court said that, because the defendant contractor prepared the plans and specifications, it was the defendant's responsibility to construct the house (in which the decedent was asphyxiated due to a faulty gas heater) with adequate subcontractors' work. This duty could not be delegated or shifted.[8]

Strict Liability In completed operations cases, a few courts have applied the strict liability in tort rule in much the same way as in holding the product manufacturer liable to the ultimate consumer or user. In one such decision, the defendant was held liable to a minor tenant of the owner who was injured by a defectively designed hot water system which was installed without a mixing valve. The house was built for the owner and accepted by him. The court refused to adopt the accepted work doctrine and instead applied the strict liability rule to the facts of this case.

Effect of the Passage of Time   The question sometimes arises as to what effect, if any, the passage of time should have on the liability of the contractor for defective work. It has been argued that the passage of a long period of time should insulate the contractor from liability, especially in cases where the owner was aware of the defective workmanship, made no claims against the contractor, and continued to maintain the premises in their defective condition. The courts have generally held that the effect of the passage of time is a question of fact for the jury to decide. It does not involve a question of law for the court. In other words, the jury would have to decide whether the negligence of the contractor—however remote in time—was the cause of the accident.

Defective Plans or Materials   Another question is the liability of a contractor or worker who constructs something from defective plans or materials furnished by another. Whether the accepted work doctrine is followed or not, the usual rule is not to impose liability for following plans that are not obviously defective.

Plans were at issue in a case where a defendant constructed grandstand seats through which a four-year-old child fell. The work was done according to plans and specifications supplied by the owner. The court found the contractor was not liable to the child because he met the owner's plans. The court added that, had he failed to follow the plans, then a question of negligence would arise.[9]

The same rule was applied to the use of materials supplied by the contractor's employer,[10] as well as where another contractor carefully carried out the plans he was given.[11] In the latter decision, the court relieved the contractor of liability where the plans were not so obviously defective and dangerous that no reasonable person would follow them.

LIABILITY ARISING OUT OF PRODUCTS

Products liability is the legal responsibility of the manufacturer, distributor, or retailer to the user or consumer of a product. The liability arises out of the manufacture, distribution, or sale of an unsafe, dangerous, or defective product, and the failure of the manufacturer, distributor, or retailer to meet the legal duties imposed with respect to the particular product. If the user or consumer sustains an injury or property damage caused by the product, liability may be imposed.

Broadly speaking, the term "products" includes all species of movable personal property and, under special circumstances, *real property*, as well. (For some purposes, the term is more narrowly defined. For example, commercial general liability policy contains a definition of "your products," which is examined in Chapter 5.) The term "products liability" is almost always used in the context of civil liability, however.

In early civil cases, negligence usually was the basis of the relatively rare actions that could be described as products cases. But contract law eventually blended with negligence concepts as courts regularly examined the presence or absence of contractual relationships between parties.

Privity

The privity doctrine developed as a means by which a manufacturer or remote seller could avoid liability to a person with whom the manufacturer or seller had no contractual relationship.

In the early years of the industrial age, the courts reasoned that only the contracting parties—the buyer and seller—were in "privity" with each other and therefore able to assert a cause of action against one another. One who was not a party to the contract of sale had no legal status with which to maintain a contract action. This was true even though third parties stood in some relationship to the buyer, such as members of the buyer's family or the buyer's employees or agents. The rule originally was laid down in 1842 in the case of Winterbottom v. Wright,[12] in which the injured driver of a mail coach brought an action against one who had contracted to sell the coach and keep it in repair. In holding that the driver had no maintainable cause of action, the court said:

> There is no privity of contract between these parties; and if the plaintiff can sue, every passenger, or even a person passing along the road who was injured by the upsetting of the coach, might bring similar action. Unless we confine the operation of such contracts as this to the parties who entered into them, the most absurd and outrageous consequences, to which I can see no limit, would ensue.[13]

Erosion of Privity Doctrine A landmark decision in 1916 resulted in the virtual extinction of the privity rule, leading the courts to recognize that a buyer can have a cause of action in tort against a manufacturer, where the product is negligently manufactured and the negligence results in damage to the buyer. In MacPherson v. Buick Motor Co.,[14] the buyer of an automobile brought an action against the manufacturer, alleging that he was injured as a result of the negligence of the manufacturer in placing a defective automobile in the stream of commerce. The court sustained the cause of action, holding that the manufacturer was under a duty to exercise reasonable care in the production of its automobiles. Its failure to meet that duty was deemed to be negligence. There was no contractual relationship between the buyer and the manufacturer, because the car was bought from a retail dealer. Yet, the buyer was allowed to recover on the tort theory of negligence.

Contract Action

Under the Uniform Commercial Code, a buyer has a cause of action based on the breach of either an express or an implied warranty. Various measures have been used to determine the amount of damages resulting from breach of warranty.

The Uniform Commercial Code Adoption of the Uniform Commercial Code in forty-nine states and the District of Columbia has had a great impact on the rules governing contractual liability. The Code, a body of law governing sales and other commercial transactions, is "uniform" in the sense that the same provisions are applicable in most states. The Code provisions relating to sales constitute a restatement of the common-law rights and duties of the parties to a contract of sale, with some clarification of areas where differences of opinion have existed between the states. The object of this legislation is to bring the applicable rules of law of the several states into conformity with each other, enhancing the predictability of the rules to be applied to business transactions. A further effect of this legislation is to overrule prior court decisions that are inconsistent with the Code and to substitute its provisions as the rule of decision in future cases.

The Code further abolishes the privity requirement in contract actions based on sales. Therefore, if a state has adopted the Uniform Commercial Code, it would follow that it has abandoned the privity rule, regardless of outstanding court decisions that have applied the rule. Section 2-318 of the Code, as drafted, provides three alternative forms of abolishing privity. Alternative A, adopted by a majority of jurisdictions, provides:

> A seller's warranty whether express or implied extends to any natural person who is in the family or household of his buyer or who is a guest in his home if it is reasonable to expect that such person may use, consume or be affected by the goods, and who is injured in

person by breach of the warranty. A seller may not exclude or limit operation of this section.

Alternatives B and C, adopted in about thirteen jurisdictions, vary slightly but are of similar import.

Express Warranties With respect to the sale of personal property, a *warranty* may be described as a statement or representation having reference to the character or quality of the goods sold. It is made by the seller of goods to induce the sale and is relied on by the buyer. It usually arises as an incident of the contract of sale. If the warranty is breached and the buyer sustains bodily injury or property damage as a result of reliance on the representation, the seller is liable in an action for damages. ″

In order to recover for the breach of an express warranty in the days before the Uniform Commercial Code, a buyer had to establish that there was reliance on the express warranty. Under the Code, the element of reliance by the buyer on the express warranty is no longer necessary in order to maintain an action for the breach—the "seller" includes anyone who placed the goods in the stream of commerce. Therefore, the term includes not only the immediate retailer but the manufacturer as well. Both may make an express warranty, in which case either or both may be held liable if the warranty is breached. Where one makes an express warranty and the other does not, then the seller making the warranty may be held liable for the breach. But one seller's express warranty does not automatically become the warranty of another farther down in the chain of distribution. In one court case, for example, the manufacturer affixed a label to each can of antifreeze attesting to its quality and safety; the purchase in issue was made in reliance upon the truth of the warranty.[15] In an action against the distributor, the court held that the distributor had neither made a warranty nor adopted the manufacturer's warranty, and therefore was not liable to the purchaser. The purchaser would probably have prevailed if the action had been brought against the manufacturer. However, it is certainly possible for a seller to adopt a manufacturer's warranty, thus binding the seller as if the seller had made the warranty.

Under Section 2-313 of the Code, "any affirmation of fact or promise" may give rise to an express warranty, although a statement that is "merely the seller's opinion or commendation of the goods does not create a warranty." This last quoted language of Section 2-313 seems to countenance "puffing" by the seller to induce a sale, and the distinction between puffery and warranty is certain to create difficulties. The nature of the product and the assertion made are relevant factors. A mere expression of opinion will not expose the seller to liability, but courts may resolve in favor of a buyer any doubt as to whether an expression was a warranty. There are cases going both ways, holding either that an expression was (1) a mere opinion not constituting a warranty or (2) a representation amounting to an express warranty. Such assertions, particularly concerning safety or suitability for a specific purpose, can be expected to be construed as warranties if such a construction is possible. Similarly, liability for breach of express warranty can result from statements made in advertisements, sales brochures, and catalogs. The plaintiff may allege that assurance of safety or quality caused a justifiable reliance upon what turned out to be a material misrepresentation and that the plaintiff's injury resulted from that reliance.

Promotional statements made by manufacturers through the advertising media can give rise to an express warranty, as explained in the *Restatement of Torts:*

> One engaged in the business of selling chattels who, by advertising, labels, or otherwise makes to the public a misrepresentation of a material fact concerning the character or quality of a chattel sold by him is subject to liability for physical harm to a consumer of the chattel caused by justifiable reliance upon the misrepresentation, even though (a) it is not made fraudulently or negligently, and (b) the consumer has not bought the chattel from or entered into any contractual relation with the seller.[16]

Advertising representations, particularly with regard to safety, have been found to be "material misrepresentations" that created express warranties to injured plaintiffs. A classic case involving a hunting and fishing knife illustrates the concepts of "material fact" and "justifiable reliance." An advertisement described the knife this way: "Handfitting Swedish Birch handle—it cannot slip or turn in the hand. No hilt to get in the way of cutting action. Knife is of such perfect design the hand cannot slip." The plaintiff purchased the knife, and when he was using it to clean fish, his hand slipped down the handle and was cut severely. The court found that the plaintiff had offered sufficient evidence for the jury to find misrepresentation of a material fact and justifiable reliance.[17]

Implied Warranties The parties to a contract of sale may agree on any terms and conditions that are mutually acceptable. Both parties will be bound by the agreed terms. Where a contract of sale is made unconditionally, the courts have recognized that the seller has superior knowledge as to the ownership of the article, the ingredients of the article, and its quality with respect to its salability and fitness for a particular purpose. Therefore, the courts impose, "by operation of law," an obligation on the part of the seller to warrant or guarantee these things about the article. The obligation is deemed to arise out of the nature of the transaction and is *implied* without any specific agreement between the parties. The implied warranties are (1) warranty of title, (2) warranty of merchantability, and (3) warranty of fitness for a particular purpose.

1. *Warranty of Title.* When an article is offered for sale, the seller warrants that the seller has title and ownership or that the seller has been authorized by the owner to pass title to another. This warranty of title has no great significance for consideration of products liability, but the other types of implied warranties require detailed discussion.

2. *Warranty of Merchantability.* The seller warrants that the goods are of such quality that they will be reasonably fit for the ordinary uses to which such products are put. Under Section 2-314 the warranty of merchantability means that a product is of medium quality or goodness, is reasonably fit for the purposes for which such products are ordinarily used, and will compare favorably with other products of like kind and description that are on the market.

Most breach-of-warranty cases are brought under the theory of breach of implied warranty of merchantability. These cases generally allege that the product was not fit for the ordinary purpose for which it was intended. In other words, the product did not do what it was supposed to do. For example, the collapse of a ladder under a person of average weight was a breach of this implied warranty.[18]

3. *Warranty of Fitness for a Particular Purpose.* Section 2-315 provides that a warranty of fitness for a particular purpose means generally that if the seller sells a commodity knowing the purpose for which it is purchased, the seller is understood to warrant it to be reasonably fit for the purpose for which it is bought. This warranty arises out of the nature of the transaction. It must be one in which the buyer can establish that the seller knew the purpose for which the product was bought and that the buyer relied on the judgment of the seller in selecting the particular product. The seller's knowledge of the purpose for which the article is bought can sometimes be inferred from the facts and circumstances of the sale.

The rule was applied in a case involving a bumper jack.[19] The plaintiff went to the defendant's store and asked for a bumper jack for a 1957 Buick. The salesman sold the plaintiff a jack that the salesman said would do the job. When the plaintiff was using it, it slipped and the plaintiff's car fell and injured him. The court held that the plaintiff did not have to prove that the jack was defective. Its ability to lift cars of different makes was immaterial. The plaintiff established a breach of an implied warranty of fitness because he proved reliance on the defendant's judgment, the defendant's knowledge of the purpose for which the product was required, and that the product did not fulfill that purpose.

Damages for Breach of Warranty Damages for breach of warranty that may be assessed against the seller consist of such amounts as will place the user or consumer in the same condition as he or she would have occupied if the breach had not occurred. This might consist only of the return of the purchase price or, more commonly in litigated cases, it could consist of damages for injury to property caused by the use of the product or damages for bodily injury sustained by the user or consumer.

Property Damage. In one property damage case, defective oil sold under an express warranty for use in the manufacture of carpets caused considerable property damage to the carpets being manufactured. Damages were awarded, based on the difference in value of the carpets made with the defective oil and the value of the carpets if they had been of merchantable quality.[20] In another case, a roof leak in a mobile home made it unfit for its intended purpose. The damages awarded consisted of the difference between the reasonable market value at the time of purchase and the original market price.[21] The same principle has been applied to sale of defective seed or animal feed. The measure of damages in such cases is the difference between the value of the crop or herd actually produced and the crop or herd that ordinarily would have been produced, less the cost of production.[22]

Therefore, in property damage claims, the measure of damages will be an amount that will reasonably compensate the user or consumer for the loss that has been sustained. The plaintiff may be able to recover for loss of profits, loss of customers, or damage to goodwill because of the defendant's breach *if* it can be shown that these were within the parties' contemplation in entering into a contract of sale and adequate proof of such losses can be offered.

Bodily Injury. When the user or consumer suffers bodily injury as a result of using a product that is the subject of a warranty, the measure of damages will be the same as those allowable in any tort cause of action. These consist of "special" and "general" damages of the type discussed in Chapter 1.

A cosmetics manufacturer was held liable for breach of warranty for injuries to the plaintiff's hair (adhesion of a gluey substance that hardened and could not be removed) when the plaintiff established that the product contained a substance not found in another purchased sample.[23] Another manufacturer was held liable for head injuries caused by a "Golfing Gizmo," an apparatus for unskilled golfers that struck the plaintiff during use. The manufacturer had warranted its safety and claimed it would not strike the user.[24]

Wrongful Death. There is a difference of opinion among the states as to whether or not a breach of warranty can form the basis of a wrongful death claim. Recovery of damages for wrongful death is a purely statutory remedy. The wrongful death statutes generally allow a recovery where the death was caused, for example, by the "wrongful act, neglect, or default" of the defendant. In some states the courts hold that a breach of warranty is not a "wrongful act, neglect, or default" so as to meet the requirements of proof necessary under the wrongful death statute.

Tort Action

The user or consumer of a product may bring a tort action against a seller—including the retailer or the manufacturer—if it can be established that the seller failed in one of the duties owed to the user or consumer. The seller's tort liability may be based on intentional deceit, negligence, or strict liability. Increasing emphasis is being placed on strict liability.

Intentional Deceit, Fraud, or Misrepresentation A seller who makes untrue statements to the buyer, either through general advertising or by direct statements, is liable to the user or consumer if the product does not meet the standards of quality that were claimed for it and the user or consumer has suffered injury to person or property through the use of the product.

Sellers, especially manufacturers, are considered to be experts when it comes to the ingredients and the properties of the article they sell. The user or consumer is not such an expert, and usually relies on the statements or advertising of the seller. Therefore, if the article does not conform to the statements or the advertising, a user or consumer who is injured may bring action in tort against the offending seller for damages, assuming justifiable reliance by the user or a misrepresentation of material fact. A good example of a case illustrating traditional concepts of fraud and misrepresentation involved the prescription drug triparanol, manufactured and sold under the name MER/29. A user of the drug who developed cataracts brought an action against the manufacturer for fraud and misrepresentation. The manufacturer untruthfully represented, both orally and through advertisements in medical journals and other promotional literature, that the drug was nontoxic, safe, and remarkably free of side effects. In fact, the manufacturer had knowledge through animal experiments that the drug caused blood changes and vision changes in most of the animals tested.[25]

(2) *Negligence* As noted earlier, the law of products liability developed in its earlier stages as a curious mixture of tort and warranty concepts. Courts were reluctant to find manufacturers liable for negligence to persons with whom they had no direct contractual relationships. But this privity of contract rule was rejected in the landmark MacPherson case.

The allegation that a manufacturer was negligent may now be raised with respect to the manufacturer's violation of a duty in (1) the product's design, (2) the construction or assembly or packaging of the product, and/or (3) the warnings, labels, and instructions that accompanied or should have accompanied the product.

Duty of a Safe Design. Many plaintiffs in products liability suits do not contest that the product may have been manufactured and put together perfectly, may have been made of good quality material, and may be functioning just as it was intended to function. The plaintiff, instead, attacks the very concept or design of the product and alleges that because of a design defect, particular articles manufactured in accord with that design were dangerous for their intended uses.

A manufacturer has a duty to design a product that is reasonably fit for its intended use and free from defects that could make it unsafe for its intended use. The design defect claim usually is based upon one of several theories.

- *Concealed defect.* In one case involving a *concealed defect*, the plaintiff sat on a lawn chair and placed his fingers close to the folding mechanism under the arm. One finger was traumatically amputated when his weight on the chair caused the mechanism to shift. The court found that the chair was defectively designed by reason of a concealed defect that rendered it unsafe for its intended use. The court found that the mechanism should have been covered with a housing to prevent the possibility of such an injury.[26]

- *Guards or safety devices.* A second theory advanced as a basis for design defect liability is failure on the part of the manufacturer to incorporate *guards or other safety devices* into products. A widely accepted rule has developed that the absence of guards or safety devices does not necessarily, in and of itself, create liability. Numerous cases have held that if a manufacturer does everything necessary to make a product function properly for the purpose for which it is designed—and if it contains no hidden or latent hazards—and if its functioning creates no danger or peril that is unknown to the user, then the manufacturer has met its duty to design a product that is reasonably safe for its intended use. In the leading case in this area[27], a worker was injured when his hands were caught in moving parts of a machine. The court held that the machine had no latent defects, that the manufacturer had done everything possible to make the machine function properly for the purpose for which it was designed, and that the danger of placing one's hands near the moving parts of the machine was an open and obvious hazard. However, some courts may find on similar facts that the manufacturer has a duty to design guards or safety devices into its product to protect users from all hazards, even open and obvious hazards.

● *Nature of the material.* A third theory used as the basis of design defect claims relates to the nature of the material specified in the design. A manufacturer was held liable for an injury caused by a nail that shattered as a result of the type of steel (and the treatment of the steel) specified for use in the product.[28] The court held that there was a defect in the design that rendered the product unsafe for the purpose for which it was intended.

● *Unintended uses.* A fourth theory used as the basis of an alleged design claim is that a manufacturer has a duty not only to design a product that is reasonably safe for its intended use but also to foresee and design against possible unintended uses of a product that are reasonably likely to occur. This issue has arisen often in the "crashworthiness" or "second collision cases," usually involving the design of automobiles. In such litigation, the claim is often made that the design of a vehicle increased or enhanced injuries occurring in an accident, and that a manufacturer has a duty to foresee that automobile accidents might occur. It therefore has a duty to design a vehicle that is relatively safe in a collision. The majority of cases that have considered this issue have concluded that because a collision is a reasonably *foreseeable* (although unintended) use of an automobile, a manufacturer has a duty to design its vehicles so as to avoid or minimize the consequences of collision. A substantial minority of jurisdictions has held that, because a collision is not one of the intended purposes of an automobile, a manufacturer has no duty to design a motor vehicle so that it will be a completely safe vehicle in which to participate in a collision.

Duty to Safely Manufacture, Construct, Assemble, and Package. With respect to the manufacture, construction, and assembly of a product, the issue is generally whether some production error caused the defect that resulted in the injury to the plaintiff. The focus is on a specific defect of production error that occurred with respect to a specific product, rather than calling into question a design that has been embodied in a large number of products following that particular design. In such a case, the plaintiff commonly alleges that in the manufacture of a particular product alleged to have caused the injury, the manufacturer was responsible for some act that constituted a failure to exercise care, which should be recognized as creating an unreasonable risk of harm to a user. Such negligence may consist of any number of problems caused by human or mechanical error or breakdown in the course of manufacture and assembly of a product, such as failure to tighten a bolt, failure to prevent foreign matter from getting into food or medical products, failure to securely attach a safety device, and so on. It is often difficult for a plaintiff to establish that an alleged product defect was caused by specific and identifiable negligent acts or omissions in the course of the manufacturing process.

The seller has a duty to properly package (as well as to design and manufacture) its product. This duty means that the seller must exercise reasonable care in adopting a method of packaging that is safe not only for the user or consumer but also for those who are concerned with transporting or storing the product while awaiting sale. For example, in one case, the consumer (a physician conducting experiments) suffered severe hand burns when a caustic chemical that he was pouring out of a bottle gushed out when the entire bakelite cap came off. The court held that the packaging was defective and that the defendant failed to exercise care commensurate with the risk of harm in packaging a dangerous chemical.[29]

Duty to Test and Inspect. Manufacturers have a duty to conduct such tests and inspections—in the course of product development, manufacture, and distribution—as are reasonably necessary to assure production of a safe product. This duty should be carried out with a degree of care commensurate with the foreseeable risk of harm. The manufacturer of a potentially dangerous prescription drug, for example, is expected to comply with tough government regulations, as well as procedures that are customary in the industry. Such compliance will constitute evidence of reasonable care.

A manufacturer of grinding wheels was held liable to a worker injured by a wheel that disintegrated while it was being operated. The accident, the court held, was caused by internal flaws that would have been discovered by a standard method of testing employed by other manufacturers in the industry.[30]

Generally, a retailer is under no duty to inspect or test products of a reputable manufacturer unless the retailer has reason to believe that a product is dangerously defective or the retailer has some special inspection opportunity or competence as a seller of such products.

Duty to Warn and Instruct. A manufacturer or seller of a product that is inherently dangerous when used for its intended purpose owes a duty to give adequate warning of that dangerous propensity to the prospective user. The same rule applies to a product that is not inherently dangerous, but may in certain circumstances cause a foreseeable injury.

A general rule has developed, however, that there is no duty to warn of "open and obvious" dangers. This rule is exemplified by a case in which a plaintiff was injured by the open rollers of a farm machine. The court, finding no affirmative duty to warn on the part of the manufacturer, denied recovery because "the very nature of the article gives notice and warning of the consequences to be expected, of the injuries to be suffered.[31] Although this rule is still followed in many jurisdictions, other courts, considering similar facts, may minimize the obviousness factor, find a duty to warn, and impose liability for negligent breach of that duty. The primary thrust of the duty is that the manufacturer must warn of hidden (or latent) danger or hazardous limitations of a product, when used for reasonably foreseeable uses, if the danger would not be reasonably apparent to the average user of the product.

The adequacy and intensity of a warning generally will be judged on the basis of the facts of a given case. The chance for a successful defense by the manufacturer seems to decrease in proportion to the smallness of the print on the warning—or in inverse proportion to the danger of the product. Thus, the manufacturer was held liable for failing to warn that a bottle of nail polish would explode if the plaintiff smoked as she applied the nail polish. The bottle was labeled in small red type: "Do not heat or use near fire." Such a warning, held to be insufficiently clear and intense to warn of the nature and seriousness of the hazard, was as much a violation of the manufacturer's duty as a complete failure to warn.[32]

Although *instructions* relative to use or maintenance differ from *warnings*, they too may have a strong bearing on safe use of a product. In one such case, the boom of a crane fell and killed a worker. It was found that the failure was due to the fact that a "safety ratchet" had not been lubricated for seventeen months and had become "frozen" with rust. The manufacturer's guide to proper lubrication failed to mention the safety ratchet. The court held that by undertaking to give lubricating instructions, the manufacturer was under the duty to make them complete and all-inclusive. Its failure to do so was a breach of that duty and led to the imposition of liability for negligence.[33]

Res Ipsa Loquitur. In negligence actions against the manufacturer, the plaintiff has the burden of establishing that the accident was caused by the negligence of the manufacturer in failing to exercise care, for example, in the production, design, packaging, or inspection of the product before it left the manufacturer's possession. Since the entire production process is in the control of the manufacturer, the plaintiff is faced with a problem of proof that may be difficult (and sometimes virtually impossible) to sustain.

In some cases the courts have applied the rule of *res ipsa loquitur,* which means "the thing speaks for itself." It is a rule of evidence that eases the plaintiff's burden of proof by creating a presumption of negligence where certain basic elements have been established. This rule tends to switch the burden of proof from the plaintiff to the defendant who must now overcome the "presumption of negligence" by evidence or attack one of the following three basic elements necessary to invoke this rule. These elements are:

1. the accident must be one that normally would not occur unless the defendant were negligent;
2. the instrumentality that caused the accident must be within the exclusive control of the defendant; and
3. the plaintiff must not have contributed in any way to the causation of the accident.

Obviously, in products cases the instrumentality that causes the accident is not in the physical control of the defendant at the time of the accident, since possession has been relinquished to the plaintiff. The courts have reasoned that, because the negligent act must have occurred while the product was in the hands of the manufacturer, that possession is sufficient to satisfy the requirements of the rule. Thus, if a bottler overfills a bottle (subjecting it to pressure beyond its capacity) or uses a defective bottle, and the bottle explodes, causing injury to the buyer or consumer, the application of the rule would be sufficient to establish a presumption that the manufacturer was negligent. The plaintiff would not have to prove facts establishing any specific act of negligence, because the circumstances of the accident would provide the evidence of negligence.

However, to invoke the application of the rule, the plaintiff would have to show that the bottle or other product was in the same condition when received by the plaintiff as it was when it left the manufacturer's hands. This would require evidence that the product had not been mishandled en route to the consumer. The failure of the plaintiff to negate any possibility of mishandling to the product while en route will deny the plaintiff the advantage of the rule.

The rule created only a *presumption* of negligence. This may be overcome by evidence offered by the manufacturer that the product was not defective or, if there was a defect, it did not occur through the negligence of the manufacturer. Once these facts have been established, the rule drops out of play and the plaintiff must prove specific acts of negligence on the part of the manufacturer in order to recover.

The courts have applied the rule of *res ipsa loquitur* most often to cases involving (1) exploding bottles, (2) foreign substances in bottled goods or goods in sealed containers, and (3) foreign substances in drugs or cosmetics. The doctrine has generally been found inapplicable to products such as heavy equipment, vehicles, and major appliances, since such products have often been used safely for an extended period of time prior to an accident giving rise to a lawsuit.

③ *Strict Liability in Tort*   The strict liability doctrine was first applied in the key 1963 decision in Greeman v. Yuba Power Products, Inc.[34] The plaintiff was a worker injured by a power lathe which had been purchased from the manufacturer by his employer. Upon suing the manufacturer, he was confronted by prior decisions refusing to extend warranty without privity beyond food products cases, as well as his failure to give timely notice of the manufacturer's "breach of warranty," as required by the applicable statute, the Uniform Sales Act. The California Supreme Court cut this Gordian knot of difficulties by holding that the case did not really involve warranty but could be resolved by imposing strict liability in tort.

In order to understand the rule of strict liability, certain terms must be defined: "seller," "user or consumer," and "defective condition unreasonably dangerous."

Seller.   The rule of strict liability in tort is applied against a seller engaged in the business of selling the type of product in question. The term "seller" is defined in Comment f (an explanatory note) to Section 402A of the *Restatement (2nd) Torts* as including an entity that is engaged in the business of selling products for use or consumption, but not including a person who makes a casual or occasional sale. One who is engaged in the business of selling products may include the manufacturer, as well as others in the chain of production or distribution, including component part manufacturers and suppliers, wholesale distributors, and retailers.

If, for example, a woman is injured when a bicycle wheel breaks and collapses while she is riding the bicycle in a normal way, she may have a cause of action against one or a number of sellers. These might include:

- the wheel manufacturer,
- the component supplier who supplied the wheels to the bicycle manufacturer,
- the manufacturer who fabricated the bicycle,
- the wholesale distributor, and
- the retail store that sold the bicycle it purchased from the distributor.

All these parties are sellers who are subject to tort liability under the strict liability doctrine. However, if the plaintiff had borrowed the bicycle from a neighbor who, in turn, had purchased it secondhand from a friend, neither of these persons would be subject to a strict liability action since they are not sellers "engaged in the business of selling such a product." A few jurisdictions have applied the strict liability rule to defendants who would not traditionally be considered sellers, such as bailors and lessors, building developers and builders of homes, testing companies, a hospital supplying blood to a patient, and a landlord renting a furnished apartment.

User or Consumer. The terms "user" or "consumer" are not limited to actual purchasers or owners of the products. The categories of user or consumer include those who ultimately benefit from the use of product, such as passengers in a vehicle, a hospital patient who is given a drug, or a worker who is repairing an appliance for the ultimate purchaser.

A few decisions have extended the doctrine of strict liability in tort to permit recovery by "bystanders" who were neither users nor consumers of the product but who suffered injury through being in the vicinity of a defective product that was in use. Examples include eye damage caused by fumes from contact cement circulated throughout a building through an air conditioning system,[35] and injuries to passengers in a vehicle that was struck by another, allegedly defective, auto that went out of control.[36]

Defective Condition Unreasonably Dangerous. To recover under the theory of strict liability in tort, a plaintiff must establish that the injury was caused by a product that was in a defective condition unreasonably dangerous to the user or consumer when it left the control of the defendant seller. A "defective condition" is one that would not be contemplated by the average consumer and that would be unreasonably dangerous to that consumer. There is no all-embracing definition of defect. What is in back of most decisions, however, is what may be called the consumer expectation test: did the product perform as a reasonable consumer would have expected? "Unreasonably dangerous" means that the article sold must be dangerous to an extent beyond that which would be contemplated by the ordinary consumer who purchases it, with the ordinary knowledge common to the community. The fact that a product is dangerous does not automatically mean that strict liability is applicable. Objects such as guns and dynamite are dangerous but can be said, based upon ordinary consumer understanding, to be reasonably so. At the other end of the spectrum, it can be said that some products, even if they have produced personal injury, are not "dangerous."

A hammer was found to be in a "defective and unreasonably dangerous condition" because it had become "work hardened" or brittle as a result of use over a prolonged period of time. A piece of metal chipped from the hammer head and struck the plaintiff in the eye while he was using the hammer. The court found that the product was in a defective condition and unreasonably dangerous because it could not stand up under repeated, foreseeable stresses that would accord with reasonable "consumer expectations."[37] Nearly every product—from food to light bulbs to plastic toys—is capable of causing injury. However, the mere fact that injury occurred in connection with the use of a product does not prove that the product was defective, since the law does not require that the product be accident-proof or foolproof.

Some courts have liberalized still further the concept of strict liability by applying it without the need for the plaintiff to establish that the product was "unreasonably dangerous." This further eases the plaintiff's burden of proof, requiring only a showing that the product was in a "defective condition." The plaintiff need not show that it was more dangerous than the average consumer would ordinarily expect.

Impact of Strict Liability. Strict liability in tort certainly has not been unanimously and uniformly accepted in all jurisdictions, and the rule remains subject to certain limitations. However, it has substantially altered the law of products liability in several respects. For example, it has eliminated from tort liability all vestiges of contractual privity, so that any user or consumer of a defective product can sue the manufacturer or retailer of the product (or, for that matter, any other seller in the chain of distribution) without regard to whether any of the sellers contracted with or extended a warranty to the user or consumer. Moreover, the rule has eliminated any necessity on the part of the user or consumer to prove negligent acts on the part of the manufacturer or other seller. Thus, the defendant may be held liable for an injury caused by a defective product, although he or she has exercised all possible care in connection with the product. Negligence is not a prerequisite to liability.

Statutory Influences

In response to pressures generated by consumer groups, Congress has passed a number of statutes regulating the manufacture and sale of consumer goods. Among these statutes are the Consumer Product Safety Act; the Pure Food, Drug and Cosmetic Act; the Federal Hazardous Substances Act; the Federal Insecticide, Fungicide and Rodenticide Act; the Occupational Safety and Health Act; the Federal Flammable Fabrics Act; and the National Traffic and Motor Vehicle Safety Act.

Statutes such as those cited above may be adopted or applied in products liability suits and can theoretically be the basis of a "negligence per se" holding. Section 286 of the *Restatement* codifies the current existing law. In essence, it provides that a plaintiff is barred from recovering on a negligence per se or prima facie evidence theory unless the plaintiff can show:

1. that the plaintiff belonged to a particular class of persons that the legislature sought to protect;
2. that the particular interest that was invaded was of a type that the legislature intended to safeguard;
3. that the legislature sought to protect that interest from a particular type of harm that occurred; and
4. that the statute was designed to guard against the kind of harm exemplified by this injury.

As to the effect of a violation of such a statute on a civil suit, there is much confusion and disparity among the various jurisdictions. Basically, there are three recognized positions:

1. The violation constitutes negligence per se, or negligence as a matter of law and, unless some justifiable excuse can be shown, the violation is conclusive as to the issue of breach of duty.
2. The violation is prima facie evidence of negligence or presumptive negligence that shifts the burden to the defendant to explain, justify, or rebut the violation.
3. The violation is merely evidence of negligence and it is to be weighed by the jury along with all other evidence.

The first two positions have the effect of creating a kind of strict liability for the product's failure to comply with statutory standards.

It is almost universally held that the defendant's compliance with a statutory standard will not insulate the defendant from potential liability. Courts have consistently held that a legislative enactment merely designates the minimum standard of care and that, in any particular case, the common-law standard may exceed that of the statute. However, the admission into evidence of the defendant's compliance with a statutory mandate is still beneficial to the defense. The fact that a defendant may be found liable despite compliance can create real policy problems for the judiciary. In one such case, a child ingested a roach killer that resulted in his death. In a subsequent negligence action, the defendant introduced evidence showing that his product and its label were both properly registered under the Federal Insecticide, Fungicide, and Rodenticide Act as well as the Texas Hazardous Substances Act. The approval of the Federal Department of Agriculture and the State Department of Health was also introduced. The defendant unsuccessfully urged "that the label was approved by proper authorities, state and federal, and he was by law *required* to use this labeling and as a matter of law he cannot be guilty of negligence. His position is that he could not market his product without the precise label, and if he did so, he would be guilty of violating the law.[38]

As federal and state standards become more stringent, allowing for less deviation, this dilemma and its consequent defense will have more appeal. However, the Consumer Product Safety Act expressly provides that compliance will not be proof of due care nor will the act affect common-law negligence actions.

Defenses to Product Actions

The plaintiff in a products liability case must establish the facts and circumstances essential to the elements of the plaintiff's theory of liability. However, certain substantive or affirmative defenses to the plaintiff's cause of action are often available to the defendant, depending on the plaintiff's theory of liability and the facts of the case.

Contributory Negligence, or Assumption of Risk Conduct on the part of the plaintiff may prove to be one of the most useful sources of effective products defense. Contributory negligence on the part of the plaintiff (that is, negligence that contributes to causation of the injury) is a valid defense to an action based on negligence. The courts and commentators have had difficulty with the application of the concept of contributory negligence to actions grounded in warranty and strict liability. Yet, conduct amounting to voluntary exposure to a known risk by the plaintiff has been widely accepted as a defense in both warranty and strict liability tort actions.

Assumption of risk, of the kind where a person proceeds unreasonably in the face of a known risk, is illustrated by two cases involving auto brakes. In one, a passenger in a car that he knew to have defective brakes was found to have assumed the risk of the injuries he sustained in a single car accident. He was knowledgeable about brakes in general (and the brakes of this car in particular) but rode in the car in disregard of the risk.[39] In another case, a truck driver was found to have assumed the risk of a steering failure because he had experienced similar failures on several occasions prior to the accident in question.[40]

One court has held that contributory negligence is a viable defense in strict liability cases. But most courts have not viewed contributory negligence as a valid defense in strict liability actions. Therefore, it is probably more useful to use the generic term "product misuse" to cover a broad range of conduct on the part of plaintiffs that may form the basis for a defense.

Product Misuse Products liability claims, whatever the theory of liability, are all concerned in some way with a question of intended, expected, or normal uses of the product:

- Under a *negligence test*, the manufacturer has a duty to manufacture a product that will be safe for the purpose for which the manufacturer should expect it to be used.
- The *warranty test* is that the product must be fit for the ordinary purpose for which such products are used.
- The *strict liability test* is that a product must be safe for normal handling and consumption and free of defects unreasonably dangerous to the user.

In determining what is intended, expected, normal, or ordinary use, the issue of foreseeability will come into play. In one case, a plaintiff garageowner sued the lessor and manufacturer of gasoline pumping equipment for damages caused by a fire. The court found that the fire was caused, not by a product defect, but by the negligence of a cab driver who drove off with the nozzle of the pump inserted in the gasoline tank. The violent stress on the hose caused a component part of the pump to rupture and leak, leading to a fire. The court held that the misuse of the product was the cause of the damage and that the manufacturer could not reasonably be expected to foresee and guard against such a misuse.[41]

In recent years, there has developed a long line of cases in which auto manufacturers have been sued by plaintiffs who were involved in collisions and claimed that the manufacturer, in effect, should have designed a vehicle in which it was safe to have a collision. Defendant manufacturers have consistently contended that collisions are not an expected, ordinary, or normal use of an auto. One line of decisions had adopted the view that the intended purpose does not include participation in collisions, despite the manufacturer's ability to foresee that such collisions will sometimes occur. Another line of decisions, on the contrary, has stressed foreseeability aspects rather than focusing on normal use. These decisions have held that a manufacturer should foresee the possibility that collisions will occur and that this concept carries with it the duty to design the product to minimize the consequences of a collision. In these cases, it is not claimed that an allegedly defective design caused the injury-producing collision in the first instance. The claim is that the design created an "unsafe environment" for an accident, in that some object in the interior of the vehicle or some change in structure as a result of collision forces *enhanced* the injuries the plaintiff received in the accident.

For all practical purposes, the manufacturer today must evaluate carefully the total environment in which its product will be used, and attempt to anticipate the ways in which it foreseeably may be misused. Realistically, the manufacturer must attempt to anticipate unintended as well as intended uses of its product and safeguard the product accordingly.

It is a general rule that the plaintiff's use with knowledge of a hazard will constitute a valid defense. Although a few recent decisions have retreated from this widely accepted general rule, it is still the law in many jurisdictions. The concept of open and obvious danger comes into play here, since these are often the types of cases in which "the very nature of the article gives notice and warning of the consequences to be expected, of the injuries to be suffered.[42]

Another common aspect of product misuse consists of using the product in disregard of warnings or contrary to instructions. Use of a product in disregard of specific warnings may be a defense, as long as the warnings are adequate to reasonably alert a person to a hazard. The following example will illustrate the potential for a sound defense. In this case, the issues of adequacy and disregard of the warning were resolved in favor of the manufacturer. The plaintiff was using contact cement in connection with his carpentry work. The container had a label that clearly and specifically warned against smoking and warned that all fires and flames must be extinguished and sparking must be prevented by turning off electric motors. An explosion occurred when the plaintiff used the cement within a few inches of a gas stove where the pilot light was left burning. The court held that the plaintiff used the product in disregard of a warning that was adequate to give notice of the hazard.[43]

Directions and warnings serve somewhat different purposes: directions are given to assure *effective* use and warnings to assure *safe* use. The two may overlap, however, since a statement directing that something be done or not be done is at least partially cautionary in nature. In a case in which the plaintiff sustained skin injuries while apparently using home permanent solution for normal purposes, the court found that she misused the product in the sense of failing to follow instructions regarding the making of a test curl. The court held that a consumer may not knowingly violate the unambiguous instruction and ignore the information supplied by the manufacturer and then attempt to hold the manufacturer liable for resulting injuries.[44]

It should be evident from this discussion of defenses based on misuse by the plaintiff that there is a considerable amount of overlap among the various defenses. For example, the conduct of a plaintiff in a single case may involve an unintended use of a product, as well as disregard of a warning and use with full knowledge of a potential hazard. One or more aspects of the plaintiff's conduct may constitute, in the terminology of a particular court, either a voluntary assumption of a known risk or contributory negligence. In short, the labels are used as convenient categories. The key point is that the types of conduct discussed above may form the basis for a tenable defense through which the defendant can attempt to establish either that the product was not defective or, even if defective, the plaintiff's conduct, rather than the defect, was the real cause of the plaintiff's injuries.

Alteration or Modification of Product by Plaintiff or Third Party   Conduct on the part of a person other than the plaintiff or the defendant may constitute the basis for a defense in a products case.

The conduct of a third person may be the actual cause of the plaintiff's injury. In one case, a successful defense resulted from proof that the negligence of a prescribing doctor in failing to follow instructions for the use of a drug caused a patient's injury. Since the drug itself was safe in the absence of the doctor's negligence, the drug company was absolved from liability.[45]

Conduct on the part of a third person can also cause an otherwise safe product to become dangerous or defective. For example, the owner of a machine may render a safety device inoperable, either by removing the device or modifying the machine to bypass it, thus allowing the machine to be operated without the safety device functioning. In such cases, the manufacturer may be relieved of liability if it can establish that such conduct was, in fact, the cause of an injury.

Other types of activity, short of such drastic modifications of a product, may form the basis of a defense. These may include mishandling or failure to follow cautionary instructions. A manufacturer is not an insurer of its product. Nor does the manufacturer impliedly warrant that its product will never deteriorate in spite of mishandling or improper maintenance.

State-of-the-Art Defense   A number of cases have held that the manufacturer's or seller's liability is to be determined solely on the basis of circumstances existing at a time of a product's design or manufacture. This "state-of-the-art defense" is well recognized in the law of products liability, and it is applicable to actions under both negligence and strict liability, where such concepts as foreseeability and reasonableness are important to the application of both theories.

It is not unreasonable for a manufacturer to follow a design or method of manufacture customary in the industry, although, through the use of hindsight when a products liability lawsuit is filed, other possible designs or methods may be conceived of as safer. In determining whether a product or its design was unreasonably dangerous or defective, it is relevant for the court to consider the conformity of the defendant's practice to that of other manufacturers in the industry at the time of the design or the manufacturing process. In a lawnmower case, the plaintiff's expert witness testified that alternative designs would have made the machine safer. The defense expert, however, established that the mower met or exceeded all safety standards, that it embodied the most advanced technology known to the industry, and the plaintiff's alternatives would create further functional and safety problems.[46]

In a case involving the crash of a chartered airplane, the injuries of the plaintiffs were allegedly aggravated because seats broke loose from the floor, blocking an exit. The plaintiffs attempted to introduce evidence of improvements in standards for installation of seats between the time the plane was manufactured in 1952 and the time of the 1970 crash. The court held that the plane was not defective, because it was in accord with the state of the art within the aircraft industry when designed, manufactured, and first sold. Proof that improved seats were available eighteen years after the manufacture of the plane was not relevant to the determination of reasonable care at the time the plane was designed.[47] On the question of reasonableness, some courts may admit into evidence proof of alternative designs or processes but restrict admissibility to alternatives that were available at the time the defendant's product was designed and manufactured.

Disclaimers Whatever the surface attraction of disclaimers in the context of products liability, it must be remembered that the law will construe them *very* strictly. According to the Uniform Commercial Code, "Limitation of consequential damages or injury to the person in the case of consumer goods is prima facie unconscionable but limitation of damages where the loss is commercial is not." In short, disclaimers may be effective in cases involving purely commercial loss, but a disclaimer is useless in an attempt to avoid liability for injuries resulting from a defective product.

Statutes of Limitations In certain circumstances, a defense may be based on a statute of limitations, asserting that the defendant is no longer subject to suit because the statutory time in which to bring an action has expired. Most jurisdictions have differing statutes for torts (including negligence and strict liability) and contracts (including breach of warranty). There may be two basic questions involved in this defense to products actions:

1. What statute (tort or contract) is to be used?
2. When does the action arise and when does the time begin to run?

Assuming an action in tort, the question of which statute applies may be relatively simple, but a more difficult question is, "When does the action accrue?"

Some courts have held that the clock begins to run at the time of the injury. In other words, if the applicable statutory limit is three years, the plaintiff will have three years from the time of the injury to bring an action. A few courts have held that the cause of action accrues at the time the product is sold, since, if an actionable defect exists, it must be present when the product leaves the seller's control. Therefore, assuming again a three-year statute, if the injury does not occur until thirty-five months after the product is manufactured and sold, the plaintiff must act with great dispatch to avoid having the action barred. The latter is a minority view, although a number of state statutes enacted by legislatures in recent years have altered statutes of limitations for the benefit of manufacturers.

CONTRACTUAL LIABILITY EXPOSURES

The parties to a commercial transaction can often foresee the possibility that one or more of the parties involved could be held liable for bodily injury or property damage that may result in connection with the transaction. The parties to such a transaction often reach an agreement that one party will bear the exposure to loss and pay any damages for which either of the parties might become liable. The various types of loss-transfer provisions were explained in Chapter 1. Additional aspects of contractual exposures are discussed in the sections that follow.

As a general rule, the courts will enforce an agreement to transfer the exposure to liability loss, if it shifts the cost of ordinary negligence to a party that is voluntarily assuming the exposure. The rule has been qualified in various ways, both by statute and by the courts, for reasons of "public policy."

Transfer of Liability Loss Exposures—Statutes and Decisions

Statutory limitations on transfers of liability loss exposures vary from state to state. In several states, statutes prohibit provisions indemnifying a party against its own negligence in a construction contract. The basic public policy underlying these statutes reflects a concern that indemnity agreements may encourage negligence. In other words, the legislators are concerned that a party who does not have to bear the cost of negligence will not be careful. Another public policy often underlying the statutes is the desire to place the burden of loss on the party most able to bear the cost.

Contractual shifting of liability is usually restricted to liability for ordinary negligence. A party may not, as a general rule, exempt itself from liability for gross negligence or willful or wanton misconduct. Again, the concern is that such an indemnity would encourage reckless action.

While many indemnity agreements are considered contrary to public policy, this is counteracted by the basic right of freedom of contract. Courts normally allow parties of roughly equal strength to allocate loss exposures in whatever manner makes sense to the parties involved.

Contractual Provisions

Contractual liability provisions may take various forms. The provisions may be tailored so that one party will assume liability for all or only a certain portion of a potential liability arising from a certain situation. For example, Subcontractor S might agree to indemnify General Contractor G for any liability G might incur for losses caused by S's own negligence. Thus, if an injured party recovers from G for injuries sustained as a result of S's negligence, General Contractor G may, under its contract with Subcontractor S, be reimbursed.

Agreements are often broader than the contractual provisions discussed above. For example, an agreement could cover nearly all injuries arising out of a particular situation, including those resulting from the sole negligence of the transferor. Thus, if Subcontractor S had executed such a broad agreement, it could be liable for a party's injuries whether they were caused by either S's or G's negligence.

An indemnity provision may not only indemnify a party for liability arising out of that party's sole negligence, but in some states it may also involve the duty of the indemnitor to defend the indemnitee. If Subcontractor S had executed an agreement of this type, S might be required to both defend and indemnify the general contractor, even for losses caused by the sole negligence of the general contractor.

Examples of Contracts and Agreements that May Involve Tort Liability Assumptions

Liability exposures are often transferred in connection with construction contracts, purchase order and sales agreements, incidental agreements, and surety agreements.

Construction Contracts Construction contracts often include agreements by a party (usually the contractor) to indemnify another party (usually the owner) against tort liability resulting from a class or classes of occurrences specified in the contract.

Courts will uphold contractual assumptions of tort liability in construction contracts that are reasonable attempts to predict and allocate the costs of possible accidents associated with a construction project, especially where the assuming party assumes liability for negligent acts or omissions connected with its own activities. Courts will also uphold intermediate assumptions, wherein the assuming party undertakes to hold the other party harmless for its partial or contributing negligence.

Common Law. Under the common law, even a broad assumption of tort liability in a construction contract was effective and enforceable (and still is, where there has been no intervening statute). Courts look to the language of the indemnity agreement, and have indemnified a solely negligent party when that obligation was within the scope of the indemnification agreement. The common law viewed broad indemnification agreements in construction contracts as part of a bargain between equally powerful parties and therefore not in violation of public policy.

Statutes. As noted, the common law has been preempted in some states by enactment of statutes relating to the assumption of tort liability for another's negligence in the context of construction contracts. For example, a statute enacted in Illinois in 1971 voids indemnity agreements in construction contracts that hold a party harmless for its own negligence. Similar statutes have been enacted in several other states.

The enforceability of a construction contract indemnification agreement that seeks to hold harmless a party for its own negligence is likely to vary from state to state. Therefore, an evaluation of the exposures in any particular situation must be based on a knowledge of the law(s) that apply in the jurisdiction involved. Note that, if an agreement is unenforceable, any insurer that agreed to insure the assuming party for contractual liability would not be required to pay under the insurance contract, and liability would rest with the negligent party, despite the attempted assumption. This is a key point that will be reemphasized when contractual liability coverage is discussed in Chapter 5.

Purchase Order and Sales Agreements Purchase order agreements and sales agreements generally involve the same considerations as other tort liability assumptions. In addition, there are problems unique to such agreements.

Unequal Bargaining Positions. A purchase order or sales agreement may include an assumption of tort liability as a result of the superior bargaining position of one party. When one party forces a shifting of liability to avoid having to bear any loss exposures, and when there are no economically or socially desirable advantages resulting from the assumption of liability, courts will usually try to avoid giving effect to the liability assumption agreement.

Indemnitor Unaware of Assumption. Purchase order and sales agreements also involve the possibility that a liability assumption will not come to the attention of the assuming party. Suppose, for example, it has been printed in small type on the back of the purchase order or sales agreement. If the entity assuming the burden is not aware of it, the provision usually will not be enforced.

"Battle of the Forms." A contract for the sale of goods often will be embodied in two separate writings—a purchase order prepared by the purchaser and a sales document prepared by the seller. These writings often include differing provisions, including inconsistencies as to which party may bear tort liability relating to manufacture or use of the goods that are the subject of the contract. A question arises as to whether a contract has been formed and, if so, *which* terms are part of the contract. This has been described as "the battle of the forms."

Under the Uniform Commercial Code (UCC), when the parties have knowledge or skill peculiar to the practices or goods involved in a transaction, the seller's use of a form that includes terms in addition to or different from terms included in the purchaser's purchase order may not prevent formation of a contract.[48] For example, if the seller's sales document contains a provision (not included in the purchaser's document) whereby the purchaser agrees to hold the manufacturer harmless for personal injury resulting from the purchaser's failure to install or properly assemble the product, that term would become a part of the final contract between the parties, with three exceptions:

1. *If the original purchase order states that the purchaser wants a contract to be formed only on the precise terms included in that order, the inclusion of additional terms may result in the failure to form a contract.*
2. *If additional or different terms materially alter the contract, no contract may have been formed.* The question as to what constitutes a material alteration is a question of fact based on all the surrounding circumstances and the customs of the trade. For example, it is likely that a term in a seller's sales form shifting liability to the purchaser for negligence in the manufacture of a product would constitute a material alteration, and therefore would prevent a contract from being formed.
3. *If either party gives notice of objection to the additional terms, the contract may not have been made.*

There is an important exception to the above UCC rules. If the conduct of both parties recognizes the existence of a contract, the UCC will hold a contract to have been established, *despite* the existence of material alterations in the seller's form or the other two circumstances that otherwise could lead to a finding that no contract has been created. In such a case, the terms of the particular contract will "consist of those terms on which the writings of the parties agree," plus those general provisions of the UCC that are needed to provide the essential terms of the agreement.

In summary, there is substantial uncertainty as to whether, in a contract for the sale of goods, an attempt by one party to shift tort liability to the other party will be effective. Such an attempt may result in one of the following:

1. There may be a failure to form a contract.
2. The shift may become a term of the contract.
3. If the liability shift materially alters the contract, but the parties nonetheless carry out the other terms of the contract, it will not be considered a part of the final agreement because the parties did not agree on that term.
4. Even if it becomes part of the contract, it may be unenforceable as contrary to public policy.

Surety Agreements In general terms, a surety is one who is *primarily liable* for the debt or obligation of another. A surety agreement thus involves three parties: (1) the *surety,* who is liable for (2) his or her *principal* (the debtor or obligor), who in turn is obligated to (3) the *obligee* or creditor. The liability of a surety is measured by and is strictly limited to that assumed by the terms of the surety agreement or "bond." (Corporate suretyship will be discussed in detail in Chapter 13.)

Circumstances When Tort Liability Cannot Be Assumed or Delegated under Contract

Under certain circumstances, the courts will hold exculpatory agreements void as against public policy. Statutory enactments have already expressed the public view that tort liability cannot be assumed or delegated under certain types of contracts.

Public Policy Whether or not a contract providing for exemption from liability for negligence is deemed void as a matter of public policy depends on a number of considerations. No clear-cut rule can be deduced from the opinions of the courts. On one hand, some courts seek to discourage negligent behavior and broadly hold that one cannot by contract avoid liability for negligence. On the other hand, many other courts emphasize the freedom of parties to contract as they wish; they condition the validity of exculpatory contracts, in any particular case, on the relations of the parties, the presence or absence of equality of bargaining power, and other circumstances. Thus, courts may strike down exculpatory provisions, under certain circumstances, in order to protect those in need of goods and services from those who have a far superior bargaining position.

Public Servants The area in which courts most often impose restrictions on people's freedom to contract for exculpatory provisions is where contracts are entered into by persons who perform public duties for compensation.

Common Carriers. Common carriers are said to perform "public duties." While common carriers may not completely exempt themselves from their tort liability, they may contractually limit the amount for which they shall be liable in case of harm to property caused by their negligence (provided they have complied with all federal and state statutory and regulatory provisions). Common carriers must also offer to render the public service at a reasonable rate without such a limitation, and the public must be given a choice between the two forms of liability and the two rates. In most instances, this limitation will take the form of a maximum valuation amount of property that the carrier transports, commonly known as the shipper's "declared value."

Others Performing a Public Duty. In addition to common carriers, numerous other categories of contracting parties are considered to be performing a public duty. Such parties are also barred from benefiting from a clause exculpating them from their own negligence.

For example, public utilities such as gas, electric power and telegraph companies have been regarded, with respect to customers, as having such a monopolistic position that they will not be allowed to exempt themselves from liability for their own negligence.

Common carriers and others performing a public service are not the only parties that will not be permitted to benefit from a contract exculpating them from their own negligence. In the precedent-setting opinion of Tunkl v. Regents of University of California,[49] the Supreme Court of California held invalid a contractual clause exempting a charity hospital from tort liability, even though the hospital had no duty to serve the public. The hospital was a nonprofit, research-oriented organization that admitted only the types of patients whose study and treatment would aid the development of a research and medical education program.

In addition to contracts that exempt a person from willful or negligent action, agreements to commit a tort or to injure third persons will also be held illegal as against public policy. This rule also encompasses agreements made for the purpose of defrauding a third person, agreements to place false and deceptive labels on goods in order to deceive purchasers, and agreements that would involve the breach of a contract with a third person.[50]

Similarly, a contract to indemnify against the consequences of illegal action may also be held invalid because of its tendency to promote illegal acts. The validity of such a contract depends upon whether the party who performs the illegal act is acting in good faith and without knowledge of the illegality. For example, an agreement to indemnify a publisher against the consequences of publishing libelous material is generally invalid. However, where it is not anticipated that any material in a book will be libelous and an exculpatory clause is inserted into the contract or publication merely as a backstop against unforeseen liability, the contract will be enforced.[51]

While the courts have generally upheld contracts that shift tort liability from one contracting party to another, subject to the numerous exceptions noted above, they often indicate their distaste for these contracts by construing them so strictly as to make the exculpatory clauses inapplicable to the particular facts of any given case. Thus, courts usually require that an exculpatory provision in a contract be expressed in clear and unequivocal language to be valid and effective. If the exculpating language is not absolutely clear, the courts may indulge in the presumption that the parties never intended to contractually shift the consequences of their own negligence from one party to another. More often, they will construe the language against the drafter of the provision and in favor of the other contracting party.

Chapter Notes

1. Andrews v. DelGuzzi, 353 P. 2d 422 (WA 1960).
2. Littleton v. B & R Const. Co., 266 So 2d 560 (LA. App. 1972).
3. Roush v. Johnson, 80 SE 2d 857 (WV 1954).
4. MacPherson v. Buick Motor Co., 111 NE 1050 (NY 1916).
5. Totten v. Gruzen, 245 A. 2d 1 (NJ 1968).
6. Standholm v. General Const. Co., 382 P. 2d 843 (OR 1963).
7. Hilla v. Gross, 204 NW 2d 712 (MI 1972).
8. Dow v. Holly Mfg. Co., 321 P. 2d 736 (CA 1958).
9. Barnthouse v. California Steel Building Co., 29 Cal. Rptr. 835 (Cal. App. 1963).
10. Johnson v. City of Leandro, 4 Cal. Rptr. 404 (Cal. App. 1960).
11. Massei v. Lettunich, 56 Cal. Rptr. 232 (Cal. App. 1967).
12. CCH Prod. Liabl. Rptr. 4501 (Eng. 1842).
13. Ibid.
14. 111 NE 1050 (NY 1916).
15. Cochran v. McDonald, 161 P. 2d 305 (WA 1945).
16. Sec. 402B.
17. Pfeiffer v. Empire Merch. Co., 305 NYS 2d 245 (App. Div. 1969).
18. Handrigan v. Apex Warwick, Inc., 275 A. 2d 262 (RI 1971).
19. Austin v. Western Auto Supply Co., 421 SW 2d 203 (MO 1967).
20. Wait v. Borne, 25 NE 1053 (NY 1890).
21. Nobility Homes v. Shivers, 539 SW 2d 190 (TX 1976).
22. Atlanta Tallow Co., Inc. v. John W. Eshelman & Sons, Inc., 140 SE 2d 118 (GA 1964).
23. West v. Alberto Culver Co., 486 F. 2d 459 (10 Cir. 1973).
24. Hauter v. Zogarts, 534 P. 2d 377 (CA 1975).
25. Toole v. Richardson-Merrell, Inc., 60 Cal. Rptr. 398 (Cal. App. 1967).
26. Matthews v. Lawnlite Co., 88 Sp. 2d 299 (FL 1956).
27. Campo v. Scofield, 95 NE 2d 802 (NY 1950).
28. Independent Nail & Packing Co., Inc. v. Mitchell, 343 F. 2d 819 (1 Cir. 1965).
29. Lorenc V. Chemirad Corp., 179 A. 2d 401 (NJ 1962).
30. Trowbridge v. Abrasive Co. of Phila., 190 F. 2d 825 (3Cir. 1951).
31. Campo v. Scofield, note 27 above at 804.
32. Whitehurst v. Revlon, Inc., 307 F. Supp. 918 (D VA 1969).
33. Jackson v. Baldwin-Lima-Hamilton Corps., 252 F. Supp. 529 (ED PA 1966).
34. 377 P. 2d 897 (Cal. 1963).
35. Tucson Industries, Inc. v. Schwarts, 487 P. 2d 12 (Ariz. App. 1971).
36. Elmore v. American Motors Corp., 451 P. 2d 84 (CA 1969).
37. Dunham v. Vaughn & Bushnell Mfg. Co., 247 NE 2d 401 (IL 1969).
38. Rumsey v. Freeway Manor, 423 SW 387, 391-92 (Tex. Civ. App. 1968).
39. Sperling v. Hatch, 88 Cal. Rptr. 704 (Cal. App. 1970).
40. Kirby v. General Motors Corp., 229 NE 2d 777 (IL App. 1973).

114—Commercial Liability Risk Management and Insurance

41. Speyer, Inc. v. Humble Oil Co. & A.O. Smith, 275 F. Supp. 861 (WD PA 1967), aff'd 403 F. 2d 766.
42. Campo v. Scofield, 95 NE 2d 802, 804 (NY 1950).
43. Borowicz v. Chicago Mastic Co., 367 F. 2d 751 (7 Cir. 1966).
44. Pinto v. Clairol, Inc., 324 F. 2d 608 (6 Cir. 1963).
45. Carmichael v. Reitz, 95 Cal. Rptr. 381 (Cal. App. 1971).
46. Welch v. Outboard Marine Corp., 481 F. 2d 252 (5 Cir. 1973).
47. Bruce v. Marin-Marietta Corp., 544 F. 2d 442 (10 Cir. 1976).
48. Article 2, the "Sales" article, has been adopted (with minor modifications in some states) in every state except Louisiana.
49. 60 Cal. 2d 92, 32 Cal. Rptr. 33, 383 P. 2d 441 (1963).
50. John D. Calamari and Joseph M. Perillo, *Law of Contracts*, 365 (St. Paul: West Publishing Co., 1971).
51. Samuel Williston, *A Treatise on the Law of Contracts*, 1749A at 133, 3rd ed. Walter H. E. Jaeger, ed. (Mount Kisco, NY: Baker, Voorhees & Co., 1972).

CHAPTER 3

Identifying, Measuring, and Controlling Commercial Liability Loss Exposures

The risk management of commercial liability loss exposures involves:

1. identifying and analyzing the loss exposures
2. selecting the technique or techniques to be used to handle each exposure
3. implementing the techniques chosen
4. monitoring the decisions made and implementing changes when appropriate

This chapter deals with how liability loss exposures may be identified, how the identified exposures may be measured, and how control techniques may be used to lower the loss frequency, reduce the loss severity and/or improve the accuracy of loss predictions.[1] Later chapters will emphasize financing techniques that may be used in risk management.

A discussion of closely related topics appears in the CPCU 3 text, *Commercial Property Risk Management and Insurance.* However, this text concentrates on liability loss exposures which differ from property loss exposures in several important ways. Special attention will be paid in this chapter to industrial injury and disease exposures, product liability exposures, other general liability exposures, and motor vehicle liability exposures.

① IDENTIFICATION OF LIABILITY LOSS EXPOSURES

Identification of liability loss exposures is an extremely important part of the risk management process. The losses associated with most liability exposures are unlimited in amount, and the failure to identify such a loss exposure usually means that the exposed entity must retain any resulting loss it otherwise would have elected to control and transfer. In other words, serious mismanagement of liability loss exposures is much less likely when such exposures have not been overlooked.

To systematize the process of identification, it is advisable to use a combination of approaches. The approaches to be discussed in this chapter are (1) the insurance survey approach, (2) the risk management survey approach, (3) the flow chart approach, (4) the financial statement approach, (5) personal inspections of premises and activities, (6) interactions with persons in production, marketing, personnel, and other departments, (7) contract analysis, (8) loss analysis, (9) analysis of the legal, social, and economic environments, (10) interaction with outsiders, and (11) insurance coverage checklists.

Insurance Survey Method

Many insurance companies, producers, and others have developed insurance survey questionnaires designed to reveal the insurable loss exposures of the prospect or client and to provide the information needed to underwrite and rate the policies that would cover these loss exposures. Exhibit 3-1 contains the section from one insurance survey that relates to commercial general liability loss exposures. Similar sections deal with other classes of exposures or other types of insurance.

The first page of the completed form consists almost entirely of application information describing the desired insurance. Coverages and limits desired are shown in the upper portion of the form. The "Schedule of Hazards" in the center section lists the classification(s) from the insurance rating manual that describe the applicant's activities at each location, along with a numerical "class code" that accompanies that classification. One such classification is "Janitorial Supplies—dealers or distributors"; the code for that classification is 14527.

For each classification, a "premium basis" is indicated—usually gross sales, payroll, area, or contract cost. Premium basis figures do indicate the extent of operations within each classification, which has some value in exposure analysis. However, the real reason for accumulating this information on the questionnaire is to compute a premium for the policy.

The "Claims Made" section of the questionnaire develops information needed to issue a commercial general liability policy that provides coverage on a claims-made basis and to rate the policy during a transition period after a change from an occurrence basis to a claims-made basis of coverage. (The claims-made concept is developed in subsequent chapters of this text.) Again, this information is important in underwriting and rating insurance coverage. It has little to do with exposure identification and analysis in the usual sense, but may help to identify exposures that are uninsured because of a gap in continuous coverage or a lack of "tail" coverage, as explained in Chapter 6.

The second page of the form asks a number of questions designed to elicit information on special hazards or on hazards that may require special underwriting consideration, coverage, or rating. The answers to these questions can also lead the user to recognize some important exposures. For example, the first question is, "Does the applicant draw plans, designs, or specifications?" Contractors generally construct items according to plans, designs, or specifications developed by others, in which case liability arising out of a design error would probably not be the contractor's liability. Some contractors, however, do varying degrees of engineering or design work. The knowledgeable user of this survey form recognizes the implications of this question, realizes that an affirmative answer indicates a professional liability exposure, knows that this exposure might not be covered by the usual commercial general liability policy, and would take a "yes" answer as a cue to investigate the need for architects' and engineers' professional liability insurance. Moreover, the user should recognize the potentially serious consequences of a professional liability claim against a design professional.

Commercial general liability coverage is examined in Chapter 5, and professional liability exposures and insurance in Chapter 12. By the time this course is completed, the reader should be in a position to recognize the implications of each item on the form. For now, it is suggested that the student examine each question to see how many are clearly understood and how many identify gaps in knowledge that need to be filled by further study of this text.

The major disadvantage of the typical insurance survey is that it is designed to reveal only *insurable* loss exposures—in some cases, only the loss exposures that are insured by the insurer distributing the questionnaire. To identify and analyze uninsurable loss exposures, the results of the insurance survey must be supplemented with information gained from other sources.

Exhibit 3-1
Insurance Survey

acord COMMERCIAL GENERAL LIABILITY SECTION

DATE (MM/DD/YY)

PRODUCER

APPLICANT (First Named Insured)

PROPOSED EFF DATE	PROPOSED EXP DATE	BILLING PLAN	PAYMENT PLAN	AUDIT
		AGENCY / DIRECT		

FOR COMPANY USE ONLY

COVERAGES

COMMERCIAL GENERAL LIABILITY

CLAIMS MADE / OCCURRENCE

OWNER'S & CONTRACTORS PROTECTIVE

DEDUCTIBLES

PROPERTY DAMAGE $ ___ $ ___ $ ___

OTHER COVERAGES, RESTRICTIONS AND/OR ENDORSEMENTS

LIMITS

		PREMIUMS
GENERAL AGGREGATE	$	PREMISES/OPERATIONS
PRODUCTS & COMPLETED OPERATIONS AGGREGATE	$	
PERSONAL & ADVERTISING INJURY	$	
EACH OCCURRENCE	$	PRODUCTS
FIRE DAMAGE (ANY ONE FIRE)	$	
MEDICAL EXPENSE (ANY ONE PERSON)	$	OTHER
		TOTAL

SCHEDULE OF HAZARDS

LOC #	CLASSIFICATION	CLASS CODE	PREMIUM BASIS	TERR	RATE PREMS/OPS	RATE PRODUCTS	PREMIUM PREMS/OPS	PREMIUM PRODUCTS
			(s) GROSS SALES					
			(p) PAYROLL					
			(a) AREA					
			(c) CONTRACT COST					
			(t) OTHER					

(s) per $1,000
(p) per $1,000/pay
(a) per 1,000 sq ft
(c) per $1,000/cost
(t) per unit

CLAIMS MADE (EXPLAIN ALL "YES" RESPONSES)

		YES	NO
1	Proposed retroactive date:		
2	Entry date into uninterrupted claims made coverage:		
3	Has any product, work, accident, or location been excluded, uninsured, or self-insured from any previous coverage?		
4	Was tail coverage purchased under any previous policy?		

COMMENTS

TRANSITION

		YES	NO
1	Has this risk or any location ever not qualified for transition?		
2	If this risk qualifies for transition, indicate the year it first qualified: _____ and:		

LOC	CLASS,	AREA	SALES

ACORD 126-S (11/85)

PLEASE COMPLETE REVERSE SIDE

IIR/ACORD CORPORATION 1985

CONTRACTORS

#	EXPLAIN ALL "YES" RESPONSES	YES	NO	FULL TIME STAFF	PART TIME STAFF
	(For any past or present operations)			DESCRIBE THE TYPE OF WORK & PERCENT SUBCONTRACTED	
1	Does applicant draw plans, designs, or specifications?				
2	Do any operations include blasting or utilize or store explosive material?				
3	Do any operations include evacuation, tunneling, underground work or earth moving?				
4	Do your subcontractors carry coverages or limits less than yours?				
5	Are certificates of insurance required from subcontractors?				
6	Does applicant lease equipment to others with or without operators?				

REMARKS:

PRODUCTS/COMPLETED OPERATIONS

PRODUCTS	ANNUAL GROSS SALES	# OF UNITS	TIME IN MARKET	EXPECTED LIFE	INTENDED USE	PRINCIPAL COMPONENTS

#	EXPLAIN ALL "YES" RESPONSES (For any past or present product or operation)	YES	NO
1	Does applicant install, service or demonstrate products?		
2	Foreign products sold, distributed, used as components?		
3	Research and development conducted or new products planned?		
4	Guarantees, Warranties, Hold Harmless Agreements?		
5	Products related to aircraft/space industry?		
6	Products recalled, discontinued, changed?		
7	Products of others sold or re-packaged under applicant label?		
8	Products under label of others?		
9	Vendors coverage required?		
10	Does any Named Insured sell to other Named Insureds?		

Please attach literature, brochures, labels, warnings, etc

ADDITIONAL INTERESTS/CERTIFICATE RECIPIENTS

#	NAME & ADDRESS (INCLUDE LOAN NUMBER FOR MORTGAGEES)	INTEREST	CERT

GENERAL INFORMATION

#	EXPLAIN ALL "YES" RESPONSES	YES	NO
	For all past or present operations		
1	Any medical facilities provided or doctors employed/contracted?		
2	Any exposure to radioactive/nuclear materials?		
3	Do operations involve storing, treating discharging, applying, disposing, or transporting of hazardous material? (e.g. landfills, wastes, fuel tanks, etc.)		
4	Any operations sold, acquired, or discontinued in last 5 years?		
	Machinery or equipment loaned or rented to others?		
6	Any watercraft, docks, floats owned, hired, or leased?		

#	EXPLAIN ALL "YES" RESPONSES	YES	NO
7	Any parking facilities owned/rented?		
8	Is a fee charged for parking?		
9	Recreation facilities provided?		
10	Is there a swimming pool on the premises?		
11	Sporting or social events sponsored?		
12	Any structural alterations contemplated?		
13	Any demolition exposure contemplated?		

REMARKS:

ACORD 126-S (11/85)   ATTACH TO APPLICANT INFORMATION SECTION

(B) Risk Management Survey Method

time consuming interviews
multiple interviews

Questionnaires not limited to insurable loss exposures can be obtained from the American Management Association, the Risk and Insurance Management Society (RIMS),[2] and the International Risk Management Institute, among others.

Exhibit 3-2 contains the premises and operations liability segment of the International Risk Management Institute *Exposure Survey Questionnaire*. The entire survey is 101 pages long.

This questionnaire is intended to solicit the data necessary for underwriters and to serve as an aid "in identifying all types of pure risks, whether insurable or not."[3] This helps to overcome the limitations of an insurance-oriented survey.

However, a broad risk management survey has its own limitations. A survey of this type can be completed only with considerable investment in time and effort. Interviews with a number of different people are required, as well as extensive research to develop much of the detailed information. While some survey questions can be answered with simple fact information, the questionnaire is most effectively used by a trained risk management professional who recognizes the implications of each item. The answers to certain questions should also prompt the knowledgeable user to probe further in order to pin down some of the more unusual exposures.

Due to its complexity, it may not be practical to complete a survey of this nature more frequently than once every several years. Moreover, the amount of detail in the form may lull the user into thinking all possible exposures have been dealt with once the questionnaire is complete. Another limitation is that the survey approach relies primarily on information supplied through interviews with other people. In order to develop a complete, reliable understanding of the exposures faced by any organization, survey information should usually be verified or supplemented with information from other sources.

(C) Flow Chart Method

A second approach that may be used in identifying a firm's liability loss exposures is to prepare and study a flow chart or flow charts of the firm's operations. In using this method, the financial statement method, and the others to be described later, the person conducting the analysis must have a sound understanding of liability loss exposures. Preparing and studying the flow chart, the financial statements, or the other data sources should reveal liability exposures that apply to this particular firm.

The number, variety, and format of flow charts that can be drawn depend on the exposures present, the amount of information available, and the creativity of the person making the flow charts. Two flow charts are reproduced here as Exhibits 3-3 and 3-4. In CPCU 3 these same charts were used to indicate the property loss exposures associated with the property and activities identified by the flow charts.[4] Here these charts are used to determine what liability exposures are associated with these properties and activities.

Exhibit 3-3 shows the movement of goods from suppliers into storage followed by three types of processing and storage of finished goods. From the finished goods warehouses, the products move to the firm's retail outlets or to miscellaneous independent retailers who in turn sell the products to consumers. This flow chart shows that the firm owns or rents one raw materials warehouse, two factories, three finished goods warehouses, and four retail outlets. Possession and use of these premises creates premises liability; rental of premises suggests possible liability assumed under lease agreements. Contractual liability may also exist because of agreements the firm makes with suppliers, subcontractors, and miscellaneous independent retailers. Auto liability exposures may be involved as property is moved from location to location. Auto loading and unloading may also create liability exposures. Employees may be injured on the job or cause injuries or damage to property of others.

Product liability may result from defective products. The flow chart in Exhibit 3-3 shows that raw materials come from four suppliers, one manufacturing process is performed by two subcontractors, and completed products reach consumers through a variety of company-owned and independent retail outlets. This information helps one visualize the problems that might be involved in tracing the source of a product defect or in recalling a defective batch of products.

Exhibit 3-4 provides a more detailed picture of the flow of goods within a plant from the receiving room to the shipping room. This chart sheds light on liability exposures by revealing more of the activities that occur within the plant.

Financial Statement Method

The financial statement method has been suggested as a way of identifying all the loss exposures faced by a firm. "The financial and operating statements mirror everything the corporation owns or does, because every business transaction ultimately involves either money or property. Budgets and forecasts project proposed activities for at least a year ahead, enabling the risk manager to anticipate future exposures."[5]

Exhibit 3-2
Risk Management Survey*

Premises-Operations Liability Exposure

Care, Custody, Control

1. a. Do you ever take possession of the *personal* property of others for any reason (i.e., storage, repair, transportation, collateral, etc.)? ☐ Often, ☐ Occasionally, ☐ Never

    b. If yes, please explain: _____

    _____

    _____

2. a. Do you rent or lease any personal property (i.e., equipment, machinery, furniture) from others? ☐ Often, ☐ Occasionally, ☐ Never

    b. If yes, explain details, obtain lease: _____

    _____

    _____

3. a. Do you rent or lease any real property from others? ☐ Often, ☐ Occasionally, ☐ Never

    b. If yes, explain details, obtain lease: _____

    _____

    _____

4. a. Do you have any parking lots, garages, etc. on your (owned or leased) properties that are used by the public? ☐ Yes ☐ No

b. If (a) is yes, complete the following:

	Annual Receipts	# Vehicles	Est. Value Exposed
Location	$		$
Location	$		$

c. If (a) is yes, do you charge a fee for parking in your lots, garage, etc.? ☐ Yes ☐ No

5. a. Do you ever occupy the *real* property of others for any reason (i.e., security, maintenance, repairs, remodeling, etc.)? ☐ Often, ☐ Occasionally, ☐ Never

b. If yes, explain details: _____

_____

_____

Environmental Impairment

6. a. Do your operations generate any "hazardous wastes?" ☐ Yes ☐ No ☐ Uncertain

b. If yes, explain details and method of disposal: _____

_____

_____

c. Discuss measures taken to comply with federal, state, local regulations, laws and ordinances. Comments: _____

_____

_____

7. a. Do your operations require the use of potentially hazardous chemicals or substances (i.e., silicon, asbestos, PCB's etc.)? ☐ Yes ☐ No ☐ Uncertain

b. If yes, explain details including quantities, uses, methods of storage: _____

_____

_____

8. a. Do you have any underground storage tanks on any of your (owned or leased) properties? ☐ Yes ☐ No ☐ Uncertain

b. If yes, give details including location, age, use: _____

_____

_____

_____

9. a. Do you own an interest in any oil or gas wells or pipelines? ☐ Yes ☐ No

b. If yes, explain type of ownership, number of wells: _____

_____

_____

10. a. Do you perform operations for others that could result in a pollution incident? ☐ Yes ☐ No

b. If yes, please explain: _____

_____

_____

11. a. Do any of your buildings or premises contain:

i. asbestos ceiling tiles? ☐ Yes ☐ No ☐ Uncertain

ii. transformers with PCB's? ☐ Yes ☐ No ☐ Uncertain

iii. formaldehyde?

b. Location(s), corrective measures: _____

12. a. Has your organization ever been cited by the EPA or the state for violations of a law, regulation or ordinance? ☐ Yes ☐ No

b. Details: _____

Advertising

13. a. What is the approximate annual advertising budget?

last year: $ _____ this year $ _____ next year $ _____

b. Do you use an advertising agency? ☐ Always ☐ Sometimes ☐ Never

c. Is advertising copy reviewed by:

risk manager ☐ Yes ☐ No
outside legal counsel ☐ Yes ☐ No
employed legal counsel ☐ Yes ☐ No

14. Indicate media used and approximate extent of use:

Television _____ %   Direct Mail _____ %
Radio _____ %   Other* _____ %
Newspaper _____ %   100 %
Magazine _____ %

*Please describe: _____

Premises Hazards

15. a. Do you own any vacant land? ☐ Yes ☐ No

    b. Explain location, area, use: _____

16. a. Do you have any swimming pools, lakes, ponds, or reservoirs on or streams, rivers running through your properties or jobsites? ☐ Yes ☐ No

    b. Explain access, uses, protective measures: _____

    c. Do you make a charge for their use? ☐ Yes ☐ No Annual receipts: $___

17. a. Do you have any grandstands or auditoriums? ☐ Yes ☐ No

    b. Explain uses, number of seats, receipts, protective measures: _____

18. a. Do you own any amusement parks, recreational parks, or exercise facilities? ☐ Yes ☐ No

    b. Explain type, purpose, protective measures: _____

19. a. Do you own any horses, livestock, or wild animals? ☐ Yes ☐ No

b. Explain type, purpose, protective measures: _____

20. a. Do you store any explosive, caustic, flammable, or volatile agents on any properties or jobsites?
☐ Yes ☐ No

b. Explain, particularly proximity to other persons or property: _____

21. a. Do you have any boilers, compressors, or pressure vessels on any of your properties or jobsites?
☐ Yes ☐ No

b. Explain nature, use, proximity to others' property/persons: _____

22. Estimate value of surrounding *nonowned* buildings and premises.

Location: _____

North	$
South	$
East	$
West	$
Total	$

Location: _____

North	$
South	$
East	$
West	$
Total	$

Location: _____

North	$
South	$
East	$
West	$
Total	$

Location: _____

North	$
South	$
East	$
West	$
Total	$

Operations Hazards

23. a. Do you have nurses, paramedics, or other medical professionals at any of your facilities? ☐ Yes ☐ No

b. If yes, explain duties, training: _____

c. Do these individuals carry personal professional liability insurance? ☐ Yes ☐ No

24. a. Do you have armed guards at any of your facilities? ☐ Yes ☐ No

b. Explain: _____

25. a. Do you use any independent contractors? ☐ Often, ☐ Occasionally, ☐ Never

b. Explain use: _____

c. Obtain sample contracts if not already secured.

d. Approximate annual expenditures: $ _____

26. a. Do you lease real property to others? ☐ Yes ☐ No

b. Obtain sample lease if not already secured.

c. Location, value, use: _____

27. a. Do you rent or lease personal property to others?

b. Obtain sample lease/rental agreement if not already secured.

c. Type of property, value, use: _____

28. a. Do you ever serve alcoholic beverages to others?

　　i. Employees　　　　☐ Frequently ☐ Occasionally ☐ Never

　　ii. Customers　　　　☐ Frequently ☐ Occasionally ☐ Never

　　iii. Members (i.e., clubs)　☐ Frequently ☐ Occasionally ☐ Never

　　iv. General Public　　☐ Frequently ☐ Occasionally ☐ Never

b. Annual receipts (if applicable): $ _____

c. States in which liquor is *sold*, if applicable: _____

29. a. Do you manufacture or distribute alcoholic beverages? ☐ Yes ☐ No

b. Annual revenues: $ _____

c. States of operations: _____

30. a. Do you lease real property to others who sell, manufacture or distribute alcoholic beverages to the public?
☐ Yes ☐ No

b. Explain: _____
_____
_____
_____

c. Applicable states: _____

31. a. Do you own or use in your operations any:

		Own†	Use
i.	Aircraft	☐ Yes ☐ No	☐ Yes ☐ No
ii.	Watercraft	☐ Yes ☐ No	☐ Yes ☐ No
iii.	Barges or floats	☐ Yes ☐ No	☐ Yes ☐ No
iv.	Docks	☐ Yes ☐ No	☐ Yes ☐ No
v.	Railroads	☐ Yes ☐ No	☐ Yes ☐ No

†Refer to aircraft or watercraft questionnaires.

b. Explain use: _____

32. a. Do any of your employees, officers, or directors own watercraft? ☐ Yes ☐ No   Aircraft? ☐ Yes ☐ No

b. If yes, is there a company policy regarding business use? ☐ Yes ☐ No
Explain: _____

c. Length of watercraft, if applicable: _____ feet

33. a. Do you ever use explosives in your operations? ☐ Often, ☐ Occasionally, ☐ Never, ☐ Subcontractors use

b. Explain use, frequency, expertise, safeguards: _____

34. a. Do your operations ever involve underground excavation? ☐ Often, ☐ Occasionally, ☐ Never

35. a. Does your organization publish any pamphlets, books, newsletters, magazines, etc.? ☐ Yes ☐ No
    b. Obtain copies or samples.
    c. Annual revenues: $ _____

36. a. Does your organization ever sponsor athletic events or athletic teams? ☐ Often, ☐ Occasionally, ☐ Never
    c. Discuss and explain: _____
    _____
    _____

37. a. Do your operations ever involve nuclear isotopes or radioactive materials of any kind?
    ☐ Often, ☐ Occasionally, ☐ Never
    b. Explain: _____
    _____
    _____

38. Do you ever perform operations on or within 50 feet of the following:

    Describe

    Yes No
    ☐   ☐   Rivers, streams _____

    ☐   ☐   Lakes, ponds, reservoirs _____

    ☐   ☐   Dams _____
    ☐   ☐   Railroads _____

☐ ☐ Chemical storage or processing facilities _____

☐ ☐ Power lines _____

☐ ☐ Oil or gas pipelines _____

☐ ☐ Airports or runways _____

☐ ☐ Aircraft _____

☐ ☐ Watercraft _____

39. a. Are any structural alterations or any construction projects currently underway or planned for the next 12 months? ☐ Yes ☐ No

b. Explain: _____

Employee Benefit Plan Exposures

40. a. Types of benefit plans in use, self-funded?

Use		Self-Funded
☐	Pension	☐ Yes ☐ No
☐	Profit Sharing	☐ Yes ☐ No
☐	Group Medical	☐ Yes ☐ No
☐	Dental	☐ Yes ☐ No
☐	Prepaid Legal	☐ Yes ☐ No
☐	Group Life	☐ Yes ☐ No
☐	Long-Term Disability	☐ Yes ☐ No
☐	Short-Term Disability	☐ Yes ☐ No
☐	Other	☐ Yes ☐ No

41. a. Are there any pension, profit sharing, or similar plans that might give rise to an exposure under ERISA?
☐ Yes ☐ No

b. If yes, explain type and name of plan(s), trustees, assets, method of funding: _____

_____

_____

42. a. Does personnel director consult with employees regarding benefit plans and personal financial planning?
☐ Yes ☐ No

Personnel Practices/Relations

43. a. Employee breakdown — indicate approximate percentages.

Total Workforce

			Executives/Officers		
Male	_____ %		Male	_____ %	
Female	_____ %		Female	_____ %	
Total	100%		Total	100%	
Caucasian	_____ %		Caucasian	_____ %
Minorities	_____ %		Minorities	_____ %
Total	100%		Total	100%

b. Is your organization an "equal opportunity employer?" ☐ Yes ☐ No

c. Has your organization ever had (i) an EEOC suit lodged against it? ☐ Yes ☐ No or (ii) wrongful termination suit lodged against it? ☐ Yes ☐ No

d. If (c) is yes, give details, result: _____

_____

44. a. Is there an employee handbook? ☐ Yes ☐ No

b. Obtain copy if not already secured.

45. a. Is your organization unionized? ☐ Yes ☐ No

b. Name of union: _____

c. Describe relationship: _____

_____

_____

* Reprinted, with permission from International Risk Management Institute, Inc., *Exposure Survey Questionnaire*, first edition January 1985, pp. E1 to E11.

Exhibit 3-3
Flow Chart Covering External Flow*

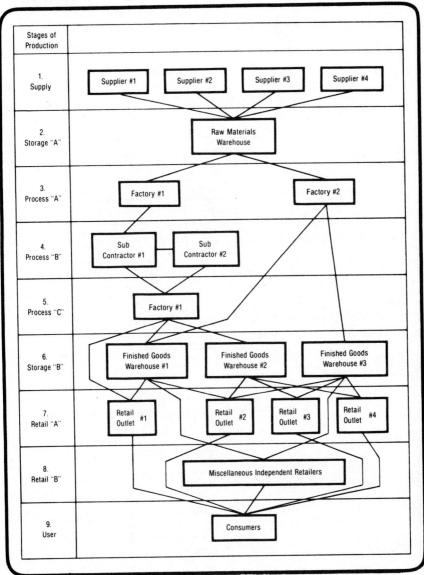

* Reprinted, with permission, from Matthew Lenz, Jr. *Risk Management Manual* (Santa Monica: The Merritt Company, 1976), p. 17.

Exhibit 3-4
Flow Chart Covering Internal Flow*

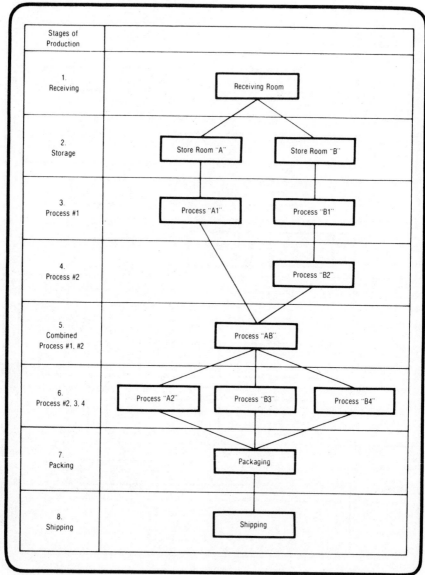

* Reprinted, with permission, from Matthew Lenz, Jr. *Risk Management Manual* (Santa Monica: The Merritt Company, 1976), p. 18.

Like the flow chart approach, the financial statement approach can be used to reveal many of the firm's properties and activities. Given a sound understanding of all liability loss exposures, the analyst seeks out the exposures arising out of property and activities revealed by the financial statements.

Take, for example, the balance sheet. Among the assets listed might be the land owned by the firm, the buildings, the furniture and equipment, machinery, raw materials, goods in process, finished goods, and motor vehicles. These items alert the analyst to the potential liability losses arising out of the ownership, use, or possession of premises; the sale, manufacture, and distribution of products or services; vehicles; and employees who may suffer a job-related injury or disease. A footnote to the balance sheet might describe the firm's pension assets and liabilities. This footnote also should remind the analyst of the existence of a workers' compensation exposure and a fiduciary liability exposure.

The income statement is also useful in identifying liability loss exposures. For example, the revenue item should cause the analyst to inquire into the activities that generate that income and the liabilities associated with those activities. The expense items can be extremely helpful. For example, the direct labor expense item may shed light on the workers' compensation exposure, as well as on liability the employer might incur for injuries or property damage employees may cause to others. Studying the expense accounts of employees may reveal some potential liability-generating activities on their part that would otherwise remain unidentified. Advertising expense indicates an activity that creates a special type of liability exposure known as advertising injury. Rental income or expense should cause the analyst to examine the rental agreements to determine what liabilities the firm may have assumed as either landlord or tenant. Finally, research and development expense may lead the analyst to discover that the firm is engaged in some projects that are potentially dangerous to others.

Associated with a review of financial statements is the organization's annual report. Such documents can provide a wealth of important data on the organization's operations, various property holdings, business environment, employee relations, subsidiaries, and pending litigation.

Personal Inspection of Premises and Activities

To supplement the information obtained from the preceding three methods, the person identifying the exposures should inspect the premises and activities for at least two reasons: (1) the inspection should confirm the existence of the exposures identified by the other methods, and (2) the inspection may reveal some exposures that would not otherwise be identified. For example, the inspection may reveal that the "old factory building" shown on a list of properties is no longer a manufacturing plant but has been converted to a retail outlet. Inspection might also show that a firm's auto maintenance garage is much more than a small repair shop; it includes a body shop with a haphazard spray-painting operation that presents significant air and water pollution exposures. By touring a firm's operating area, one might also see first-hand whether necessary personal protective equipment—such as safety glasses and hard hats—is in use and whether public areas are kept free of unnecessary hazards.

Some organizations' premises and activities may be so extensive that it is impossible—or at least not practical—to inspect everything. In this case a sampling of several premises and activities might determine if further inspection would be justified. For example, the sampling may reveal substantial deviations from what was known prior to the sample inspection.

Interactions with Other Departments

Another method that can provide important supplementary information is to visit personally and obtain periodic reports from operating, supervisory, and management personnel. The people to interview will depend on the type of organization. For example, the production, marketing, quality control, personnel, and other departments of a manufacturing firm could be interviewed. In a bank, one might desire to interview trust, leasing, data processing, funds transfer, and lending personnel. When working with a municipality, the chief of police, fire chief, director of parks and recreation, and maintenance department personnel might be interviewed. The persons in those departments are not trained in exposure analysis, but they know much more about their own departments than any outsider who relies mainly on financial statements, flow charts, and periodic inspections. For example, an inspection might not reveal that the parks and recreation department of a city erects playground equipment for the local school district, which creates a completed operations liability exposure for the municipality. Also, the department personnel are much more likely to be aware of new exposures soon after they are developed. For example, the legal or property management department of a corporation may be aware of new provisions in property leases creating new liability exposures that, unless transmitted to the exposure analyst, might remain unidentified for some time.

Contract Analysis

identify transferred & assumed Contractual liab.

A sixth approach (analogous to personal inspection of the premises and activities) is a personal analysis of the contracts into which the firm has entered. The goal here is to identify what types of liability the firm has transferred or assumed under those contracts, the types and amounts of insurance required of the parties, and all other exposure-related provisions of the contracts. Interaction with other departments is also necessary to reveal these contracts on a continuing basis and to help with their analysis.

To illustrate how contract analysis helps identify liability loss exposures, consider the following provision in an office lease from the perspective of the tenant.

WAIVER OF CLAIMS:
A. Damage from Water and Similar Sources
    To the extent permitted by law, Landlord shall not be liable for any damage to any property, or person, at any time in the Premises, or the Building of which they are a part, from steam, gases, or electricity, or from water, rain, or snow, whether they may leak into, issue or flow from, any part of said building, or from the pipes or heating or air conditioning apparatus of the same, or from any other place. Tenant shall give Landlord prompt notice of any accident to or defect in the pipes, heating or air conditioning apparatus or electric wires or system.
B. Damage from Other Causes
    Tenant, to the extent permitted by law, waives all claims it may have against Landlord, and against Landlord's agents and employees for injury or damage to person or property sustained by Tenant or by any occupant of the Premises, or by any other person resulting from any part of the Building or any equipment or appurtenances becoming out of repair, or resulting from any accident in or about the Building or resulting directly or indirectly from any act or neglect of any tenant or occupant of any part of the Building or of any other person, unless such damage is a result of the negligence or contributory negligence of Landlord, or Landlord's agents or employees. If any damage results from any act of neglect of Tenant, Landlord may, at Landlord's option, repair such damage and Tenant shall thereupon pay to Landlord the total cost of such repair. All personal property belonging to Tenant or any occupant of the Premises that is in or on any part of the Building shall be there at the risk of Tenant or of such other person only, and Landlord, its agents and employees shall not be liable for any damage thereto or for the theft or misappropriation thereof unless such damage, theft or misappropriation is a result of the negligence or contributory negligence of Landlord or Landlord's agents or employees. Tenant agrees to hold Landlord harmless and indemnified against claims and liability for injuries to all persons and for damage to or loss of property occurring in

or about the Building, due to any act of negligence or default under this lease by Tenant, its contractors, agents or employees.

In analyzing any contract, it is of crucial importance to examine the *entire* contract. Nonetheless, for the sake of brevity, it will be assumed that the remainder of the lease contains no further provisions that would modify or relate to the quoted provisions.

Under the first quoted paragraph of this lease, the tenant has excused the landlord from responsibility for any losses to the tenant caused by steam, gases, electricity, water, rain, or snow. The tenant here has relieved the landlord of some of its liability loss exposures (to the extent permitted by law and enforced by the courts). However, the tenant has assumed no extra liability exposure itself.

For losses *to the tenant* from other causes, as stated in the second quoted paragraph, the landlord remains responsible if the landlord's negligence contributes to the loss. For losses *to others*, however, due in part to negligence on the part of the tenant, the tenant has agreed to indemnify the landlord for any amount for which the landlord may be held liable. The tenant, therefore, has assumed some contractual liability.

The lease could have been written to impose more or fewer responsibilities upon the tenant. Other lease arrangements may vary.

Analysis of Legal, Economic, and Social Environment

The legal, economic, and social environments affect the types of events that will lead to a liability loss, as well as the frequency and severity of the claims arising from such events. For purposes of loss exposure identification and analysis, it is particularly important to monitor changes in the environment.

For example, the enactment and periodic revision of workers compensation, environmental pollution, and other statutes have imposed liability exposures that never existed or differed sharply under the common law alone. Courts also have been expanding the range of activities that may result in legal liabilities, and such statutory and judicial changes are likely to continue in the future.

Macroeconomic conditions such as unemployment rates and consumer price increases can also affect liability exposures. For example, strong competition within an industry may force a firm, especially a firm with inferior bargaining strength, to assume some contractual obligations under lease, sales, or purchase agreements. Changing regulations may also impose some special obligations on the firm.

The social environment must be considered. Social conditions affect the types of events that occur—such as riots, peace rallies, demonstrations, and political campaigns. While such events do not necessarily create liability, they may create a highly charged atmosphere that leads to some unfortunate action. Moreover, the claims consciousness of the population at any given time greatly affects the types of accidents that result in a liability claim.

Loss Analysis

Information on past losses is useful for exposure identification purposes, because history often does repeat itself. Clearly, the exposure analyst should study past losses to determine whether they might happen again. On the other hand, one should realize that many types of losses the firm will incur in the future never have happened before. The larger the firm, the more useful the information on past losses is likely to be for exposure identification purposes, because the firm is more likely to have already experienced many types of losses. A small firm is likely never to have experienced some very common types of losses. Furthermore, as will be described later in this chapter, analysis of past loss experience is an important part of predicting and controlling future losses.

Interactions with Outsiders

Interactions with outsiders can take various forms. Reports by insurance agents and brokers, risk management consultants, attorneys, loss control specialists, and others providing services to the firm may suggest exposures that otherwise might not be identified. Meetings with other exposure analysts in the same industry can be highly informative, as can the reading of insurance, risk management, or trade publications.

Using Insurance Coverage Checklists

Coverages Applicable, a publication by the Rough Notes Company, shows for each of a number of different entities an outline of the insurance coverages that might be applicable. An excerpt is shown in Exhibit 3-5. This checklist is quite useful as a listing of insurance coverages to be considered. As a loss exposure identification aid, however, it is limited to insurable loss exposures, and it needs to be supplemented by a careful review of the specific policy forms to which it refers.

Exhibit 3-5
Excerpt from Coverages Applicable*

Communications†

INCLUDING: *Blueprinters • Bookbinders • Broadcasting (Radio & TV) Electrotypers • Engravers • Letter Shops • Lithographers • Magazines Monotypers • Multigraphers • Newspapers • Photo-printers • Printers Publishers • Stereotypers • Typesetters • Typographers*

General Liability Insurance: Printing firms are Liability insurance conscious. Though manufacturers of all kinds generally discourage promiscuous wandering about by members of the public in rooms where machinery is in operation, this category is special from the public interest standpoint. Newspapers constantly conduct tours through their plants; job printers have frequent visitors in their shops. Machinery must be carefully watched. Third party injury and property damage claims may be insured against under the following policies and divisions of General Liability insurance:

COMPREHENSIVE GENERAL LIABILITY: Insures against all graphic arts establishment's declared existing liability hazards and any additional liability hazards which may occur during the policy term, arising out of operator's business operations, building and premises. Product Liability is optional and may be included or excluded. Though lease of premises and elevator or escalator maintenance agreements are covered without special treatment or charge, important contractual agreements such as construction agreements are not automatically covered. The policy must be endorsed to cover them. (271.4)

Divisions of General Liability insurance applicable to risks in this category, that may be made effective under Comprehensive General Liability insurance or by combination of desired coverage parts with the provisions of a Premises-Operations in Progress coverage part, include the following (Elevator Liability is incorporated in basic Premises-Operations coverage):

CONTRACTUAL LIABILITY: Covers the insured's liability assumed under specifically described contracts, as distinguished from liability imposed by law. (Liability assumed under a building lease or under an elevator or escalator maintenance agreement is covered under basic Premises-Operations insurance.) (272.1)

OWNERS' OR CONTRACTORS' PROTECTIVE LIABILITY: Covers accidents resulting from acts performed for an insured building owner or contractor by independent contractors. This division should be made effective whenever there is major building alteration or construction. (272.4)

PRODUCT LIABILITY: This may be considered the least necessary form of General Liability insurance for printing firms. It assumes greater importance when other products are sold in conjunction with printed material, such as office supplies and furniture. (272.5)

MEDICAL PAYMENTS: May be added to take care of injuries to third parties, regardless of the insured's liability, arising out of the insured's premises or operations. Frequency of public visiting in the shop or plant has a bearing on the need for this optional addition to the policy. (272.8)

BROAD FORM COMPREHENSIVE GENERAL LIABILITY: When added by endorsement, extends basic Comprehensive General Liability insurance to cover such additional hazards as contractual liability, personal injury, advertising injury, premises medical payments, host liquor law liability, real property fire legal liability, broad form property damage exposures, incidental medical malpractice, non-owned watercraft liability, worldwide exposures, protection for employees as insureds, bodily injury resulting from intentional act, and newly acquired organization exposure. (271.4-1)

WORKERS COMPENSATION AND EMPLOYERS LIABILITY: Insures against claims for work-related injuries or diseases, suffered by employees, that are compensable by statute and/or are imposed by law as damages. Other States insurance is incorporated in the 1984 "plain language" policy and is activated by appropriate entry. Voluntary Workers Compensation and Employers Liability coverage may be made effective for workers not subject to a Workers Compensation law. (280.1)

Motor Vehicle Insurance: Trucks, delivery vehicles, and passenger cars are required equipment for almost all printing businesses and newspapers. Pickup and delivery are expected by customers and salesmen are constantly busy on the outside (with cars) to keep up a flow of business. These coverages apply:

AUTOMOBILE LIABILITY INSURANCE: The rapid delivery and pick-up services operated by or contracted for by newspapers and printing service agencies are important objects of this coverage. Protects insured against loss by reason of liability for bodily injury or property damage to members of the public from operation of owned vehicles used in his business. Automobile Comprehensive Liability, for large risks, covers all possible third party claims arising from the use of automobiles. (221.1, 221.2)

EMPLOYERS NON-OWNERSHIP AUTOMOBILE LIABILITY: Protects the employer to the extent of liability imposed by law and within policy limits against claims for accidents due to employees and other agents operating their own automobiles in the employer's interest. (221.3)

PARTNERSHIP NON-OWNERSHIP LIABILITY: Protects partnership on a contingent basis for liability arising from business use by partner of his or her automobile. (221.3)

HIRED CARS: Covers use, if any, of hired cars. Can be included in minimum premium charged for Non-Ownership Liability. (221.5)

MEDICAL PAYMENTS: Reimburses for reasonable hospital and funeral expenses for persons other than employees injured while passengers in an insured automobile. (221.1-1)

VEHICLE COMPREHENSIVE (INCLUDING FIRE & THEFT): Insures operator's motor vehicles from physical damage from fire, theft and other perils, including glass breakage. (111.1)

COLLISION: Insures operator's vehicles against loss from collision or upset. (111.1)

BUSINESS AUTO POLICY: The business counterpart of the Personal Auto Policy, this single unit, self-contained contract eliminates the use of separate coverage parts and employs fewer words and language that is more understandable. Coverages described above may be made effective under it, with the option to select Combined Physical Damage coverage with a single deductible. (222.1)

UMBRELLA LIABILITY INSURANCE: Provides Excess General Liability, Automobile and Aircraft Liability limits and also protects the insured from the exclusions and gaps of the primary Liability policy or policies. An Umbrella Liability policy comes into play when the limits of the primary insurance have been exhausted, or when a claim develops that is not covered by the primary insurance. (272.10)

†Numbers at the end of paragraphs refer to detailed coverage analyses in the Rough Notes PF&M Analysis Service.

PUBLISHERS OR BROADCASTERS LIABILITY POLICIES: Publishers, newspapers and radio and TV broadcasters are constantly exposed to claims for libel and slander. Errors, mistakes or omissions of employees can be the cause of suits. Although great care is exercised in the selection of material, the owner or operator may find himself the subject of court action. A few companies, underwriting each risk separately and individually, offer protection against this paramount publishing and broadcasting hazard. (361.2)

FIDUCIARY LIABILITY INSURANCE: Pays, on behalf of the insured, legal liability arising from claims for alleged failure to prudently act within the meaning of the Pension Reform Act of 1974. "Insured" is variously defined as a trust or employee benefit plan, any trustee, officer or employee of the trust or employee benefit plan, employer who is sole sponsor of a plan and any other individual or organization designated as a fiduciary. Group Life and Medical Expense plans, as well as Pension and Retirement plans, are within the scope of the law. (384.8, 384.8-1)

COMMUNITY ANTENNA TELEVISION LIABILITY POLICY: Protects cable telecast systems against suits alleging libel and slander, invasion of privacy, infringement of copyright and other perils similar to those covered by comparable insurance written for broadcasters using the air. Legal expenses are included in the coverage. (361.2)

SEXUAL HARASSMENT DEFENSE COVERAGE: Protects an employer against sexual harassment lawsuits and/or administrative proceedings. The Civil Rights Act of 1964, as amended, holds employers responsible for sexual harassment and provides a legal basis for women and men to take action against it.

BUSINESS LEGAL EXPENSE POLICY: Designed to cover the gap in unforeseen business related legal expenses not covered by Liability policies.

* This exhibit contains liability and auto insurance-related coverages that may apply to firms in the communications industry, as excerpted from Roy C. McCormick, Coverages Applicable, Rough Notes Co., Inc., 1984, pp. 43-47.

MEASURING LIABILITY LOSS EXPOSURES

After a loss exposure has been identified, it should be measured.

Dimensions to be Measured

The dimensions of a loss exposure may be determined and analyzed by obtaining the following information:

1. *Loss frequency*—the number of events (e.g., industrial injuries or auto accidents) that are likely to occur within some time interval, such as 1 year, 5 years, or 100 years. (For a loss that occurs rarely, expected loss frequency is usually expressed in terms of loss probability. For example, if expected loss frequency is 1 out of every 100 years, the probability of a loss next year is 1/100, or 0.01. Even if loss probability is low, the exposure may be a matter of considerable concern if the potential loss severity is high.)

2. *Loss severity*—how serious the losses caused by these individual occurrences are likely to be. This dimension is particularly important for liability loss exposures, because the losses are among the most difficult to predict and the largest an entity may incur. Liability losses are also much more likely to involve payments over a long period of time. For example, a worker who is permanently and totally disabled by a work injury may receive a weekly income for life.

3. *Total dollar losses*—how serious the total losses are likely to be. The "expected total dollar losses" are equal to the expected loss frequency times the expected loss severity (the expected number of events times the average dollar loss per occurrence). The annual expected dollar loss is the *average* annual loss that can be expected over a long period of time if the exposure and its environment remain unchanged. It is by no means a reliable prediction of the losses that will actually occur next year.

4. *Credibility of the loss predictions*—the confidence the risk manager can place in predictions of the loss frequency, the loss severity, and the total dollar losses. This credibility is inversely related to the likely variation in the number of occurrences, the dollar loss per occurrence, and the total dollar losses. Although prediction is possible and desirable, *no one entity* can with complete confidence predict the *maximum* liability loss it will incur in a future time period. The measures described are at best useful in selecting deductible size.

Why This Information Is Useful

→ 1. *It reduces uncertainty concerning loss.* For a loss exposure that has been measured, there is greater ability to predict the future than for an exposure of unknown dimensions.

→ 2. *It indicates which exposures should receive more immediate or concentrated attention.* When loss exposures have been measured, it becomes easier to identify those exposures that are most serious.

→ 3. *It helps the risk manager determine what risk management techniques would be most appropriate for the particular exposure.* By evaluating how different risk management techniques affect each measurement, the risk manager can test the effects of possible risk management techniques.[6]

Data Sources

To measure a loss exposure precisely, the risk manager must know for each of the following all the possible outcomes and the relative loss frequency for each of those outcomes:

1. the number of occurrences per year (or other budget period),
2. the dollar losses per occurrence, and
3. the total dollar losses per year (or other budget period).

For example, suppose one knew that the number of occurrences during a given time period could not exceed five and that the relative loss frequencies for the six possible outcomes were as follows:

Number of Occurrences	Relative Frequency
0	.60
1	.20
2	.10
3	.06
4	.03
5	.01
	1.00

The relative frequencies tell the probability that each of the various numbers of losses will occur. For example, the probability that no losses will occur is .60. The probability that the maximum number of five will occur is .01. The probability that the number of occurrences will be three or more is $.06 + .03 + .01 = .10$. The expected number, which is the number that will occur on the average in the long run (i.e., over a period of many years), is obtained by summing the products of each possible number of losses times the probability of that number occurring. For this illustration, therefore, the expected number is $0(.60) + 1(.20) + 2(.10) + 3(.06) + 4(.03) + 5(.01) = .75$. Less than one per year can be expected on the average in the long run (since .75 is clearly less than 1).

A frequency distribution also sheds light on the predictability of the number of occurrences. Listed below are two alternative distributions, one of which depicts a much more predictable situation than the other.

Number of Occurrences	Alternative Relative Frequency	
	More Predictable	Less Predictable
0	.60	.60
1	.35	.08
2	.05	.08
3	—	.08
4	—	.08
5	—	.08
	1.00	1.00

Under the more predictable situation only three possible outcomes exist and the probability that the number will be zero or one is .95 (that is, .60 + .35). Under the less predictable situation the number of possibilities for zero occurrences is the same as in the original example, but the probabilities are the same for one through five occurrences.[7]

A similar analysis can be conducted for the other two types of frequency distributions—the dollar losses per occurrence and the total dollar losses per year (or other budget period).

Where can one get information such as this? In a few cases a firm may have enough experience from the past to provide a rough estimate of the probability distribution. For example, a firm with a large number of vehicles may have enough property damage liability claims for the experience to be credible. Similarly, a firm with many employees may have experienced each month enough nondisabling injuries and short-term disabilities to construct a fair estimate of its probability distribution for future losses of these types. For the experience to be credible the experience period must be long enough to include enough exposure units for the law of averages (or law of large numbers) to work effectively. The larger the number of exposure units (for example, auto years or employee months), the more stable the experience of those units becomes. On the other hand, because conditions change over time, the longer the experience period becomes, the more this past experience must be adjusted or "trended" to reflect price increases, increased internal or external hazards, changes in loss control measures, or other factors affecting loss frequency and loss severity. Except for large firms, and even for them in many cases, past experience is likely to be too limited to provide useful estimates of future loss probability.

Trade associations, insurers, and government agencies may provide supplementary information, some of which will be described below. Usually, however, at best this information is limited to the average number of occurrences per exposure unit and the average dollar loss per occurrence. Although very useful, these data are less helpful than a frequency distribution. Furthermore, they are based on the pooled experience of many firms grouped into the same class as the firm in question, but different from it in many ways.[8]

One does not need to have a complete frequency distribution to be better informed than one would be without such information unless one assigns too much credibility to incomplete information. One can also assign too much credibility to *complete* information about the past—as a guide to the future—especially for tort losses. One way of handling incomplete information would be to group liability losses into categories, for example:

0 to $1,000
$1,001 to $10,000
$10,001 to $100,000
over $100,000

One can also err by relying too heavily on statistical projections. It is always important to remember the changing nature of the liability exposure and the fact that potential loss severity is not limited by any natural factors.

An Example: Industrial Injuries and Diseases

Three important sources of data on industrial injuries and diseases are the data gathered (1) under the Occupational Safety and Health Act, (2) according to standards established by The American National Standards Institute, and (3) in the booklet, *Accident Facts*.

OSHA Data Under the Occupational Safety and Health Act almost all private sector employers are required to prepare and maintain records of occupational injuries and illnesses. Not generally required to keep such records are (1) employers with no more than ten employees (full-time or part-time) at any one time in the previous calendar year and (2) all employers in retail trade; finance, insurance, and real estate; and, subject to some exceptions, service industries.

These employers must, however, report to OSHA within forty-eight hours any accident that results in one or more fatalities or the hospitalization of five or more employees. (As will be explained below, a few of these exempt employers are selected each year to participate in the Annual Survey of Occupational Injuries and Diseases.) Employers of domestics and employers engaged in religious activities are also exempt from the record-keeping requirements.

Participating employers are required to keep a log of all recordable occupational illnesses and injuries. Because firms are required to keep these records they should be readily available for risk management analysis.

All illnesses and all fatal injuries are recordable. Nonfatal injuries are recordable if they involve loss of consciousness, restriction of work or motion, transfer to another job, or medical treatment other than first aid.

For all recordable cases the employer must enter the following information on the log within six days after learning of its occurrence:

1. the case or file number,
2. date of the injury or onset of the illness,
3. occupation,
4. department, and
5. description of the injury (for example, amputation of first joint right forefinger, strain of lower back).

For injury cases the employer must also provide the following information:

1. if death occurred, the date of death;
2. if the injury involves days of work or days of restricted activity—
   * whether the injury involves days away from work or just days of restricted activity,
   * the number of days away from work, and
   * the number of days of restricted activity.

The number of lost workdays should not include the day of injury or onset of illness or any days on which the employee would not have worked even though able to work. For example, if the employee would normally never work on Saturdays or Sundays, these two days of the week are not included in the number of lost workdays. A day of restricted activity is one on which because of injury or illness (1) the employee was assigned to another job on a temporary basis, (2) the employee worked at a permanent job less than full time, or (3) the employee worked at a permanently assigned job but could not perform all duties normally connected with it.

For illness cases, the employer must state, in addition to the information provided for injury cases, which of the following seven classes describes the worker's illness:

- occupational skin diseases or disorders,
- dust diseases of the lungs,
- respiratory conditions due to toxic agents,
- poisoning,
- disorders due to physical agents,
- disorders associated with repeated trauma, or
- all other occupational illness.

The logs containing this information must be retained for at least five years following the end of the calendar year to which they relate. If during this five-year period the worker's condition changes, the log entry should be revised accordingly. For example, a worker without any lost workdays during the calendar year of the injury may later die or be unable to work.

One important instruction affecting loss severity measures states that if an employee's loss of workdays is continuing at the time the totals are summarized, the person completing the log should estimate the number of future workdays the employee will lose and add that estimated number to the workdays already lost. Continuing cases are not reported in next year's log. Thus, if a disabled worker has already lost 100 days of work during the calendar year for which the log is being prepared and is expected to be disabled for 50 more workdays, the number of lost workdays for that case would be 150. For a worker who is permanently and totally disabled at a young age, the number of workdays lost would be very large (for example, the number of days lost during the calendar year plus 250 days times the future worklife expectancy). Most employers, however, apparently fail to add the estimate of workdays to be lost in the future, thus understating the loss severity.[9]

The individual entries on this log and the totals under each heading provide considerable information concerning the frequency and the severity of occupational injuries and illnesses in the risk manager's firm.

To make a meaningful comparison of the totals with (1) the firm's experience in earlier years or (2) the experience of other firms during a specified time period, the numbers need to be related to the total hours of employee exposure. For example, if the firm had twenty persons who missed work this year compared with ten persons last year, the number of injured persons (the frequency) has doubled. However, if the total hours worked also doubled, the frequency *rate* has remained constant.

If the total hours worked had tripled, the frequency rate would actually have declined.

The logs for the current year and the previous five years must be available for inspection and copying by representatives of the Department of Labor, the Department of Health and Human Services, or the state if it has been accorded jurisdiction. Employees, former employees, and their representatives also must have access to these logs.

A copy of the totals and the individual entries (but not the case number, date of injury or illness, occupation, department, or description of the injury or illness) in the log for the most recent calendar year must be posted no later than February 1 and must remain in place until March 1.

The risk manager can compare the loss frequency and loss severity date for his or her firm with that of other firms by consulting *Occupational Injuries and Illnesses in 19XX: A Summary*, published annually by the United States Department of Labor Bureau of Labor Statistics. Prior to publishing this report, the Bureau issues a much earlier press release that contains much important information.

The BLS data are based mainly on an annual sample survey of occupational injuries and illnesses. About 280,000 private employers are included in this survey, the sample being stratified by state, industry, and size. For rare characteristics, such as fatalities, the sampling error can be large, but for most other characteristics and industry groups, the numbers are subject to relatively small sampling errors.[10] Each sample firm must provide the following information:

- annual average employment during the year,
- total hours worked that year,
- nature of business,
- month of OSHA inspection, and
- recordable case information that consists of the totals of the individual entries in the firm's OSHA logs.

The sample firms include some firms that are otherwise exempt from the OSHA record-keeping requirements. These employers are notified in advance that they must participate in the survey. They are provided with the necessary forms and instructions.

The sample represents virtually all employers except the self-employed; farmers with fewer than eleven employees; private households; railroad, coal, metal, and nonmetal mining employers; federal, state, and local government agencies; and, for 1983 and 1984, nonfarm employers with fewer than eleven employees in low-risk industries. To provide in its summary total private sector estimates of occupational injuries and diseases except for farmers with fewer than eleven employees, the BLS obtains data on excluded industries from the Mine Safety and Health Administration, the U.S. Department of Labor, and the Federal Railroad Administration. For nonfarm employers in low-risk industries with fewer than eleven employees, the Bureau estimated the experience during 1983 and 1984 based on the data reported by small employers in 1980, 1981, and 1982 surveys. The federal government compiles a similar report on its employees. About half the states maintain comparable reports.

Exhibit 3-6 shows the 1982 occupational injury and illness incidence rates by major industry classification. The *incidence rates* are the number of injuries and/or illnesses or the number of lost workdays reported by the participating firms divided by the total hours worked by all employees during the calendar year, the quotient then being multiplied by 200,000.

Because 100 full-time employees working 40 hours a week for 50 weeks would work 200,000 hours, the incidence rates state the number of injuries and/or illnesses or the number of lost workdays per 100 full-time equivalent employees. If the risk manager wants to compare the data for the firm with the BLS summary data, the OSHA log totals must be divided by the number of hours worked by the firm's employees, the resulting quotient being then multiplied by 200,000.

Exhibit 3-6 shows the rates for injuries and for injuries and illnesses combined. No separate information is provided for illnesses because the reported cases are subject to substantial sampling error. Illness accounted for only about 2 percent of the total cases reported, 3 percent of the lost workday cases, and 2 percent of the lost workdays. Because relatively few cases involve fatalities, these cases are included in the total cases but are not reported separately.

The incidence rates for the number of cases show the frequency rates for recordable cases, lost workday cases (divided into cases that involve days away from work and those that involve restricted work activity only) and nonfatal cases with no lost workdays. The final column states the average lost workday case, a measure of the severity per case. This number times the incidence rate for lost workday cases yields the number of lost workdays per 100 employees. For example, for the total private sector, 17 times 3.4 yields 57.8, which is close to 52.9 plus 4.6, or 57.5. The difference can be explained by rounding errors.

The BLS report provides similar information for much smaller, less heterogeneous categories. For example, for insurers the injury numbers are as follows:

Total cases per 100 full-time employees	1.8
Lost workday cases	.8
Away from work	.7
Restricted work activity only	*
Nonfatal cases with	
no lost workdays	1.0

Exhibit 3-6

Occupational Injury and Illness Incidence Rates, By Major Industry Category, 1982*

	Total Cases	Away from Work	Restricted Work Activity Only	Non-fatal Cases With no Lost Workdays	Days Away From Work	Restricted Work Activity Days	Lost Workday Per Lost Workday Case
	Number of Cases				**Lost Workdays**		
	Lost Workday Cases						
			INJURIES				
Agriculture, forestry, and fishing	11.3	5.4	0.2	5.6	79.2	5.0	15
Mining	10.3	5.2	0.2	4.9	131.1	5.6	25
Conservation	14.5	5.8	0.2	8.5	109.3	5.3	19
Manufacturing	9.9	3.8	0.5	5.6	64.7	7.7	17
Transportation and public utilities	8.4	4.4	0.4	3.5	87.6	8.2	20
Wholesale and retail trade	7.1	2.9	0.1	4.1	42.0	3.0	15
Finance, insurance and real estate	2.0	0.8	*	1.1	11.6	1.2	15
Services	4.8	2.2	0.1	2.5	32.8	2.2	15
Total Private Sector	7.6	3.2	0.2	4.1	52.9	4.6	17
			Injuries and Illnesses				
Agriculture, forestry, and fishing	11.8	5.9		5.9	86.0		15
Mining	10.5	5.4		5.0	137.3		25
Conservation	14.6	6.0		8.6	113.1		19
Manufacturing	10.2	4.4		5.8	75.0		17
Transportation and public utilities	8.5	4.9		3.6	96.7		20
Wholesale and retail trade	7.2	3.1		4.1	45.5		15
Finance, insurance and real estate	2.0	.9		1.1	13.2		15
Services	4.9	2.3		2.6	35.8		15
Total	7.7	3.5		4.2	58.7		17

* Reprinted from *Occupational Injuries and Illness in the United States by Industry, 1982*, Bulletin 2196, U.S. Department of Labor, Bureau of Labor Statistics, April 1984.

Lost workdays per 100 full-time employees	10.7
Days away from work	9.7
Restricted work activity days	1.0
Lost workdays per lost workday case	14

Incidence rates by major industry category for total cases are provided for employer size groups ranging from one to nineteen employees to 2,500 employees or more. The rates are lowest at both extremes and highest for firms with 50 to 499 employees.

The report also categorizes occupational illness cases by major industry divisions and the illness category. Fatalities are classified by the cause (such as a heart attack, an over-the-road motor vehicle accident, or a fall) and industry division.

2) *American National Standards Institute Data*   In addition to using the OSHA approach to keeping records of accidental injuries, many firms use the standards (ANSI Z16.3) prescribed by the American National Standards Institute.

The Institute defines the accident frequency rate as the number of disabling injuries per million manhours worked. The severity rate is the number of days lost by the injured employees per million man-hours worked.

For temporary total disability cases, the number of days lost is defined as the number of full calendar days on which the employee is unable to work because of the injury or disease. The number does not include the day the employee was injured nor the day he or she returned to work. All intervening days, regardless of whether they would be workdays, are counted. If the worker's disability has not terminated when the report is being made, the reporter is supposed to add an estimate of the number of days the disability will continue in the future.

For death, permanent total disability, and permanent partial disability cases the number of days lost is in most cases prescribed by a table of scheduled charges, regardless of the actual number of days lost. For example, for death and permanent total disability cases, the charge is 6,000 days. For permanent partial disability cases involving the loss of a finger, thumb, hand, toe, foot, ankle, arm, or eye or the impairment of the function of eyes or ears, the charges are illustrated by the following:

Index finger, middle phalange	200
Hand at wrist	3,000
Foot at ankle	2,400
Arm above elbow, including shoulder joint	4,500

Leg above ankle but below knee	3,000
Loss of sight in one eye	1,800
Loss of sight in both eyes	6,000

If a person loses some of the use of a specified member, the estimated number of days lost is the scheduled charge for loss of that member times the percentage loss of use estimated by the attending physician.

If the permanent injury does not involve a member or function listed in the schedule (for example, a back injury or loss of speech), the number of days lost is considered to be 6,000 times the estimated percentage of permanent total disability.

The ANSI data thus differ from the OSHA data in some important ways:

1. The ANSI data provide information only on cases that result in lost workdays.
2. For temporary total disability cases the ANSI data on days lost include all calendar days between the day of the injury and the return-to-work day.
3. For death and permanent disability cases, the ANSI data on days lost are based not on the actual days lost but on prescribed estimates of the number of days to be lost by the average worker because of this death or disability in the current calendar year and the future.
4. ANSI incidence and severity rates are stated per 1 million hours worked. OSHA incidence and severity rates are reported per 200,000 hours worked.

Until 1977 most firms used the ANSI standards for their management reports. The National Safety Council used reports based on these standards for reporting aggregate and industry experience and for its contests and awards. Effective in 1977, the NSC changed for these purposes from the ANSI approach to the OSHA system. Many firms, however, continue to compile data according to the ANSI approach or both the ANSI and OSHA approach. For example, Exhibit 3-7 shows a monthly summary of injuries and diseases from an NSC publication that uses both approaches. The reasons for the continued use of the ANSI approach are that (1) some firms that are subject to the OSHA record-keeping requirements have not changed their ways, (2) many firms prefer the severity measures provided by ANSI or believe it provides additional information, and (3) ANSI data permit comparisons with past periods, when that was the only approach used.

Accident Facts   A third source of information on work accidents is *Accident Facts,* published annually by the National Safety Council.

ANSI and OSHA Monthly Summary of Injuries and Illnesses

Company __ABC Mfg. Co.__ Plant _____ Department _____ Dayton, Ohio All

Average Number of Employees	Number of Man-Hours Worked	Z16.1 CASES — Disabling Injuries and Illnesses — Fatal. Permanent Total	Permanent Partial	Temporary Total	Total Z16 Cases	Frequency Rate	Time Charges — Fatal. Permanent Total	Permanent Partial	Temporary Total	Total Z16 Charges	Severity Rate*	COSTS (Compensation, Other)	OSHA CASES — Fatals	Lost Workday Cases	Non Lost Workday Cases	Total OSHA Cases	Incidence Rate†	Total Lost Workdays	FIRST AID CASES ONLY
2,060	345,000	0	1	1	2	5.80	0	150	18	168	487	284.50	0	3	18	21	12.2	42	20
2,010	298,000	0	0	3	3	10.07	0	0	22	22	74	42.65	0	4	27	31	20.8	34	36
	643,000	0	1	4	5	7.78	0	150	40	190	295	327.15	0	7	45	52	16.2	76	52
2,080	353,000	0	0	1	1	2.83	0	0	42	42	119	72.82	0	1	9	10	5.7	12	10
	996,000	0	0	5	6	6.02	0	150	78	232	229	404.97	0	8	54	62	12.4	88	66
2,000	332,000	0	0	4	4	12.05	0	0	47	47	142	92.64	0	5	35	40	24.1	64	42
2,150	1,328,000	0	1	9	10	7.53	0	150	125	275	207	497.61	0	13	89	102	15.4	152	108
2,150	375,000	0	0	5	5	13.33	0	0	63	63	168	123.24	0	7	45	52	27.7	88	55
	1,703,000	0	1	14	15	8.81	0	150	203	353	207	620.85	0	20	134	154	18.1	240	163
1,800	303,000	0	1	0	1	3.30	0	1000	0	1000	3300	985.54	0	1	13	14	9.2	25	15
	2,006,000	0	2	14	16	7.98	0	1150	203	1353	674	1606.41	0	21	147	168	16.7	265	178
1,825	295,000	0	1	3	4	13.56	0	250	23	273	925	368.18	0	5	40	45	30.5	91	51
	2,301,000	0	3	17	20	8.69	0	1400	226	1426	707	1974.59	0	26	187	213	18.5	352	229
1,800	285,000	0	0	4	4	14.04	0	0	31	31	109	63.24	0	5	43	48	33.7	123	53
	2,586,000	0	3	21	24	9.28	0	1400	251	1457	641	2037.83	0	31	230	261	20.2	479	282
1,875	301,000	0	0	0	0	0.00	0	0	0	0	0	843.66	0	0	9	9	6.0	0	12
	2,887,000	0	3	24	24	6.31	0	2300	275	2575	871	2881.49	0	31	239	270	18.7	479	294
1,795	302,000	0	0	0	1	3.31	0	0	17	14	46	45.60	0	1	5	6	4.0	10	6
	3,189,000	0	4	21	25	7.84	0	2300	212	2529	793	2927.09	0	32	244	276	17.3	489	300
1,665	280,000	0	0	2	2	7.14	0	0	17	17	61	36.76	0	3	23	25	17.9	13	26
	3,469,000	0	4	23	27	7.78	0	2300	246	2546	737	2963.85	0	34	267	301	17.4	502	326
1,620	275,000	1	0	0	1	3.64	6000	0	0	6000	2818	6763.25	1	1	7	8	6.5	2	8
	3,744,000	1	4	23	28	7.48	6000	2300	246	8546	2283	9748.10	1	35	274	310	16.6	504	334

* Z16 Rates: Frequency rate is the total number of Z16 cases per 1,000,000 man-hours worked. Severity rate is the total Z16 charges per 1,000,000 man-hours worked.

† OSHA Rate: Incidence rate is the total number of OSHA cases per 200,000 man-hours worked.

Issued by: National Safety Council, 425 N. Michigan Ave., Chicago, Illinois 60611

The latest BLS survey report, described above, is summarized in a Work Accident section. This section also provides more recent comparable information, using the OSHA definitions, based on the experience of those firms who report directly to the National Safety Council.

To make some rough estimates that are informative from a macro point of view, the National Safety Council uses work accident and illness data from a number of other sources, including the National Center for Health Statistics, state industrial commissions, insurers and insurer associations, and industrial associations. For example, the NSC estimates that 11,377,000 persons were injured annually in work accidents during 1979-1981, of whom 24 percent were bed disabled and 76 percent suffered some lesser activity restrictions. Disabling work injuries totaled about 1,900,000 in 1982, about 11 percent of which involved motor vehicles and 89 percent resulted in permanent impairments. Work accidents in 1982 cost $31.4 billion distributed as follows:

Wage loss	5.2
Medical expenses	3.6
Insurance administration	5.9
Fire loss	2.0
Time lost by noninjured workers because of injury	14.7

The cost per worker was $320. The total days lost from work in 1982 because of accidents that year was 40,000,000, the estimated time loss in future years from the 1982 accidents being 110,000,000 days.[11]

CONTROLLING LIABILITY LOSS EXPOSURES: INTRODUCTION

The discussion to this point has been concerned with the first two steps of risk management: identifying and measuring liability loss exposures. As noted earlier, the third step is to select which of the risk management techniques the firm should use to treat its loss exposures. The remainder of this chapter will be devoted to the control techniques that should be considered in making that selection. The financing techniques that should be considered, especially insurance, will be the major topic of the remaining chapters in this text. Financing techniques are designed to provide funds to handle the losses that do occur. Financing techniques include transfers of the financial loss to others (including but not limited to insurers) or, if one does not transfer the loss to others, retention.

Control techniques attempt to change the loss exposure itself by reducing the loss frequency and/or loss severity or by improving the organization's ability to predict losses with greater confidence. Before examining specific techniques that may be used to control losses, it is helpful to examine the various theories on accident causes and effects. An understanding of accident causes helps to show that it is often possible to eliminate some of the causes, thus preventing accidents. Similarly, it is often possible to limit the effects of some accidents that cannot be prevented, thus reducing their severity.

Accident Theory: Causes and Effects

Two theories of accident causes and effects are summarized below with particular reference to liability exposures. A basic understanding of these two theories and their interrelationship will make more meaningful the subsequent discussion of loss control measures and their application.

Heinrich's "Domino" Theory The "domino" theory was developed by H. W. Heinrich, a safety engineer for a leading insurer and a pioneer in the field of industrial safety.[12] According to this theory, an "accident" is the fourth of five factors in a sequence that may result in an "injury," the fifth factor in the sequence. The first factor is "ancestry and social environment," the second "fault of person," and the third an "unsafe act and/or mechanical or physical hazard." Each factor can occur only if the preceding factor occurs. These five factors can be visualized as a series of five dominoes standing on edge, as shown in Exhibit 3-8. Each domino will fall only if the preceding domino falls. In other words, an injury can occur only as the result of an accident; an accident is always the result of an unsafe act or a mechanical hazard; unsafe acts or mechanical hazards can always be attributed to the faults of persons; and faults of persons are inherited or acquired as a result of their environment.

The converse, however, is not true. Accidents can occur that do not cause injuries; unsafe acts or mechanical hazards do not always lead to accidents; persons with faults do not always commit unsafe acts or permit mechanical hazards to exist; and persons may not develop the faults associated with their ancestry or social development. Nevertheless, if the first domino falls, all five dominoes *may* fall unless one or more of the dominoes is removed from the sequence (see Exhibit 3-9).

For example, a worker's social environment may cause him or her to be reckless and ignorant of safe practices. These character traits may in turn cause the worker to remove a safeguard from a machine and to operate the machine in an unsafe manner. Five times the worker

Exhibit 3-8
Heinrich's Domino Theory*

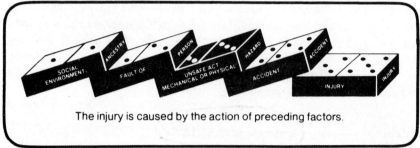

The injury is caused by the action of preceding factors.

* Reprinted, with permission, from H. W. Heinrich, *Industrial Accident Prevention*, 4th
ed. (New York: McGraw-Hill Book Company, 1959), p. 15.

Exhibit 3-9
Loss Prevention in Heinrich's Domino Theory*

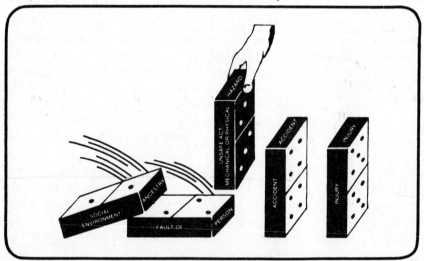

* Reprinted, with permission, from H. W. Heinrich, *Industrial Accident Prevention*, 4th
ed. (New York: McGraw-Hill Book Company, 1959), p. 16.

may catch his or her clothing in the machine, without further incident.
The sixth time the worker may suffer a broken arm.

In this example, five times only four dominoes fell; the accidents
did not result in injuries. The sixth time all five dominoes fell; the
accident did result in an injury. In his writings, Heinrich placed great
emphasis on the fact that accidents usually do not produce injuries.
Based on a study of industrial injuries he estimated that, on the
average, workers suffered major disabling injuries only one time per

300 accidents. In 270 of these similar accidents, not even a minor injury would result.

Heinrich argued that loss control specialists should be primarily concerned with removing the third domino—unsafe acts and/or mechanical or physical hazards. Unsafe acts of persons should receive special attention because, in a study of industrial injuries, he found that 88 percent of the injuries could be charged to such unsafe acts, but only 10 percent to dangerous physical or mechanical conditions.

A present day safety expert, Dan Petersen, has endorsed Heinrich's domino theory and the emphasis on unsafe acts of persons. He has, however, introduced a modified version. Instead of five factors, he includes six in the accident sequence. The first is "management fault," which sets Heinrich's five factors in motion. Management, therefore, becomes responsible for all injuries by fostering an environment in which the other factors can exist.[13]

Heinrich's theory was developed in the context of industrial injuries, but its principles are applicable to most other accidents as well. For example, an error in the design of a power lawnmower may cause a customer to have an accident causing a serious injury which, in turn, may result in a liability suit against the manufacturer.

Haddon's Energy Release Theory   Instead of concentrating on human behavior, Haddon treated accidents as a physical engineering problem. Accidents result when energy that is out of control puts more stress on a structure (property or a person) than that structure can tolerate without damage. Accidents can be prevented by controlling the energy involved or by changing the structures that the energy could damage. More specifically, Haddon suggested ten strategies designed either to suppress conditions that produce accidents or to enhance conditions that retard accidents.[14] In brief, these ten strategies, with examples of each, are as follows:

1. *To prevent the creation of the hazard in the first place.* (Examples: prevent production of plutonium, thalidomide, LSD.)
2. *To reduce the amount of the hazard brought into being.* (Examples: reduce speed of vehicles, lead content of paint, mining of asbestos; make less beverage alcohol—a hazard itself and in its results, such as drunken driving.)
3. *To prevent the release of the hazard that already exists.* (Examples: pasteurizing milk, bolting or timbering mine roofs, impounding nuclear wastes.)
4. *To modify the rate or spatial distribution of release of the hazard from its source.* (Examples: brakes, shutoff valves, reactor control rods.)

5. *To separate, in time or space, the hazard and that which is to be protected.* (Examples: isolation of persons with communicable diseases; walkways over or around hazards; evacuation; the phasing of pedestrian and vehicular traffic, whether in a work area or on a city street; the banning of vehicles carrying explosives from areas where they and their cargoes are not needed.)

6. *To separate the hazard and that which is to be protected by interposition of a material barrier.* (Examples: surgeon's gloves, containment structures, childproof poison-container closures, vehicle air bags.)

7. *To modify relevant basic qualities of the hazard.* (Examples: altering pharmacological agents to reduce side effects, using breakaway roadside poles, making crib slat spacing too narrow to strangle a child.)

8. *To make what is to be protected more resistant to damage from the hazard.* (Examples: immunization, making structures more fire- and earthquake-resistant, giving salt to workers under thermal stress, making motor vehicles more crash resistant.)

9. *To begin to counter the damage already done by the environmental hazard.* (Examples: rescuing the shipwrecked, reattaching severed limbs, extricating trapped miners.)

10. *To stabilize, repair, and rehabilitate the object of the damage.* (Examples: posttraumatic cosmetic surgery, physical rehabilitation for amputees and others with disabling injuries—including many thousands paralyzed annually by spinal cord damage sustained in motor vehicle crashes—rebuilding after fires and earthquakes.)

Professors Mehr and Hedges, in their book *Risk Management: Concepts and Applications,* suggested a useful summary of Haddon's ten categories into five broader strategies:

1. Control the energy buildup (Haddon's 1 and 2)
2. Control the injurious release of built-up injury (Haddon's 3 and 4)
3. Separate the released energy from persons and objects susceptible to injury (Haddon's 5 and 6)
4. Create an environment that minimizes injurious effects (Haddon's 7 and 8)
5. Counteract injurious effects (Haddon's 9 and 10)[15]

The Two Theories Compared The difference between the Heinrich and Haddon theories can be viewed as a difference in emphasis. Both the Heinrich and the Haddon theories explain a sequence or chain that leads to damage or injury. Heinrich's sequence starts with ancestry and social environment and ends with an injury or property damage. Haddon starts with the build-up of energy and ends with an injury or property damage. Haddon's theory can be viewed primarily (Strategies 1 through 8) as an expanded analysis of *part* of the third domino in Heinrich's sequence—mechanical or physical hazards that cause accidents—and what to do about them.

Unlike Heinrich, who places most of the blame for accidents on human behavior that leads to mechanical or physical hazards, Haddon concentrates on the physical engineering aspects of the conditions that give rise to accidents. To illustrate, assume that an auto being driven at eighty miles an hour crashes into a rigid roadside sign causing serious bodily injuries to the occupants of the car and extensive physical damage to the car. Heinrich's approach would emphasize the unsafe act of speeding as a personal fault of the driver and the fault of the highway department in installing the rigid sign. Haddon's approach would emphasize the amount of energy created by speeding and the contact surface that increases the injury or damage that results from the impact. In other words, Haddon's analytical framework is more concerned about the physical conditions surrounding the accident than who was responsible for those conditions. He was also more optimistic about what can be done to control accidents by correcting mechanical or physical causes. Consequently, Haddon would have had greater faith that more sturdily built cars would reduce injuries from auto accidents even if driving habits and attitudes remained unchanged. (On the other hand, correcting the physical conditions that led to the uncontrolled release of energy may require some change in human behavior.) Haddon did not claim, however, that his ten strategies were exhaustive or that he had detailed all the causes of accidents.

Both the Heinrich and Haddon analyses are worthy of study by all students of loss control.

Four Categories of Control Techniques

The four categories of control techniques are (1) avoidance, (2) loss control, (3) combination, and (4) transfers of the exposure itself. Each of these categories is explained briefly below. Later discussions will highlight the application of these techniques to various types of liability exposures.

(1) *Avoidance*   One way to control a loss exposure is never to have assumed it. If a person does not have any interest in a piece of property, he or she does not have any of the liability loss exposures

associated with interests in that property. The person has avoided that loss exposure.

A second example of avoidance is to abandon or discontinue the property or activity that formerly created a liability loss exposure. Discontinuing the manufacture of some product or filling a swimming pool with dirt would permit a firm to avoid future liability loss exposures associated with the product or swimming pool.

Avoidance should be distinguished from loss control and transfers. Loss control assumes that the firm will keep the property or continue the activity creating the liability loss exposure, but that the firm will conduct its future operations in a safer manner. Unlike avoidance through abandonment or discontinuance, transfers pass the liability loss exposure to someone else.

Loss Control Loss control is the most important, most frequently used control technique. Loss control techniques can be classified as loss prevention measures, loss reduction measures, or both.

- *Loss prevention measures* are designed to reduce the number of occurrences. Examples are product quality control and driver training courses.
- *Loss reduction measures* attempt to reduce the severity of those losses that do occur. Examples are antidote instruction on products it is dangerous to consume and rehabilitation of injured workers.

Although conceptually possible, loss control techniques never eliminate completely some chance of loss, though they may greatly minimize certain hazards.

Loss control always deserves consideration because, if successful, it reduces losses in material and human resources. Firms often underestimate the benefits of loss control because they underestimate the losses that might be associated with a given event whose frequency or severity might have been reduced through loss control.

One special form of loss control is *separation.* Separation breaks up a loss exposure into more units, the major objective being to reduce loss severity. For example, instead of carrying 100 passengers in one vehicle a firm might carry 10 passengers in each of 10 vehicles. The maximum liability exposure per vehicle is thus reduced. A by-product of separation is an increase in the number of exposure units, which makes future loss experience more predictable. In the illustration given, the number of motor vehicles exposed to loss was increased tenfold. Because of the larger number of vehicles carrying the same number of passengers, the chance that at least one vehicle will be involved in a liability suit is much higher, but the maximum possible or probable loss is much less and the future is more predictable.

3)Combination Combination means the acquisition of more independent exposure units through growth or merger. The benefit derived from combination is that increasing the number of independent exposure units makes the future more predictable.

Combination differs from separation in that combination is not a *loss control* measure—other things being equal, it does not reduce either the loss frequency or the maximum possible loss. Like separation, however, it increases the chance that at least one unit will be exposed in a loss.

Many firms experience combination of their pure loss exposures through merger, acquisition, and growth. As part of their attempt to meet a much broader objective, such as to increase their market share or to better their customer service, they increase their loss exposures. Insurers are the only firms who, at least until they reach a certain size, use combination for the purpose of making their future losses more predictable.

4) Transfers Transfers can control liability loss exposures in three ways:

1. *Transferring the property or activity that creates the liability exposure to somebody else.* The transferor thus transfers the liability exposure to someone else, along with the property or activity.

2. *Transferring legal responsibility under an exculpatory contract.* Under an exculpatory contract, a person who might suffer a bodily injury or a property loss because of the acts of another party agrees not to hold the other party responsible for any such injuries or losses. The party is thus relieved of a liability loss exposure that it previously had. Note that under these exculpatory contracts A can agree to relieve B only of legal responsibilities that B would have toward A, not the responsibilities B might have toward C or other persons. Note also that courts tend to interpret exculpatory contracts literally and to abrogate those that, to the courts, seem unconscionable.

3. *Deleting a hold-harmless provision from an agreement under which one is the transferee.* For example, under the lease arrangement cited earlier, the tenant might be able to relieve itself of liability for covered acts of the landlord by deleting the lease provision or, if that is not possible, by refusing to renew the lease with that provision.

These control transfers are different from financing transfers.

Financing transfers obligate the transferee to provide money for the transferor if certain losses should occur. Insurance is the clearest example of loss financing, but many noninsurance examples exist. For example, under a lease, the landlord may require the tenant to hold the landlord harmless if the landlord's negligence leads to injuries to a visitor to the premises. The landlord's liability loss exposure remains (the tenant cannot change the law insofar as third parties are concerned), but the tenant agrees to *pay* the landlord's share of any damages. If a visitor is injured and the tenant does not pay, the transfer is ineffective and the landlord must pay.

CONTROLLING WORKPLACE INJURY AND DISEASE LOSSES

For a variety of reasons, industrial injury and disease have been the subject of more loss control literature than any other liability exposures.

- Claim frequency is higher for these exposures than for most others, so employers are well aware of this exposure.
- Loss control efforts have been highly effective in dealing with industrial injuries and diseases. Historical comparisons of the loss experience of all industries, specific industries, and specific firms can be cited to document this effectiveness.
- Publicity given to workers compensation laws alerts employers and their workers to the potential losses from these exposures.
- Insurers first recognized the loss experience of individual employers through experience and retrospective rating plans applied in workers compensation insurance. Large employers have also frequently retained this exposure for many years.
- For humanitarian reasons and good industrial relations alone, employers should concern themselves with these exposures.
- State and federal laws require some loss control activities.

The costs of providing workers compensation benefits are only part of the losses employers sustain because of an industrial injury or disease. The incentive for controlling industrial injuries or diseases is thus greater than the resulting compensation benefit savings alone would suggest.

In addition to his other major contributions to industrial safety, Heinrich studied the total costs associated with a large sample of accidents. In addition to the cost of workers compensation benefits, he analyzed such costs as the time lost by other employees who stop work to assist the injured employee or for some other reasons; the time lost by supervisors to assist the employee, investigate the accident, secure a replacement, and fill out forms and answer questions; and damage to machines or spoilage of material. For the cases he studied, he found that the non-workers-compensation-benefit costs (called "incidental" or "hidden" costs) were four times the compensation benefit costs.[16]

Other writers have suggested that the four-to-one ratio is too high or that the ratio varies with the type of case. For example, Grimaldi and Simonds argue that the other costs vary depending upon whether the accident produces no bodily injuries, first-aid treatment only, doctors' care only, or disability.[17]

In its estimate of the dollar cost of work accidents cited earlier, the National Safety Council "conservatively" estimates that the money value of the time lost by noninjured workers is equal to the workers compensation costs. All these sources agree that workers compensation benefits are only part of the costs associated with industrial injuries or diseases.

Recognition of this principle emphasizes the importance of the three major categories of techniques used to control industrial injury and disease loss exposures: (1) avoidance, (2) loss control, and (3) noninsurance transfers.

Avoidance

Business may avoid a workers compensation or employers liability exposure by (1) never having an exposure, or (2) abandoning an existing exposure.

Small individual proprietorships or partnerships may be able to avoid workers compensation or employers liability exposures simply by hiring no employees. While this may be feasible for a one-person insurance office or a "Ma and Pa" grocery store, such avoidance is not feasible for a majority of business enterprises. Even such small proprietorships or partnerships might find it desirable to hire an occasional part-time employee for maintenance work or temporary help.

Liability under workers compensation statutes may be avoided if only those operations are performed that do not fall under the statutes requiring compulsory insurance. A business enterprise might choose to locate in a state where that enterprise's type of operations does not fall within the statute, or an enterprise might keep the number of employees and/or the type of business operations to the point where the statute does not apply. Although such methods might make it possible for an employer to avoid providing compulsory workers compensation benefits, they do not avoid the exposures at common law. These exposures must still be retained or covered with employers liability insurance.

At other times, an entire project may have to be avoided or

abandoned because the potential consequences may be detrimental to the health of employees, or workers compensation insurance may be too expensive or unavailable.

Loss Control

Most workers compensation and employers liability exposures cannot be avoided. Even if it is possible to avoid being subject to a workers compensation law, there is still an exposure to employees or independent contractors. Even the individual proprietorship or partnership with no employees has an interest in preventing, controlling, or reducing the direct and indirect costs that might be incurred if an owner is injured.

Five aspects of loss control of industrial injuries and diseases will be discussed here: (1) the importance of a loss control policy statement, (2) the roles of loss control specialists and line managers, (2) loss and hazard identification analysis, (4) the major classes of loss control measures, and (5) compliance with the Occupational Safety and Health Act.

Loss Control Policy Statements A loss control policy statement describes the loss control objectives of the firm, the various activities the firm will employ to achieve those objectives, who will be involved in these activities and in what capacity, what standards of performance are expected, and how compliance with these standards will be measured. Such a policy statement, endorsed by top management, is an important part of loss control.

In endorsing such a statement, top management becomes more aware of loss control and its importance. Top management's endorsement will make it easier for those charged with implementing the policy statement to secure the cooperation of other employees. The statement of the goals, activities, and performance standards focuses the attention of the firm's employees on specific targets.

Loss Control Specialists and Line Managers Both loss control specialists and line managers play important roles in controlling industrial injury and disease exposures. Loss control specialists are experts in loss control, but they usually know less than line managers about the jobs and the people employed to do these jobs in their departments. Most control specialists also have only staff authority, not line authority. They cannot command line managers or the employees in their departments to do anything. Line managers, on the other hand, may order their subordinates to practice job safety. The specialist, therefore, relies largely on motivation and persuasion of both employees and their supervisors. Specialists will be more successful to the extent that their requests are considered reasonable and worthwhile, they provide services and advice that make compliance relatively easy, their expertise in the field is acknowledged, and they have the backing of top management.

③ Loss and Hazard Identification and Analysis Loss and hazard analysis is a crucial first step in controlling industrial injuries and diseases. The objective is to analyze:

1. the losses experienced by the firm, and
2. the hazards that led to these losses or might lead to losses in the future.

Some of the liability loss exposure identification and measurement principles presented earlier are applied in this process. In identifying liability loss exposures, the risk manager was instructed to study the losses that have occurred in the past and the property or activities that were the source of those losses. In measuring these loss exposures, the analyst was told to measure the potential loss frequency and loss severity plus the predictability of the loss experience. How firms might keep records that would provide this information and permit comparisons with the experience of other firms was also discussed.

The analysis of these accidents for industrial safety purposes requires relatively detailed information and comparisons. For example, in order to determine the hazards that caused those accidents, the loss control specialist needs to know who was involved, what specific operation was being performed, the time of the accident, the department or section in which the accident occurred, how the employee was injured (for example, slipped and fell or caught between vehicles), whether the employee was committing an unsafe act prior to the act, whether the unsafe act was the fault of the employee or management, whether defective tools, equipment, materials and facilities contributed to the accident, and whether any environmental factors such as noise, temperature extremes, or poor illumination were present.

Accident report forms should be designed to provide as much of this information as possible but still be relatively easy to understand and not too burdensome to complete. These forms are almost always completed by line managers or those subordinates who are close to the scene of the accident but who may see little value in the report itself.

The accident data gathered through these formulas can be analyzed in various ways. Personal computers and common software programs such as Lotus 1-2-3™ can be extremely useful in this analysis. Accident rates can be compared with respect to individual employees; supervisors; departments; operations; the month, day of the week, or time of day; whether an unsafe act was involved and, if so, whether the fault was attributable to the worker or management; whether defective tools, equipment and the like were involved; and whether an environmental problem existed. With this information the loss specialist is alerted to what caused these accidents and how they might be controlled. The data also provide a base for allocating loss costs among departments or plants that can be used to provide financial or other incentives for loss control.

Many hazards may exist that have not yet produced any accidents. To identify these hazards, the loss specialist must use some of the methods suggested earlier for identifying loss exposures: personal inspection of the premises and activities, interactions with other departments, and a study of the legal, social, and economic environment—particularly changes in workers' compensation laws and their interpretation, and interactions with outsiders. The information so gathered may also be useful in estimating the probable frequency and severity of the potential losses. For example, a worker drilling a hole with a drill press may sometimes leave a wrench in the chuck and turn the switch on, causing the wrench to hit the worker. Such an accident has never occurred but supervisors estimate the probability of its occurrence to be 1/500. A major but not catastrophic loss probably would result.[18]

To analyze further the hazards revealed by the accident data or separate hazard identification, several methods have been developed, two of which will be described here.

Failure Mode and Effect Analysis can be illustrated as follows. For a worker drilling a hole with a drill press, the example cited above, five components might be identified: a drill, the motor, a bolt, a switch, and an operator. For each component one or more modes of failure are identified. The drill may break, the switch may stick "on," the operator may fail to secure a workpiece, use excessive speed, or do both of these things. The effect of each mode of failure on (1) personnel, (2) hardware, and (3) the system is identified. If the drill breaks, the personnel and the hardware are not affected but the system is rendered inoperative. If the worker fails to secure the workpiece and uses excessive feed, the operator will be hit by the work drill, the drill will be broken, and the system will become inoperative. For each mode of failure the probability of that failure is estimated (for example, 1/1000 for a drill break and 1/20 for the operator to use excessive feed). The severity is classified as nil, minor, major, or catastrophic.[19]

Fault tree analysis, a more commonly used technique, traces a particular accident back to its roots. For example, a part thrown from the table of a drill press must have been caused by the part not being secure on the table and excessive torque on the drill. The reason the part was not secure on the table must be that no clamp was provided or the item was not clamped. If the item was not clamped, the cause could be either poor instruction or carelessness or both. If the fault lies with management, which provided the machine, excessive torque on the drill may have been caused by a dull drill, too high a feed, or too large a drill. The cause, here, could also be either poor instruction or carelessness, or in the case of the drills, the provision of defective or improper drills by management. Fault tree analysis would express this line of reasoning in a diagram.[20]

Major Classes of Loss Control Measures   The measures used to control exposures to industrial injury or disease can be classified into five categories:

1. a safe workplace,
2. employee screening, training, and supervision,
3. supervisor selection, training,
4. claims management including rehabilitation, and
5. human factors engineering

These categories are not independent, but overlap with one another.

Safe Place to Work.   A safe place to work means a safe plant or office together with safe equipment and products. The goals are accident prevention or reduction and a healthy environment.

A wide variety of measures may be taken to improve and maintain workplace safety.

To illustrate the broad range of measures in this category consider the chapter headings in Part III, "The Workplace Environment," and Part IV, "Equipment Design," of *Safety Engineering*, a text by Gilbert Marshall:[21]

> The Workplace Environment:
>> Atmospheric conditions
>> Walking and standing surfaces
>> Egress and line safety
>> Noise and noise control
>> Fire prevention and suppression
>> Explosion
>> Radiation
>> Hazardous materials
> Equipment Design:
>> Mechanical hazards
>> Electrical hazards
>> Tools and machine controls
>> Principles of machine guarding

A related chapter on personal protective equipment appears earlier in the Marshall text.

Because *falls* cause more injuries than any other factor except motor vehicle accidents, Marshall's discussion of walking and standing surfaces is of special interest. One common cause of falls is tripping. Tripping may be caused by rough surfaces or by objects on the floor. Whether a person trips depends upon how attentive they are to the condition of the surface as to the actual condition. Extension cords and open file and desk drawers are an important problem in offices; stub ends of welding rods, screws, and balls from ball bearings are often found on the floor in manufacturing or maintenance areas. Construction site paths may be obstructed by temporary water lines, loose boards, broken boxes, and the like. The solution is level surfaces, the removal of obstructions, and making workers and others more aware of possible hazards.

Slipping is another reason people fall. The slipperiness of a floor is commonly determined by the static coefficient of friction between various floor and shoe sole materials. The higher the coefficient, the less slippery the floor. The coefficient of many materials is less when they are wet than dry. For example, for leather soles, the coefficient is 0.46 for dry vinyl asbestos, 0.30 for wet vinyl asbestos, and 0.27 for dry linoleum. For neoprene soles, these three coefficients are higher. Using floor materials with a high coefficient, keeping the floor drier, and providing safe work shoes should reduce the number of slips. Some flooring is impregnated with abrasive materials in order to make it less slippery.

A third problem is falling through openings in the floor. Barriers must be placed around such openings and workers alerted to the presence of the openings.

Other items requiring special attention are ramps, stairs, fixed and portable ladders, and temporary and movable elevated platforms.

In his chapter on the principles of *machine guarding*, Marshall notes that the first priority in loss control is to eliminate the hazard or to reduce it to an acceptable level. If the hazard cannot be so eliminated or reduced, the next step is to isolate the hazard. One way to isolate the hazards associated with industrial machines is to separate the hazard from the worker by distance. For example, overhead belts should be at least seven feet above the floor. Distance, however, is usually not an effective way of isolating machine hazards from workers in which case a barrier or guard must be placed between the machine and the worker. Examples of guards and related devices are enclosure guards, guards that push away the worker's body, fail-safe brakes, and remote controls.

Personal protective equipment is a related approach. However, instead of isolating the worker completely from the hazard, it usually merely reduces the effects of exposure to the hazard. Marshall considers this approach to be a last resort because the equipment tends to be heavy and uncomfortable, it is expensive, the worker's effectiveness may be reduced, and workers may choose not to use it when they should. Sometimes, however, no other approach is possible or feasible. Personal protective equipment can be used to protect the worker against the impact of moving objects, respiratory problems, heat and corrosives, noise, and falling.

Atmospheric conditions in the workplace are an important concern of industrial hygienists. These conditions include the temperature, humidity, air cleanliness, illumination, and background color. Workers tend to be more comfortable and more alert if the atmospheric conditions are satisfactory. Otherwise, work accidents may become more frequent. If the air is not clean, workers may over time incur industrial diseases that have attracted more attention in recent years. For example, the air may contain asbestos or some other toxic material that is injurious to a worker's lungs. Among the measures used to control air cleanliness are not generating any harmful material in the first place and proper ventilation. If the air being discharged requires some treatment, several devices are available including mechanical separators, filtration devices, gas absorbers, and combustion incinerators.

Radiation is an extremely important concern of industrial hygienists and an increasingly common source of occupational disease claims. Radiation is a form of energy emitted from many sources. The higher the frequency, the higher the energy and the more serious the loss potential. Radiation may cause excessive heating of body tissues and in more serious cases, permanent cell deformation. Control methods include eliminating the radiation, absorbing shields, time and distance delays, warning signs, and personal protective equipment.

The preceding discussion has emphasized the engineering approach to controlling industrial injuries and diseases. The remaining four control categories use the human relations approach.

2. Employee Screening, Training, and Supervision. Unsafe acts of workers can be reduced by proper screening, training, and supervision.

In hiring persons and assigning them to a job the firm should consider not only their ability to do the job, but also their ability to do it in a way that will not result in injuries to themselves or to their fellow employees. Proper training and supervision also includes attention to workers' safety, in addition to productivity.

In its _Accident Prevention Manual for Industrial Operations: Administration and Programs_, the National Safety Council illustrates the importance of these practices. Workers and management, the Council states, may cause an accident by doing what they should not do or by not doing what they should do. Four common unsafe acts, which represent deviations from standard job procedures are (1) using equipment without authority, (2) operating equipment at an unsafe speed or in any other improper way, (3) removing safety devices or rendering them inoperative, and (4) using defective tools.[22] Possible explanations of why these unsafe acts occurred and how they might be avoided include the following:

Explanation	Countermeasure
No standard or well-known procedure	Develop such a procedure and include in training
Employee knew the procedure but did not follow it	Test the validity of the procedure and include compliance in evaluating employee
Employee knew the procedure but did not follow it because of work pressures or supervisor's influence	Consider changes in work pressures; counsel worker and supervisor
Handicapped worker unable to follow the procedure	Consider changing work requirements or more training, counsel employee

③ *Supervisor Selection and Training* If supervisors are responsible for job safety, they need to be selected and trained with this responsibility in mind. The purpose of the training is to emphasize the continuing importance of job safety and to provide the supervisors with the technical and human relations knowledge they need to be effective.

④ *Claims Management, Including Rehabilitation.* Although workers compensation benefits are only part of the total cost of industrial injury and disease, they are an important part. After an accident occurs or a worker is exposed to some disease, the firm's objective should be to minimize the severity of the loss to the worker and the firm. How the worker's claim is managed has been found to influence greatly the final outcome. Consequently, the firm should have a plan that assigns responsibility to someone within the firm to implement a plan that becomes effective following an injury. The plan should include procedures for providing emergency care, communications to and from the worker's supervisors and fellow workers, investigation of the accident, and, most importantly where necessary, transportation of the injured worker to proper medical facilities and close, compassionate, contacts with the worker and family while the worker is undergoing medical treatment and subsequent convalescence. If the employer demonstrates at an early stage sincere concern for the welfare of the employee, the employee is much less likely to be negative toward the employer or to seek the help of an attorney, which on the average, tends to increase the magnitude of the loss. After the worker reaches maximum medical improvement, he or she should be encouraged to return to active employment, preferably with the same employer. Where appropriate, the worker should receive physical and vocational rehabilitation. Where possible, the firm should have a return-to-work program that includes light-duty assignments, part-time schedules, and job modifications.

5) *Human Factors Engineering.* Also called "ergonomics," human factors engineering is designed to make controls, machines, and workplaces "more convenient and more comfortable and less confusing, less exasperating, and less fatiguing to the user."[23] This approach combines the human relations and engineering approaches into a system. The five factors considered in this approach are (1) the selection of workers, (2) training of workers, (3) operating rules, procedures, and instructions, (4) design of equipment, and (5) design of the environment.

5) ***Compliance with the Occupational Safety and Health Act*** In controlling industrial injuries and diseases it is important to comply with the safety and health standards promulgated by the Secretary of Labor or approved state plans under the Occupational Safety and Health Act of 1980 (OSHA). This Act is applicable to all employers with one or more employees engaged in a business affecting commerce. Specifically excluded are all federal, state, and local government employees and some employers such as coal mine operators subject to separate safety laws.

OSHA standards incorporate by reference many standards developed by private organizations such as the American Society for Testing and Materials (ASTM), the Society of Automotive Engineers (SAE), and Underwriters Laboratories (UL). The Occupational Safety and Health Administration has also promulgated many other standards following publication of the proposed standard in the *Federal Register,* inviting comments on the proposal, and, if requested, holding a hearing.

OSHA officers check compliance with these standards by periodic inspections of selected businesses. Unless the employer demands a search warrant, the officers can enter the premises any time. Employers have demanded a warrant in less than 3 percent of the inspections because this demand usually delays the inspection only a day or two. An employer representative and an employee representative are permitted to accompany the officer during the inspection. OSHA has assigned most of its inspection time to some high-priority situations: investigation of imminent dangers, accidents that have resulted in fatalities or several hospitalized employees, investigations of employee complaints alleging imminent danger, high-hazard industries, and reinspection of establishments cited earlier for serious violations.

If the inspection reveals some violation of a specific standard or the general duty to provide a safe workplace, the officer may issue a written citation that the employer must display at or near the place where the alleged violation occurred. Citations for serious violations must be accompanied by a monetary penalty of $500 to $1,000 per violation. Citations for lesser violations may or may not carry a monetary penalty ranging from $0 to $1,000. In either case the employer must correct the penalty by a specified date. Failure to correct an uncontested violation by that date may result in a penalty after that time of up to $1,000 per day.

In case of willful or repeated violations, OSHA may impose a $10,000 civil penalty. Multiple violations can result in a sizable fine, such as the $1.38 million fine against Union Carbide proposed in April 1986.[24] An employer who, by willfully violating a standard, causes the death of an employee may face criminal penalties as well.

Although compliance with OSHA standards is not a sufficient condition for employee safety, it is a necessary condition.

Transfers

State workers compensation laws specifically prohibit employees from signing an exculpatory contract that would excuse employers from any responsibility for industrial injuries or diseases. Consequently, control transfers relating to industrial injuries and diseases are limited to arrangements between businesses, as discussed in later chapters.

CONTROLLING PRODUCT LIABILITY LOSS EXPOSURES

Control techniques are especially important with respect to product liability loss exposures. Some product liability exposures are not insurable at any cost—but too serious to be retained. Other exposures are insurable—but only at considerable cost. Exclusions in product liability insurance policies expose all purchasers to some serious losses. Avoidance, loss control, and transfers are again the most important control techniques.

Avoidance

Avoidance, as a noninsurance technique for treating the products liability exposure, can take one of two forms. One is where a firm never creates the exposure. For example, a pharmaceutical firm decides against the production of a new drug product because of the potentially severe repercussions that can result from claims and suits and the unavailability of adequate insurance. Another example is the firm that decides against expanding into an unrelated field, such as the production of paints or toys, because high loss frequency, large court judgments, and sharp increases in insurance premiums would be likely. The approach of never creating an exposure was seldom practiced when exposures could be covered by insurance at relatively low prices. Today, the public is more claims conscious, courts are more generous with judgments, federal agencies are more stringent in upholding the laws to protect the public, liability of product producers and sellers is nearly absolute, and liability insurance, as an aid to handling products loss exposures, has become very costly.

The second form of avoidance is where a firm already has an exposure and decides to eliminate it. An actual situation in the early 1970s involved the makers of certain diet soft drinks containing cyclamates as a sugar substitute. Following a series of tests by a federal agency over a long period, it was determined that the consumption of cyclamates in very large quantities could be a cause of cancer. The Federal Food and Drug Administration therefore halted the production of diet soft drinks containing cyclamates. The avoidance of that exposure, though federally imposed, was eventually overcome when soft drink manufacturers substituted saccharin for cyclamates. Subsequently, much of the saccharine in soft drinks has been replaced with aspartame.

Products liability exposures sometimes present so serious a threat that a firm has no other choice but to avoid them altogether by going out of business. Havir Manufacturing Company, a builder of punch presses, is believed to be one of the first to take that approach voluntarily. That firm had seventy-five employees and annual sales between $2 and $3 million based upon production of about 1,000 punch presses annually. Two major problems confronted Havir. First, it was being sued by individuals who were operating some of its 25,000 punch presses that were sold prior to 1969. In fact, some of the lawsuits against it involved punch presses that were thirty years old. Havir's second problem was that its product liability insurance became too expensive to purchase. Its bids for insurance had an annual average price of $150,000 for $500,000 coverage and a minimum deductible of $5,000. The company executives decided that since matters would get worse before they would improve, the only alternative was to liquidate the business.[25]

Loss Control

Loss control is an indispensable technique, whatever the exposure. Loss control is especially important in dealing with product liability loss exposures because (1) the loss potential is great, (2) the firm must comply with the Consumer Product Safety Act and similar legislation, and (3) a liability suit and the accompanying publicity may tarnish the reputation of the firm and reduce its market share.

Firms should exercise special precautions to see that their products are free from defects and reasonably safe for their intended purposes. Because these measures are almost never completely effective, they should also establish strong legal defenses by documenting the positive steps they take to reduce the likelihood or severity of losses.

Company Policy and the Role of Management and Personnel No products loss control program, however carefully structured, will produce results, unless it has the backing of top management and personnel at all levels. All personnel should be made to understand their role in maintaining the quality of products.

In order to assure a properly coordinated loss control program, many firms establish products reliability or safety committees that include top management, personnel from research, production, sales, industrial relations, legal services, purchasing, engineering, and risk management. It is the committee's function and responsibility to develop corporate policy on loss control and see to it that line and staff responsibilities are carefully communicated and executed. Each committee member usually is directly involved in the production of a safe product from the time it is first researched and designed to the time when the product is ready for sale.[26]

Since motivation also is an essential characteristic of a workable loss control program, it has been suggested that a program be related in "terms of profits and bonuses for management personnel and wages and jobs for the work force," because this is language everyone understands. Complementing this approach, an internal cost control program also is advisable, so that employees know what their efforts are doing to reduce losses. Each department and division can then be rewarded or penalized, depending upon its successes or failures.[27]

Implementing Effective Loss Control Measures Effective loss control is an expensive and a complicated undertaking involving every facet of the manufacturing process. As Exhibit 3-10 shows, products liability suits arise from all phases of the manufacturing process, and loss control measures should form an integral part of design and engineering functions, manufacturing and assembly, including materials and components, advertising and sales literature, warranties, packaging, instruction manuals, and sales, service, and parts.

While this discussion deals with loss control measures of manufacturers, some of the measures also can apply to wholesale distributors, dealers, and retailers that package or assemble goods, such as heavy equipment dealers and bicycle shops.

Most of the loss control measures to be discussed are applied before the product passes to the customer. Measures involving instruction manuals, sales, services, and parts control the exposure while the customer has the product. Product recalls may become effective after some (hopefully, not many) customers have been injured or the defect is otherwise discovered. Record keeping is a continuous process covering all those phases.

Design and Engineering. Since the function of design and engineering primarily is devoted to the planning, designing, and testing of new products, it is considered to be one of the more crucial functions in the manufacturing process. It stands to reason that if a product is improperly designed or inadequately tested, it is seldom possible to prevent an exposure to loss, even though the product is manufactured and assembled according to all specifications of the design plan.

In planning and designing a product, a manufacturer should keep in mind that a safe product is not one that it believes to be safe, but one that the average consumer believes to be safe. Manufacturers, some have suggested, practically have to make their products "idiot proof" to avoid complications following the sale of their products.[28]

It is nearly impossible to anticipate all the possible uses and abuses to which products may be subjected, particularly durable goods with use expectancies of many years. It is also difficult to design and produce a competitively priced product that will meet the standards of safety of the future. Consider the example of the punch presses sold as long as thirty or forty years ago. Though the presses were properly designed and manufactured by then existing standards, the manufacturers of those old machines are now being held legally accountable for injuries to machine operators because the machine did not have the safety controls on them that are currently required.

This particular trend runs counter to the customary precautions that manufacturers have been following for years. Industrial products have been designed according to the specific standards of government or industry; or, when specific standards were lacking, manufacturers, to be safe, were required to search out unwritten standards referred to as "customs of the industry." In some cases, standards had to be disregarded altogether because they were not keeping pace with technological changes. Manufacturers in these situations have been

Exhibit 3-10
Where Product Liability Suits Arise*

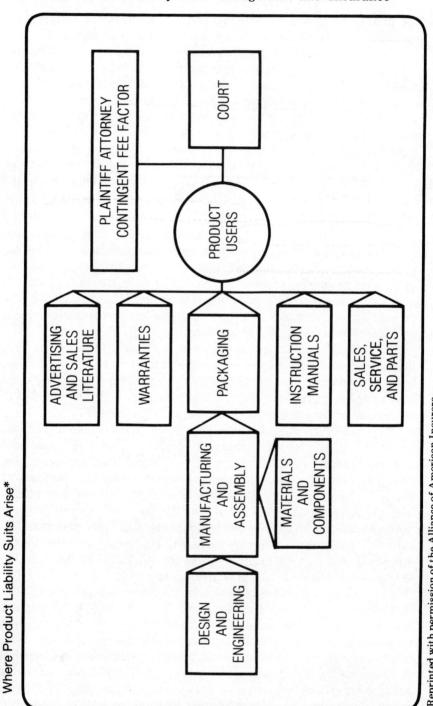

*Reprinted with permission of the Alliance of American Insurers.

required to design economically feasible products corresponding to the "current state of technological knowledge." Yet, in spite of all the care exercised by manufacturers, they are still being held liable for injury stemming from their products from a variety of causes, including negligence of the product users.[29]

Manufacturing and Assembly, Including Materials and Components. Following the design and testing of what a manufacturer considers to be a safe, reasonably priced, and usable product, the next crucial step in the production process involves the actual manufacturing of the product, usually with raw stock or component parts supplied by others. This is a crucial stage, because an otherwise properly designed and tested product still can produce adverse exposures when it is improperly manufactured or incorrectly assembled.

It is impractical to provide any detailed discussion on the elements of the manufacturing process. However, the following points commonly are considered to be fundamental to the typical exposure:

1. quality control on incoming goods,
2. proper storage of materials and component parts,
3. spot checks during the manufacturing process,
4. need for records on critical parts,
5. control of rejects or reworked items (large amounts of reject materials along the assembly line should be an indication that something is inherently wrong with the system),
6. full testing before shipment,
7. proper marking of products or containers, and
8. the need for modifications of products and the effects of such modifications.[30]

The importance of properly handling, inspecting, and testing raw materials of others that are transformed into a finished product, or component parts of others that are assembled as part of a complete product cannot be overemphasized. Exposures to loss from materials and components confront many manufacturers, since many do not desire to produce a product in its entirety and some would be incapable of doing so.

The average American-made automobile, for example, consists of over 7,000 parts, ranging from the frame, engine block, fuel tank, and sheet metal pieces to the nuts, bolts, and rivets. While any one of those parts may be faulty or may malfunction, it has been stated that approximately 2,000 parts of an auto may relate to the cause of accidents and to injuries.[31] Producers of autos, as well as of other products that use components in order to assemble the complete product should be just as careful about components as they are about handling products or parts of their own manufacture.

Furthermore, the overwhelming weight of case law clearly shows that a manufacturer can be held accountable for damages stemming from the components of others. The rule is that, if a defective component is incorporated into a product of another manufacturer and the defect could have been discovered by conducting reasonable tests and inspections, the manufacturer of the ultimate product can be held liable if the inspections or tests were not performed or were performed negligently. As noted in Chapter 2, the manufacturer can be held liable for damages in tort, by breach of warranty and, in some states, by strict liability in tort.

Advertising and Sales Literature. A firm whose product is properly planned, designed, tested, manufactured, and assembled can still face tremendous exposures to loss when its advertising or sales literature is misleading or lacks sufficient warning or instructions. It is for this reason that sales literature and advertising should be coordinated with the engineering, legal staff, or products safety committee to see that all material clearly represents the use and capabilities of the product.

As difficult as it often is to sway consumers in a competitive marketplace, manufacturers must be extremely careful not to make statements in their advertising that are exaggerated or untrue. Costly losses have all but eliminated the practice of manufacturers describing their products in such absolute terms as "safe" and "foolproof." The misuses of advertising seals of approval also have caused difficulties. In his testimony before the National Commission on Product Safety, Irving D. Gaines, a Milwaukee attorney, said about advertising seals:

> The public is lulled into a sense of security by these so-called "seals of approval." The consumers of this nation would be appalled to learn that most anyone who contracts with *Good Housekeeping* and *Parents' Magazine* for a stipulated amount of annual advertising in their publications can usually obtain the "seals of approval" for their product in the same package.[32]

Many products, particularly durables, cannot be designed and produced to withstand all unforeseeable or even foreseeable abuses, nor can they be built to operate without the exercise of some special precautions. It therefore is important that sales literature, advertising, and warranties be made to communicate precisely what products can and cannot do, and what must be done to operate or use them safely. The advertising division of manufacturers should make this point clear to all of its personnel, to its outside advertising firms, and to all of its distributors and retailers.

Warranties. When statements in advertising and in sales literature are held to be warranties, the results can be damaging to manufacturers. Thus, care in the wording and use of warranties is an important element in any products loss control program.

Packaging. Product packaging provides a double-barreled exposure. A package is both used as a container for a product and considered to be a product itself. Paper product containers usually do not present too many problems. But packaging takes in a wide spectrum of uses, including containers for liquids, flammables, and heavy expensive machinery. What all of this means is that the design, production, and advertising of packaging is just as important as the requirements of any other product. If a package is defective or not suitable for its intended purposes as designed or advertised, the package can give rise to a products liability loss.

Instruction Manuals, Sales, Service, and Parts. Instruction manuals may relate to the installation, operation, maintenance, service, or repair of products. Their purpose is to assist persons in learning about the product, how it is made, how it works, and what to look for and to avoid. To this end, there are several basic points that should be considered in preparing such manuals.

1. What may appear clear to the technical writer of the manual may not necessarily be clearly understood by others. Terminology and language, therefore, should be used with the consumer in mind.
2. Reference should be made to standards and codes that govern the installation and operation of the product.
3. Instructions should emphasize the critical and/or procedural steps that are important in minimizing start-up or final operation failures.
4. Appropriate warnings may be necessary when materials are flammable or hazardous.
5. Pictures and photos may be necessary to illustrate the product with proper guards and an operator wearing protective gear.[33]

Since the function of product service affects completed operations loss exposures, a considerable amount of competence is required of service personnel; and, of course, there should be a good rapport between such personnel and the manufacturer. Since those who install or service products usually are the first to know whether a product is not functioning properly, they should be the first to notify the manufacturer. In fact, early identification of product difficulties will not only control the size of problems but also will reduce the expenses that usually accompany them. Training, competence, and a direct line of communication between service personnel and the manufacturer therefore is considered necessary.[34]

Record Keeping. Maintaining records is a key factor in any loss control program, whether an entity produces the whole product or only a component and regardless of how sophisticated its loss control program may be. To be effective, records normally should be kept on all materials that go into the product, including the components of others, and on the quality control standards of the entire manufacturing process, from research, design, and testing to sales and service. It is also vital that these records be maintained for at least the anticipated use expectancy of the product.

Records are essential in any loss control program, for at least three reasons:

1. They can be used in locating the division or department and the source of the production process that consistently causes the production of poor-quality products that have to be rejected or recalled, or that cause a frequency of similar losses. Records, for example, may show that the component of a supplier was not properly tested before being used, or that proper quality control standards were not maintained as required during the production process. Without records, it may be impossible to determine problem areas, or possible only at considerable expense.

2. They can facilitate the systematic withdrawal of products from the market or from use when they are known or suspected of being defective or unreasonably dangerous.

3. Records also can serve as post-loss measures in aiding firms with the defense of lawsuits. In the majority of cases, manufacturers do not learn about their products liability losses until they are served with a summons and a complaint. When this happens, manufacturers must move quickly to produce detailed records which will enable their attorneys to prepare their cases. The more comprehensive the records, the easier it is for manufacturers to support their arguments. Many manufacturers have won cases with records by illustrating that it was not their product that caused injury or damage but negligence of the user.

Three types of documentation have proved to be important in products litigation.

1. _Performance documents_ include (a) in-house guideline documents such as a drafting standards manual, a safety code manual, and a manual of engineering test procedures, (b)

checklists used in design, construction, testing, inspection, or warnings, and (c) external relations documents such as suppliers' manuals and customer relations manuals.

2. *Audit manuals* relate to monitoring whether the firm is meeting the requirements stated in the performance documents including the use of checklists. Audits by the board of directors and staff groups are important. So are external certifications by private testing groups, consumer associations, accreditation agencies, and government regulators.

3. *Genealogy tracing documents* include all records that enable the firm to trace the life history of the product by serial and model numbers or by batch and production-run numbers.[35]

Product Recall Programs. Since a producer of products can control but not entirely eliminate its exposures to loss without going out of business, the potential always exists for actual or threatened claims or suits. And, while a firm's loss control program may be effective in locating and correcting the source of problems, a firm cannot afford to ignore the further threat of loss from products that are in use. The problem may become especially critical when a "laser beam" endorsement is attached to a renewal claims-made policy or future occurrences from the hazardous product are excluded under an occurrence policy, as explained in later chapters. What an entity needs to complement its loss control program, therefore, is an organized system of communicating and, if necessary, of recalling its products from the market or from use. This system must be so structured that notice of a defective or unreasonably unsafe product can be given to distributors, retailers, and customers as promptly as possible. It also must be organized to facilitate, if necessary, the prompt, orderly withdrawal, inspection, repair, or replacement of products that are known to be or suspected of being harmful.

Organizing and maintaining an effective product recall program can be an expensive proposition. Yet, if the initiative is not taken to implement such a program, the repercussions can be far-reaching, whether a firm handles its products loss exposures with a funded retention program and/or with products liability insurance. Furthermore, the whole purpose of a loss control program is defeated if measures are not taken to prevent or reduce losses from exposures known to exist. Consumers also can lose confidence in a firm that does not seem to care enough about the safety of its own products. If a product comes within the jurisdiction of the Consumer Product Safety Act, a firm also faces serious penalties for any failure to comply with the commission's requirements dealing with the notification and the withdrawal of products.

Manufacturers realize that product recalls can be damaging to their image, if only by the implication that something is wrong with their quality control standards. But, in one study on the subject of product recalls, the two authors, George Fisk and Rajan Chandran, maintained that recalls can be viewed as an opportunity rather than a threat. Although some of their examples are obviously dated, the reasons they gave remain sound:

First, the ability to show that a product safety problem is being handled professionally can be proof that quality control systems work to protect the customer even after the product is sold. Service after sale offers many unexploited opportunities for extending customer loyalty. An excellent example is American Motors "Buyer Protection Plan": the company recalls and repairs manufacturing defects at company expense—even providing the customer, in some cases, with a replacement car and lodging expenses for the duration of the repairs. These services, highlighted in creative advertisement, have not only helped AMC's image but have enlarged its market share as well.

Second, a product traceability and recall system, along with good quality control procedures, can provide a good-faith legal defense in many product liability cases.

Third, a product traceability and recall system can also help a manufacturer understand his distribution system better. For instance, recall strategies offer an opportunity to devise a reverse and backward channel of distribution for recycling wastes—a goal of many ecologists.

Fourth, a system can enable the manufacturer to keep in touch with the consumer. Companies expend great effort and skill to determine what customers will buy, but they rarely find out whether customers are harmed by the product after purchase. For example, no effort has been made to recall "clogs" (high platform shoes), despite repeated warnings by leading doctors about their hazards and news reports of broken and twisted ankles.

Fifth, a product traceability system can supplement a test program under direct factory control. The findings of a test program, in conjunction with field usage studies, can be valuable in developing better products in the long run.[36]

In spite of those suggested measures that possibly can produce opportunities for manufacturers, it has been argued that:

... recall campaigns, contrary to the expectations of some writers, will not allow the manufacturer of a defective product, that may be unreasonably dangerous, to shift the risk of loss on a large scale simply by notifying consumers that their products have been recalled. The law has created a duty to recall that will in many instances prevent the manufacturer from shifting responsibility for his defective products to someone else.[37]

Fisk and Chandran also maintain that since speed is of the essence in recalling products, a firm should have a "predetermined structure and procedures" that can be implemented the moment the need arises to recall products.

Whether a product has to be recalled depends upon a number of factors. At Sears, Roebuck & Company, a product safety committee assesses the seriousness of the exposure and decides whether the product should be recalled, replaced, or repaired. If the potential exposure to the public is minimal, a "stop shipment order" may be sufficient. If, on the other hand, the exposure is minimal but additional sales could increase the exposure, a "stop selling order" may be issued. If the ultimate decision is to recall products, the action taken will depend on the procedures of "advance planning, speed, and accuracy."[38]

Record keeping, mentioned earlier, is also an essential part of any product recall program. One reason is that records can help identify the particular batch or serialized group of products that need to be recalled, repaired, or replaced, as well as the distributors and the geographical areas of sale. As a product is designed, produced, tested, coded, and shipped, records should be made and retained at all stages. Depending upon the product, sales invoices of distributors and retailers may be useful in identifying buyers of that product. Otherwise, other media will have to be used to put consumers on notice. The second reason record keeping is important is that it is a prerequisite to purchasing products recall insurance.

Limitations The levels of exposures that can be controlled, the mechanisms required to control them, and the costs of actually implementing controls are variables that differ for each firm. Some firms can afford safety committees, a staff of loss prevention engineers, a full-time risk manager, and all types of sophisticated measures to handle their product liability exposures. Others must do the best they can with available resources, including the services provided by insurance companies.

Regardless of the intensity of loss control efforts, losses still will occur. Accordingly, firms should have the foresight to determine how the losses should be handled by yet other techniques.

Transfers

Manufacturers, distributors, and retailers sometimes find noninsurance transfer helpful in dealing with some or all of their products liability loss exposures. This technique can be employed in one of two ways. First, the activity that produces a particular exposure can be transferred to another entity. And, second, the activity that produces the exposure can be transferred to another through an exculpatory contract.

An example of the first method, involving the transfer of an activity-producing exposure, is the manufacturer of a particular component or ingredient that discontinues its own production and hires another firm to produce the product instead. Or, faced with too great a products liability loss exposure and no economically feasible means to handle it, a firm may decide to transfer its production exposure entirely by selling out to another firm. Note again the distinction here between the noninsurance techniques of transfer and avoidance. In a transfer, the activity, its loss exposure, and potential financial consequences continue to exist. The only difference is that the exposure now confronts the firm that accepts the transfer of that activity. With avoidance, the exposure either is not created in the first place or it is eliminated entirely.

An example of the second method of transfer would be an exculpatory contract under which a customer or some other party would excuse the business from liability for losses that party sustains while consuming, transporting, storing, or otherwise handling its products. Unless the transfer seems reasonable, courts are likely to rule them invalid.

CONTROLLING OTHER GENERAL LIABILITY LOSS EXPOSURES

The premises and operations of a business create many general liability exposures. This section deals separately with the techniques used to handle (1) the "pure" premises-operations liability loss exposures and (2) contractual liability loss exposures.

"Pure" Premises-Operations Liability Loss Exposures

Many liability exposures relate in some way to a firm's premises or operations. Discussion here centers on those exposures that do not more specifically relate to occupational injury and diseases, products liability, auto liability, or contractual liability.

The basic techniques used to handle "pure" premises-operations liability loss exposures are the usual three: (1) avoidance, (2) loss control, and (3) transfers. The techniques may also be classified according to whether they are designed to (1) reduce bodily harm or property damage to others or (2) establish legal defenses against claims made by persons asserting legal responsibility of the firm for losses they incur.

Avoidance Although avoidance is not often used for the treatment of premises and operations liability exposures, avoidance of some narrowly defined liability exposures may be desirable, and it may even be essential when liability insurance is either unavailable or unaffordable. Isolating the "pure" premises and operations liability exposures confronting businesses for purposes of citing examples of situations that sometimes can be avoided effectively, is not an easy task.

Examples of avoiding such exposures include:

- the owner of a business premises who refuses to lease the premises to an operator of a restaurant or bar for fear of the liability implications created by various liquor liability or dram shop acts;
- the appliance dealer who sells but refuses to install goods in order to avoid losses to a purchaser's property which may be in the care, custody, or control of the seller during the actual course of installing such appliances;
- the landscape contractor who refuses the offer to perform certain excavation work in areas of underground piping or wiring; or
- the roller skating rink that goes out of business because it can obtain no insurance (see Exhibit 3-11).

An example of a more broadly defined exposure that may be avoided through abandonment is the firm that decides to go out of business because it does not have the financial resources either to meet federal and/or state environmental standards concerning pollution or contamination controls or to survive potentially catastrophic losses of the uninsurable type.

So, while avoidance is sometimes the proper method for handling narrowly defined aspects of a firm's premises and operations liability exposures, it is impossible to use it for all exposures if the firm wants to stay in business. To deal with the many important exposures that invariably remain, the firm must look to other methods and combinations of methods.

Loss Control Regardless of its size or the nature and scope of its operations, a firm always should take the initiative to adopt and administer a workable program of loss prevention and control.

Many premises liability hazards take the form of physical conditions in buildings, structures, and grounds, often due to poor maintenance of the premises. Examples of such hazards include sidewalks in need of repair, defective stairways, unmarked glass door panels, exposed floor plugs and wiring, poor lighting, insufficient means of

Exhibit 3-11

This roller skating rink went out of business when it could not obtain liability insurance.

—Photo by Kim Holston

access from buildings, sidewalks not properly and promptly cleared of ice and snow, signs and billboards weakened through weathering and not periodically inspected, and sidewalk canopies not raised during closing hours or during severe weather conditions. These and other hazards can be found and controlled by making sufficiently frequent inspections and timely corrections and repairs.

Since most structural hazards of premises are relatively fixed in time and place, they can be eliminated or controlled, in most cases, through the exercise of foresight and care. An auto repair shop, for example, may be able to reduce bodily injury claims emanating from accidents within its work areas by strictly enforcing rules that preclude access to customers within these areas. Or a commercial firm may be able to reduce or control certain liability losses by fencing its premises.

Less easy for firms to handle, generally speaking, are the liability exposures that arise out of business operations away from premises owned, maintained, or used by them, particularly those that stem from operations performed on premises of others. Whereas many hazards *on* the firm's own premises stem from defective conditions that usually can be sought out and corrected, hazards *away from* the firm's premises are actively created as work is performed, and, by their nature, these hazards are often more difficult to anticipate and control.

For instance, a manufacturing plant that is not open to the public may have little in the way of an on-premises liability exposure. But its operations away from these premises can produce a variety of costly losses, particularly since an employer is vicariously liable for its employees' negligent acts or omissions in the course of their employment.

Construction contractors, unlike those who operate predominately from fixed locations, may be confronted with somewhat different hazards at every location. Work in many instances is conducted in populated areas over which contractors have little control. A demolition contractor, for example, is not always permitted to disrupt the flow of traffic during its operations, in which case it should proceed with special caution and take care not to injure members of the public or to damage adjoining buildings or structures. An excavation contractor, on the other hand, should be careful to determine the location of underground hazards such as telephone cables and natural gas lines. It also should see that properly lighted barriers are installed to warn pedestrians and motorists of hazardous conditions.

In all likelihood, businesses will not establish programs of loss control solely for purposes of handling their premises and operations liability exposures. Well managed firms have loss control programs that encompass all facets of their liability exposures, including auto, products, completed operations, and workers' compensation exposures. In designing a comprehensive loss control program and pinpointing corrective measures that need to be taken, large firms rely primarily on their own staff specialists, while smaller firms rely primarily or entirely on advice from insurance agents, consultants and/or insurers. Yet, even the best designed loss control program will not produce results unless it is genuinely supported by top management, effectively communicated to all employees, and meaningfully enforced.

Transfer Businesses frequently have opportunities, under the terms of common business contracts, to transfer some part of their losses to others. Examples of such "noninsurance" transfers of "pure" premises and operations exposures include:

- the sale of a building or business or the employment of a subcontractor to perform a portion of a construction project; and
- a lessee (the firm that desires to occupy all or part of another's premises) who could sustain a loss caused by the lessor (property owner) nevertheless agrees in the lease to vindicate the lessor from blame.

Contractual Liability Loss Exposures

If defined broadly, a firm's "contractual liability" exposures would include all loss possibilities to which the firm is exposed by virtue of its enforceable obligations under written or oral contracts or agreements, including all losses the firm might incur as a result of its breach of a contract or its assumption of the tort liability of another party. This broad notion of contractual liability is not devoid of conceptual merit, but it is not what is customarily meant by contractual liability in the jargon of risk managers or insurance practitioners. The typical risk manager does not have the responsibility or authority for managing breach-of-contract exposures as such. And most insurers are not willing to provide insurance coverage for losses due solely to a breach of contract. Hence, risk managers and insurance practitioners frequently use the phrase "contractual liability" as a short-cut way of referring to the *insurable aspects* of contractual liability.

In forms providing insurance coverage for contractual liability exposures, the insurer usually intends to cover only that portion of a contract under which the insured has assumed the tort liability of another party to pay damages to a third person who is not a legal party to the contract. The coverage under some forms is further restricted to written contracts, contracts entered into prior to loss, specified classifications of contracts, and/or contracts that are designated and identified in the policy. While the language of widely used policy forms has not always been explicit or clear enough to avoid litigation and misunderstanding, the standardized contractual liability forms are not intended to cover an insured's liability for breach of contract or any contractual liability the other party may have to a third person. Instead, the intent is to cover only the insured's contractual *assumptions* of the *tort* liability of another party to the contract.

Avoidance Contractual liability exposures can be avoided by an entity only to the extent that it refuses to be a party to any contract under which it would be required to assume the tort liability of another party. Such a refusal might be advisable in situations where the entity's bargaining power is so superior that it can dictate the terms of a contract without losing valuable business to a competitor who does not object to the liability-assumption provision. Yet, in other situations it would not be advisable for the entity to risk losing an otherwise lucrative contract, especially when contractual liability insurance is available and the tax-deductible premium can either be absorbed by the entity or included in the price it charges for its products or services. This is indoubtedly one reason why the technique of avoiding contractual liability exposures is not more widely used than it is. Another reason is that a great many business contracts have already been executed by the time the risk manager or insurance adviser is aware of their existence. Thus, the contractual liability exposures cannot be avoided but must be insured, retained, and/or controlled.

Loss Control Contractual liability exposures can sometimes be reduced—or their potential impact lessened—by amending the terms of the contract(s) involved. Whether the terms of any hold harmless agreement can or should be amended in any given case depends upon the specific situation. As was pointed out earlier, a complex and ambiguously worded contract may be interpreted by a court in a way that is detrimental to either party to the contract. Likewise, a loss that exceeds the scope of any contractual liability insurance can place additional burdens on both parties, particularly when the party that assumes the contract terms is financially unable to handle the defense and the settlement of any such uninsured loss.

So, if a prospective transferee feels that a particular contract assumption provision is too much to handle, it is better to act on it early while the terms still stand a chance to be altered, instead of being forced to react when the harsh terms are enforced later. The possibility of amending the contract depends in part on the relative bargaining power of the parties involved. If the terms of a contract cannot be amended to more suitable conditions, the prospective indemnitor must then make a thorough assessment of the exposures involved to determine whether contract terms can be met if it ever becomes necessary. Of course, the economic profits to be gained under the contract must also be weighed against the probability of a loss because of the contract.

CONTROLLING MOTOR VEHICLE LIABILITY EXPOSURES

Mentioned throughout this chapter, a firm can choose among three types of control techniques in handling its loss exposures: (1) avoidance, (2) loss control, and (3) transfer. In dealing with its motor vehicle loss exposures, the firm faces the same options.

Avoidance

Although avoidance guarantees absolute safety from loss, few firms find avoidance practical. For example, a corporation that decides against the purchase of a subsidiary company whose operations utilize a large fleet of trucks operated on a competitive basis in a geographical area in which the corporation desires to expand avoids the chances of sustaining any losses as the owner of that subsidiary. However, that corporation also loses the opportunity to expand its operations and to obtain a better return on its investment.

Certain motor vehicle liability exposures nonetheless can be avoided in isolated cases. For example, a firm in the business of trucking goods of others on a local basis (within a fifty-mile radius of its principal place of business) may decide against the expansion of operations on a long-haul basis because of the stringent rules and regulations imposed by the Interstate Commerce Commission and the possibility of more serious losses. A firm in this situation may avoid certain hardships and losses stemming from accidents by not creating an interstate exposure in the first place, but this avoidance also reduces its chances for growth.

Loss Control

Loss control is the single most important technique for preventing and minimizing virtually all types of liability losses.

Of importance to a firm that embarks upon a loss control program for its motor vehicle liability loss exposures is the first stage wherein troublesome exposures are identified. Although poorly maintained vehicles, severe weather conditions, road conditions, and faults of other motorists can contribute to a firm's adverse loss experience, the annual statistics of the National Safety Council repeatedly show that motor vehicle losses are largely attributable to the human element, i.e., to the driving habits and ages of drivers (over 50 percent of all accidents in 1982 being caused by drivers of age twenty-nine and under).[38] Thus, when a firm begins identifying its principal sources of motor vehicle liability exposures, the firm that has records and statistics on the frequency and severity of its past losses is at an advantage because it may be able to predict losses likely to recur and identify employees who are more likely to become involved in accidents.

Whether or not these records of accident loss histories are available, a firm still has to screen new employee-drivers from the standpoint of their driving experience, as well as their past loss experience and moving traffic convictions. Motor vehicle reports (MVRs) can usually be obtained from the state licensing authority. The information on driver experience should be obtained whether employees simply park customers' autos in storage garages or drive owned passenger buses coast-to-coast.

When appropriate measures are taken to identify sources of frequent and/or severe motor vehicle losses and violations, the management of a firm is in a position to determine what has to be done to prevent and control losses. If any individual drivers have had a series of serious moving violations and/or accidents, it may be wise to replace those drivers. On the other hand, for drivers who have had few traffic violations and one or two minor accidents, it may be to the firm's advantage to require the drivers to attend special classes. It may even help if the firm requires its better drivers to attend driver safety classes merely as a preventive measure. Of course, when a firm is subject to ICC jurisdiction, the firm must comply with certain rules and regulations concerning qualifications of vehicles and operators. The ICC requires that drivers meet certain physical requirements and that drivers not be permitted to drive their vehicles longer than a certain specified number of hours in any day.

If a firm does not take corrective measures with problem drivers and does not monitor its program on a periodic basis to see if adjustments are necessary, the whole program of loss control may be in vain.

While this discussion of loss control as a technique for handling motor vehicle liability losses has dealt primarily with drivers, many of the points that have been made in these pages apply equally well to other employees who are in some way involved with motor vehicles. Thus, firms should formulate and enforce standard safe operating procedures for anyone who is in any way involved with motor vehicles. For example, material handlers who load and unload motor vehicles, as well as mechanics who have responsibility for maintaining vehicles, are just as important to a company's loss control program as its vehicle operators.

This emphasis on driver selection, training, supervision, and monitoring is not meant to diminish the importance of other measures such as the acquisition of safe vehicles, proper maintenance, and proper routing and scheduling. For example, drivers should not be required to meet a schedule that causes them to drive too fast or too long.

Transfers

An activity-producing exposure involving motor vehicles can be transferred when a firm sells out to another firm. The buyer is then confronted with the exposures that were once the seller's alone. On the other hand, a firm that decides to sell its fleet of owned autos for some reason, such as high maintenance and insurance costs or poor loss record, probably will not effect a transfer of an activity-producing exposure, because, in all likelihood, it may still be confronted with certain liability exposures stemming from the use of nonowned and/or hired motor vehicles.

CONCLUSION

Chapters 1 and 2 dealt with the nature of the liability exposure in general and with the legal liability exposures affecting a number of types of activities or operations. Chapter 3 has dealt with methods for identifying and analyzing these exposures and with the various control measures that can be used to deal with them. The remainder of this text deals primarily with means of financing losses that occur despite the controls. However, where necessary, further information on specific exposures and control measures will be integrated with the discussion of applicable types of insurance.

Chapter Notes

1. The basic risk management principles summarized here are developed in greater detail in the CPCU 1 text by C. Arthur Williams, Jr., George L. Head, Ronald C. Horn, and G. William Glendenning, *Principles of Risk Management and Insurance*, 2nd ed. (Malvern, PA: American Institute for Property and Liability Underwriters, 1981).
2. A. E. Pfaffle and Sal Nicosia, *Risk Analysis Guide to Insurance and Employer Benefits* (New York: Amacom, Division of American Management Association, 1977).
3. *Exposure Survey Questionnaire* (Dallas: International Risk Management Institute, Inc., 1985), p. iii.
4. William Rodda, James S. Trieschmann, Eric A. Wiening, and Bob A. Hedges, *Commercial Property Risk Management and Insurance*, vol. I, 2nd ed. (Malvern, PA: American Institute for Property and Liability Underwriters, 1982), pp. 37, 38.
5. A. Hawthorne Criddle, "The use of Financial Statements in Corporate Risk Analysis," *Identifying and Controlling the Risks of Accidental Loss, Management Report 73* (New York: American Management Association, 1962), p. 33.
6. Williams, Head, Horn, and Glendenning, vol. I, p. 157.
7. The example here relies on intuition to show that some exposures are more predictable than others, as indicated by a probability distribution. Ways of measuring this predictability are explained in CPCU 1.
8. Insurance data may relate the losses to the premiums instead of the number of exposure units, thus limiting their usefulness. Workers compensation and automobile liability insurance data, however, are available on a per exposure unit (per 100 employees or per vehicle) basis.
9. Phone conversation between author and Chao Wang, Biostatistician, Bureau of Labor Statistics, December 1984.
10. The report indicates the size of the sampling errors for most characteristics and industries and tells one how to use this information.
11. *Accident Facts* (Chicago: National Safety Council, 1983).
12. H. W. Heinrich, *Industrial Accident Prevention*, 4th ed. (New York: McGraw-Hill Book Co., 1959), pp. 14-16.
13. Dan Petersen, *Techniques of Safety Management* (New York: McGraw-Hill Book Co., 1971), pp. 12-16.
14. William Haddon, Jr., "Strategies to Reduce Damages from Environmental Hazards," *Status Report*, XV, No. 17 (21 November 1980, published by The Insurance Institute for Highway Safety).
15. Robert I. Mehr and Bob A. Hedges, *Risk Management: Concepts and Applications* (Homewood, IL: Richard D. Irwin, 1974), p. 426. Mehr and Hedges based their analysis on an earlier version of Haddon's theory.

198—Commercial Liability Risk Management and Insurance

16. Herbert W. Heinrich, *Industrial Accident Prevention*, 4th Ed. (New York: McGraw-Hill Book Co., 1959), pp. 50-52.
17. J. W. Grimaldi and R. H. Simonds, *Safety Management*, 3rd Ed. (Homewood, IL: Richard D. Irwin, Inc., 1975), pp. 397-404.
18. Gilbert Marshall, *Safety Engineering* (Monterey, CA: Brooks/Cole Engineering Division, 1982).
19. Marshall, pp. 45.
20. Marshall, pp. 42-43.
21. Marshall.
22. *Accident Prevention Manual for Industrial Operations: Administration and Programs*, 8th Ed. (Chicago: National Safety Council, 1981), pp. 63-64.
23. *Accident Prevention Manual*, p. 276.
24. "Carbide Appealing Record Fines," *Business Insurance*, April 7, 1986, pp. 1, 41.
25. Susan Alt, "Product Liability Costs Force Machine Builder to Liquidate Company," *Business Insurance*, 25 October, 1975, pp. 1, 2.
26. Gerald L. Maatman, "Interpret Product Safety As Profit, Bonus," *Business Insurance*, 8 December 1969, pp. 26, 34.
27. Maatman.
28. Paul C. Nelson, "Manufacturing Irregularities Often Crux of Product Cases: Attorney," *Business Insurance*, 30 June 1975, p. 3.
29. *Products Liability Reports*, Commerce Clearing House Inc., 1971, p. 4733.
30. *Products Liability Loss Prevention Manual*, Chicago: Alliance of American Insurers (formerly American Mutual Insurance Alliance), August 1976, pp. 11, 12.
31. Dennis D. Skogen, "Product Liability Claims Related to Automobile Accidents," p. 1.
32. "Product Safety Hearing Examines Seals, Advertising Claims," *Business Insurance*, 17 March 1969, p. 12.
33. *Products Liability Loss Prevention Manual*, pp. 20-22, 24-25.
34. *Products Liability Loss Prevention Manual*, pp. 20-22, 24-25.
35. Irwin Gray, "Product Liability Prevention," *Product Liability: A Management Response* (New York: AMACOM, 1975).
36. George Fisk and Rajan Chandran, "How to Trace and Recall Products," *Harvard Business Review*, November-December 1975, p. 91.
37. David L. Ramp, "The Impact of Recall Campaigns on Products Liability," *Insurance Counsel Journal*, January 1977, pp. 83-96.
38. Recordkeeping Key to Product Recall Program," *Business Insurance*, 30 June 1975, p. 3.
39. *Accident Facts*, p. 54.

CHAPTER 4

Liability Insurance Basics

This chapter is the first of many dealing directly with liability insurance policies. The purpose of this chapter is to provide the reader with (1) a set of questions to keep in mind when analyzing any commercial liability insurance policy, (2) the most common answers to those questions, and (3) some of the ramifications of the various possible answers.

The present chapter encompasses basic principles underlying all forms of commercial liability insurance, including auto liability, workers compensation and employers liability, and general liability insurance. Frequent references are made to standard policies of these types. However, discussion is by no means limited to the basic approaches of the standard forms. Alternative approaches and policies are also relevant.[1]

GENERAL CONTENT

All liability insurance policy provisions fit into one or more of six categories:

1. declarations,
2. insuring agreements,
3. exclusions,
4. conditions,
5. definitions, and
6. miscellaneous provisions.

Declarations

In some policies, notably the workers compensation policy, the declarations are known as the *information page.* The declarations are the part of the liability insurance contract that make it applicable to a specific situation by identifying the named insured(s) and describing the activity to be insured. The declarations also specify the policy number, the forms that are attached, the inception and expiration dates, the policy limits, the deductibles, if any, and the premium bases, rates, and premiums.

Insuring Agreements

Insuring agreements tell what the insurer agrees to do, subject to the declarations, conditions, exclusions, definitions, and other policy provisions. In other words, an insuring agreement generally provides a very broad statement of coverage that is narrowed by other policy provisions. They are conditional promises to pay. For example, when the insurer promises to pay sums that the insured becomes legally obligated to pay as damages because of bodily injury or property damage "to which this insurance applies," the meaning of the phrase "to which the insurance applies" is determined largely by policy provisions in other categories.

Exclusions

Exclusions state what the insurer does not intend to cover. The purpose of exclusions may be one or more of the following:

1. eliminate coverage the insurer considers uninsurable;
2. reduce the impact of moral and morale hazards;
3. eliminate coverage duplication;
4. eliminate coverage not needed by the typical insured;
5. eliminate coverages requiring special rating, underwriting, and/or reinsurance arrangements; and
6. lower the premium rate by limiting the events covered.

Though virtually all exclusions have the effect of reducing the premiums that would otherwise be required, some exclusions have premium reduction as their sole or primary purpose.

Conditions

Conditions have been defined as all the qualifications the insurer attaches to its promises. Many conditions deal with the insured's duties and rights following an insured event. Some deal with the insured's obligation to provide information needed for premium computations and the right of the insurer to inspect the premises and audit the named insured's books and records. Other conditions govern the insurer's rights and duties.

Definitions

Many words and phrases used in insurance policies are given a special meaning in the policies in question. Some policies use **boldface** type to distinguish words and phrases that are defined elsewhere in the policy. Other policies, including those recently introduced or revised by the Insurance Services Office (ISO), use quotation marks to offset defined words and phrases.

Many policies or forms contain a section titled *definitions*. Such a *definitions* section generally defines terms used throughout that policy or form. Sometimes a *definitions* section appears near the beginning of the policy to clarify terms that will be used. A *definitions* section may also appear at the end of the policy, where it forms a sort of glossary. Definitions also appear within certain sections of a policy, in which case they are usually located close to the place where the defined term is used.

Since many modern policies refer to the insurer as "we" and the named insured as "you," those pronouns are used extensively throughout the policy. These and pronouns such as "us," "our," and "your" are often defined in a preamble to the policy, rather than in a definitions section per se.

Miscellaneous Provisions

Miscellaneous provisions are provisions not included under the other categories. For example, a policy issued by a mutual insurer may state the date of the annual meeting and the right of the policyholder to cast a ballot.

Where These Provisions May Be Found

The contract itself may or may not be divided into parts bearing the preceding headings. In fact, policy provisions are often found under a seemingly unrelated heading.

To illustrate: A definition may contain an exclusion. The CGL provides liability coverage for losses arising out of the operation of mobile equipment, but the definition of mobile equipment does not encompass self-propelled vehicles with permanently attached street cleaning equipment. The portion of the definition that effectively precludes coverage for streetcleaners could be considered an exclusion.

As a further illustration, note that insuring agreements can sometimes be found within the exclusions section of a policy. Many such insuring agreements are worded as exceptions to exclusions. An example is provided in personal auto policies that contain an exclusion precluding coverage while the auto is used to carry persons or property for a fee, but then adding "this exclusion does not apply to a share-the-expense car pool." This exception to the exclusion is actually an insuring agreement, since it clearly states that there is coverage for vehicles used in nonprofit car pools—subject, of course, to other exclusions and conditions in the policy. (As noted in later chapters, such exceptions to exclusions are sometimes referred to as "coverages." For example, the above-mentioned exception might be referred to as "car pool coverage.")

POLICY CONSTRUCTION

Liability insurance policies can be (1) preprinted or (2) manuscript. They may also be (1) self-contained or (2) assembled by combining two or more parts.

Preprinted or Manuscript

- Preprinted contracts are ready-made documents prepared in volume by the insurer or by a rating bureau. Insureds may be able to select from among a number of preprinted contracts, but the contract is not prepared "from scratch" to meet the needs and desires of the individual insured.
- Manuscript contracts, usually typewritten or word-processed, are drafted jointly by the insurer, the producer, and the insured for one particular account with the insured's specific needs and desires in mind.

The most obvious distinction between preprinted and manuscript forms lies in the area of flexibility. Even though insurance forms are designed to be versatile enough to meet a broad range of needs of many different types of insureds, situations arise for which no ready-made form is available.

A less obvious ramification involves policy interpretations. Courts nearly always apply the *doctrine of adhesion* when interpreting a contract that has been drafted solely by one party to the contract. If a court believes a contract provision is ambiguous, the court will select the interpretation most favorable to the party who did not draft the contract. Preprinted policies are generally contracts of adhesion, drafted by the insurer and accepted or rejected by the insured. On the other hand, the insured has a hand in drafting manuscript policies. If there is a dispute over policy wording, the insured under such a manuscript policy cannot rely upon a court to interpret an ambiguity in the manner most favorable to the insured.

Self-contained or Assembled

Some liability insurance contracts, such as many professional liability contracts, are self-contained. Except for endorsements, which may modify the contract in some way but are not essential to complete the contract, the contract is a stand-alone document.

In contrast, many liability insurance policies are assembled by adding one or more declarations and coverage forms to a "jacket" or pages containing policy conditions that are common to a number of coverage forms. The policy may also contain endorsements that modify the basic contract. The commercial general liability insurance contract illustrates this approach and clarifies some of the terminology used in ISO's commercial lines simplification program.

- A *coverage part* consists of:
  - one or more *Line of Business Declarations*
  - one or more *coverage forms,* and
  - any applicable *endorsements.*
- It becomes a *monoline policy* (see Exhibit 4-1) with the attachment of:
  - *common policy declarations* (which may be combined with the Line of Business Declarations to make one form), and
  - *common policy conditions.*
- Or, the coverage part may become part of a *package policy* (see Exhibit 4-2) in combination with:
  - one or more other *coverage parts,*
  - a *common policy declarations,* and
  - a *common policy conditions.*[2]

A POLICY ANALYSIS FRAMEWORK

A systematic approach can be used to analyze any liability insurance contract. The following framework has been suggested: [3]

1. Who is insured against the losses covered by the contract?
2. What events are covered?
   a. What activities are covered?
   b. What causes of loss are covered?
   c. What loss consequences are covered?
   d. During what time period is coverage provided?

Exhibit 4-1
Commercial General Liability Policy*

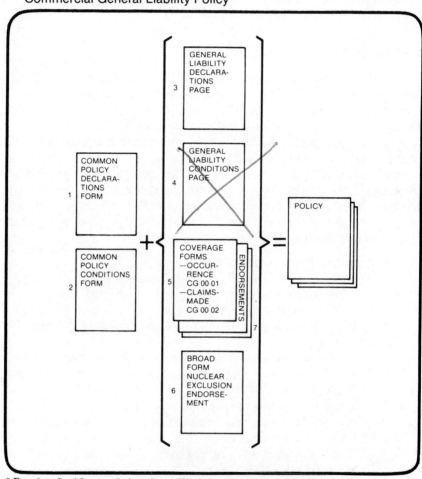

* Reprinted with permission, from *Workshop Leader's Guide,* ISO Commercial Lines
Policy and Rating Simplification Project© Insurance Services Office, 1985, p. 52.

    e. At what locations is coverage provided?

    f. Must any other conditions or circumstances not included in the above be present or not present for the loss to be covered?

3. If the event is covered, how much will the insurer pay?

4. What are the rights and responsibilities of the insured and the insurer following a loss?

The remainder of the chapter will examine the matter of how these questions are answered in various liability policies.

Exhibit 4-2
Contents of the Commercial Package Policy (CPP)*

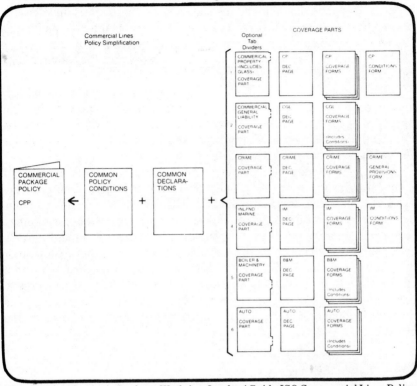

*Reprinted with permission from *Workshop Leaders' Guide*, ISO Commercial Lines Policy
and Rating Simplification Project, © Insurance Services Office, 1985, p. 52.

WHO IS INSURED?

Who is insured by any given liability insurance contract depends on
(1) who can have an insurable interest and (2) what interests are
insured under the specific provisions of the insurance policy in question.

Insurable Interests

While property insurers frequently deny claims made by persons
who do not have a legally recognized insurable interest, the lack of an
insurable interest is a problem that is not faced by liability insurers. A
person has an insurable interest in the occurrence of an event whenever
that person would suffer a financial loss as a result of that occurrence.
Liability insurance applies only to claims alleging that an insured under

the policy is legally liable for an occurrence that resulted in damages covered by the policy. Therefore, any claim that would come within the scope of a particular liability insurance policy inherently involves an occurrence in which an insured has a valid insurable interest, as long as the person against whom the claim was made was an insured under the policy at the time of a covered loss. This means that no liability claim can be denied for lack of an insurable interest as such.

If property such as an auto or a building is involved in the liability situation, the person need not have an insurable interest in that property to be insured for liability claims arising out of that property. For example, a person driving a borrowed car may be held responsible for negligent driving of that auto.

Any person may be held responsible for an unlimited amount of money for bodily injury or property damage to others. The practical exception is when the legal liability arises out of damage to some specific property. For example, bailees may be responsible for damage to specific property in their care, custody, or control. A tenant may be responsible for damage to the premises it occupies, and a contractor may be responsible for damage to a building under construction. As a practical matter the liability for loss to a specific item of property is limited to the cost of repairing or replacing that item of property, plus whatever dollar amount a court might award for loss of use of the property.

What Interests Are Insured?

Not all parties who have insurable interests in a given liability situation are necessarily covered under the same liability insurance policy. However, most liability insurance policies do cover more than one insured. The insureds are either (1) named insureds or (2) other insureds who have a specific relationship to named insureds.

Named Insureds Named insureds are those who are listed by name in the relevant block of the policy declaration. Although the named insured is commonly one person, partnership, corporation, government body, or other entity with a liability insurable interest, multiple named insureds may be listed. Many simplified language policies subsequently refer to the named insured(s) as "you."

Named insureds typically receive broader liability insurance protection under the contract than most other insureds. For example, under a business auto coverage form, the named insured may be protected against a liability suit involving the operation of owned or other insured types of vehicles by either the named insured or another insured. Other insureds are protected only against liability arising out of their operation of insured vehicles, not against liability arising out of the operation of their own vehicles.

First Named Insured. According to explicit provisions in some policies—notably the latest editions of the ISO commercial policies and the NCCI workers compensation and employers liability policy—the *first named insured* (the first "named insured" listed in the declarations) has some special rights and duties. Basically, the first named insured acts as the legal agent for all named insureds in initiating cancellation, receiving notice of cancellation, requesting policy changes, and accepting any return premiums; the first named insured is also responsible, in some forms, for the payment of premiums.

Regardless of the sequence of names in other documents pertaining to a business, the liability insurance policy should name first the individual or organization who handles insurance transactions.

Other Insureds The other insureds covered under a liability insurance policy are identified by class, not by name. The covered classes are based on specified relationships to the named insured. Some of these insureds are *separate* insureds; others are acceptable legal *substitutes* for the named insured.

Depending in part on whether the named insured is an individual or a business organization, the separate insureds may include the insured's spouse, members of the insured's family, the insured's employees, the insured's employers, persons who manage the insured's real property, operators of the insured's vehicles, anyone else responsible for the use of those vehicles, and others described in the policy. Normally an auto liability policy covers more classes of persons than a general liability policy.

Possible substitute insureds are legal representatives such as executors, administrators, and receivers in bankruptcy proceedings; the insured's personal legal representatives; and the insured's heirs. Because these other insureds are substitutes for the named insured, they receive the same protection as the named insured but only in their capacity as a substitute. For example, an executor would have liability protection for a claim arising on premises that are part of the insured's estate, but would not have coverage for personal or business activities unrelated to the estate.

WHAT EVENTS ARE COVERED?

As noted earlier, what events are covered depends upon what activities, causes of loss, loss consequences, locations, and time periods are covered.

Covered Activities

Every liability insurance policy provides coverage for only certain activities or sources of liability. Two approaches are possible:

- Comprehensive liability insurance covers all activities or sources of liability that are not specifically excluded.
- Specific liability insurance contracts state the activity or source of liability that is covered.

The comprehensive approach is analogous to "all-risks" or "special" property insurance policies, except that these property policies cover all perils, rather than all activities, that are not specifically excluded. Specific liability insurance contracts are likewise comparable to specified perils, (or specified causes of loss) property insurance policies.

The commercial general liability policy is one example of the comprehensive approach. The insuring agreement does not list the activities or sources of liability that are covered, but uses the phrase "to which this insurance applies." However, exclusions and other policy provisions restrict or eliminate coverage for activities to which the policy is not intended to apply. For example, coverage is excluded for losses that can be covered by business auto liability insurance or workers compensation insurance.

An example of the specific approach is an aircraft liability coverage, which promises to pay damages arising out of the ownership, maintenance, or use of aircraft.

The word "comprehensive" used to appear in policy names, such as the "comprehensive general liability policy" and the "comprehensive auto liability policy." The names of these policies have been changed, for much the same reason that the phrase "all-risks" has been dropped from most property insurance policies. The term "comprehensive" implies coverage of such an all-encompassing nature that insureds and courts might overlook the fact that even very broad insurance policies contain exclusions.

The activities specified in these contracts are, of course, also subject to exclusions. Some excluded exposures can be covered by other forms of insurance or by endorsements.

Covered Causes

The causes covered under liability insurance policies are the liabilities imposed upon the insured and arising out of covered activities or sources of liability. As noted in previous chapters, tort liability may be (1) imposed by common law, (2) imposed by statute, or (3) assumed under a private contract. The coverage of liability policies also depends partly on whether the wrongful act or omission is (1) a breach of contract or (2) a particular kind of tort.

Common Law, Statutes, or Contracts Liability insurance policies do not protect insureds against liability for criminal activities. To do so would be against public policy. Liability for civil actions may be covered whether the obligation arises out of common law, statute, or contract. However, coverage is often restricted in one of two ways.

1. *The policy may limit the coverage to a specific kind of statute or a specific kind of contract.* For example, the promise to pay workers compensation claims (not the promise to pay employers liability claims) under the standard workers compensation and employers liability policy is a promise to protect the employer against statutory legal obligations under applicable workers compensation acts. The personal injury protection (no-fault) endorsement to an auto insurance policy covers the insured only against statutory obligations under a particular state's no-fault automobile law. Contractual liability insurance protects the insured only against tort liability assumed under contract.
2. *The policy may specifically exclude one or more types of liability.* Contractual liability is commonly excluded under various liability insurance contract. Obligations under workers compensation statutes or state temporary disability insurance legislation are also commonly excluded from general liability insurance because these obligations are covered under separate contracts. As will be explained shortly, some common-law liabilities may be excluded under the policy, to clarify the insuring agreements.

Breach of Contract Standard *general* liability insurance policies do *not* provide coverage for an insured's breach of a contract. For example, an insured may fail to honor its contractual obligations under an enforceable lease, a construction contract, or a sales agreement. Breaches of such contractual obligations are viewed by most insurers as uninsurable "business risks." Even when so-called contractual liability insurance is purchased, it applies only to an insured's contractual assumption of the *tort* liability that another party may have to a third person.

Products liability insurance forms do provide coverage when at least one of the claimant's allegations is that an insured breached an express or implied warranty and the claimant suffered bodily injury and/or property damage as a proximate result of the breach. Whether the courts treat such a breach as a tort or a breach of contract, it is a covered cause of loss under all products liability forms. Only in this limited sense is it customary for insurers to provide coverage for breach-of-contract actions.

Torts As previously explained, tort liability may be imposed on the grounds of (1) negligence, (2) strict liability, or (3) intentional interference. While all three grounds are generally insurable, the extent to which specific kinds of torts are covered depends on the policy. The methods of providing the tort coverage also may vary from one policy to another.

Negligence. The tort of negligence is a covered cause of loss under *all standard* policies providing tort liability coverage. Many liability policies also provide coverages that are not preconditioned on a finding of tort liability. For example, coverages such as medical payments, auto physical damage, and workers compensation are provided without regard to whether an insured may have been negligent. Even so, under all tort-based portions of all liability policies, negligence is among the covered torts.

The word negligence is not specifically mentioned in the policies. It is quite clearly a covered tort, nonetheless, because (1) it is not excluded and (2) it is conduct for which an insured may be legally obligated to pay damages to others for bodily injury or property damage caused by an accident or an occurrence, according to the definitions of the policy and the legal meaning of damages.

Two policies that illustrate how negligence is covered without being specifically mentioned are as follows. Under the business auto coverage form the insurer agrees to:

> pay all sums the "insured" legally must pay as damages because of "bodily injury" or "property damage" to which this insurance applies, caused by an "accident" and resulting from the ownership, maintenance or use of a covered "auto."

Under the ISO commercial general liability coverage form the insurer promises to:

> pay those sums that the insured becomes legally obligated to pay as damages because of "bodily injury" or "property damage" to which this insurance applied ....The "bodily injury" or "property damage" must be caused by an "occurrence."

"Occurrence" is defined elsewhere in the policy as:

> an accident, including continuous or repeated exposures to substantially the same general harmful conditions.

Notice that the policy language is deliberately broad enough to cover the vicarious liability an insured may have for the negligence of another, as well as its direct liability for its own negligence. Both direct and vicarious liability are also covered in policies providing strict liability coverage.

Strict Liability. As a general rule, an insured under a commercial liability insurance policy has coverage for strict liability in tort, whether direct or vicarious, to the extent that the *activity* giving rise to strict liability is a covered activity under the policy or form in question. Stated another way, a commercial entity may insure most of its strict liability exposures by purchasing the policies and forms that cover the activities for which strict liability may be imposed on the kind of commercial entity in question. While these activities are customarily referred to as "hazards" in some insurance policies and rating manuals, they are not necessarily hazardous conditions to a particular buyer. They are activities or groups of activities that are distinguishable from other activities, from the viewpoint of insurers, for the purpose of rating, underwriting, and policy design.

Examples of strict liability exposures that can be insured under specific policies or forms (subject to all applicable exclusions, conditions, and definitions thereof) are as follows:

- Strict liability that may be imposed on sellers of products can be insured only under forms covering the products hazard or the "products-completed operations hazard."
- Strict liability under workers compensation statutes can be insured only under the standard workers compensation policy (or its nonstandard equivalent).
- Strict liability that may be imposed upon a possessor of land for ultrahazardous activities or abnormally dangerous instrumentalities can be insured only under forms covering the premises hazard.
- Contractual assumptions of the strict liability that another party may have to a third person can be insured only under forms covering the contractual liability hazard.
- The vicarious liability an insured entity may have for the negligence of another is a form of strict liability that is automatically insured under all forms covering negligence.
- Strict liability under "dram shop" laws can be insured only under forms providing liquor liability coverage.
- Strict liability for acts of pollution can be insured, to some extent, under pollution liability forms or policies, but only for accidental pollution.

Intentional Interference Torts. As a general rule, most commercial entities are now able to purchase liability insurance coverage for at least some of the major torts in the intentional interference category. This was not true in the earlier days of liability insurance. To understand the initial reluctance of insurers and the modern restrictions on the availability and nature of intentional interference coverage, one needs to know a little about the history of its development.

The earliest casualty insurers had gained experience in writing first-party insurance for persons who negligently or otherwise sustained bodily injury as a result of railroad and auto accidents. Likewise, fire insurers had profitably written fire insurance, even though many fires were the result of the negligence of an insured or a third party. As the demand for third-party liability insurance began to emerge, it was not such a drastic step to cover accidental bodily injury and property damage caused by an insured's negligence. Even if the negligent act or omission is conscious or deliberate, the resulting injury to others is accidental, It is therefore the kind of "fortuitous" event considered insurable, then and today.

In contrast, an intentional act like assault and battery is not fortuitous from the standpoint of the person committing the act. If persons who secretly planned to commit such acts (or knew of their own propensity to do so) were given the free and unfettered choice, they could easily select against the insurer. In recognition of this "adverse selection" potential, standard liability forms routinely excluded from coverage any damages resulting from intentional acts committed by or at the direction of an insured.

An optional endorsement was ultimately developed to provide so-called "personal injury" coverage—a term selected because most of the package of covered torts did not cover *bodily* injury per se. However, as recently as the early 1970s, "personal injury" was viewed by many insurers as a coverage that could be granted only after careful underwriting evaluation of the specific exposures involved in each individual case.

To the surprise of some observers, personal injury coverage did not generate an avalanche of claims. During the mid-1970s, insurers included "personal injury" coverage in the package of other broadening coverages routinely offered in a broad form comprehensive general liability endorsement. In many instances these broadening coverages were added to commercial liability insurance policies without any specific underwriting of the personal injury hazard. Apparently personal injury coverage has not been a problem for insurers, despite the nature of intentional interference torts that are covered. Practically speaking, it is doubtful whether accurate information on "personal injury claims" is available, since aggregate general liability claims data do not distinguish among most of the various "hazards" or "coverages" that give rise to claims. (An exception is products liability claims, for which separate data are required to be reported to regulatory authorities.)

Today, personal injury coverage is a standard part of the package of liability coverage offered to most commercial insurance buyers. One of the major changes in the 1986 ISO commercial general liability insurance contract (to be examined in Chapter 5) is the inclusion in the basic policy of a coverage titled "Personal and Advertising Injury Liability."

- Personal injury liability is covered if it arises out of one or more of the following offenses: (1) false arrest, detention, or imprisonment; (2) malicious prosecution; (3) wrongful entry into or eviction of a person from premises occupied by the person; or (4) oral or written publication of material that slanders or libels some person or violates that person's right of privacy.
- Advertising injury liability is covered if it arises out of (1) oral or written publication of material that slanders or libels some person or violates his or her privacy rights, (2) misappropriation of advertising ideas or style of doing business, or (3) infringement of a copyright, title, or slogan.

Under both personal injury and advertising injury, the insurer is not responsible if the insured knows that the oral or written information is false or if the injury arises out of the willful violation of a penal statute or ordinance committed by or with the consent of the insured.

Some business firms may not be able to obtain primary coverage for all of the intentional interference torts that they desire to insure. They may even experience difficulty obtaining excess or umbrella coverage for certain types of torts. For example, some basic forms do not provide coverage for such intentional interference torts as assault and battery, conversion, trespass, and some of the specific torts in the general category of wrongful interference with a business relationship. Furthermore, some publishers are known to have had an unusually large number of libel actions brought against them in the past. Such publishers have found that they cannot obtain coverage for defamation torts or cannot obtain coverage for any torts in the available intentional interference packages.

Covered Loss Consequences

If a person faces the potential of a liability claim, the possible financial consequences are not limited to the payment of damages that may be the result of an out-of-court settlement or a tort lawsuit. Regardless of whether he or she is ultimately held responsible, if not insured, that person will also incur various expenses defending himself or herself and otherwise investigating the situation. Under a liability insurance policy the insurer agrees to pay at least part of the costs of defending the insured and investigating the claim, and also to pay the out-of-court settlement or statutory or court award. The insurer's promise is, of course, conditioned upon the person being a covered insured, the event being a covered event, and the damages and expenses within the dollar limits imposed upon its obligations. The insurer's obligation is not limited to claims that result in decisions against the insured. Indeed, the insurer agrees to defend and investigate any claim that would otherwise be covered, even if the allegations of the suit are groundless, false, or fraudulent.

Damages As more thoroughly explained in Chapter 1, damages can be divided into two broad categories: (1) compensatory and (2) punitive. Compensatory damages are covered under all liability insurance policies. Variations exist in the coverage of punitive damages. The three possibilities are that punitive damages are (1) excluded, and (2) not mentioned, or (3) specifically covered.

In some states, insurers are prohibited from paying punitive damages. The insurance policy might not limit the insurer's payments of these damages, but the state law does. In theory, punitive damages are assessed only for willful and wanton misconduct or for gross negligence, and these states reason that the insureds should themselves bear the financial penalties that are assessed because of such serious misconduct. To permit insurance coverage of punitive damages would shelter these insureds against financial consequences of their acts that they should not be able to transfer to someone else. Furthermore, forcing insureds to pay punitive damages reduces the likelihood of socially undesirable conduct.

In other states insurers have, through policy language, tried to eliminate payments for punitive damages. Their reason for seeking this relief was that during the seventies and eighties courts began to award punitive damages in a larger proportion of tort cases. Consequently, insurers found that their punitive damage payments were becoming much larger than the allowances they had included or wanted to include in their rates for these extra awards. Although a few states approved insurers' requests to exclude coverage for punitive damages, most did not. Many insureds strongly opposed the elimination of punitive damage coverage for two reasons. First, they argued that payment of punitive damages was not socially undesirable in most cases because courts were actually awarding such damages in cases involving only ordinary negligence. Second, insurers were eliminating punitive damage coverage without any corresponding rate reduction. Responding to this opposition, insurers withdrew the policy language excluding punitive damages from almost all, if not all, liability insurance policies.

The usual procedure—in states that prohibit payments for punitive damages as well as those that do not—is for the policy to promise to pay damages with no specific reference to special, general, or punitive damages. Hence, all three types are paid unless the law in a given state prohibits insurers from paying punitive damages.

Defense Costs and Other Related Benefits   In addition to paying damages, all liability insurance policies obligate the insurer to pay the cost of defending the insured and providing other related benefits. For example, the business auto coverage form states that the insurer will defend any suit asking for damages. It also agrees to pay for the insured:

1. All expenses incurred by the insurer.
2. Up to $250 for cost of bail bonds (including bonds for related traffic law violations) required because of a covered accident. The insurer does not, however, have to furnish the bonds.
3. Premiums on bonds to release attachments in a suit it defends but only for bonds up to its limit of liability.
4. All costs taxed to the insured in a suit the insurer defends.
5. All interest accruing after the entry of the judgment in a suit it defends. Its duty to pay interest, however, ends when it pays or tenders an amount equal to its limit of liability.
6. Up to $100 a day for loss of earnings because of time off from work because the insured attends hearings or trials or expends other time at the insurer's request.
7. Other reasonable expenses the insured incurs at the insurer's request.

Similarly, under the ISO commercial general liability coverage form, the insurer acknowledges its right and duty to defend any suit seeking the covered damages. It also promises to pay for the insured the seven items noted above. In addition, the commercial general liability policy obligates the insurer to pay pre-judgment interest awarded against the insured on any judgment paid by the insurer. *Pre-judgment interest* is an amount intended to compensate the claimant for interest that could have been earned on the sum awarded if payment had been made at the time of the covered occurrence, rather than at the time of judgment—which might be years later in the event of a "long-tail" claim. In cases where the insurer offers to pay the applicable limit of insurance to the claimant, the insurance policy states that the insurer will not pay any pre-judgment interest based on time that elapses after the offer is made. Further delays in such circumstances are caused by the insured, the claimant, or other parties.

Most liability policies state that the insurer's right and duty to defend the suit end when the insurer has used up the applicable limit of insurance in the payment of judgments or settlements.

Locations at Which Coverage Is Provided

Liability insurance policies cover activities occurring in a broadly defined location ranging from, say, the United States and Canada to anywhere in the world (and possible in outer space), subject to some exclusions.

For example, the business auto coverage form covers accidents and losses that occur in the United States, its territories or possessions, Puerto Rico, and Canada. The "coverage territory" under the new ISO commercial general liability coverage form is broader. Specifically, this territory includes:

1. the United States, its territories and possessions, Puerto Rico, and Canada;
2. International waters or airspace, provided the injury or damage does not occur in the course of travel or transportation to or from any place not included in 1; or
3. All parts of the world if
    a. the injury or damage arises out of
        (1) goods or products made or sold by the insured in the territory described in 1, or
        (2) the activities of a person whose home is in the territory described in 1 but is away for a short time on the insured's business, and
    b. the insured's responsibility to pay damages is determined in a suit on the merits in the territory described in 1 above or in a settlement the insurer agrees to.

Umbrella liability policies generally provide worldwide coverage, or coverage anywhere—including outer space and other planets.

Covered Time Periods

The time period covered has become extremely important in determining whether a particular event is insured under a liability insurance policy. In addition to the policy term and cancellation provisions, the covered time period depends upon whether the policy is written on an occurrence or a claims-made basis.

Policy Term Liability insurance policies usually have a term of one year, but shorter (for example, six months) or longer (for example, three years) term policies also exist. If the policy is written for a term of longer than one year, the insured usually pays the premium in annual installments with rate changes being permitted on each installment date. (Various alternative payment approaches are discussed in Chapter 14.) A one-year policy starts on a specified date at 12:01 A.M. standard time at the named insured's address stated in the declarations and ends at 12:01 A.M. standard time on the same date the next year. Note that the change to daylight time is to be ignored in determining the starting and ending times and dates. Note also that if the covered event occurs in some time zone other than the zone for the specified named insured's address, coverage is determined by the time at the named insured's stated address.

Cancellation Coverage may be cut shorter than the policy term if either the insurer or the insured elects to cancel the contract. A typical liability insurance cancellation provision permits the insurer to initiate cancellation of the contract by mailing to the named insured notice of its intent, at least ten days prior to the effective date of the cancellation. Common-law interpretations of this provision are that the ten day period begins at 12:01 A.M. of the day the insured receives the notice of cancellation. To protect itself against failure of the insured to receive the notice the insurer typically takes several steps. First, the policy generally states that the notice is to be mailed to the last address known by the insurer. Second, the policy usually says that "proof of mailing" of any notice will be sufficient proof of notice. Third, insurers often send the cancellation notice by registered or certified mail with a return receipt requested.

The common policy conditions of the ISO commercial policies state that notice of cancellation will be mailed or delivered to the "first Named Insured's last mailing address known to us." This underscores the importance of determining which named insured should be listed first in the policy declarations.

Even when an insurance policy gives the insurer a right to cancel coverage at any time after giving proper notice, state statutes or regulations often restrict this right. During the 1980s a number of states specifically restricted insurers' ability to cancel or nonrenew coverage in response to a tightening insurance marketplace that threatened many businesses with the potential loss of essential insurance coverage. Even before then, nearly all states had statutes restricting an auto insurer's right to cancel.

If the insurer cancels the policy, it need not give any reason for this action to comply with the terms of the insurance policy. It must, however, return a pro rata portion of the premium. For example, if the premium is $50,000 and the policy is canceled after one quarter of the time has expired, the insurer must return to the insured three quarters of the premium, or $37,500. This pro rata return penalizes the insurer because it will already have incurred most of the expenses (not losses) it expected to incur during the policy period.

The insured (in ISO's commercial policies, only the first named insured) may also cancel the contract. It must give the insurer advance notice of the cancellation, but the cancellation can become effective as soon as the insurer receives the notice. The notice may be given orally or in writing; no reason need be given for the cancellation. The insured is entitled to a premium refund, but the refund may be less than a pro rata return. The refund may be determined by a short-rate procedure that recognizes the expenses the insurer has already incurred relative to its expectations for the term and some extra costs associated with the cancellation itself.

Trigger How coverage is triggered is a crucial question. The two major approaches are "occurrence" and "claims-made" triggers.

Occurrence policies replaced earlier "accident" policies. Under accident policies the coverage trigger was an accident. If the bodily injury or property damage arose from an accident and occurred when the policy was in effect, the injury or damage is covered—even if the negligent act that caused the accident occurred prior to the effective date or some consequences of the accident occurred after the termination date. For example, under an auto policy written on this basis, the insured could have neglected to have his brakes fixed for months prior to the accident, the brakes could fail causing a collision with another car during the policy period, and the occupants of the other car could incur most of their medical expenses, wage loss, and pain and suffering after the policy expired. The insurer whose policy was in force at the time of the accident would defend the insured against suits arising out of this accident and, subject to the policy limits, pay the out-of-court settlements or court awards.

As long as events occur suddenly, the accident approach provides the necessary protection. For some liability exposures—such as those arising out of the ownership, maintenance, or use of autos—most insured events are sudden. (During the past two or three decades, however, courts have increasingly held businesses liable for damages caused not by a sudden event but by continuous or repeated acts that, over time, cause bodily injury or property damage to others.) Many courts, however, held that because these continuous or repeated acts were not "sudden" events, they were not covered under accident-based policies.

To broaden the coverage to meet this changing legal environment, insurers replaced most accident liability insurance policies with "occurrence" policies. The insurer agreed to pay on behalf of the insured all sums that the insured shall become legally obligated to pay as damages because of bodily injury or property damage, to which this insurance applies, caused by an "occurrence." "Occurrence" was defined as "an accident, including continuous or repeated exposure to conditions, which results in bodily injury or property damage neither expected nor intended from the viewpoint of the insured."

- *Bodily injury* means bodily injury, sickness, or disease sustained by any person which occurs during the policy period, including death at any time resulting therefrom.
- *Property damage* means (1) physical injury to or destruction of tangible property which occurs during the policy period, including the loss of use thereof at any time resulting therefrom, or (2) loss of use of tangible property which has not been physically injured or destroyed provided such loss of use is caused by an occurrence during the policy period.

In other words, for an event to be covered during the policy period, the bodily injury or the property damage must occur during the policy period. For sudden events, the accident and the occurrence of the bodily injury or property damage are likely to happen almost simultaneously. For nonsudden events, however, coverage trigger can be highly significant, especially with respect to latent diseases.

Partly because of the development of new drugs and toxic substances and partly because of the improved ability of medical service to prove that current diseases are related to past long-term exposures, businesses have become increasingly responsible for the latent diseases incurred by their customers, employees, and others. Asbestosis is a case in point. Asbestos manufacturers and installers have been held responsible for bodily injury to many victims of asbestosis. With latent diseases like asbestosis, it is not clear when the bodily injury "occurs." If a business purchased insurance from Insurer A the first five years and Insurer B the next ten years, the date the bodily injury occurred determines which insurer is obligated to pay the loss. If it is determined that injury occurred over time, both insurers may be liable. In addition to its obvious relevance to insurers, the question, "When did bodily injury 'occur'?" can be highly relevant to the insured, if liability insurance policy limits were higher during some years than others. This is often the case; since there has been a trend toward higher liability limits over the years, the more recent policies usually have higher limits.

In interpreting the trigger definition, some courts say the bodily injury occurs when it becomes "manifest." Others argue that the injury occurs when the injured party is first "exposed" to the drug or toxic substance. Although the *manifestation* and *exposure* theories have attracted a lot of attention, others have also been suggested. For example, a third doctrine would hold all insurers responsible who had policies in effect from the time the claimant was exposed to a toxic substance until the claim for the injury is made. How the insurers should share the responsibility has also been the subject of considerable debate.

Because the events that trigger auto liability insurance policies are usually referred to as "auto accidents," auto policies state that they pay for bodily injury or property damage caused by an auto accident. In the business auto coverage form, accident is defined to include continuous or repeated exposure to the same conditions.

The "occurrence" version of the ISO commercial general liability coverage form continues the position that the trigger is the occurrence of a bodily injury or property damage caused by an accident including continuous or repeated exposures to substantially the same general harmful conditions.

Policies covering personal injury liability arising out of specified intentional torts resemble the old accident policies in that the offense must be committed during the policy period, a concept that will be clarified in Chapter 6.

Insurers have encountered many problems with occurrence policies. Pricing these policies, in their view, has become extremely difficult, if not impossible. The reasons have been stated as follows by representatives of the Insurance Services Office:[4]

1. Litigation ... has been costly and time consuming. For the most part such litigation ... has centered on latent bodily injury and long-term exposure issues involving substances such as asbestos and DES. A key issue in dispute is: When did the injury or damage occur? That's extremely important in the context of insurance because the answer determines which "occurrence" policy or policies apply. Litigation over that question is likely to affect more and more insureds of all sizes in all types of business, as new cases arise where the time when bodily injury or property damage occurred is at issue.

2. Some courts have adopted legal theories in latent-injury or long-term exposure cases, which hold that injury occurred during a long series of "occurrence" policies. That leaves many contracts—and sometimes many insurers—with primary defense and indemnity obligations for a single claim. Often, such situations arise when there are many claims for similar or related injury. As a result, insurers do not know how much is at stake, and for how long, under these contracts. That makes it difficult to determine accurate premiums and loss reserves. And beyond that, such

"stacking" of limits poses a serious threat to the very solvency of some insurers . . . .

3. [Under the pre-1986 occurrence policy] the only limit that applies to some parts of the coverage is a per-occurrence limit so that the insurer's limit for injury that occurs during the policy period increases with the number of "occurrences" held to have produced the injury. That liability could be astronomical depending on how courts interpret the term "occurrence." "Stacking" per-occurrence limits within a single policy further threatens insurance availability and insurer solvency.

Not only insurers, but also insureds also have encountered some difficulties with "occurrence" policies. Again in the words of ISO spokespersons:

Many insureds have to rely on policy limits provided by old "occurrence" policies to respond to current claims, because the injury or damage may have occurred long before the claim is made. These old policies may have been purchased many, many years before claims emerge; settlements are reached and judgments rendered—and years before inflation eroded the value of the old policies' limits.

This lag between the date of occurrence and the date of the claim also complicates insurance company pricing and reserving.

Workers compensation policies handle some of these problems by stating that bodily injury or disease must be caused or aggravated by the conditions of the employment provided by the employer. The employee's last day of last exposure to the conditions causing or aggravating such bodily injury or disease must occur during the policy period. State laws typically state how the responsibility for so-called "second injuries" will be shared among employers.

Liability insurers see "claims-made" policies as a potential solution to these problems. The basic idea of claims-made is that the insurer is responsible only for claims made during the policy period, regardless of when the injury or damage took place. For example, suppose Policy A is in effect throughout calendar year 19X1, Policy B is in effect throughout 19X2, and Policy C is in effect through 19X3. For Policy A to cover a loss, the claim must be made during 19X1. For Policy B to cover a loss, the claim must be made during 19X2. Likewise, claims made during 19X3 are covered only by Policy C, and so on.

Few, if any, claims-made policies are as simple as suggested by the basic idea depicted above. Many claims-made policies have a *retroactive date*. For coverage to apply, the injury or damage must have occurred after the retroactive date (*and*, of course, the claim must be made during the policy term). The basic reasons behind a retroactive date are that most insureds purchasing a claims-made policy have previously been insured on an occurrence policy, that the retroactive date is set to coincide with the inception date of the first claims-made policy, and that same retroactive date will be kept on all future claims-made policies. To illustrate, suppose Policy A, an insured's first claims-made policy, replacing occurrence-basis coverage, goes into effect on January 1, 19X1 and also bears a retroactive date of January 1, 19X1. The occurrence policy covers claims made at any time, including during 19X1 and future years, for injury or damage that took place while that occurrence policy was in force. The new claims-made policy is therefore not needed to cover claims that might be made for injury or damage that occurred while a previous occurrence-basis policy was in force. (The claims-made policy might, however, in the absence of a retroactive date, provide higher limits for claims based on earlier injury or damage.)

Assuming the retroactive dates on Policy B, effective throughout 19X2, and Policy C, effective during 19X3, are also January 1, 19X1, then

- Policy B provides coverage for claims made during 19X2 based on injury or damage that occurred on or after January 1, 19X1, and
- Policy C provides coverage for claims made during 19X3 based on injury or damage that occurred on or after January 1, 19X1.

and so forth.

According to ISO the three major advantages of claims-made forms are as follows:

1. "The claims-made version of the new policy form reduces arguments and expensive litigation over which policy responds to a particular claim for injury or damage. By responding to claims first made during the policy term, the 'claims-made' version generally makes it unnecessary to determine when injury or damage occurred." This ISO argument assumes the original retroactive date is not advanced.
2. "With 'claims-made', *today's* claims are covered by *today's* policy with up-to-date not out-of-date limits of insurance." This feature of claims-made policies also enables insureds to purchase policy limits reflecting the current economic and legal environment.
3. "The 'claims-made version of the policy form reduces the potential under legal theories for stacking the limits of several policies in long-term exposure or latent-injury cases. The 'claims-made' form is designed to have one and only one precisely identified policy respond to a claim for covered injury or damage. 'Claims-made' introduces greater certainty and continuity into claims-handling and improves the accuracy of

rates and loss reserves while covering exactly the same kinds of injury and damage as the 'occurrence' alternative."

The major disadvantage of a claims-made form is that if either the insured or the insurer cancels or does not renew the policy, the insured would have no coverage against claims made after the cancellation or non-renewal date for injuries or damage that occurred prior to that date. A similar problem arises if, upon renewing a policy, the retroactive date is advanced closer to the inception date of the renewal period.

To counter this disadvantage claims-made forms often contain provisions extending the time period during which claims can be reported or guaranteeing the availability of a "tail" endorsement which the insured can elect to purchase when the claims-made policy expires. Several such provisions are found in the ISO commercial general liability (CGL) policy; these will be explained in detail in Chapter 6.

Other criticisms that have been levied against claims-made forms include the following:

- The insurer might change the retroactive date upon each policy renewal.
- The claims-made form is difficult to understand and to explain to insureds.
- The contract reduces insurers' uncertainties by reducing the coverage, and therefore increasing the insureds' uncertainties.
- The policy will encourage insureds to solicit the filing of claims before the policy expires.[5]

A variety of steps have been taken to address these issues, as detailed in Chapter 6.

HOW MUCH WILL THE INSURER PAY?

If the person and the event is covered under a liability insurance policy, how much will the insurer pay? The major policy provisions that answer this question are the policy limit or limits. The insurer's net payment may also be affected by deductibles, other insurance, and subrogation provisions.

Policy Limit or Limits

Several policy limits, or sets of policy limits, may be found in a single policy. Policy limits state the maximum obligation of the insurer. The functions of policy limits can be summarized briefly under four headings.

1. Policy limits clarify the insurer's obligations. Without policy limits the insurer might be exposed to large infrequent losses that are difficult to predict, even on the average. In liability insurance the policy limits often affect (though in principle they should not) awards or settlements. It is sometimes stated that without policy limits claims payments might be much larger. On the other hand, since there can be a tendency to "go for the limit" when making a claim or settlement, there may be cases where payments would actually be lower without policy limits.

2. A related function of policy limits is that they help the actuary achieve the goals of adequacy, reasonableness, and equity. Because policy limits make loss predictions more reliable, the price structure is less likely to be too high or too low. When the actuary is able to confidently predict future losses for groups of insureds, the price structure is also more likely to treat insureds equitably.

3. Another related function of policy limits is that they enable insurers to limit their obligations to exposures that they believe they can handle. In other words, coverage is related to the insurer's financial capacity.

4. By offering insureds a choice of policy limits, insurers permit consumers to adapt the coverage to their own needs, desires, and financial resources.

Liability insurance policies typically contain either (1) split limits or (2) single limits per occurrence. Many also contain (3) aggregate limits. Despite what has been said above concerning the functions of policy limits, some liability policies do not contain dollar limits as such. These special cases will be discussed separately.

Split Limits   Split limits per occurrence specify separate maximum amounts for which the insurer will be responsible per occurrence in case of (1) bodily injury or (2) property damage. For example, the insurer may limit its responsibility per occurrence to $1 million for bodily injury and $500,000 for property damage. If a third-party claimant is entitled to $800,000 for bodily injury and $700,000 for property damage, the insurer would then pay $800,000 for the bodily injury and $500,000 for the property damage. Unless the bodily injuries were valued at $1 million or more, or the property damage at $500,000 or more, the insurer would pay out the total amount of the award.

The insurer's maximum obligation is the same regardless of the number of persons who suffer injuries or damage because of a single occurrence. Under older liability insurance policies (and perhaps some current ones but not usually) the bodily injury liability limit was a stated amount per occurrence subject to another, usually lower, stated amount per person. For example, if the $1 million per occurrence limit in the previous example had been coupled with a $500,000 per person limit and only one person suffered bodily injuries, the insurer's responsibility for the $800,000 claim (or multiple claims based on the injury to one person) would have been limited to $500,000. If two persons had been injured, one to the extent of $700,000 and the other $100,000, the insurer would pay $500,000 + $100,000, or $600,000. If one person had a judgment of $500,000 and the other $300,000, the insurer would pay $800,000. In this last case the per person limit would not cap the recovery in any way.

If, after applying the per person limit to each claim, the sum of the insurer's obligations exceeds the per occurrence limit, then the insurer's responsibility is capped by that limit. For example, suppose that three persons are injured resulting in awards of $900,000, $400,000, and $300,000. The sum of the insurer's obligations under each of the claims would be $500,000 + $400,000 + $300,000, or $1,200,000. The per occurrence limit caps the insurer's total payment for damages at $1 million.

Per occurrence limits may not reflect an insurer's total obligation under a given policy. Courts sometimes hold that more than one "occurrence" has caused a given bodily injury or accident. Because per occurrence limits provide the same coverage for each occurrence, regardless of the number of "occurrences," the insurer's maximum responsibility for a given injury or damage may be the limits applicable at the time of each occurrence times the number of occurrences. The net effect could be a finding of virtually unlimited coverage. To reduce the likelihood of such interpretations, insurers have included in their policy some language directed specifically at this problem.

For example, the Business Auto Coverage Form (which uses the word "accident" instead of "occurrence" but defines accident to mean an occurrence) states that:

> All "bodily injury" and "property damage" resulting from continuous or repeated exposure to substantially the same conditions will be considered as resulting from one "accident."

The ISO commercial general liability forms contain an "each occurrence limit" which limits the amount the insurer will pay for claims arising out of any one "occurrence," which is then defined in the usual manner.

Single Limits The trend in liability insurance is to replace split bodily injury/property damage limits with single limits per occurrence (or per claim). The single limit states the most the insurer will pay for all bodily injuries and property damage arising out of one occurrence. Neither the number of claims made because of that occurrence nor the mix of bodily injury and property damage amounts affects the amount the insurer will pay (unless the sum of all claims exceeds policy limits).

Aggregate Limits   Under a per occurrence limit, if the insured is responsible for, say, twenty "occurrences" during a single policy period, the insurer could conceivably be held responsible for twenty times the "per occurrence" limit. To cap the maximum aggregate responsibility of the insurer per policy period, many insurance policies contain aggregate limits.

Under earlier ISO forms, aggregate limits applied only to liability arising out of certain hazards. Separate aggregate limits applied to recoveries for bodily injury and for property damage. The bodily injury aggregate limit was the most the insured would pay for all "occurrences" during the policy period that resulted in bodily injury because of (1) the products hazard or (2) the completed operations hazard (as defined in the policy). The property damage aggregate limits applied only to the damage arising out of (1) the products or (2) completed operations hazards plus those arising out of certain types of premises or operations exposures.

The current commercial general liability form, which also includes a "per occurrence" limit, contains two aggregate limits.

- A *products-completed operations* aggregate limit applies to bodily injury and property damage arising out of the products or completed operations hazard.
- A *general aggregate limit* is the most the insurer will pay under other coverages.

Defense Costs and Supplementary Benefits

Many liability insurance policies provide that the defense costs and supplementary benefits are not subject to the policy limits. In other words, except for the small dollar limits imposed on some supplementary benefits (noted earlier), the insurer's defense obligation is not subject to any dollar limit whatsoever.

To illustrate the implications of this approach, assume a policy limit of $100,000. If the damages were $30,000 and the insurer's defense costs and supplementary payments $20,000, the insurer would pay $30,000 and take care of $20,000 defense costs. If in a different situation the facts were the same but the damages were $130,000—$30,000 more than the policy limits—the insurer would pay $100,000 of the damages, and also the $20,000 in costs. However, as noted earlier, the insurer would be responsible for the full $20,000 in defense costs only if the insurer had incurred these costs prior to its $100,000 payment. If, for example, the insurer is willing to admit defeat and settle for the $100,000 policy limit plus defense costs, but the insured appeals the $130,000 judgment and thereby incurs $15,000 additional defense costs, win or lose the insured—not the insurer—must take care of the $15,000.

In many cases defense costs may exceed the amount paid as an award or settlement. This obviously is the case when the defense is successful and no award or settlement is payable, but it may also happen when the insured loses the case. During recent years legal costs have increased dramatically, resulting in a much higher ratio of defense costs to award and settlement amounts. For example, from 1978 to 1983 defense costs rose at a pace more than twice the rate for damages.

Under a proposal that ISO is considering, the commercial general liability policy would state that defense costs are subject to the two aggregate limits. (They would not be subject to the occurrence limits.)[6] Insurers argue that they can no longer provide unlimited defense cost coverage. They also argue that subjecting defense costs to some limits creates incentives for all parties to reduce defense costs. Critics, however, argue that insureds would lose important coverage against costs over which they have little control. One possible reaction is that insureds will seek a more active role in how and by whom the defense is conducted.

No Limits

Despite the benefits of policy limits, cases exist where, for special reasons, insurers issue coverage with no stated dollar limit. Two major examples of this practice are found in (1) workers compensation insurance, and (2) auto no-fault insurance.

The *workers compensation and employers liability* policy states under Part One that the insurer

> will pay promptly when due the benefits required of you by the workers compensation law.

It also reserves the right to defend any claim and promises to pay litigation costs, premiums for bonds to release attachments, and so on.

While the policy does not contain a dollar limit for workers compensation coverage, the state law does limit the employer's—and hence the insurer's—liability. State laws vary greatly, but they essentially limit the employer's responsibility to medical expense reimbursement, disability income replacement, funeral expense allowances, income to survivors, and rehabilitation expenses. All states prescribe unlimited medical expense reimbursements, but the other benefits are subject to dollar or duration limits. For example, a worker who is temporarily totally disabled, typically receives a weekly benefit equal to two-thirds of the wage loss, subject to maximum and minimum amounts. Payments start after the worker has been disabled for a few days (usually three or seven) and continue for the duration of the disability but in some cases no more than, say, fourteen days, the worker receives a retroactive benefit for the waiting period.

The practical effect, for accidents involving individual workers, is that the law limits the insurer's responsibility. However, the de facto limitation on payments to individual workers does not resolve the catastrophic exposure of an accident in which multiple employees may sustain injuries. When the workers compensation exposure is insured, the insurer accepts the possibility that many workers will be involved in one accident or that the employer may experience many accidents within one year.

Auto no-fault insurance is provided by a "personal injury protection" (PIP) endorsement to an auto insurance policy. Like workers compensation insurers, auto no-fault insurers are subject to the compensation benefits prescribed by state law. Limits may not be stated in the policy because they are stated in the law.

Deductibles

Deductibles state the amounts the insured has agreed to retain. For example, a deductible may state that the insured will be responsible for the first $1,000, $5,000, or $50,000 per occurrence or claim. Deductibles may apply to each claim, each occurrence, the total losses during the policy period, or some other base. They may take several forms such as a specified amount, a percent of the loss, or a waiting period (such as that used in workers compensation), or benefits provided under a base policy. Finally they may apply to all losses covered under the contract or be limited to certain losses.

Deductibles are attractive to insureds when they reduce premiums significantly. Small losses tend to be more common than large losses. If this tendency is strong and loss frequencies are high, the premium reductions may be substantial because the insurer's loss payments and loss adjustment expenses may be substantially reduced. Deductibles may also encourage the insured to be more careful and thus further reduce losses.

Insurers also find deductibles useful because they eliminate troublesome small claims, enable them to price their product more attractively, and may heighten the insured's interest in loss control.

Deductibles are much less common in liability insurance policies than of property insurance policies. Few, if any, liability insurance policies contain small deductibles. The premium savings associated with small deductibles would generally be too small (nonexistent for very small deductibles) to create a market for this approach. Generally speaking, small losses do not outnumber large losses as much in liability insurance as in property insurance. Exceptions exist, however. Contractors, for example, may be prone to a frequency of small property damage liability losses, and a department store may have a frequency of small bodily injury liability claims (slips and falls). Also, liability insurance claims tend to be less frequent on the whole than property insurance claims. Third parties with small claims may find the effort involved in pursuing their rights more costly than their loss, particularly if they have received some no-fault payment such as those provided under medical payments coverage, a personal injury protection endorsement, or damage to property of others coverage. Insurers are also reluctant to grant such deductibles because claims that seemed small initially often turn out to be large claims. For this reason, they may continue to investigate all claims, thus incurring about the same loss adjustment expense as they would without a deductible. Usually insurers want to remain in control of liability claims so they handle the defense and seek reimbursement of the deductible amount from the insured. Finally, small deductibles may not be consistent with auto financial responsibility, auto no-fault, or workers compensation laws that require insurance to guarantee the insured's financial responsibility. On the other hand, some auto no-fault laws specifically authorize deductibles. Insurers are exploring the use of small deductibles in workers compensation insurance. In these no-fault areas, however, claims are more frequent than in the typical liability lines and small losses are relatively more important.

Large deductibles, on the other hand, are common, though less so than in property insurance. Beyond a certain point, losses below that boundary line do tend to become much more common than losses above that point. Insurers may at some point also be willing to investigate only those claims that have a reasonable chance of exceeding the deductible amount. The result is a substantial reduction in premiums. When the deductible is very large, the coverage is considered to be excess insurance.

Large businesses may elect to purchase excess insurance in connection with a retention program for most of the events that are expected to occur. Workers compensation and general liability exposures are commonly handled in this way by the largest firms.

Some liability insurance policies such as directors and officers and umbrella liability insurance contracts, contain mandatory deductibles. For example, umbrella liability insurance requires that the insured have certain basic auto and commercial general liability insurance. For events that would also be covered under these basic policies, the retained amount is the policy limits in the basic policies. For losses not covered under these base policies, the retention is usually a stated amount per occurrence.

Other Insurance

An insured may have two or more liability insurance policies covering the same loss. Policies contain provisions designed to (1) avoid duplicate payments and (2) determine the responsibility, if any, of each insurer.

Other insurance provisions found in liability insurance policies may be classified into four categories.

1. Clauses that prohibit other insurance as a policy condition or shift responsibility to the other policies. This approach is rare, but it is found, for example, in some directors and officers liability policies.
2. Clauses that limit the insurer's responsibility to some fraction of the loss. The shares can be determined in various ways.
3. Clauses that make the policy excess over other applicable insurance.
4. Clauses that make the policy primary with respect to other applicable insurance.

Proportional Sharing Provisions Of the various approaches to proportional loss sharing, two are by far the most common in liability insurance: (1) contribution by equal shares and (2) proration by policy amounts.

For example, the new ISO commercial general liability contract uses both approaches. The policy states that:

> If all of the other insurance permits contribution by equal shares, we will follow this method also. Under this approach each insurer contributes equal amounts until it has paid its applicable limit of insurance or none of the loss remains, whichever comes first. If any of the other insurance does not permit contribution by equal shares, we will contribute by limits. Under this method, each insurer's share is based on the ratio of its applicable limit of insurance to the total applicable limits of insurance of all insurers.

To illustrate how this provision works, assume two policies—one with a per occurrence limit of $1 million, the other with a $500,000 limit. The covered loss is $900,000. If both contracts permit contribution by equal shares, the two insurers share the loss equally. The $500,000 limit of the second insurer exceeds its $450,000 equal share of the loss. If, however, the loss was $1.2 million instead of $500,000, the second insurer's liability is limited to $500,000. The first insurer must pay the remaining $700,000.

If the second insurer's contract does not permit contribution by equal shares, the first insurer's obligation is determined by the ratio of its $1 million limit to the $1.5 million total of the two limits. The first insurer would therefore pay two-thirds of the two losses: $600,000 of the $900,000 loss and $900,000 of the $1.2 million loss.

The Business Auto Coverage Form states that if two or more policies or coverage forms cover on the same basis, the insurer's share is the proportion that the limit of the form bears to the total of the limits of all forms and policies covering on the same basis. This approach, therefore, illustrates proration by policy amounts.

Excess Insurance Excess insurance provisions are common in liability insurance. For example, the ISO CGL contract contains an extensive section on excess insurance as follows:

> b. Excess Insurance
> This insurance is excess over any of the other insurance, whether primary, excess, contingent or on any other basis:
> (1) That is effective prior to the beginning of the policy period shown in the Declarations of this insurance and applies to "bodily injury" or "property damage" on other than a claims-made basis, if:
>   (a) No Retroactive Date is shown in the Declarations of this insurance; or
>   (b) The other insurance has a policy period which continues after the Retroactive Date shown in the Declarations of this insurance;
> (2) That is Fire, Extended Coverage, Builders' Risk, Installation Risk or similar coverage for "your work;"
> (3) That is Fire insurance for premises rented to you; or
> (4) If the loss arises out of the maintenance or use of aircraft, "autos" or watercraft to the extent not subject to Exclusion g. of Coverage A (Section 1).
> When this insurance is excess, we will have no duty under Coverages A or B to defend any claim or "suit" that any other insurer has a duty to defend. If no other insurer defends, we will undertake to do so, but we will be entitled to the insured's rights against all those other insurers.
> When this insurance is excess over other insurance, we will pay only our share of the amount of the loss, if any, that exceeds the sum of:
> (1) The total amount that all such other insurance would pay for the loss in the absence of this insurance; and
> (2) The total of all deductible and self-insured amounts under all that other insurance.
> We will share the remaining loss, if any, with any other insurance that is not described in this Excess Insurance provision and was not bought specifically to apply in excess of the Limits of Insurance shown in the Declarations of this Coverage Part.

Excess insurance is also a prominent feature of the Business Auto

Coverage Form. For any covered auto not owned by the named insured, the BAC insurance is excess over any other collectible insurance. Since this policy may cover the operation, maintenance, or use of any auto, many opportunities arise for liability to arise out of the use of a nonowned car. For example, Horst Johnson may drive a rented car, a borrowed car, or his own car on company business. If the owner of each of these cars has liability insurance on these cars, that insurance is primary. Horst's policy is not activated until the primary insurer has exhausted its limits. One effect of this provision is that the named insured has higher limits of protection if the liability arises out of the use of nonowned cars instead of ~~used~~ *owned* cars.

Primary Insurance Except for separate excess insurance, liability insurance policies are designed to provide primary insurance for some exposures. For example, the business auto coverage form states, that, for any covered auto owned by the named insured, the BAC provides primary insurance. The ISO commercial general liability insurance policy states that it is a primary insurance policy except under those conditions that it explicitly states, as explained above, that it is excess.

Subrogation

Sometimes the insured has other sources besides the insurer against whom he or she can assert a claim because of the liability generated by a covered occurrence. This claim may arise out of the tortious conduct of some other person who was solely or partly responsible for the occurrence or it may be based on a contractual right. Subrogation gives the insurer the right to take over the rights of the insured against that other party to the extent that it has made payments on behalf of the insured. Subrogation prevents the insured from recovering more than once for the same loss and reduced the cost of insurance. The subrogation rights of the insured are spelled out in a provision with a title such as "Recovery From Others."

For example, if an injured worker sues the manufacturer of some machine that caused an injury, the workers compensation insurer states that:

> We have your rights to recover our payment from anyone liable for an injury covered by this insurance. You will do everything necessary to protect those rights for us and to help us enforce them.

The business auto coverage form statement is even more explicit:

> If we make any payment, we are entitled to recover what we paid from other parties. Any person to or for whom we make payment must transfer to us his or her rights of recovery against any other

party. This person must do everything necessary to secure these rights and must do nothing that would jeopardize them.

A similar statement appears in the ISO commercial lines program common policy conditions forms:

> If the insured's claim against the other parties exceeds the insurer's limit of liability the insured may proceed separately or jointly with the insurer to pursue its rights not subject to the subrogation clause.

INSURED'S DUTIES FOLLOWING A LOSS

Following a loss covered under the contract, the insured has certain duties to perform in order to collect from the insurer. The four major duties deal with (1) prohibition of certain actions by the insured following the accident, (2) notice to the insurer that an occurrence has taken place, (3) notice that a claim or suit has been brought against the insured, and (4) cooperation with the insurer. For example, under the ISO commercial general liability policy, a section titled, "Duties in the Event of Occurrence, Claim or Suit" reads as follows:

a. You must see to it that we are notified as soon as practicable of an "occurrence" which may result in a claim. *To the extent possible, notice should include:*
   (1) How, when and where the occurrence took place;
   (2) The names and addresses of any injured persons and witnesses; and
   (3) The nature and location of any injury or damage arising out of the "occurrence."

   Notice of an "occurrence" is not notice of a claim.

b. If a claim is received by any insured you must:
   (1) Immediately record the specifics of the claim and the date received; and
   (2) Notify us as soon as practicable. You must see to it that we receive written notice of the claim as soon as practicable.

c. You and any other involved insured must:
   (1) Immediately send us copies of any demands, notices, summonses or legal papers received in connection with the claim or a "suit;"
   (2) Authorize us to obtain records and other information;
   (3) Cooperate with us in the investigation, settlement or defense of the claim or "suit;" and
   (4) Assist us, upon our request, in the enforcement of any right against any person or organization which may be liable to the insured because of injury or damage to which this insurance may also apply.

d. No insureds will, except at their own cost, voluntarily make a payment, assume any obligation, or incur any expense, other than for first aid, without our consent.

Similar words appear in other liability insurance policies.

Prohibition of Certain Acts

Insureds are told not to assume voluntarily any liability, make any payment, or incur any expense, other than for first aid without the consent of the insurer. The reason is clear. Such actions by the insured may prejudice the ability of the insurer to defend the insured against the claim. In determining how strictly they will enforce this position, insurers consider how much their defense ability has been prejudiced. Similarly, in judging whether they should uphold an insurer's denial of a claim based on a violation by the insured of this condition, courts consider the effect of this violation on the ability of the insurer to defend the insured.

Notice of the Occurrence

The insured must tell the insurer promptly about any occurrence that *may* result in a claim. The insured should not wait until the third party brings a claim or a suit against the insured. The reasoning again is that failure to notify the insurer promptly may prejudice the insurer's defense of the claim. Prompt notice permits the insurer to investigate the situation immediately and commence negotiations with the injured party at the optimum time.

Despite the importance of this notice requirement, courts and insurers have excused some short delays unless the insurer can demonstrate prejudice. As the delay period increases, the burden of proof shifts to the insured who must demonstrate some mitigating circumstances that explain the delay or that the insurer was not hurt by the delay. The mitigating circumstances argument tends to be less persuasive the longer the delay. Business insureds are held to a higher standard of performance with respect to this notice requirement than are insureds under personal policies.

If the insured fails to notify the insurer promptly, the third party claimant may suffer as well as the insured. If the insurer is not obligated to defend the insured, the insured will be less financially able to pay the claimant any damages. For that reason the claimant may notify the insurer directly. As long as the notice is timely and reasonably complete and the insurer's defense rights are not prejudiced, courts will accept this notice as satisfying the notice requirement. In states with direct action statutes the claimant can proceed directly against the insurer.

Notice of Claim or Suit

Insureds involved in occurrences that should be reported often fail to report them because no one appeared to have suffered any bodily injury or property damage. When they receive notice of a claim or a suit, however, they should realize that the insurer should be notified promptly. For this reason insurers and the courts interpret the claim or suit notice provision even more strictly than the occurrence notice requirement.

Cooperation with the Insurer

If the insurer so requests, the insured must attend hearings and trials and assist the insurer in securing and giving evidence, obtaining witnesses, and effecting settlements where that seems appropriate.

If an insurer wishes to deny a claim on the basis of non-cooperation, the insurer must show that the insured in bad faith did not cooperate and that as a result the insurer's defense ability was prejudiced. The clearest example would be false information provided by the insured, particularly if he or she is acting in collusion with the claimant.

Chapter Notes

---

1. The method of addressing this topic closely follows the system used in the CPCU 1 text *Principles of Risk Management and Insurance*, Williams, Head, Horn, and Glendenning, second edition, 1981, The American Institute, Vol. II. However, while CPCU 1 presents an overview of principles applicable to personal and commercial property and liability insurance, discussion here emphasizes those points most relevant to commercial liability insurance.
2. Domenick J. Yezzi, CPCU, Assistant Manager, Industry Relations, Insurance Services Office, in a letter dated January 29, 1986.
3. Robert Mehr and Emerson Cammack first suggested such a framework in Mehr and Cammack, *Principles of Insurance* (Homewood, IL: Richard D. Irwin, Inc., 1952), Chapters 7-11. The framework shown here is based on Williams, Head, Horn, and Glendenning, op.cit.
4. This section is based heavily upon *Insurance Services Office, Inc.'s New Commercial General Liability Program* (New York: Insurance Services Office, Inc., 1984), pp. 1-3.
5. For a more extensive list see "RIMS Criticizes ISO's CGL Forms at Insurance Hearing," *Risk Management*, Vol. 32, No. 7 (July 1985), pp. 50-56.
6. "At its December 11, 1985 meeting, the ISO Board of Directors ... approved a revised program for discussion with the NAIC which would provide that an amount equal to 50% of policy aggregate could be spent on legal defense before additional defense cost expenditures begin to reduce the aggregate available for both indemnity and defense. An optional endorsement would be made available to vary the defense cost threshold from the basic policy provision's 50% to values ranging from 0% to 300%." ISO Chief Executive Circular CE 86-18, May 23, 1986, Copyright Insurance Services Office, Inc., 1986.

CHAPTER 5

General Liability Insurance

This is the first of two chapters devoted to a description and analysis of the most widely used commercial general liability (CGL) policies. In a fundamental sense, there are two versions of such policies—an "occurrence" version and a "claims-made" version. Chapter 5 examines the similarities between the two, while Chapter 6 examines the differences. Among other things, Chapter 6 will explain the application of the coverage triggers, the retroactive date concept, extended reporting periods ("tails") the so-called "laser beam endorsements," limits, and other related concepts.

BACKGROUND

General liability insurance did not develop overnight. Indeed, modern CGL policy forms are the result of a lengthy process of evaluating and revising the numerous forms that have been used over the years. Thus, to provide the needed historical perspective, this chapter first traces the evolution of general liability insurance coverages.

Early Policies

Liability insurance began to develop in the United States over a century ago. Its root is commonly said to be accident insurance. One of its earlier outgrowths was employers' liability insurance, introduced in 1886 to meet the demands of employers who feared financial loss because of suit by employees.

Over time, as new kinds of claims surfaced and became more frequent, corresponding insurance coverages were developed. For example, the contractors' public liability coverage was introduced in 1886, followed in 1892 by the manufacturers' public liability policy. Two years later, in 1894, the owners', landlords', and tenants' policy was introduced to cover specified liability exposures of businesses.[1]

As each new liability insurance coverage was developed, whether it concerned elevators, horse teams, automobiles, or products, it was provided on a separate policy, and it excluded all losses that could be insured under another policy. This monoline approach was probably necessary in the early experimental stages of liability insurance. Each insurer wanted (and probably needed) the freedom to (1) confine its writings to particular types of liability policies and (2) exclude from these policies any loss exposures that the insurer regarded as undesirable, uninsurable, or insurable only for an additional premium.[2] Each business buyer was likewise free to purchase and pay for only the coverages that were desired and/or needed by the firm. However, to insure all of its important liability exposures, the firm was forced to buy a number of different policies, often from several different insurers (and sometimes through several different producers). While this proved to be a complicated, cumbersome, and potentially dangerous way of preserving the range of choices needed by insurance buyers, there was no other practical alternative at the time. Comparatively few insurers were willing to write *all* of the liability coverages that were desired by many business buyers.

As more insurers gained experience in writing a wider variety of liability coverages, the separate policy approach of obtaining liability protection eventually gave way to a "schedule liability approach" that permitted buyers to insure several loss exposures in one contract. The desired coverages were simply designated on the policy declarations. For example, a firm could purchase liability protection for the loss exposures associated with its premises, operations, elevators, and work performed for the firm by a contractor, all on one insurance policy.

The schedule liability approach may have been a step in the right direction for both insurers and insureds, yet it also had its pitfalls, described by one author as:

> ... a veritable patchwork of complexity and a heterogeneity, not always rational, of cover, rating base and underwriting rules. Particularly for larger risks, a combination of policies or endorsements is required to secure coverage, and the often arbitrary dividing lines among covers confuse agent and insured, encourage the insured to select from the total hazard and leave a twilight zone of hazards unprotected because they are not specified in any combination of policies. There is also probably less incentive to prevention when part of the total hazard only is covered, and several insurers split the subhazards.[3]

The Comprehensive General Liability Policy

It was primarily to address the aforementioned concerns that the so-called comprehensive general liability insurance policy was developed. The earliest liability policy was introduced for use in 1941 through the combined effort of the stock and mutual casualty rating bureaus after several years of planning.

The comprehensive general liability policy or CGL, as it came to be called, was devised to provide, in one contract, virtually all of the coverages that previously were available under the schedule liability policies. In concept the CGL was the opposite of the schedule policies and covered all liability exposures of a business known to exist at policy inception and all hazards created during the policy period. The CGL policy was viewed as especially attractive for the businesses that found it difficult to identify all of their present exposures to loss, as well as those that might develop during the policy term, and then to select the coverages they thought necessary.

The first "bureau" CGL policy contained two insuring agreements. One applied to bodily injury liability and the other to property damage liability. Either coverage could be purchased without the other.

Interestingly, the earliest "bureau" CGL policy contained five groups of exclusions that still apply to some extent, in current-day forms. These exclusions eliminated coverage for:

1. liability assumed under any contract or agreement, except otherwise defined;
2. liability stemming from the ownership, maintenance, or use of aircraft, automobiles or watercraft while away from the insured's premises—except with respect to operations performed by independent contractors;
3. the statutory exposures of workers compensation and employers liability;
4. under property damage liability, to injury to or destruction of property owned, occupied by, rented, or used by the insured; premises alienated; or to any goods or products manufactured, sold or distributed, or work completed by or on behalf of the named insured out of which the accident arose; and
5. water damage liability.

The CGL policy was first revised in 1943. It was not until 1955 that it was again revised. Subsequent revisions took place in 1966, 1973, and 1986. The primary reason for the revisions was to clarify the policy provisions that consistently led to arguments, litigation, and/or findings of coverage where none was intended.

The 1955 policy revision was said to be "a step backward"

according to some courts and "ambiguous and confusing—or even unintelligible."[4] This also was the policy that substituted the words "legally obligated to pay" in the insuring agreement for the phrase "imposed by law or assumed under any contract, as defined in the policy" of earlier policy editions. Some earlier contracts limited coverage to liability imposed by law. When contractual liability coverage was added to earlier liability policies, it was believed necessary to add the words "liability assumed under contract" to the language of the insuring agreement, because liability imposed by law might not be construed to include liability voluntarily assumed under contract. Since the 1955 policy offered coverage against all legal obligations of the insured, except as otherwise excluded, it was no longer necessary to make the distinction between liability imposed by law and the liability assumed under contract.[5]

The comprehensive general liability policy was considered to be the deluxe form of protection. It automatically included coverage against five distinct exposures:

1. premises and operations,
2. elevator liability,
3. independent contractor operations,
4. products liability and completed operations, and
5. limited contractual liability.

Any new exposures that arose during the policy period were also covered automatically—for an additional premium, of course. For those that did not require or desire such broad protection (or when insurers did not wish to provide it), insurers offered more limited versions, such as the owners', landlords', and tenants' (OL&T) policy and the manufacturers' and contractors' (M&C) policy.

Owners', Landlords', and Tenants' (OL&T) Policy

The OL&T policy was devised to provide liability coverages to buyers whose exposures were centered primarily on premises. The only coverages automatically provided by the basic OL&T contract were premises and operations—including contractual liability for *incidental contracts*, and liability for structural alterations performed by or on behalf of the named insured—provided the operations did not involve changing the size or moving an existing structure or building. The OL&T policy was not intended for use when a significant exposure existed for either products or completed operations. Therefore, it was suited only for such entities as lessors and lessees of building office complexes; firms that operate auto parking lots; municipalities with exposures concerning firehouses, golf courses, street signs, and banners; and individuals who rented one or more private dwellings or apartment houses to others.

Manufacturers' and Contractors' (M&C) Policy

The M&C policy was similar to the OL&T policy, except that the M&C form was devised to provide liability coverages for those whose exposures were predominately *away* from premises. Those for whom the M&C policy might have been appropriate included auctioneers, marine divers, funeral directors, and sales and service organizations. Strangely enough, the fact that the M&C policy was not designed to include products and completed operations liability coverage made the policy inadequate for manufacturers and contractors, since the former usually require products liability coverage and the latter usually require completed operations coverage.

1966 Revision

The 1966 revision involved a major overhaul of the commercial liability insurance contract's format and content. The policy was designed to be flexible. A variety of protection suited to the particular needs of business entities could be written in one policy, using single policies or appropriate combinations of the CGL, OL&T, M&C, storekeepers, garage liability, owners and contractors protective, products and completed operations, and contractual liability coverage parts. It also was with this policy revision that coverage was "officially" changed from an accident to an occurrence basis. (Some insurers had independently offered occurrence basis coverage before 1966.)

1973 Revision

The 1973 revision was not as extensive as the 1966 revision, but it did make some significant changes. For example, it expanded the written definition of "property damage" to explicitly include loss of use of tangible property that was not physically injured. This new definition of property damage also attempted to preclude coverage for diminution in value or the economic loss associated with tangible property where there had been neither loss of use of tangible property nor its physical injury or destruction. Another significant change dealt with the so-called "failure to perform" exclusion. When this exclusion first made its appearance in 1966, complex language was deemed to be necessary to accomplish the desired results of preventing insurers from covering losses of the kind that are better treated as part of the normal costs of producing products or work. As it turned out, the revised language still resulted in interpretations detrimental to insurers and it required additional changes in the 1986 revision.

Broad Form CGL Endorsement

During the mid-1970s, some insurers introduced their own independently filed packages of coverage extensions to use with CGL forms. Such a package typically included, in one endorsement, many of the broadening coverages that otherwise required separate endorsements. Subsequently, ISO introduced a broad form comprehensive general liability insurance endorsement similar to many of these independent filings. This endorsement provided the following twelve coverage extensions:

1. blanket contractual liability,
2. personal injury liability and advertising injury liability,
3. premises medical payments,
4. host liquor liability,
5. fire legal liability on real property,
6. broad form property damage, including completed operations,
7. incidental medical malpractice,
8. nonowned watercraft liability,
9. limited worldwide coverage,
10. additional persons insured,
11. extended bodily injury coverage, and
12. automatic coverage on newly acquired organizations.

This optional broad form CGL endorsement gradually became a part of the complete package of general liability insurance coverages purchased by many commercial insurance buyers.

1986 Revision—*Commercial* General Liability

The 1986 revision of the general liability forms represented a major overhaul. It incorporated for the first time the so-called "plain English" approach to overcome the criticism that the policy language was difficult to read and comprehend—and also to meet state statutes on readability. The latest general liability format also combines into a single form nearly all of the coverages of the 1973 edition of the CGL policy and the ISO Broad Form CGL endorsement, subject to numerous revisions made necessary by court decisions adverse to both insureds and insurers.

The first name of the form was also changed from "comprehensive" to "commercial" to avoid the danger that some courts might be disinclined to uphold exclusions and limitations in a policy that had the word "comprehensive" in its title. Yet, rather than starting with narrow coverages expandable by endorsement, the commercial general liability policy begins with a broad set of coverages that can be narrowed by endorsement(s).

Of particular significance (and controversy) is the fact that there are now two general kinds of forms: a "claims-made" form and an "occurrence" form. The chief difference between the two lies in the "trigger," or means of activating coverage for bodily injury and/or property damage liability.

The Coverage Trigger—Evolution

The coverage trigger has taken on a special significance in recent years as a result of the so-called "latent" disease cases. An example is the lung disease, silicosis, caused by the inhalation of silica dust. A disease of such a prolonged nature may encompass many policy periods, from the time a person was first exposed to a hazardous condition through the period during which an illness is developing in the person so exposed, and finally to the period when the illness first becomes manifest or a claim is made. If different insurance policies were in effect during these three time periods, the question arises as to which of the policies provide coverage. The coverage trigger of all relevant policies is important to claimants, insurers, and insureds. The more policies of the past that can be triggered and the more policy limits that can be stacked, the better the claimants' chances of collecting their damages from insurers. When one or more of the previous policies are deemed by the courts to be inapplicable, the insurer(s) involved are relieved from the obligation to pay damages, while the insured may be out-of-pocket for the damages, defense costs, and the costs of litigation with its own liability insurer(s). Some corporations have even been forced into bankruptcy.

The first general liability policies to be introduced were on an "accident" basis. That is to say, for coverage to apply under the earliest policies, an accident must have taken place during the policy period. While bodily injury and/or property damage often result simultaneously with an accident or instantly thereafter, it did not matter when the bodily injury or property damage actually occurred so long as a policy was in force at the time of the accident itself. The word "accident" was not defined in the policies, but most courts defined accident in terms of an event that was unintended, unpredictable, unforeseen, and sudden in nature.

Astute insurance buyers often demanded coverage that was not limited to sudden events. Thus, for a number of years following the introduction of the comprehensive general liability policy, some insurers were willing to endorse their policies to cover injurious exposure to conditions as well as accidents in a narrower sense.

Although these broader endorsements were in use as early as the 1940s, it was not until the 1966 revision of the bureau general liability forms that coverage was officially provided on an occurrence basis. However, it was the policy period during which the bodily injury or property damage took place that triggered the coverage, rather than the accident or event that fostered the injury or damage. The 1973 revisions move from the definition of occurrence to the respective definitions of bodily injury or property damage must take place during the policy period.

The occurrence forms prompted a number of questions and a great deal of controversy, particularly with respect to so-called "long-tail" exposures and claims, such as those associated with medical malpractice, defective products, and latent diseases.[6] The problem, briefly, is that many years often elapse between the time the premiums are charged for long-tail exposures and the time the losses are reported and paid. In the meantime, insurers find it extremely difficult to predict future losses, establish adequate premium levels and loss reserves, and avoid premature conclusions about their underwriting results for a particular year.

It was mainly long-tail exposures, unprecedentedly large and unpredictable court judgments, the latent disease cases affecting a growing number of industries, and the ability of plaintiffs to stack the limits of previously expired liability policies that prompted the introduction of "claims-made" liability coverage, as an alternative to "occurrence." Although the topic of triggers is discussed more extensively in Chapter 6, it will be sufficient for the immediate purposes to note:

- The trigger of the modern *occurrence* form activates the policy in force at the time of the bodily injury or property damage.
- The trigger of the *claims-made* form, on the other hand, activates the policy in force at the time a claim is first made against insured or insurer.

The choice between forms is to be dictated by underwriting judgment the idea being to encourage the use of the claims-made form when long-tail exposures are involved.

MODERN COMMERCIAL GENERAL LIABILITY INSURANCE

Modern policies of commercial general liability insurance may be "standard" or "nonstandard" in nature. Within each of these broad classifications, there are also noteworthy variations.

- *Standard* policies comprise preprinted forms and endorsements that are used, without alteration, by a large number of insurers. Though the standard policy required or approved in a particular state may differ sharply from its counterpart(s) in other states, the standard commercial general liability policies of most states tend to be identical or substantially similar over time. At present, the most widely used of the standard forms and endorsements are those that have been drafted by ISO and approved by the majority of states.
- *Nonstandard* policies comprise forms and endorsements that are somewhat unique, in a sense, either to each insurer or to each buyer. The language of one nonstandard policy is not uniform with the language of other such policies. Some nonstandard policies are preprinted, while others are "manuscripted."

Nonstandard policies constitute an important source of general liability insurance for commercial entities. Even so, the remainder of this discussion is devoted to an analysis of the standard ISO commercial general liability policy (CGL). It is a widely used policy in its own right. It also provides a norm or point of departure for anyone who wishes to grasp the nature and purpose of language differences in nonstandard forms. In fact, many provisions of the various nonstandard forms are identical or similar to provisions in the CGL.

Organization of the CGL

The current standard CGL policy, which was introduced for use in 1986, consists of five parts:

- *Common policy declarations* which identify the named insured, the mailing address of the named insured, the forms applicable to the respective coverage parts, and the annual premium for each coverage. The common declarations can be used when the insurer is also to write one or more of the other standard policies (such as the commercial property, inland marine, crime, and/or boiler and machinery policy).
- *Common policy conditions* which apply to all of the standard coverage parts.
- *Commercial general liability declarations* which contain all of the variable information pertinent to the liability exposures

of the named insured. (This page and the common policy declarations can sometimes be combined.)

- Either of two *coverage forms.* One is the "occurrence" form and the other is the "claims-made" form. Except for their bodily injury and property damage triggers and related provisions, they are otherwise similar.
- A *broad form nuclear exclusion* endorsement. It remains a separate part of the contract because it can apply to other liability provisions included in a package policy.

The combination formed by the commercial general liability declarations page, claims-made or occurrence coverage form, the broad form nuclear exclusion endorsement and other applicable endorsements is referred to as the *coverage part.*

Combining the *coverage part* with the *common policy declarations* and *common policy conditions form* results in a *monoline policy.* If combined with other coverage parts, it may form a *package policy.* Various *endorsements* are also available to narrow the coverage of the CGL to a scope that would be somewhat comparable to the unendorsed former edition of the CGL policy (or to narrow the coverage even further, if desired).

CGL Forms

Both the occurrence and the claims-made CGL forms are divided into the following sections:

Section I—Coverages Three major groups of coverages are provided, each with its own insuring agreement, trigger, and exclusions. Apart from the triggers, the coverages can be summarized as follows.

Coverage A. Bodily Injury and Property Damage Liability. This coverage encompasses all premises and operations liability exposures, as well as products and completed operations liability exposures, unless otherwise excepted.

- The premises include those that are known to exist and are designated on the general liability declarations page, plus all other premises exposures that arise during the policy period.
- The operations encompass those on and away from the business premises, including any contingent or vicarious liability stemming from the acts or omissions of others and for which the insured may be liable.

Other "coverages" provided separately on earlier policies but integrated into this section are blanket contractual liability; fire legal liability; broad form property damage; host liquor liability; incidental malpractice; nonowned watercraft liability; limited world wide products liability; explosion, collapse, and underground property damage liability; and extended bodily injury liability coverage.

Coverage B. Personal Injury and Advertising Injury Liability. The protection provided here covers liability from such offenses as libel, slander, false arrest, malicious prosecution, and some advertising activities.

Coverage C. Medical Payments. This coverage applies to the medical expenses incurred as a result of accidental bodily injury on or away from the premises.

Section II—Who Is An Insured Those who are considered to be insureds under these forms include individuals; partnerships or joint venturers, as designated; or any other type of organization—including, where applicable, executive officers, directors, stockholders, and employees. Newly acquired organizations are also eligible for automatic coverage up to a maximum of ninety days.

Section III—Limit of Insurance This section addresses the application of the two aggregate limits and the sublimits. The *general aggregate limit* is the maximum amount payable during the policy period for claims or suits under Coverages A, B, and C, except for products and completed operations liability. The latter coverages are subject to a separate annual *products-completed operations aggregate limit.*

Section IV—Commercial General Liability Conditions These conditions are the ground rules that both parties to the contract must follow. Since these conditions apply solely to the two CGL forms, they must necessarily be separated from the other conditions which are common to all commercial lines contracts and are therefore contained in a separate form.

Section V—Extended Reporting Periods This section is found only in the claims-made form and describes the conditions under which the reporting period for claims may be extended.

Section VI—Definitions The definitions section is the fifth section of the occurrence form and the sixth in the claims-made form.

WHO IS OR IS NOT AN INSURED

Throughout the CGL policy, the words "you" and "your" refer to the named insured listed in the policy declarations. The named insured can include an individual, a partnership, a corporation, or an unincorporated association. It could also include two or more partnerships involved in a joint venture, a parent company and its subsidiaries, or a corporation and its individual shareholders.[7] To be covered as a *named* insured, a person or entity must be specifically designated in the policy declarations. If the number of named insureds is large, a list can be attached to the policy as an endorsement.

The provision that clarifies who insureds are appears as Section II of the CGL forms. This provision also contains many exclusionary phrases that explain which parties are not insureds. Though these phrases are not specifically labeled "exclusions," they do indeed function as exclusions and may properly be referred to as such. The following may be considered insureds under this policy:

1. An *individual*, when designated in the policy declarations as the named insured. Covered are the named insured and spouse, but only with respect to the conduct of a business of which the named insured is sole owner.
2. A *partnership or joint venture*, when designated in the policy declarations as the named insured. The named insured's members, partners, and their spouses are also insureds, but only with respect to the conduct of the named insured's business.
3. Any *organization other than a partnership or joint venture*, when such organization is designated in the policy declarations as the named insured. Included as insureds are the named insured's *executive officers and directors. Stockholders* also are considered to be insureds, but only with respect to their liability as stockholders.

Employees Insured and Excluded

The Who Is Insured provision also includes as insureds the named insured's employees, other than executive officers—but only for acts within the scope of their employment. However, employees are not protected as insureds under certain circumstances, as explained in the following paragraphs.

Fellow Employees and Cross Liability The first circumstance under which employees are not insured occurs when bodily injury or personal injury is sustained by the named insured or by a co-employee while in the course of his or her employment.

The reference to injury to co-employees is commonly referred to as the *fellow employee exclusion*. This exclusion can sometimes be deleted. However, it is intended to serve two purposes:

1. to help ensure that workers compensation insurance is the only source of coverage for employment-related injuries, and
2. to discourage the instituting of suits against fellow employees.

Similarly, injury sustained by the named insured at the hands of a fellow employee is excluded. The effect here is comparable to the so-called *cross liability exclusion*, which keeps a person from being both an insured and a claimant simultaneously. A fellow employee who allegedly injures the named insured would not be protected by the policy if the employee were to be sued for injuries sustained by the named insured. This exclusion reduces claims or suits involving internal disputes and the duplication of coverage with workers compensation insurance.

Medical Professional Liability An employee is not insured for bodily injury or personal injury that arises when an employee provides or fails to provide professional health care services. The purpose of this exclusion is to encourage such an employee, who is a physician, nurse, qualified emergency medical technician, or other medical professional, to obtain his or her professional liability insurance.

Note who is not excluded by this provision:

- Only the liability of professional employees is excluded.
- The named insured, as employer, would be protected against any vicarious liability it might incur because of an employed medical professional's acts or omissions.
- This exclusion is limited to professional liability exposures of the medical profession only.
- An additional endorsement excluding other professional liability exposures, such as architects, engineers and design-build contractors, might be added, however, if the insurer does not want to cover those exposures.
- If the employee who administers first aid is not a medical professional, protection should apply both to the employee and to his or her employer. For example, both employees and their employer are protected if an employee inadequately administers medical treatment to a customer who is injured while on the named insured's premises.

Coverage of this latter exposure is commonly referred to as *incidental malpractice coverage*. As with many so-called "coverages," this is not actually a separate affirmation of coverage within a distinct insuring agreement. Rather, it is a special category of exposures that is covered simply because it is not excluded. One reason insurance practitioners tend to refer to such things as "coverages" is that they were, in fact, separate and distinct coverages under earlier general liability policies or endorsements.

Employees' and Partners' Property The third circumstance excluding classification as an insured involves employees, as well as members and partners of partnerships. None of these people is insured for property damage to real or personal property that is owned, occupied, rented, or loaned to them.

Real Estate Managers

Apart from the foregoing, coverage applies to any person or organization acting as a real estate manager for the named insured, other than an employee of the named insured. The term *real estate manager* is not defined in the policy. However, it presumably includes any person or firm that manages the real property (buildings and grounds) of the named insured. A real estate manager's duties could involve maintaining the premises, making minor repairs, collecting rents, advertising for prospective tenants filling vacancies, and answering complaints.

Legal Representatives

In the event of the named insured's death, coverage applies to the named insured's legal representative. Coverage also applies to a person who has temporary custody of the named insured's property. This provides coverage for liability that may arise out of the maintenance or use of the property until the named insured's legal representative has been appointed.

Operators of Mobile Equipment

The Who Is Insured provision also contains a so-called *omnibus clause* that designates those who are and are not considered to be insureds while operating "mobile equipment" (defined later) registered and driven by the named insured (or by others with the named insured's permission) on public highways. (Omnibus, in this context, does not refer to a particular kind of vehicle, but to the fact that the clause handles many things at once.)

Persons Insured Persons insured in these circumstances are:

- any person while driving such equipment along a public highway with the named insured's permission, and

- any other person or organization responsible for the conduct of the above person, but only when liability arises out of the operation of such equipment and no other insurance of any kind, i.e., primary or excess, is available to such person or organization.

Persons Not Insured   A person or organization is not an insured while operating mobile equipment of the named insured on public highways in circumstances involving:

- bodily injury to a co-employee of the person operating the equipment, or
- property damage to property owned by, rented to, in the charge of or occupied by the named insured or the employer of any person who is an insured under this omnibus provision.

Newly Acquired or Formed Organizations

Any organization acquired or formed by the named insured is automatically protected as a named insured under the Who Is Insured provision until the new firm is specifically added to the policy or for ninety days, whichever is the shorter period. If a newly acquired or newly formed firm is not added to the policy by the ninetieth day (or by the end of the policy period, if it comes first), such firm is without further protection. The conditions that must be met to receive this automatic coverage are that:

1. the named insured either owns or has a majority interest in the newly acquired organization,
2. no other similar insurance is available to that organization,
3. coverage does not apply to "bodily injury" or "property damage" that occurred *before* the named insured acquired or formed such organization, and to "personal injury" or "advertising injury" that arises out of an offense committed *before* the named insured acquired or formed the organization, and
4. the newly acquired or newly formed organization is not a joint venture or partnership.

Unnamed Partnerships or Joint Ventures

Unless modified, the CGL policy does not include as an insured any person or organization with respect to the conduct of any *current or past* partnership or joint venture that is not listed in the policy declarations as the named insured. This provision prevents covering a liability exposure that is not contemplated by the basic premium charge of the policy. If coverage is desired for additional partnerships or joint ventures that arise during the policy period, they must be specifically declared and added to the policy by endorsement. Note that no coverage would apply to liability of a past partnership or joint venture if claim for damages is brought within the current policy period.

COVERAGE A: BODILY INJURY AND PROPERTY DAMAGE

An insurer makes the same basic promise, paraphrased below, in the insuring agreement of the CGL coverage forms—both claims made and occurrence:

> We will pay those sums that the insured becomes legally obligated to pay as damages because of "bodily injury" or "property damage" to which this insurance applies... The "bodily injury" or "property damage" must be caused by an "occurrence." The "occurrence" must take place in the "policy territory."

In the first part of the insuring agreement, the phrase *to which this insurance applies* is especially noteworthy. An insurer does not have to fulfill its promise to pay damages if the claim or suit does not allege a "bodily injury" or "property damage," as those terms are defined, or if the claim or suit is otherwise excluded. However, the insurer's duty to *defend* is broader than its duty to pay damages. Even if a suit is later found to be groundless, false, or fraudulent, the insurer must defend an insured whenever the plaintiff alleges facts that could conceivably fall within the coverage of the policy. In determining whether the insurer has a duty to defend, some courts have based their findings solely on the allegations expressed in the complaint or petition of the plaintiff, while other courts have looked beyond the allegations and considered the actual facts and/or the reasonable expectations of the plaintiff.

Occurrence

For coverage to apply under either form, the "bodily injury" or "property damage" must be caused by an "occurrence." This term is defined in the forms to mean "an accident, including continuous or repeated exposure to substantially the same general harmful conditions." The term accident is not defined in the policy, but the intent is to provide coverage for any adverse condition that continues over a long period and eventually results in bodily injury or property damage, as well as an event that happens suddenly and results in immediate bodily injury or property damage. In either case, the bodily injury or property damage would be caused by an occurrence.

Coverage Territory

Coverage applies only to occurrences that take place in the "coverage territory," as defined, and the "coverage territory" is not necessarily the same for activities as for products, completed operations, or property in transit. Also relevant to some claims is the question of where the suit is brought.

Activities From the standpoint of an insured's activities, the coverage territory is worldwide. However, this broad territorial scope applies only if the bodily injury or property damage (or personal injury or advertising injury of Coverage B) arises from activities of an insured who is domiciled in the United States, its territories or possessions, Puerto Rico, or Canada.

Products and Completed Operations With respect to injury or damage arising from the named insured's goods or products, the coverage territory is worldwide only when the goods or products are made *or* sold by the named insured in the United States, its territories or possessions, Puerto Rico or Canada. In addition, the insurer has an obligation to pay any damages only when the suit is filed within one of the aforementioned jurisdictions, unless the insurer agrees to a settlement.

To illustrate, if a product made by the named insured in the United States is sold abroad, coverage would be afforded, provided the named insured's liability is determined in a suit brought within the United States, its territories or possessions, Puerto Rico, or Canada.

From the viewpoint of the plaintiff, there are definite advantages to filing suit within the United States rather than in a foreign country. The American courts are said to be relatively attractive to foreign plaintiffs because of the (1) availability of trial by jury, (2) availability of the contingency fee approach, (3) pre-trial discovery, and (4) recognition of strict liability in products.[8] While American courts will permit original suits based on occurrences in other countries, not all foreign plaintiffs file their suits within the United States. The latter may lead some firms to seek worldwide liability protection—particularly if they are multinational corporations that cater to the foreign market.

The coverage territory for any injury or damage stemming from completed operations, on the other hand, is limited solely to the United States, its territories or possessions, Puerto Rico, or Canada. For example, the construction contractor who conducts operations in a foreign country would have limited protection while operations are in progress; but once those operations have been completed, there would be no coverage for claim or suit, even if it were to be filed within the coverage territory.

In Transit While the coverage territory of the CGL forms is defined to include international waters and airspace, no claim or suit is covered if the injury or damage arises out of and in the course of an insured's travel to or from any place other than the United States, its territories or possessions, Puerto Rico, or Canada:

- Coverage would be applicable while an insured is upon international waters or in air space between the United States and its territories or possessions, Puerto Rico, or Canada; between the continental United States and Hawaii or Alaska; or between the United States, it territories or possessions, Puerto Rico, or Canada and off-shore towers in international waters.
- No coverage would apply during the course of the insured's travel or transportation between two foreign countries, or between the United States and a foreign country other than Canada, or between Canada and a foreign country.

Where Suit Must Be Brought Any "suit" for damages also must be brought within the United States, its territories or possessions, Puerto Rico, or Canada. For example, if an employee of a firm negligently injures someone while on a business trip to the Far East:

- If a suit against them is filed within the United States, its territories or possessions, Puerto Rico, or Canada, both the employer and the employee will be protected.
- If the suit is instituted in the foreign country of injury, neither the employer nor the employee will be protected—unless the insurer, at its option, agrees to a settlement there. An insurer may investigate and settle a claim, if it can, in order to prevent a suit.

Legally Obligated to Pay Damages

The insuring agreement states that coverage applies in situations where the insured becomes *legally obligated* to pay *damages*. An insured may become legally obligated to pay damages as the proximate result of any type of legal wrong for which the civil law provides a remedy in the form of an action for money damages, whether the wrong is committed by an insured or by another person for whose conduct an insured is vicariously liable. Such wrongs include any type of tort, the breach of a contractual obligation, an antitrust violation, or any other wrong for which money damages are payable. However, the policy does not cover all legal obligations to pay damages; it covers only the kinds of obligations that are within the scope of the complete insuring agreement and are not excluded in the exclusions, conditions, definitions, and/or other policy provisions.

The damages that may be imposed by a court of law can take the form of *special damages* for such out-of-pocket costs as loss of earnings and medical expenses; *general damages* for such intangibles as pain and suffering; and, in many jurisdictions *punitive damages*. (Though the language of the CGL gives the insurer the contractual duty to pay all such damages, to the extent that an insured is legally obligated to do so, a few states do not recognize the concept of punitive damages; some states do not permit insurers to pay punitive damages on behalf of an insured; and, in states that do allow insurers to pay punitive damages, insurers are not likely to pay them in the absence of a court order.)

Defense and Legal Costs

The insurer also promises to provide a defense and pay for various legal costs associated with a claim or suit against the insured. This provision of the CGL form reads:

> We will have the right and duty to defend any "suit" seeking those damages.... Our right and duty to defend end when we have used up the applicable limit of insurance in the payment of judgments or settlements under Coverages A or B or medical expenses under Coverage C. The word "suit" is defined in the CGL forms to mean:
>
> ... a civil proceeding in which damages because of "bodily injury." "property damage," "personal injury" or "advertising injury" to which this insurance applies are alleged. "Suit" includes an arbitration proceeding alleging such damages to which you must submit or submit with our consent.

Note that this definition of "suit" is broad enough to include informal civil proceedings and arbitration, as well as formal lawsuits under the defense and supplementary payments benefits of the policy.

As noted earlier, the insurer has the duty to defend an insured whenever the petition or complaint of a lawsuit contains allegations that are potentially within the scope of coverage. In some jurisdictions, the insurer's duty to defend also extends to lawsuits in which the actual facts would fall within the scope of coverage, whether or not the actual facts are contained in the written allegations. And some courts base the insurer's duty at least partly on the grounds that the insured could reasonably have expected its defense by the insurer. Presumably, the insurer's duty to defend a claim in a less formal proceeding is as broad as its duty to defend a formal lawsuit in the particular jurisdiction involved.

Exhaustion of Limits   An insurer is not obligated to pay any claim or to defend any suit after the insurer's limit of liability has been exhausted by the payment of any judgments or settlements under any one or more of the Coverages A, B, or C of the forms. Thus, suppose an insured is confronted with two bodily injury liability suits brought by separate claimants at different times but for damages arising from the same covered occurrence. If the settlement of the first exhausts the limit of liability, the second suit need not be defended by the insurer. Also, if the two bodily injury liability suits were to arise from separate occurrences, the insurer's obligation to defend would hinge on how much of the annual aggregate limit has not been reduced following the payment of the first claim. In light of the across-the-board aggregate limit on coverages, A (bodily injury and property damage), B (personal injury and advertising injury), and C (medical payments), along with the separate annual aggregate limit applicable to products and completed operations, the insurer's duty to defend could disappear rapidly with a combination of claims under Coverages A, B, and C. Limits of liability are discussed in greater detail in Chapter 6.

Suits in Equity   Another important provision of the insuring agreement reads:

> No other obligation or liability to pay sums or perform acts or services is covered unless explicitly provided for under the Supplementary Payments—Coverages A and B.

A growing number of suits seek injunctive relief or the required performance or prohibition of an act. In the area of environmental impairment, for example, injunctions to restrain activities dangerous to the health and welfare of the community have become common. In fact, the only recourse under some environmental statutes, such as the Resource Conservation and Recovery Act (RCRA), is injunctive relief. Injunctive relief, an action in equity, does not involve money damages, but it does involve legal costs for both parties to the litigation.

While defense costs are payable when a covered suit seeks money damages, the CGL forms attempt to make clear, by the above provision, that no *other* obligation or liability is covered unless *explicitly* provided for under the supplementary payments provision. The net effect is this:

- The legal costs of an action solely in equity are not covered by the CGL forms, because an action in equity alone does not seek money damages.
- However, if a suit involves an action in equity and *also* seeks money damages on other grounds, the legal costs of the entire

action would likely be covered by the CGL forms (assuming the suit seeking damages is one that the insured has a duty to defend).[9]

COVERAGE A: BODILY INJURY AND PROPERTY DAMAGE EXCLUSIONS

The commercial general liability forms are subject to fourteen exclusions. Each of these exclusions will be examined here. However, detailed discussion of exclusions directed toward preventing the duplication of coverage of other liability policies—such as workers compensation and auto policies—will be discussed more fully in other chapters.

Although the CGL labels the various exclusions only with letter designations (a, b, c, and so forth), this chapter will refer to them by descriptive names. It will be helpful to have a copy of the policy at hand while these exclusions are discussed.

Intentional Injury Exclusion

The intentional injury exclusion is designed to preclude the payment of any damages and/or legal costs associated with bodily injury or property damage that is either *expected or intended by the insured.* Since the exclusion is couched in terms of bodily injury or property damage, rather than an act or omission, the coverage of the policy would seem to apply when an insured intended to commit an act but neither expected nor intended it to result in bodily injury or property damage to another (assuming the claim was not excluded by the application of some other policy provision). Coverage would likewise seem to apply when the act or omission was negligent or unintentional and no injury or damage was intended by the insured. A serious coverage question could arise, however, if a court holds that the insured could have reasonably expected or foreseen that bodily injury or property damage would be the natural consequence of his or her acts or omissions. For example, a firm that has a serious premises liability hazard and fails to take steps to eliminate it could conceivably be denied protection, particularly if repeated bodily injury claims result from the unsafe condition.

The language of the policy specifically stipulates that the intentional injury exclusion does not apply to bodily injury resulting from the use of reasonable force to protect persons or property. Here, as elsewhere, what is "reasonable" is a question of fact that would ultimately be decided by the trier of fact (normally a jury), if the reasonableness of the force is disputed.

Contractual Liability Exclusion

The contractual liability exclusion precludes coverage for liability assumed by the insured under any contract or agreement—except as otherwise provided for by the policy. Coverage for many of the exposures that are excluded can be purchased, either through other policies or by attachment of a coverage form to the CGL policy.

Despite the contractual liability exclusion, the CGL provides protection for business firms and other entities to whom the legal liability of others has been transferred under many contracts or agreements. In a sense, it might be more appropriate to refer to the CGL's *contractual liability coverage*.

To determine the scope and nature of contractual liability exposures covered, it is necessary to examine the contractual liability exclusion. This exclusion states that no coverage applies for "bodily injury" or "property damage" for which the insured is obligated to pay damages by reason of the insured's assumption of liability under any contract or agreement—with two exceptions. The exclusion does not apply to liability for damages (1) assumed under an "insured contract" or (2) that the insured would have in the absence of the contract or agreement. Liability for all other instances is intended to be excluded.

Insured Contracts Whether an exposure is covered depends partly on the meaning of the term "insured contract", which is defined in both forms to mean: (a) a lease of premises; (b) a sidetrack agreement; (c) an easement or license agreement in connection with vehicle or pedestrian private railroad crossings at grade; (d) any other easement agreement, except in connection with construction or demolition operations on or within 50 feet of a railroad; (e) an agreement required by a municipality, except an agreement required in connection with work for a municipality; (f) an elevator maintenance agreement; or (g) that part of any other contract or agreement concerning the named insured's business under which the named insured assumes the tort liability of another to pay damages because of bodily injury or property damage to a third person or organization, and tort liability is defined by the policy to mean "a liability that would be imposed by law in the absence of any contract or agreement."

The following are specific illustrations of the types of written or oral agreements that are considered to be within the scope of an "insured contract" and therefore covered.

a. *Lease of Premises.* Landlords commonly require a tenant to sign a lease before the tenant is permitted to occupy the property. Leases not only specify conditions dealing with rental or lease financing arrangements, but also specify the respective responsibilities of landlords and tenants for such matters as alterations, repairs, general upkeep, the payment of utilities, and damages caused by neglect. For example, a tenant may agree to hold the landlord harmless under a lease agreement for any bodily injury or property damage arising from any physical defects of the premises or from any negligent operations within the tenant's control. Because a lease of premises is an "insured contract," the liability the tenant assumes thereunder would automatically be covered under the CGL forms. (However, any agreement by a tenant to indemnify a landlord for fire damage to rented premises is not an "insured contract." This exposure may be covered by the policy's fire legal liability coverage, discussed later.)

b. *Sidetrack agreements.* Railroads require business firms, as a condition precedent to installing sidetracks or spurs to facilitate private operations, to hold the railroads harmless from losses arising from the ownership, maintenance or use of the sidetracks. Such agreements may also hold firms responsible for any damage to the property itself.

c. *Easement or license agreement involving vehicle or pedestrian railroad crossings at grade.* Although easements involve a variety of legal complexities, they can be thought of as limited rights to use land belonging to others. Such rights can benefit owners and users, or only users. For example, in order to extend railroad tracks into a refinery, it may be necessary that the tracks cross public property over which motor vehicles and pedestrians pass. The refinery may be required to hold harmless not only the railroad but also the entity on whose property the rails are located. Such as easement agreement would be an "insured contract."

d. *Any other easements.* In addition to the specific type of easement referred to in (c) above, any other easement is an "insured contract" under CGL forms, with one exception. The policy does not cover any easement agreement required in connection with any construction or demolition operations on or within fifty feet of a railroad. ("Railroad protective liability" coverage, discussed in Chapter 7, is required to cover this latter exposure.) Examples of easements for which coverage would apply include those involving the use of private land by a public utility for maintenance of an underground natural gas pipeline, and those involving the use of a right-of-way on property owned by a township that gives access to a body of water.

e. *Agreements required by municipalities*. Municipalities often have ordinances that require others to hold the municipalities harmless for any liability stemming from devices or obstructions that can cause bodily injury or property damage to members of the public. Store owners, for example, often are required to enter into such agreements if they desire to erect signs or canopies that will hang over a public walkway, or to install sidewalk elevators that could obstruct the public thoroughfare. The owner agrees to hold the city harmless for any claims that may arise because of that sign, canopy, or sidewalk elevator. (The owner also will be required to obtain and file a license and permit bond that guarantees the city that any claims will be paid by the owner if it is required to do so. License and permit bonds are discussed in Chapter 13.) Such assumed liability automatically is covered, provided that the indemnification is required by a municipal ordinance. Road construction contractors and other firms that perform work for a municipality may also be required by ordinance to sign an indemnification agreement. Such agreements are not within this portion of the definition of "insured contract." They may, however, fall within the "other tort liability assumptions" category discussed under (g) below.

f. *Elevator maintenance agreements*. Building owners and lessees are frequently required to hold harmless firms that install and/or service elevators. The resulting contractual liability of the owner or lessee is covered automatically.

g. *Tort liability assumptions*. At some time or another, most organizations are required to assume the liability of others under a contract or agreement. The CGL policy provides coverage only for an insured who has contractually assumed, prior to injury or damage, the *tort* liability that the other contracting party may have to a third person who is not a legal party to the assumption agreement or the insurance policy. As noted earlier, the policy defines "tort liability" to mean "a liability that would be imposed by law in the absence of any contract or agreement."

"By limiting 'insured contracts' to tort liability assumptions, the CGL avoids providing coverage for warranty agreements. For example, BIM Company, a computer manufacturer, may warrant that it will replace any computer that breaks down during the first ninety days of use. Although BIM has assumed a responsibility in this warranty contract, it has not assumed *tort* liability—and the warranty therefore is not an 'insured contract.' "

What an "Insured Contract" Does Not Encompass
Contractual liability "coverage" is limited by certain exclusions describing exposures that are not deemed to be "insured contracts." Specifically precluded from contractual coverage of the CGL policy are various aspects of the professional and fire legal liability exposures.

Professional Liability Exposures. An "insured contract" does not include that part of any contract or agreement with two specific aspects of professional liability.

- First, the policy does not cover the part of any contract or agreement that obligates an insured to indemnify an architect, engineer, or surveyor for injury or damage arising out of preparation, approval, or failure to prepare or approve maps, drawings, opinions, reports, surveys, change orders, designs or specifications; or the giving of directions or instructions or the failure to give them, if that is the primary cause of the injury or damage. For example, the insured who agrees to hold harmless and indemnify an architect would not be able to look to its CGL policy for the protection of the architect, even if the architect would be liable for injury or damage in absence of this agreement.
- Second, the policy does not cover that part of any contract or agreement under which the insured, if an architect, engineer, or surveyor, assumes liability for injury or damage arising out of its rendering or failure to render professional services, including those listed above and supervisory, inspection, or engineering services.

This exclusion, which is one of many found in the definitions section, avoids providing coverage for exposures that insurers prefer to cover, if at all, under professional liability insurance forms with appropriate premiums.

Fire Liability Exposures. An "insured contract" also does not include that part of any contract or agreement that indemnifies any person or organization for damage by fire to premises rented or loaned to the named insured. This type of indemnification clause is common in lease agreements.

For example, suppose a lease requires the tenant to indemnify the landlord for fire damage to premises rented to the tenant, even if the fire is caused by the landlord. If damage is sustained because of the *tenant's* negligence and the tenant is the insured under a CGL, the tenant would have the responsibility to repair the damage even in the absence of any contractual obligation—it is not, in this case, liability assumed under contract. (As noted later, exclusion (j)—the general property damage exclusion—would eliminate coverage for damage to property rented to the named insured. However, an exception located at the end of the exclusions section of the policy applies coverage for fire damage. The coverage granted by this exception to the exclusions is sometimes referred to as *fire legal liability coverage* discussed later.)

Suppose, however, the *landlord* is burning brush near the building and the fire spreads to the building. The landlord can require the tenant to pay for the fire damage because of the cited lease provision. The CGL insurer would not be obligated to respond for this tenant's liability for fire damage assumed under contract. A tenant's contractual liability for *fire* damage to premises is excluded by the contractual liability exclusion.

No protection is available to the insured who agrees to such contractual assumption. Insureds must be careful to identify this exposure since it can be dealt with by purchasing property insurance.

Liability in Absence of a Contract   As noted, there are only two exceptions to the exclusion for liability assumed under a contract or agreement:

1. when the assumption takes place under an "insured contract," and
2. when the liability would have prevailed at law despite the contractual assumption.

To illustrate the latter circumstance, consider Arrow Builders, a construction firm, hired to construct a manufacturing plant for Quiver Manufacturing. Arrow agrees to hold harmless and indemnify Quiver for bodily injury or property damage sustained by any person because of the acts or omissions of Arrow. During the course of construction, an employee of Arrow's subcontractor is injured because Arrow allegedly failed to provide proper safeguards. The injured employee files suit not only against Arrow, but also against Quiver based on the failure of both parties to warn the employee of any unsafe conditions and to remove the hazards. It ultimately is determined that Quiver is free from any fault. Assuming no other policy exclusion is applicable, Arrow's CGL policy should respond to the claim because Arrow would have been liable at law because of negligence even the absence of its contractual assumption. The contract had nothing to do with Arrow's liability to the injured employee.

Going one step further, suppose Arrow, the builder, agrees to hold harmless and indemnify Quiver, the plant owner, in every instance except when any injury or damage as alleged is due solely to Quiver's negligence. If, in the foregoing example Quiver were to be held partially liable for failure to warn the injured employee of a hazardous premises condition, Arrow's CGL policy should respond here as long as the liability of the plant owner would be imposed by law. In this case, Quiver's portion of the claim would be attributable to liability assumed under an "insured contract"; Arrow's would be liable in the absence of contract.

Going still further, assume that Quiver is ultimately found to be solely responsible for the worker's injuries. Arrow's CGL policy would cover Arrow's contractual assumption of Quiver's liability—assuming the contract is enforceable. However, additional factors might come into play. For example, there may be a statutory prohibition against the assumption of another's sole liability; the contractual assumption may not be as explicit as a court generally requires; or because of the unequal bargaining power of the parties, the contractual assumption may be deemed to be unconscionable and, therefore, against public policy.

A Word of Caution Transferees and transferors are often under the mistaken impression that the entire assumption, as agreed upon, is covered by insurance—especially when contractual liability coverage is listed on a certificate of insurance. However, as has been pointed out, certain types of assumptions are beyond the scope of the contractual liability coverage automatically provided by the CGL policy. Furthermore, certain types of contractual assumptions have been declared void under the applicable statutes of some states. And, even in absence of statute, a court of law may hold the terms of a contract to be in violation of public policy. In such instances, despite the contract, the transferor has not transferred the exposure.

Liquor Liability Exclusion

The so-called *liquor liability exclusion* is aimed at firms in the business of manufacturing, distributing, selling, serving, or furnishing alcoholic beverages. The exclusion precludes bodily injury and property damage coverage for claims in which any insured may be held liable:

1. for causing or contributing to the intoxication of any person;
2. for furnishing alcoholic beverages to a person under legal drinking age, or to a person under the influence of alcohol; or
3. for violating any statute, ordinance, or regulation relating to the sale, gift, distribution, or use of alcoholic beverages.

The laws mentioned in (3) above, which apply in varying degrees in many states, are sometimes referred to as *dram shop acts* or *alcoholic beverage control acts*. While the application and scope of these laws vary by state, their general purpose is to give a person, when injured by an intoxicated adult or by a minor who is served alcoholic beverages, a right of action against the dispenser of the beverages. In some states, the common law creates liability even when a statute may or may not apply. In any event, a seller of alcoholic beverages confronted with a liquor liability suit does not have any protection under an unendorsed commercial general liability policy.

It is not always easy to determine whether an entity is "in the business of" selling, serving, or furnishing alcoholic beverages. For example, would a nonprofit organization that sells liquor without profit motive be considered "in the business"? How about an organization that conducts a special event where alcoholic beverages are sold? Would the fact that the entity requires a license be the determinant? These are all important questions that may require answers before any coverage is to be expected by exception to the exclusion. For example, if the insured is not considered to be *in the business*, then by inference the insured could be considered a *host* and covered by exception to the exclusion. This "coverage" is sometimes referred to as *host liquor liability coverage*.

A liquor host, or an enterprise with no known connection to the liquor business, can also become involved with liquor liability exposure through contractual assumption. Consider the following situation. Concord Company desires to hold a picnic for its employees and their families. Concord engages Booz, a wholesale distributor of alcoholic beverages, to dispense beverages at the picnic. As a condition precedent to the undertaking, Concord signs a contract to hold Booz harmless from any liability that could result from serving such beverages. A member of an employee's family becomes intoxicated and causes an auto accident after the picnic. As a result, suit is brought against both Concord and Booz. Concord's CGL policy should offer protection to Concord because Concord was not in the business of serving the alcoholic beverages, but was a host. Booz's CGL would not protect Booz because it was in the alcoholic beverage business.

If Booz seeks protection from Concord because of the latter's contractual assumption, the CGL policy of Concord also should apply to Booz's claim because the suit is considered to be an "insured contract," (that part of any contract in which the named insured (indemnitor) assumes the tort liability of another (indemnitee) to pay damages to a third person). However, Booz's contract transferring its liquor liability to Concord might not be upheld by the courts if it is considered to be against public policy.

Note finally that the liquor liability exclusion does not apply to the owner or lessee of premises used by others for liquor businesses. The owner or lessee therefore would be protected by the CGL policy for any claim or suit against the owner or lessee alleging that had the owner or lessee been more careful in the selection of tenant (vendor), the injury might not have occurred.

Workers Compensation (and Similar Laws) Exclusion

The CGL policy (and virtually all commercial liability policies) excludes coverage for any obligation for which the insured may be held liable under any workers compensation, disability benefits, unemployment compensation, or similar law. The purpose of the exclusion is to avoid a duplication between the CGL policy and other policies that are specifically designed for such employee protection.

Employers Liability Exclusion

No protection applies under the commercial general liability policy for bodily injury sustained by any employee of the insured when the injury arises out of and during the course of an employee's work. This exclusion makes employers liability insurance, rather than the CGL policy, the exclusive source of coverage for tort actions against the employer by employee with job-connected injuries or diseases. Employers liability insurance coverage is usually included in the same policy that provides statutory workers compensation coverage.

Claims by Spouses and Families A portion of the employers liability exclusion also precludes coverage for any claim or suit by spouses and other close relatives seeking damages as a consequence of a job-connected injury sustained by an employee of an insured. Claims or suits of this nature generally seek damages for loss of consortium.

Claims Under Dual Capacity Doctrine Another portion of the employers liability exclusion makes it clear that the exclusion is applicable whether the insured may be liable as an employer or in any other capacity. The phrase "in any other capacity" is directed toward claims or suits against employers based on the so-called *dual capacity doctrine*, a doctrine under which it is sometimes possible for the employee to collect twice for injuries. For the employee to prevail, however, he or she must allege and show, among other things, that the employer occupied two independent and unrelated relationships with the employee.

In one actual case, the plaintiff was injured while he was a passenger in a truck owned by a manufacturer.[10] One of the truck tires blew out and that caused an accident. At the time of injury, the plaintiff was a "borrowed employee" of the manufacturer and therefore subject to the statutory benefits of the manufacturer's workers compensation insurance. The twist here was that the tire that blew out was made by the manufacturer who hired the borrowed employee. Thus, a second cause of action against the employer was based on products liability. This latter cause of action was upheld by the court on the basis that the exposure was not employment-related but rather common to the public as well (in other words, the employee would have been exposed to injury had he been a consumer of the product at the time of injury).

The dual-capacity doctrine is also referred to as the "two-hat" theory. The employer wears two hats. The first connotes its capacity as an employer and the other signifies its role as a third-party tortfeasor.

In light of the dual-capacity exclusion of the CGL policy, any such actions of persons who seek a second source of recovery would be payable, if at all, under the employers liability portion of the workers compensation policy, or stop gap coverage in monopolistic fund states. (These policies are discussed in Chapter 11.)

Third-Party-Over Actions Another part of the employers liability exclusion precludes coverage for so-called *third-party-over actions.* A third-party-over action can arise when an injured employee sues and recovers from a negligent third party. The third party, in turn, sues the employer for at least partial recovery based on joint negligence of the employer.

For example, as illustrated in Exhibit 5-1, an employee is injured by a machine which the employer, with knowledge of a safety defect, allows to be operated. The employee sues the manufacturer of that machine, rather than accepting the compensation benefits of the applicable statute, in order to obtain a judgment for a larger dollar amount. The manufacturer then sues the employer on the basis that the employer was also negligent in permitting the machine to be operated in an unsafe condition. Specific reference to the phrase of the exclusion reading "... to any obligation to *share* damages or to *repay* someone else..." means that no coverage applies whether the obligation of the employer to pay damages in a third-party-over action takes the form of contribution (share) or indemnification (repay).[11]

The reason for this exclusion is that protection for third-party-over actions is available under employers liability coverage, except when liability of the insured (employer) for the bodily injury is assumed by the insured under an "insured contract." (In these latter instances, coverage is available under the CGL policy to the extent of the applicable contractual liability protection. This subject is discussed in more detail in Chapters 10 and 11.)

Exhibit 5-1
Third-Party-Over Action Illustrated

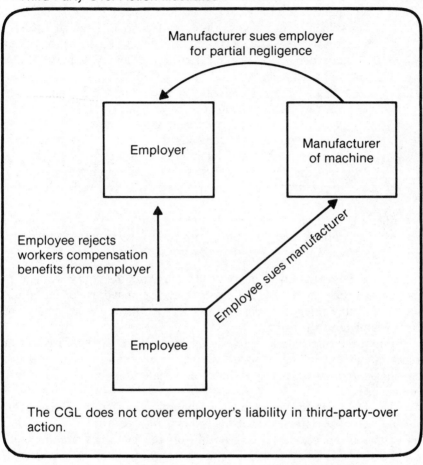

Manufacturer sues employer
for partial negligence

Employer

Manufacturer
of machine

Employee rejects
workers compensation
benefits from employer

Employee sues manufacturer

Employee

The CGL does not cover employer's liability in third-party-over
action.

Pollution Exclusion

The pollution exclusion is a broadly worded provision which, with a
few exceptions, represents nearly a total exclusion of the exposure. The
exclusion eliminates coverage for:

*(1) "Bodily injury" or "property damage" arising out of the actual,
alleged or threatened discharge, dispersal, release or escape of
pollutants:
    *(a) At or from premises you own, rent or occupy;

(b) At or from any site or location used by or for you or others for the handling, storage, disposal, processing or treatment of waste;

(c) Which are at any time transported, handled, stored, treated, disposed of, or processed as waste by or for you or any person or organization for whom you may legally responsible; or

(d) At or from any site or location on which you or any contractors or subcontractors working directly or indirectly on your behalf are performing operations:

  *(i) if the pollutants are brought on or to the site or location in connection with such operations; or

  *(ii) if the operations are to test for, monitor, clean up, remove, contain, treat, detoxify or neutralize the pollutants.

(2) Any loss, cost, or expense arising out of any governmental direction or request that you test for, monitor, clean up, remove, contain, treat, detoxify or neutralize pollutants.

A policy endorsement, introduced soon after the policy was put in use, states that the asterisked portions of the above exclusion do not apply to bodily injury or property damage caused by heat, smoke, or fumes from a hostile fire.

Pollutants means any solid, liquid, gaseous or thermal irritant or contaminant, including smoke, vapor, soot, fumes, acids, alkalis, chemicals and waste. Waste includes materials to be recycled, reconditioned, or reclaimed.

This pollution exclusion is discussed again in Chapter 7. However, it is important to note here that the following exposures are intended to be excluded: emissions (1) originating on the insured's premises, (2) from a waste disposal or treatment site, regardless of its location, (3) from a site where the operations are being performed by or on behalf of the insured and the pollutants are brought on the site for purposes of having work performed on them, including containment or treatment. Also excluded are cleanup costs prompted by any government direction or request, whether such cleanup costs are incurred directly by the insured or indirectly by assessment following such cleanup by others.

What coverage may apply must be inferred from what is not excluded by the exclusion. In essence, coverage is provided for products-completed operations losses and off-site emissions, provided the pollutants are not in the nature of waste or brought to the jobsite in connection with the insured's or subcontractor's operations. For example, coverage is said to apply to a firm that sold a tank, now on premises of the buyer (other than a waste disposal or treatment site), which in time leaks and releases a pollutant that results in claims for bodily injury or property damage. Protection applies whether the leak was sudden or gradual, if the leak was accidental. But no coverage would apply under the CGL belonging to the owner of the tanks on whose premises the event occurred. If, at the time of the leak, the seller of the tank is out of business, the owner might be faced with a costly uninsured loss that could not be charged to another party unless other measures had been taken. Also, coverage is provided for heat, smoke, and fume damage arising out of a hostile fire.

Exclusion of Aircraft, Autos, and Watercraft

This exclusion is designed to eliminate the coverage duplications and substantial overlaps that would otherwise exist between the CGL policy and the policies customarily used to cover aircraft, watercraft, and auto exposures. To gain the proper perspective on the scope of this exclusion, it is necessary to examine the meaning of the terms "auto" and "mobile equipment," as defined in the CGL policy.

Auto Almost all auto liability exposures are excluded under the CGL policy. The term "auto" is defined as meaning *a land motor vehicle, trailer or semitrailer designed for travel on public roads, including any attached machinery or equipment. But "auto" does not include "mobile equipment."* While the precise meaning of an auto hinges on the definition of "mobile equipment," note that an auto—as a land motor vehicle designed for public road travel—does not include aircraft, watercraft, locomotives operated on rails, and self-propelled equipment such as contractors' cranes and bulldozers, even when the latter equipment travels on public roads. On the other hand, the term "auto" is not limited to four-wheeled vehicles, as is the case under many personal policies designed to cover private passenger automobiles. Thus, an "auto" as defined in the policy can consist of vehicles with one or more wheels, if they do not otherwise qualify as "mobile equipment." Note, finally, that machinery or apparatus that is attached (towed or carried) to a land motor vehicle is deemed to be as much a part of the auto liability exposure as the powered unit that conveys such machinery or apparatus.

Mobile Equipment The definition of "mobile equipment" is important, because the liability exposure of any land vehicle that qualifies as such equipment is automatically covered under the CGL policy. On the other hand, the business auto coverage form covers auto liability exposures, but excludes mobile equipment liability. To qualify as mobile equipment, a land vehicle, whether or not self-propelled, must come within at least one of six categories listed in the policy.

It is not always easy to distinguish "autos" from "mobile equipment," but the distinction can be crucial—especially in cases where (1) there is no applicable auto insurance, (2) there is no applicable general liability insurance, (3) the auto liability and general liability coverage have different limits of liability available, or (4) the two coverages are with different insurance companies.

"Mobile equipment" is defined as any of the following types of land vehicles, including any attached machinery or equipment:
a. Bulldozers, farm machinery, forklifts and other vehicles designed for use principally off public roads;
b. Vehicles maintained for use solely on or next to the premises the named insured owns or rents;
c. Vehicles that travel on crawler-treads;
d. Vehicles, whether self-propelled or not, maintained primarily to provide mobility to permanently mounted:
    (1) Power cranes, shovels, loaders, diggers or drills; or
    (2) Road construction or resurfacing equipment such as graders, scrapers or rollers;
e. Vehicles not described in a., b., c., or d. above that are not self-propelled and are maintained primarily to provide mobility to permanently attached equipment of the following types:
    (1) Air compressors, pumps and generators, including spraying, welding, building cleaning, geophysical exploration, lighting and well servicing equipment; or
    (2) Cherry pickers and similar devices used to raise or lower workers;
f. Vehicles not described in a., b., c., or d. above maintained primarily for purposes other than the transportation of persons or cargo. However, self-propelled vehicles with the following types of permanently attached equipment are not "mobile equipment" but will be considered "autos":
    (1) Equipment designed primarily for:
        (a) Snow removal;
        (b) Road maintenance, but not construction or resurfacing;
        (c) Street cleaning;
    (2) Cherry pickers and similar devices mounted on automobile or truck chassis and used to raise or lower workers; and
    (3) Air compressors, pumps and generators, including spraying, welding, building cleaning, geophysical exploration, lighting and well servicing equipment.

These definitions and their implications will be examined more closely in Chapter 8, in the context of the business auto coverage form. However, it was necessary to examine briefly the meaning of "auto" in order to clarify the scope of the CGL exclusion for autos.

Scope and Rationale of Exclusion The CGL aircraft, automobile, and watercraft exclusion precludes coverage for bodily injury or property damage claims that arise from the ownership, maintenance, use, entrustment, or loading or unloading of aircraft, auto or watercraft, when they are owned, operated, rented, or loaned to any insured. If coverage for employees, as additional insureds, is not otherwise deleted by endorsement, this exclusion will also preclude liability from aircraft, autos, and watercraft operated by any person who is considered to be an insured, such as an employee.

The reference to *entrustment* is intended to preclude any attempt to circumvent this exclusion by maintaining that liability did not arise from the ownership, maintenance, or use of the vehicle, but instead because the insured negligently entrusted the vehicle to another party. Such attempts have been made with rental autos where the plaintiff sues the auto owner because the owner entrusted the auto to a person who was not competent to operate it. Any such allegations must be handled under the respective auto liability policies of those vehicles.

However, it can be inferred that an insured may be protected if implicated in a claim involving the use of a nonowned aircraft, auto, or watercraft operated by any person or firm that is not deemed to be an insured under the policy, when such vehicle is used in the furtherance of the insured's business.

As with other exclusion, some coverage is specifically granted by way of exceptions. Coverage applies to liability arising:

- *from watercraft of any size while ashore on premises owned or rented to the named insured.*
- *from a watercraft the named insured does not own, wherever it is used, so long as it is (a) less than 26 feet long and (b) is not being used to carry persons or property for a charge.*
- *from the parking of an "auto" on, or on the ways next to, premises the named insured owns or rents, provided the auto is not owned, rented, or loaned to the named insured or the insured.* Restaurants, hotels and office complexes that provide parking for their customers or clients and provide attendants to park them have coverage for their liability because of bodily injury or property damage arising from the parking of such autos of others. Damage to the autos themselves is not covered, however, because of the care, custody, or control exclusion mentioned later. A business that desires physical damage insurance should purchase garagekeepers insurance.
- *from the assumption of liability under an "insured contract" dealing with the ownership, maintenance, or use of any aircraft or watercraft.* No coverage applies from the contractual assumption of liability dealing with auto because that exposure can, and should, be handled under the business auto policy.

- *from the operation of equipment under paragraphs (f) (2) and (f) (3) of the definition of "mobile equipment."* As was noted earlier, a truck, as a self-propelled vehicle to which building cleaning equipment is attached, is considered to be an "auto" rather than "mobile equipment." If a claim were to be prompted by a traffic accident involving the truck, it would be the business auto coverage form that would be applicable, rather than the CGL. If a claim for damages because of bodily injury or property damage were made against the insured stemming from the *operation* of the equipment, coverage would be subject to the CGL policy.

Mobile Equipment Exclusion

The CGL policy is the primary form of coverage against the liability exposures of mobile equipment. However, there are two circumstances when the liability exposures of mobile equipment are not covered under the CGL policy.

1. *When bodily injury or property damage arises out of the transportation of mobile equipment by an auto that is owned, operated, rented, or loaned to any insured.* The reason for this exclusion is that mobile equipment in this circumstance is considered to be part of the auto and, therefore, covered by the business auto coverage form.
2. *When the bodily injury or property damage arises out of "the use of mobile equipment in, or while in practice or preparation for, a prearranged racing, speed or demolition contest or in any stunting activity."* In light of the fact that the exclusion is subject to a so-called "while clause," the bodily injury or property damage is excluded only "while" the mobile equipment is being used in those activities.

War Exclusion

Also excluded under this and other forms of liability insurance are bodily injury and property damage losses due to war, whether or not declared, or any act or condition incident to war if the liability for such losses is assumed under a contract or agreement. The term *war* is defined here to include "civil war, insurrection, rebellion or revolution." The rationale for excluding war and war-related losses is that most insurers regard such losses as uninsurable by private insurers. Coverage for war-related losses is sometimes available (and of particular interest to those whose operations extend into foreign countries), but the cost may be prohibitive.

Exclusions Related to the Products-Completed Operations Hazard

All remaining exclusions of the commercial general liability policy in some way pertain to premises and operations exposures and/or products-completed operations exposures. More specifically, exclusions (j) and (l) relate to completed operations exposures, exclusion (k) relates to products exposures, and exclusions (m) and (n) affect both products and completed operations exposures.

"Products-Completed Operations Hazard" Definition The CGL policy contains a detailed definition of "products-completed operations hazard." Losses arising out of the "products-completed operations hazard" are subject to a Products-Completed Operations Aggregate Limit, which is separate and distinct from the General Aggregate Limit. For this reason, it is often important to distinguish products and completed operations losses from premises and operations losses. Although the CGL does not handle the products-completed operations hazard under a separate insuring agreement, it is sometimes convenient to use the terms *products liability coverage* and *completed operations liability coverage* to refer to coverages that fall within the definition of the "products-completed operations hazard."

Each part of the "products-completed operations hazard," as defined in the CGL forms, must be fully understood. The first part concerns products liability. The products hazard uses the term "your product." The second part deals with the completed operations hazard. The completed operations hazard uses the term "your work."

Products Hazard Two conditions generally must be met, as stated under the policy definition of "products-completed operations hazard," before a loss is considered to be one of products liability.

1. The bodily injury or property damage arising out of the named insured's product (which is either defective or does not serve the purpose for which it was warranted or represented by the named insured) must occur *away* from the owned or rented premises of the named insured.
2. The product must be in the physical possession of one other than the named insured.

Both of these conditions must be met. One or the other will not do. For example, if a person purchases a product and sustains an injury from its use at the seller's owned or rented premises, the loss will be treated as a premises and operations loss, subject to an entirely different aggregate limit than the one earmarked for losses within the scope of the "products-completed operations hazard."

The named insured's product ("your product") means goods or products (other than real property) manufactured, sold, handled, distributed or disposed of by (1) the named insured, (2) others who are trading under the named insured's name, or (3) someone whose business or assets the named insured has acquired. The term also includes any containers of products (other than vehicles). It does not include vending machines or other property rented to or located for the use of others but not sold.

Containers are Products. Containers of goods or products, such as bottles, cardboard cartons, cans, jars, boxes, oil drums, propane tanks or cylinders, and wood crates are products within the meaning of the policy, as are materials, parts or equipment furnished in connection with goods or products. And the term container has been broadly interpreted by some courts. For example, one court held that steel bands and straps keeping steel coils in place on a skid, which came apart and injured a person, were considered to be a container.[12]

Containers may still be products, even if ownership of the containers remains with the manufacturer, distributor, or dealer. Returnable beverage bottles and refillable propane gas cylinders are examples. As previously mentioned, the products liability hazard is defined to include only bodily injury and property damage that occurs away from the premises and *after physical possession* of the products has been relinquished by the named insured. The definition does not require that ownership of such products must also be relinquished by the named insured. Hence, when not in the physical possession of the named insured, returnable fuel oil drums are products of the named insured, and any compensable injury or damage they may cause is covered as part of the products hazard.

Vehicles Are Not Containers. The policy specifically indicates that vehicles are not containers within the meaning of the term "your product." This is intended to eliminate products liability coverage for exposures that are more appropriately handled under other forms of liability insurance. However, because the term *vehicle* is not defined in the policy, its meaning—in terms of what may or may not be deemed a container—is ultimately a question of fact for a court to decide. And the courts have defined vehicle rather broadly over the years.

Vending Machines. From the viewpoint of its manufacturer or seller, a vending machine is clearly a product, presenting an exposure within the scope of the products hazard. From the standpoint of the machine's owner, the vending machine is in the nature of a container that dispenses other products. The question is whether claims against the machine's owner, for bodily injury or property damage caused by the machine itself, fall within the products hazard. It is not difficult to imagine the possibilities:

- Vending machines may malfunction, leading to fire or water damage to the premises where they are located.
- People may be cut by sharp corners or broken glass on a vending machine.
- Vending machines may be responsible for bodily injury if located where they block a passage or exit.

Claims resulting from these situations would not fall within the products hazard, but would be considered a part of the machine owner's premises and operation exposure.

The contents dispensed by vending machines are considered to be products. Whether bodily injury or property damage arises on or away from premises owned or rented to the named insured, the losses from the contents of a vending machine normally would be within the products hazard.

Leased Property. The term "your product" does not include real property or goods or products that are merely rented to others, but protection for such exposures is provided under the coverage for the premises and operations hazard.

If the rental of property is incidental to a business (e.g., a hardware store that handles wallpaper and paints also rents a wallpaper removing machine to its customers), coverage is automatically provided at no additional charge.[13] However, when a business's principal function is to rent or lease equipment or appliances, such as lawn mowers, lawn rollers, ladders, post hole diggers, floor polishers and sanders, refrigerators, stoves, and machines—on a short or long term basis, a separate premium charge is made.

Warranties or Representations. The term "your product" includes warranties or representations made at any time with respect to the fitness, quality, durability, or performance of the named insured's products and containers, materials, parts and equipment furnished in connection with such containers. As mentioned in Chapter 2, liability from products can arise from breach of warranties (express or implied), including warranties of merchantability or fitness for a particular purpose. If coverage is to apply, however, there must be bodily injury or property damage resulting from such warranty or representation.

Exclusion of Damage to the Named Insured's Product No coverage applies for "property damage" to "your product" arising out of it or any part of it, whether the product is physically damaged or is

merely rendered useless. This exclusion prevents an insurer from having to pay for the repair or replacement of a product that is incorrectly designed or defectively produced.
Two aspects of this exclusion deserve emphasis.

1. When damage arises out of a portion of a product and such damage makes the remaining part of the product useless, the exclusion applies to the whole product—not just to that part from which the damage arises.
2. Damage to a product arising from it or any part of it is also excluded, whether the underlying cause is attributable to the work of a manufacturer, an assembler, or a supplier of any component.

For purposes of illustration, assume Alpha Manufacturing Company is under contract to produce electric generators that Baker Manufacturing Company uses in its steam turbines (see Exhibit 5-2). One of Alpha's electric generators is defective. It burns out and causes damage (physical injury or loss of use) to the remaining part of the steam turbine while in the possession of a utility company.

- Baker Company, in this circumstance, would be without liability protection under its CGL for damage confined to the electric generator and to the turbine, because both are considered to be Baker Company's products. (While Baker Company initially may be responsible for repairing or replacing the electric generator or the entire unit, depending on the resulting loss to the product, it has a right of recourse against Alpha Company whose defective component is the proximate cause of loss).
- Alpha Company has responsibility for the costs of repairing or replacing its defective component, without benefit of insurance, because that component is considered to be its product.
- On the other hand, products liability coverage of Alpha Company's CGL, should respond for the payment of damage to Baker Company's steam turbine, since that turbine is not Alpha Company's product; i.e., the turbine was not manufactured, sold, handled, distributed, or disposed of by Alpha Company.

If physical injury to the generator and to the steam turbine were sudden and accidental, the situation would change:

- Baker Company would at least have protection under its product liability insurance (for loss of use of other undamaged tangible property sustained by the utility company) under the exception of the so-called *failure to perform* exclusion (m). Adjustments between the insurers of Alpha and Baker Companies would then be required, depending on the proximate cause

Exhibit 5-2
Exclusion of Damage to Named Insured's Product Illustrated

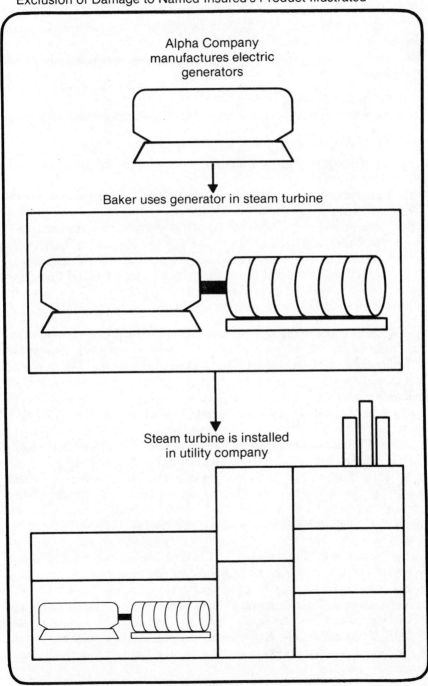

of that loss. But damage to the product itself is still excluded from insurance coverage.

Suppose, however, that Alpha's defective component were to make the entire turbine inoperable. In other words, the electric generator does not burn out and the turbine does not break down, but the entire unit simply does not work.

- Baker Company, again, would have no coverage for its own product because of the exclusion of damage (including loss of use) to the named insured's product. It would also have no liability protection for loss of use of the utility company's undamaged tangible property because of the failure to perform exclusion.

- Alpha Company more than likely will have to assume the costs of repairing or replacing its defective component, because that component is considered to be its product and, therefore, excluded under its products liability coverage. It will also have to assume those costs representing loss of use of undamaged tangible property of the utility company for two reasons: (1) the loss was caused by its product; and (2) such loss is not covered under the failure to perform exclusion.

While damage to the named insured's products is excluded whether the products are made by one entity or by several, coverage does apply to bodily injury and to other property damage, including loss of use of any tangible property arising out of those products. So, for example, if the defective steam turbine were to damage other property of the utility company, that damage and any loss of use of such property stemming from that damage is covered under Baker Company's CGL.

While the above illustrations deal with situations involving component products that are clearly distinguishable, many losses are much more complicated. For example, finding the exact source of food poisoning can be extremely difficult and costly, particularly if the product comprises many ingredients from several sources. Bodily injury by food poisoning is covered, of course, if it ultimately is determined that the product contained botulism or some harmful foreign substance. But the insured's loss of use of the product is not covered, nor are the costs of withdrawing the food product from the market and destroying it (the latter costs are not covered due to the so-called "sistership" exclusion (n) discussed hereafter). Yet, determining which ingredient is responsible for this kind of loss is sometimes difficult, if not impossible. Every entity involved may be required to pay a portion of the damages, even though one entity alone may have caused the loss.

Completed Operations Hazard The completed operations hazard is defined to include only bodily injury and property damage occurring away from premises the named insured owns or rents and arising out of that portion of the named insured's work ("your work") that has been completed or abandoned.

Time of Completion.

- When loss occurs after an operation is completed or abandoned and away from the premises owned or rented to the named insured, it comes within the completed operations portion of the "products-completed operations hazard."
- When a loss occurs while operations are in progress, it is not within the completed operations hazard, but is a premises and operations loss.

Each type of loss is subject to a different set of aggregate limits.

To minimize arguments about the question of when a particular operation is deemed completed, the definition of the "products-completed operations hazard" lists three time periods, and it specifies that "your work" will be deemed completed at the earliest of the following three times:

1. When all of the work called for in the named insured's contract has been completed.
2. When all of the work to be done at the site has been completed if the named insured's contract calls for work at more than one site.
3. When that part of the work done at a job site has been put to its intended use by any person or organization other than another contractor or subcontractor working on the same project.

Time Period (1). Time (1) arrives when all of the work to be performed under contract is completed, whether the work is performed in whole or in part by the named insured or by someone else (such as a subcontractor) on behalf of the named insured.

If certain work is only partially done and the one performing it intends to return at a later date to finish it, the work already performed is not deemed to be completed.

For example, suppose an electrical subcontractor is hired to do the wiring and other related work on a new one-story building. The contractor does the rough work, but is unable to install the switches, plugs, and light fixtures until the walls and ceilings are finished. If someone on the work site, such as a carpenter, should sustain injury from an electrical shock, or if a fire should start from within the circuit breaker box before work is fully completed, the resulting loss would be covered as a premises and operations loss, but it would not be within the scope of the completed operations hazard.

Time (2).   At Time (2), work is deemed completed as soon as all work that has to be done *at the site of operations* is finished. Work under this second category usually involves the performance of like operations at two or more different sites. Much depends on how the word *site* is interpreted, because it is not defined in the policy. For example, each utility pole removed by a contractor might be considered a completed operation at each site—no matter how many poles must be removed under contract, or each sewer line laid and connected to a new house might be considered to be a completed operation at that site, even though the work must be performed on a whole tract of new dwellings. Each newly constructed and completed story of a high-rise building could in some cases be considered as a separate site of operations.

As each utility pole is removed, each sewer line is laid and connected, and each story of building is finished, contractors need completed operations coverage against any bodily injury or property damage arising from the completed work. They also need premises and operations coverage against any bodily injury or property damage stemming from operations while additional poles are being removed, new sewer pipes are being laid and connected, and work is being performed on additional levels of a building.

Time (3).   Time (3) operations are considered completed when some portion of the work, out of which bodily injury or property damage arises, has been put to its intended use by anyone other than contractor or subcontractor who is performing operations on the project. Occupancy or use of work for its intended purpose therefore marks completion, even when the work has not been officially inspected and accepted.

Thus, if a boiler is put to use by its owner before work on the entire heating system is completed, and the boiler causes bodily injury or property damage, loss is considered to be the result of a completed operation. The same results are intended to apply when bodily injury or property damage arises from a portion of a new highway that the public is permitted to use before it is officially opened, or from a building that is partially occupied before it is fully completed. However, when the boiler, the highway, or the partially completed building is being used by other contractors on the same project, the operation is not considered a completed operation.

As explicit as the provisions of Time (3) may appear, they can be a source of argument, especially if one does not keep in mind the following:

1. It is not work *used by* others that is the controlling factor. It is work that has been *put to its intended use* by others.
2. Bodily injury or property damage must arise out of that portion of the work that has been put to its intended used by others.

Completed Operations Requiring Service, Maintenance, Correction, Repair, or Replacement. Another important provision of the completed operations hazard deals with operations that may require some kind of ongoing attention. The relevant provision states that work that may need service, maintenance, correction, repair, or replacement, but which is otherwise complete, will be treated as completed.

Were it not for this provision, firms under a continuing obligation to service, maintain, or repair their work would never need completed operations coverage. Firms simply could maintain that operations requiring further service or repair work would be considered still in progress (and therefore not within the "products-completed operations hazard").

In any event, operations are deemed to be completed at the earliest of the three points in time previously mentioned, even if ongoing attention is required. For example, assume a firm installs an elevator and promises to inspect and service it periodically, and to repair it when necessary. As soon as the elevator is installed and accepted by its owner, it is considered to be a completed operation (unless one of the other points in time arrives first).

- The elevator firm, of course, has a premises and operations *exposure* because bodily injury or property damage may result *while* it is inspecting, servicing, or repairing the elevator.
- If the elevator should *subsequently* malfunction, fall, and injure its passengers because of the way it was installed or because of neglect in servicing it properly, loss is considered to be within the scope of the completed operations hazard.

Operations not within the Scope of Products-Completed Operations Hazard The policy stipulates that bodily injury or property damage arising out of the following operations are outside the scope of what is meant by the "products-completed operations hazard," unless otherwise noted:

1. The transportation of property, unless the injury or damage arises out of a condition in or on a vehicle created by the "loading or unloading" of it.
2. The existence of tools, uninstalled equipment, or abandoned or unused materials.

3. Products or operations for which the classification in this Coverage Part or the insurer's manual or rules includes products or completed operations.

Transportation of Property. To comprehend the full scope of this first exclusion, as well as the exception to it, one must also examine the scope of the CGL *exclusion of aircraft, autos, and watercraft,* and the *mobile equipment exclusion* discussed earlier.

To briefly recap, this exclusion removes coverage under the CGL policy for bodily injury or property damage arising from the ownership, maintenance, use, or entrustment to others of any aircraft, auto, or watercraft owned, operated, rented, or loaned to any insured. By exception, therefore, the CGL policy covers bodily injury or property damage stemming from any aircraft, auto, or watercraft that is not owned, not operated by, and not rented nor loaned to any insured. An example of a covered exposure within the meaning of that exception is any liability the named insured may have for the operation of aircraft, auto, or watercraft by an independent contractor.

In light of that exception, the CGL policy also applies to bodily injury or property damage stemming from operations in connection with the transportation of an insured's property on vehicles of others. For example, following an accident, White Company is sued along with the independent trucker of its goods. White (but not the independent trucker) has protection under White's CGL policy, even though the operations of loading that vehicle have been completed. This type of loss is not within the scope of the completed operations hazard, but it is not excluded from the premises and operations coverages of White Company. However, if bodily injury or property damage arises out of a condition in or on a vehicle created by its loading or unloading, loss is covered within the completed operations hazard. The vehicle, of course, must be one that is not owned, not operated by, not rented, nor loaned to any insured. And, in line with other criteria of the completed operations hazard, bodily injury or property damage must occur away from premises owned by or rented to the named insured. The losses that would be covered are those allegedly caused by an insured, or by a person for whom the insured is responsible, who improperly loads or unloads cargo and causes dangerous conditions that result in bodily injury or property damage to others.

Existence of Tools, Uninstalled Equipment, or Abandoned or Unused Material. Bodily injury or property damage arising from the existence of tools, uninstalled equipment, or abandoned or unused materials is covered, but is not within the scope of the completed operations hazard. This is true even when such tools, equipment, or unused materials were used or were intended to be used in performing operations that have since been completed or abandoned away from premises the named insured owns or rents.

Manual Classifications Automatically Including Products and Completed Operations. The rating manual shows separate premises/operations premium rates and products/completed operations premium rates for most classifications. However, a few classifications show no separate premium charge for products and completed operations coverages; the charge for products or completed operations liability coverage is automatically included along with an entity's premises and operations premium.

This means that the named insured in those categories has products liability or completed operations coverage even though the declarations do not show a products-completed operations limit, and any products or completed operations losses are subject to the general aggregate limit.

General Property Damage Exclusion

Because of its length and nature, exclusion j will first be stated and then discussed section by section. The policy does not cover

"Property damage" to:
(1) Property you own, rent, or occupy;
(2) Premises you sell, give away or abandon, if the "property damage" arises out of any part of those premises;
(3) Property loaned to you;
(4) Personal property in your care, custody or control;
(5) That particular part of real property on which you or any contractors or subcontractors working directly or indirectly on your behalf are performing operations, if the "property damage" arises out of those operations; or
(6) That particular part of any property that must be restored, repaired or replaced because "your work" was incorrectly performed on it.

Paragraph (2) of this exclusion does not apply if the premises are "your work" and were never occupied, rented or held for rental by you.

Paragraphs (3), (4), (5) and (6) of this exclusion do not apply to liability assumed under a sidetrack agreement.

Paragraph (6) of this exclusion does not apply to "property damage" included in the "products-completed operations hazard."

Exclusion of Insured's Property Paragraph (1) of the general property damage exclusion precludes any protection for damage to real or personal *property* that is owned, rented, or occupied by the insured. This exclusion avoids paying for damage to property that should and normally would be covered by some form of first-party property insurance. Because the CGL policy automatically includes a certain amount of fire legal liability coverage, explained later, the only exception to this exclusion is liability for fire damage to real property rented to a named insured.

Exclusion of Alienated Premises   Paragraph (2) of the general property damage exclusion is commonly referred to as the *alienated premises exclusion.* (Earlier policies used the word "alienated.") This exclusion is designed to preclude coverage for liability for property damage to premises sold by a firm that is negligent in not informing the purchaser about latent premises defects, when the property damage arises out of and is confined to the sold premises. For example,

- A firm sells its building that is known to have a latent electrical defect, and the seller, as a matter of oversight, does not make the defect known to the purchaser. The latent defect causes a fire that damages the building.
- The insured created a structural defect in the building by making modifications to the building or by overloading the floors beyond their load-bearing capacity.

In either case, the policy is not designed to cover the property damage results of any dangerous condition that should have been corrected by the seller before the sale or should have been communicated to the purchaser.

However, it can be inferred from this exclusion that coverage does apply to bodily injury emanating from defective, sold premises, as well as to property damage to other than the sold premises. If the electrical fire in the example were to spread to an adjoining building, the seller would have protection, provided coverage was not precluded by other policy provisions.

Exception.   Note that, by exception, the alienated premises exclusion does not apply if the premises are the named insured's work and were never occupied, rented, or held for rental by the named insured. What this means is that the alienated premises exclusion does not eliminate coverage for liability emanating from premises constructed by or on behalf of the named insured. Neither does it exclude liability stemming from use of materials, parts or equipment furnished in connection with such work or operations.

This exception to the exclusion applies only when the premises were never occupied, rented or held for rental before they were relinquished. For example, if either the developer or general contractor were to rent out the premises, and then sell them, and a claim subsequently arose from such premises, the insurer would be permitted to invoke this exclusion and deny the claim.

(The fact that the alienated premises exclusion might not apply in some of the examples noted above, does not mean that the insured necessarily will have coverage, since other exclusions yet to be mentioned may apply.)

Exclusion of Personal Property in the Named Insured's Care, Custody, or Control This exclusion, referred to as the *care, custody, or control exclusion*, is designed to preclude any coverage for damage to personal property that is best handled through the exercise of care or by insuring the exposure under some form of property or inland marine insurance.

Note, however, that there is an exception to the property damage exclusion under paragraphs (3) and (4), affecting also paragraphs (5) and (6) to be discussed subsequently, concerning liability assumed under a *sidetrack agreement*. This exception means that the CGL policy provides a business with protection for any liability stemming from the use of a sidetrack spur, as well as protection for any liability because of damage to the sidetrack spur itself.

Exclusion of Property On Which Work Is Being Performed Paragraphs (5) and (6) of the general property damage exclusion address property damage liability exposures that are deemed to be uninsurable under the CGL policy. The exclusions apply to losses taking place while operations are in progress by or on behalf of the named insured. Following damage to real property while operations are in progress, the liability coverage that may apply must be inferred from the exclusions.

Thus, there is *no coverage* for "property damage" to:

- that particular part of *real* property on which operations are being performed by the named insured or on behalf of the named insured by any contractor or subcontractor, if the "property damage" arises out of those operations being performed.

The key words are *"that particular part."* No coverage applies to that particular part of the real property that is damaged while work is being performed on it. But, by inference, *coverage does apply* for damage to:

- other parts of the real property, on which work was performed by or on behalf of the named insured, resulting from that particular part of the work on which operations are being performed at the time ~~of the time~~ of the occurrence.

An example is the developer who hired a general contractor to construct condominiums. While employees of the general contractor are positioning one of the beams, it slips, falls, and bends so that it is no longer usable. At the time it falls, it also damages other steel beams that had already been erected. Both the developer and the general contractor would be protected for damage to the real property that was damaged by the beam that fell because operations were not being performed on it at the time of the accident. However, no coverage would apply for damage to the fallen beam because it was the particular part on which operations were being performed. The damaged beam could be excluded under paragraphs (4) and (6) of the exclusion.

Damage to work involving separate, identifiable parts—such as the steel beams erected and being erected—should present no problems. But when work is being performed on one unit from which damage arises, such as a machine or a switchboard, it may be difficult to determine the particular part from which damage arises.

Also *not covered* is "property damage" to:

- that particular part of any property that has to be restored, repaired or replaced because work or operations performed by or on behalf of the named insured ("your work") was incorrectly performed on it.

This situation does not necessarily require property to be physically damaged, but only that the work be performed so improperly that it has to be redone. The painter who uses the wrong shade of paint, the plumber who places pipes in areas not designated in the work plans, and the elevator installer who installs a unit that does not perform properly following its installation would have no coverage because of paragraph (6). In each case, the insured will undo or repair the faulty work at its own expense.

However, paragraph (6) of the exclusion does not apply to "property damage" within the "products-completed operations hazard." This means that paragraph (6) applies only to losses while operations are in progress. Once the operation has been deemed completed under the criteria set down by the definition of the "products-completed operations hazard," paragraph (6) cannot be relied on by the insurer to deny a claim. But the property damage may still be excluded by virtue of exclusion (l) concerning damage to the named insured's work as explained next.

Exclusion of Property Damage to the Named Insured's Work The property damage to "your work" exclusion (l), also referred to as the *injury to work performed exclusion,* is designed to prevent an insurer from having to pay for replacing, repairing, or otherwise redoing faulty work of the named insured. Under exclusion (l), no coverage applies for liability because of "property damage," (i.e., physical injury to tangible property, including all resulting loss of use of that property, and loss of use of tangible property that is not physically injured) to "your work" arising out of it or any part of it and included in the "products-completed operations hazard." The term "your work" is defined to mean (a) work or operations performed by you or on your behalf; and (b) materials, parts or equipment furnished in connection with such work or operations. "Your Work" includes includes warranties or representations made at any time with respect to the fitness, quality, durability or performance of the items in (a) and (b) above. However, the exclusion of "your work" does *not* apply if the damaged work or the work out of which the damage arises was performed on behalf of the named insured by a subcontractor.

Two points are important:

1. This exclusion *applies only to the "products-completed operations hazard"; it does not exclude coverage for property damage liability that occurs while operations are in progress. Recall that paragraph (5) of the general property damage exclusion, dealing with damage to property being worked on, will control the extent to which coverage may or may not apply during the period when operations are in progress.*

2. This exclusion does not apply if the damaged work or the work out of which the damage arises was performed by a subcontractor on behalf of the named insured. By inference, *damage to all work performed by the named insured is excluded* (unless it arises out of a subcontractor's work), as well as damage to all materials, parts and equipment furnished in connection with such work as performed solely by the named insured. The net effect is to exclude the particular part of any work that causes damage, as well as any portion of the work performed that is adversely affected by that damage.

The following illustration should help to clarify just how all-encompassing this second exclusion actually is.

Work Performed By Named Insured. Assume a contracting firm was hired to build a one-family dwelling on a concrete slab. Part of its work involved placing pipes for steam heat on impacted soil and pouring concrete over them in constructing the slab. Because a coupling on one of the pipes was not tightened, steam eventually escaped, condensed, and caused leakage into the dwelling. The contracting firm was required not only to tear up a large portion of the slab and retrieve and replace the loose coupling, but also to replace the concrete slab. All costs incurred by that contracting firm in performing that work would be excluded. The damage to "your work" exclusion (1) precludes coverage for property damage to "your work," i.e., work or operations performed by or on the named insured's behalf (installing the piping and constructing the concrete slab) when damage arises out of the work or any part of it, or out of materials, parts, or equipment furnished in connection with such work (e.g. a defective coupling). The only coverage the contracting firm may have is for property damage to the dwelling owner's carpeting by water leakage, provided the carpeting was not supplied and installed by that contracting firm. (As for a defective coupling and the damages caused by it, the contracting firm's only recourse would be against the distributor or manufacturer of that coupling).

Suppose the condensation remains undetected and the water eventually causes the ground to sink, the slab to crack, and the dwelling to tip to the point that it becomes uninhabitable. The contracting firm is required to raze and rebuild the dwelling. The exclusion in question will preclude coverage for all damages, including loss of use of the dwelling, for two reasons.

1. The entire dwelling is considered to be work performed by that contracting firm, and physical injury or destruction to work performed is excluded (even if the underlying cause of loss is a defective coupling).
2. Loss of use of the dwelling by its owner is not covered, since the definition of property damage includes all resulting loss of use of that property. When damage to property is covered, any resulting loss of use is also covered; but, when damage to property is excluded, any resulting loss of use is also excluded.

Work Performed on Behalf of Named Insured. Assume now that the general contracting firm did not perform any of the work on the dwelling but, instead, subcontracted all of its work out to another firm. If the general contractor were to be sued for the resulting damages or were to become liable for damage to work performed on its behalf by the subcontractor, this exclusion should *not* apply to the general contractor. To repeat, this exclusion does not apply if the damaged work or the work out of which damage arises was performed on behalf of the named insured.

It is important that the ramifications of this exclusion be fully understood because the financial consequences can be overwhelming.

Impaired Property Exclusion

Referred to as the "failure to perform exclusion" in earlier general liability policy editions, the impaired property exclusion deals with (1) property damage to "impaired property," and (2) damage to property that has not been physically injured whether the occurrence arises during the course of operations or after operations are completed. Both (1) and (2) hinge on a defect, deficiency, inadequacy, or dangerous condition of the named insured's product or work, or from a delay or failure to perform any contract or agreement. However, this exclusion is not applicable when a product or work of the named insured causes physical damage to tangible property of others, including its loss of use following damage. The exclusion also does not apply when failure of a product or work causes bodily injury, or when there is loss of use of other property arising out of the sudden and accidental physical injury to the named insured's product or work after it has been put to its intended use.

Damage to "Impaired Property" To understand the scope of the first part of this exclusion dealing with property damage to impaired property, it is first necessary to refer to the definition of "impaired property."

"Impaired property" means tangible property, other than "your product" or "your work," that cannot be used or is less useful because:
a. It incorporates "your product" or "your work" that is known or thought to be defective, deficient, inadequate or dangerous; or
b. You have failed to fulfill the terms of a contract or agreement;

if such property can be restored to use by:

a. The repair, replacement, adjustment or removal of "your product" or "your work;" or
b. Your fulfilling the terms of the contract or agreement.

Defect in Product or Work. As an example of a loss that would be *excluded* by the impaired property exclusion, consider the manufacturer that sells a steam turbine with the guarantee that it will produce a specified level of power within a certain period. The turbine fails to produce power to expected levels, causing its owner to lose the use of certain machinery that depends on that power, and also causing loss of production and revenue. Since the machinery (other tangible property) is impaired because the named insured's boiler ("your product") is inadequate, the manufacturer will have no protection under its CGL if confronted with a suit for damages filed by the turbine's owner.

If the same steam turbine were to suddenly and accidentally break apart or its electric generator were to suddenly and accidently burn out while being used by its owner, the manufacturer *would have coverage* against loss of use of tangible property, other than the turbine.[14] Such other property could even include the owner's entire buildings and contents, if the loss were serious enough to cause its temporary unoccupancy. Coverage applies because the impaired property exclusion makes exception for loss of use of other property arising out of sudden and accidental physical injury to "your product" or "your work." The only prerequisite, and it is an important one, is that someone has put the product or work to its intended use. For example, if the purchaser of a turbine were to be operating the turbine and the turbine's failure to perform were to cause fire damage to the purchaser's premises, including temporary interruption of business and/or bodily injuries, the manufacturer of the turbine would have protection for any such resulting liability. But damage to the turbine, being the named insured's product, is excluded.

Failure to Fulfill Contractual Obligations. The impaired property exclusion also can apply when an insured does not fulfill its contractual obligations. An example is the general contractor who agrees to complete construction of an office building within a certain period. The general contractor fails to complete the contract, and the building owner has to return rental payments it collected in anticipation of the grand opening. Here, it is not because of a defect, deficiency, inadequacy, or dangerous condition to the contractor's product or work that the impaired property is excluded. Instead, it is excluded because of the delay or failure of the named insured (or the failure of others acting on behalf of the named insured, such as subcontractors) that there is property damage to impaired property, and the resulting damages are excluded.

Property That Has Not Been Injured The other part of the impaired property exclusion deals with property that has not been physically injured (because of the same two general groups of conditions that affect property damage to impaired property exposures, i.e., defect or deficiency, a dangerous condition in "your product" or "your work" or failure to perform a contract). This part of the impaired property exclusion addresses claims that the value of property has been reduced even though there was no (1) physical injury to property caused by the named insured's product or work or (2) loss of use of tangible property.

One example of a diminution in value claim is the poorly constructed condominium. There is no physical damage to the condominium and it can, in fact, be occupied, but the workmanship that went into its construction was so poor that the condominium is worth thousands of dollars less than the price paid by purchasers. Another example is the farmer's reduction in the yield of a certain food crop prompted by negligent application of a fertilizer.[15]

The impaired property exclusion applies both to products and to work of the named insured. An example concerning the named insured's work is the auto mechanic who rebuilds an engine on a stock car. When the stock car is raced, it does not perform properly. Each time the driver accelerates, the motor cuts out. The owner and its sponsor not only sustain loss of use of that car but also forfeit the entry fee for the race. Damages for loss of the stock car's use are excluded because of the impaired property exclusion.

If, on the other hand, the motor were to suddenly and accidentally blow up in the race pit while the driver was preparing for the start of the race, the mechanic who rebuilt the motor would have liability protection against any bodily injury and property damage other than to the motor and other work it performed. Such other property damage could include the remainder of the stock car not worked on, damage to equipment in the pit, and even physical damage to and loss of use of the pit area.

The net effect of the impaired property exclusion is to prevent coverage for losses that are normally considered to be part of the costs of producing products or performing work. It stands to reason that when a product or work does not function properly, the burden of any loss of use stemming from that product should fall on its maker or assembler, who is the best judge of that product or work and its capabilities, and who has certain responsibilities to make that product or work workable warranted or represented.

Sistership Liability (Recall) Exclusion

(13)

As explained by Norman Nachman, of ISO, in his 1972 study titled *Products Liability Insurance,* "sistership liability" is terminology used by the aircraft liability insurers to signify the liability for damages that usually follows the withdrawal, inspection, repair, replacement or loss of use of aircraft, because of known or suspected defects. When one aircraft, for example, has a suspected defective condition because of its design or production error, all the aircraft of the same manufacturer—all sisterships—also are grounded until they are fully inspected. Sistership liability is used to refer to all kinds of products that must be withdrawn from the market or from use when they are known or suspected of being defective.

The so-called "sistership" liability exclusion can be thought of as an exclusion of product "recall" losses. It precludes coverage for the costs incurred by an insured for the loss of use, withdrawal, recall, inspection, repair, replacement, adjustment, removal or disposal of the named insured's product, work or impaired property, when the product, work or impaired property is withdrawn or recalled from the market or from use because of a known or suspected defect, deficiency, inadequacy, or dangerous condition in the product.[16]

Product recalls are common today. Manufacturers and distributors of autos, food, drugs, toys, and other products must sometimes recall products that are suspected of being unsafe. It is not unusual, for example, to read or to hear about auto manufacturers recalling thousands of their vehicles of a certain type in order to make adjustments or modifications.

Reasons for Exclusion Damage for product recalls or withdrawals are not covered under the basic provisions of the CGL policy for at least two reasons:

1. *Product recalls involve extraordinary costs* that are not contemplated in the basic rate structure of products liability insurance. Considerable expense can be incurred in communicating a recall campaign to wholesalers, retailers, and the general public. The seller must also pay for the transportation costs of recalled products, as well as the costs of inspecting and repairing them. If the products are instead destroyed, the producer loses not only the value of those products in terms of raw stock, labor, and sales value, but also incurs costs of replacing recalled products with new ones. Damages claimed for loss of use of recalled products by consumers can also be costly. Such damages, of course, will depend on the type and usage of the product. It is doubtful that a consumer of canned goods purchased for future consumption would be able to argue that it sustained any loss of use. But a firm whose defective fleet of buses is recalled may have a justifiable claim for loss of use.

2. *Separate insurance, sometimes referred to as product recall or recapture insurance, is available for this exposure.*

Withdrawal Before or After Marketing The exclusion applies whether the damages are claimed for the withdrawal of products from the market or loss of use of products before or after they are marketed. For example, a manufacturer of canned goods has no coverage for the expenses it incurs in withdrawing spoiled goods from its wholesalers or retailers or from the possession of consumers. It is also without coverage for the costs of inspecting and testing the contents of those withdrawn products, as well as dealing with any products that are ready for shipment to the market. And, finally, there is no CGL coverage for the disposal of spoiled canned goods, the replacement of the product, or loss of use claims.

Component Products The sistership exclusion applies to the withdrawal of products produced by one firm, as well as to situations involving several producers of component products. The latter situation can become complicated. In either case, the intent of the exclusion is to preclude coverage for the loss of use, the costs of withdrawing, recalling, inspecting, repairing, replacing, adjusting, removing or disposing the named insured's products, either as a direct expense of the entity that initiates such withdrawal, or as a liability of another entity whose product includes the named insured's component that is responsible for the known or suspected defective condition of the whole product. In other words, whether the damages claimed are by the named insured or by others who incurred certain costs caused by the named insured's products, the damages are not intended to be covered.

For example, assume that several of Alpha Company's steam turbines are suspected of causing Baker Company's electric generators to produce insufficient levels of power. Baker Company therefore decides to withdraw certain generators from use in order to inspect them and to repair them, if necessary.

- The expenses incurred by Baker Company in withdrawing the generators from use are not covered by Baker's CGL because of the exclusion in question.
- The expenses that Baker Company will seek to recover from Alpha Company for these purposes are also not covered by Alpha Company's CGL policy.

The sistership exclusion refers to "Damages claimed for any loss, cost or expense incurred by you or others...." Thus, no coverage applies whether the damages are claimed by Baker Company, as incurred expense, or by Alpha Company, as its liability. The exclusion applies in both instances.

Damages claimed against Baker Company for loss of use of undamaged tangible property by owners of those generators and turbines are also excluded by the impaired property exclusion. The exclusion of damage to the named insured's products will prevent Baker Company from claiming protection under its policy for loss of use claims imposed by owners of the turbines. Because of the impaired property exclusion, the products liability coverage of Alpha Company will not respond for the payment of any loss of use claims sustained by Baker Company customers who are unable to use their turbines. Alpha Company will also have to assume the costs of repairing or replacing any defective electric generators that are withdrawn from the market because of the sistership liability exclusion. If Baker Company also were to sue Alpha Company for loss of its goodwill, Alpha Company would be without protection, because goodwill is considered to be an intangible, and property damage liability insurance deals strictly with tangible property.

Duty to Withdraw   Note, finally, that if an entity does not take reasonable steps to withdraw its products from the market or from use following a series of similar losses to its product, it may be without future protection for its liability to others. This is because the CGL excludes bodily injury or property damage expected or intended from the standpoint of the insured.

Applicability to Completed Operations   The sistership liability exclusion also applies to work of the named insured or work performed on its behalf. In fact, it applies in the same way that it applies to products. The potential exposures involving the withdrawal of materials, parts, or equipment can be costly, particularly when they already form a part of the completed work. Examples include removing defective concrete blocks that already form a part of a building, removing defective wall paneling that is known to blister, and retrieving defective couplings on piping, even if it involves tearing up concrete to secure them.

Fire Legal Liability "Coverage"

The last provision in the exclusions section of the CGL policy under Coverage A concerns the fire legal liability exposure. It states that exclusions (c) through (n) do not apply to damage by fire to premises rented to the named insured. By inference, therefore, the named insured is given certain protection for damage to rented property for which the insured may be held liable because of damage by fire.

The fact that exclusion (a)—the intentional injury exclusion—does apply means that the applicability of fire legal liability coverage hinges on the negligence of the insured. Any damage either expected or intended by the insured would be excluded.

Since exclusion (b)—the contractual liability exclusion—also applies, the insured would not be protected for fire damage to rented property if the insured agreed by contract to be responsible for such damage and the insured would not otherwise have been accountable in absence of such agreement. An example is an agreement whereby the tenant agrees to be accountable for damage to the rented premises because of acts or omissions of the landlord. Since a tenant would not be accountable for such liability in the absence of a contract or agreement, such liability of the tenant would not be covered by the CGL policy. This point was explained earlier.

Leases must be examined closely to determine whether they are subject to exculpatory agreements, because property insurance may be necessary. Care also should be exercised in determining what causes of loss, other than fire, may be the obligation of the insured under the lease. Obviously, if there are other potential causes of loss, such as water damage, the insured may be required to seek out a broader form of protection.

COVERAGE B: ADVERTISING AND PERSONAL INJURY LIABILITY

Both advertising and personal injury liability coverages, Coverage B of the CGL, are automatically included, unless they are excluded by endorsement.

Scope of Coverage

The insuring agreement of advertising and personal injury coverage parallels the insuring agreement pertaining to bodily injury and property damage liability coverage. The insurer agrees to pay the sums that the insured becomes legally obligated to pay as damages because of "personal injury" or "advertising injury," (as those two terms are defined in the policy), as long as an exclusion or some other policy provision does not rule out coverage.

The trigger of these two coverages will be explained in Chapter 6. For the moment, it should suffice to mention that the CGL policy applies to personal injury only if caused by an *offense* (1) committed in the coverage territory, (2) during the policy period, and (3) arising out of the conduct of the named insured's business, other than advertising, publishing, broadcasting, or telecasting done by or for the named insured. Publishers, broadcasters, and telecasters should have special insurance coverage; advertising liability is covered by the CGL—not as "personal injury," but as a separate item.

Like personal injury, advertising liability is conditioned on an offense (1) committed in the coverage territory and (2) during the policy period, but only for injury arising in the course of advertising the named insured's goods, products, or services. This coverage is not intended for a firm that is in the advertising business. Rather, is intended for the business that *buys* advertising in order to sell its own goods or products.

Definitions Of obvious importance in determining the scope of coverage are the definitions of "advertising injury" and "personal injury."

Advertising Injury. "Advertising injury" means injury arising out of one or more of the following offenses:

    a. Oral or written publication of material that slanders or libels a person or organization or disparages a person's or organization's goods, products, or services;

    b. Oral or written publication of material that violates a person's right of privacy;

    c. Misappropriation of advertising ideas or style of doing business; and

    d. Infringement of copyright, title, or slogan.

While defamation is not specifically mentioned as an offense, defamation is a generic term that includes both libel and slander, and the terms defamation or defamation of character also refer to the nature of the injury when a public utterance is libelous or slanderous. Thus, if defamation is alleged without any specific mention of libel or slander, coverage should still apply.

In recent years firms have been quite open in publicizing the presumed disadvantages of competitor's products or services. It seems likely that this practice could lead to an increase in claims of advertising injury. The allegation that the insured has made an untrue statement about a competitor's goods or services in order to influence the customer would qualify as disparagement, an offense listed under the definition.

Personal Injury. "Personal injury" is defined in the CGL policy as follows:

> "Personal injury" means injury, other than "bodily injury," arising out of one or more of the following offenses:
> a. False arrest, detention or imprisonment;
> b. Malicious prosecution;
> c. Wrongful entry into, or eviction of a person from, a room, dwelling, or premises that the person occupies;
> d. Oral or written publication of materials that slanders or libels a person or organization or disparages a person's or organization's goods, products, or services; or
> e. Oral or written publication of material that violates a person's right of privacy.

In the same insurance policies the term "personal injury" encompasses bodily injury and other offenses as well. In the CGL, "personal injury" is defined to mean *injury*, other than "bodily injury," arising out of one or more of the offenses listed above. "Bodily injury," as defined in the CGL, represents physical harm or impairment. The word *"injury"* is not defined in the policy, but can encompass any other wrong inflicted on another such as mental anguish or injury, fright, humiliation, loss of reputation, and shock.

Such intentional torts as false arrest, detention, and malicious prosecution are offenses frequently alleged in claims against law enforcement agencies. However, it is not likely that Coverage B of the CGL will be written for such agencies, whether privately owned or part of municipal government, because an endorsement is available to exclude such exposures. Nonetheless, false arrest or malicious prosecution can be committed easily by citizens who are not law enforcement officials.

Exclusions

Coverage B is subject to eight exclusions. Four of them apply to both advertising and personal injury, and the remaining four apply only to advertising injury.

Exclusions Common to Both Coverages   Coverage B is stated not to apply to "advertising injury" or "personal injury":

1. *arising out of oral or written publication of material if done by or at the direction of the insured with knowledge of its falsity.* While personal injury and advertising injury deal with intentional torts, it is not the purpose of the insurance to cover a tortfeasor's liability stemming from acts that are willful malicious.
2. *arising out of oral or written publication of material whose first publication took place before the beginning of the policy period.* This exclusion commonly is misunderstood. It resembles somewhat the restriction of some claims-made policies for special exposures that do not cover claims or suits based on *prior* acts before the inception of the policy. Its purpose is to prevent adverse selection in those cases, for example, where personal injury coverage is desired based on some past misdeed which could give rise to claim or suit in the future.
3. *arising out of the willful violation of a penal statute or ordinance committed by or with the consent of the insured.* This exclusion addresses the matter of penal statutes which, in general, are both federal and state laws that define *criminal* offenses and impose fines and punishment. A person may commit a tort without violating a penal statute. However, a single act can be both a tort and a crime.
4. *for which the insured has assumed liability in a contract or agreement. This exclusion does not apply to liability for damages that the insured would have in the absence of contract or agreement.* Considering the potentially serious nature and consequences of intentional torts, insurers generally do not want to inherit any liability an insured may have based solely on its contractual assumption of the disabilities of

another party. Real estate leases often include the term "personal injury," rather than "bodily injury." Unless this policy exclusion can be deleted (which is possible), it would be to the insured's advantage to clarify any lease agreement that refers to personal injury, rather than bodily injury, and preferably to have the contract changed; otherwise, the insured could be without insurance if the landlord seeks indemnification . from the tenant because of a suit alleging wrongful eviction or other intentional tort.[17]

Some earlier forms of personal injury liability coverage contained an exclusion for personal injury sustained by any person as a result of an offense by the named insured directly or indirectly related to the employment of any person. This exclusion, which often was deleted for an additional premium, was directed at personal injury claims against an employer who, for example, slanders an employee. It also could apply if an employee of the personnel department of a company were to divulge privileged information about a former employee. Some part of the exposure may still be excluded since the Who Is Insured provision does not include employees as insureds for " 'bodily injury' or 'personal injury' to you or to a co-employee while in the course of his or her employment."

The other four exclusions limited to advertising injury preclude coverage for any insured arising out of:

(1) Breach of contract, other than misappropriation of advertising ideas under an implied contract;
(2) The failure of goods, products, or services to conform with advertised quality or performance;
(3) The wrong description of the price of the goods, products, or services; and
(4) An offense committed by an insured whose business is advertising, broadcasting, publication, or telecasting.

The latter exclusion, in effect, requires any such business to obtain special coverage, such as advertisers' or broadcasters' liability insurance. The other three exclusions deal with *business risks* for which insurance is not readily available.

COVERAGE C: MEDICAL PAYMENTS

Premises medical payments coverage was optional with former general liability policies, but is automatically included in the CGL. This coverage has its own trigger which will be discussed in Chapter 6.

The medical payments coverage under the CGL policy is not a form of liability insurance in a strict sense, because negligence of the insured need not be established as a condition precedent to payment by the insurer. Medical payments are made if there is reason to believe that the resulting bodily injury would not have occurred had it not been for some condition on the insured premises or for operations conducted by the insured.

Specifically, payments are made for medical expenses incurred by members of the public who sustain injuries caused by an accident (1) on premises the named insured owns or rents; (2) on the ways next to such premises as described in (1); or (3) because of the named insured's operations (whether caused by the named insured or by other insured's on behalf of the named insured) in the coverage territory, and during the policy period. Another condition is that medical expenses must be incurred *and* reported to the insurer within one year of the date of accident. An accident that requires an injured person to undergo a series of treatments that extend beyond the period of one year apparently would not be covered by medical payments. A claim for any injury that serious would likely be filed under bodily injury liability coverage.

Note that if the named insured does not have bodily injury liability coverage for the circumstances under which injury occurs, the named insured is not covered for the claimant's medical bills.

CONCLUDING REMARKS

The CGL is a complex document designed to serve as the basic liability insurance contract for an organization of almost any type. After briefly describing the historical roots of the current form, this chapter has closely examined the policy's coverages and exclusions.

Several important issues have not yet been covered in detail but will be deferred to Chapter 6. These include the coverage triggers, the limits of liability, and some of the options available by endorsement.

Chapter Notes

1. G. F. Michelbacher, *Casualty Insurance Principles*, 2nd ed. (New York: McGraw-Hill, 1942), p. 10.
2. "Report of Committee on Casualty Insurance," *Insurance Counsel Journal*, (Chicago: International Association of Insurance Counsel, July 1944), pp. 8-9.
3. C. A. Kulp, *Casualty Insurance*, 2nd ed. (New York: The Ronald Press Company, 1928), p. 241.
4. George H. Tinker, "Comprehensive General Liability Insurance—Perspective and Overview," *FIC Quarterly*(Spring 1975), p. 221.
5. For interesting article on the development of the policy wording dealing with "legally obligated," "liability imposed by law" and "liability assumed by contract," see Edward I. Taylor, "The Liability Imposed by Law," *Insurance Counsel Journal*, Oct. 1945, p. 38.
6. *Customer Analysis of the Comprehensive General Liability Policy* (New York: American Society of Insurance Management, Inc., 1968), pp. 24-28.
7. A joint venture is not automatically covered under the CGL policy. If coverage is desired, a joint venture must be specifically declared to the insurer and listed on the policy.
8. Sheila L. Birnbaum and Barbara Wrubel, "Foreign Plaintiffs and the American Manufacturer: Is A Court In The United States A Forum Non Conveniens?" *The Forum* (Chicago: Tort and Insurance Practice Section, American Bar Association, Fall 1984), p. 59.
9. Donald S. Malecki, "Actions in equity: Do they have a place with liability insurance policies?" *CPCU Journal*, Malvern, PA: The Society of Chartered Property and Casualty Underwriters), Vol. 37, No. 3, Sept. 1984, p. 139.
10. Mercer v. Uniroyal 361 N.E. 2d 492, (1976).
11. Insurance Company of North America v. Dayton Tool & Die Works Inc., 443 N.E. 2d 457, (1982).
12. Whittaker Corporation v. Michigan Ins. Co., 1975 C.C.H. (Fire and Casualty) 817.
13. Sun Insurance Co. of New York v. Hammanne Center, 306 A. 2d 786, held that the rental of a wallpaper machine was incidental to the business of a hardware store under the premises and operations coverage of an OL&T policy.
14. Liability of the named insured for damage to the steam turbine is not covered under products liability insurance, because of the exclusion of property damage to the named insured's products. It therefore is up to the owner of that turbine to settle with the manufacturer on the matter of damage to its turbine. However, if the owner has boiler and machinery insurance covering the turbine against breakdown of burnout, the matter of having to settle loss with the manufacturer of the turbine can be avoided.

The owner, instead, can receive its settlement from the insurer of the boiler and machinery policy. It would then be up to the insurer to seek reimbursement of the damages.

15. For further discussion of diminution in value claims, see Laurie Vasichek, "Liability Coverage for 'Damages Because of Property Damage' Under the Comprehensive General Liability Policy," *Minnesota Law Review*, 68 (1984), 809.

16. *Black's Law Dictionary* (St. Paul, MN: West Publishing Company,) 5th ed., 1979.

17. For a further discussion of this exposure and others created by leases, see *Insuring the Lease Exposure*, Cincinnati Chapter of the Society of Chartered Property and Casualty Underwriters. (Cincinnati, OH: The National Underwriter Company), 1981.

CHAPTER 6

General Liability Insurance—II

Chapter 5 discussed the coverage provisions of the Insurance Services Office's commercial general liability (CGL) form, introduced for use in 1986. Although two CGL forms are available, the basic coverages of each are identical. The differences in the two forms lie in their triggers—the bases on which the coverage of these forms is activated.

A large part of this chapter is devoted to the triggers of both forms, especially the features of the claims-made form. The next section discusses CGL policy limits for all basic coverages, a topic that is somewhat interrelated with the "triggers" discussion. A brief discussion of CGL premium rating follows; emphasis here is on the differences in claims-made and occurrence form rating.

The final part of this chapter summarizes the unique liability coverage features of the farmowners forms. In past years, the businessowners program for small stores, offices, and apartments also contained liability provisions that varied somewhat from then-available standard CGL forms. As of 1987, ISO intends to introduce business-owners program liability forms providing coverage essentially identical to that of the occurrence-basis CGL. Consequently, there is no need for a separate analysis of businessowners liability coverage.

TWO CGL FORMS DISTINGUISHED

The occurrence and claims-made versions of the commercial general liability forms provide identical coverages.

- Coverage A encompasses bodily injury and property damage liability.
- Coverage B covers personal and advertising injury liability.

- Coverage C handles premises medical payments losses.

The scope of coverage under both forms was discussed in Chapter 5, but little attention was given to the "trigger" provisions affecting Coverage A that distinguish these two CGL forms from each other.

Coverage Triggers   *deff · for Cov. A only*

The term *trigger*, as commonly used with the occurrence and claims-made forms, can be defined as the basis on which coverage of the policy is activated. The gun analogy is fairly obvious—"pulling the trigger" sets off a response from the insurer; if coverage is not "triggered," there is no response. The only difference between the two CGL policies is in the concepts surrounding the Coverage A trigger. The triggers of Coverages B and C are identical under both forms.

Coverage A Triggers   The event that triggers coverage under the occurrence form is bodily injury or property damage that is sustained by a third party during the policy period. Although a claim must be made before insurance coverage is invoked, it does not matter when a claim is eventually filed. So long as the coverage of an occurrence policy was triggered and the event is otherwise covered, the insurer of the triggered policy has the obligation to respond on behalf of its insured—even if the claim is not presented until years after the event and years after the policy expired.

On the other hand, *the coverage of a claims-made policy is triggered at the time notice of claim is received and recorded by the insured or insurer (whichever is first).* In light of some unique characteristics of the claims-made CGL form, such as the retroactive date and extended reporting periods, the claims-made form that ultimately is triggered is not always the policy with an expiration date later than the date the claim is first made, as noted later. For now, it is enough to remember that the time of the bodily injury or property damage is *not as important* a factor under the claims-made approach as it is with the occurrence approach. In fact, one of the reasons for the claims-made approach is to overcome the difficulty in determining a point in time when bodily injury or property damage[1] actually occurs; it is often easier to pinpoint the date when the claim is made.

Apart from provisions relating to the Coverage A triggers, both CGL forms are identical. "Bodily injury" and "property damage" under both forms must be caused by an "occurrence," as these terms are defined in the forms. "Occurrence" means an accident, including continuous or repeated exposure to substantially the same general harmful conditions.

Coverage B and C Triggers   Both Coverages B and C have their own triggers and are therefore unaffected by the occurrence and claims-made form triggers under Coverage A. Under Coverage B, personal injury or advertising injury, the trigger is the *offense* committed during the policy period. The nature of an offense and its implications for coverage are discussed later in this chapter. Under Coverage C, medical payments coverage, the trigger is the *accident,* during the policy period, that results in bodily injury.

Background

As noted in Chapter 5, general liability policies since 1966 have been written on an "occurrence" basis. The CGL revision introduced in 1986 added a claims-made form and also continued to provide an occurrence form. In short, the claims-made CGL form was introduced to overcome the drawbacks of the occurrence approach with respect to the so-called *long-tail* or latent injury exposures; an occurrence form CGL was retained because of some drawbacks in the claims-made approach.

While an occurrence and resulting bodily injury or property damage are often simultaneous (as when a person trips and falls, breaking a leg), there are cases where the bodily injury or property damage is deemed to be prolonged to the point where it can span a number of years. Such bodily injury cases have involved substances such as asbestos, beryllium, formaldehyde, and the drug diethylstilbestrol (DES). Toxic wastes that may impair the environment present long-tail exposures.

Since occurrence policies are triggered by bodily injury or property damage, the crux of the problem has been determining the point in time at which bodily injury or property damage is considered to have occurred. The occurrence policy in force at that time is deemed to provide coverage.

Manifestation Theory   Some insurers have maintained that an injury occurs at the time of its manifestation and, thus, it is the occurrence policy in force at the time the bodily injury becomes manifest that is triggered. This line of reasoning is referred to as the *manifestation theory.* Under the manifestation theory, it does not matter when the claimant was first exposed to the hazardous substance; what is important is the date the claimant knew or should have known of the illness or injury. Many courts have rejected the manifestation theory and accepted the broader exposure theory.

Exposure Theory   Under the *exposure theory,* it is said that bodily injury occurs during the entire period a claimant is exposed to the hazardous substance. For example, if a person is exposed to a hazardous substance for ten years, all insurance companies that provided insurance under occurrence forms during those ten years would be contractually accountable.[2]

Continuous Exposure, or Triple-Trigger, Theory Other courts have extended the exposure theory to encompass not only (1) the entire period of exposure, but also (2) that period, after a person has been exposed to a hazardous substance, during which the condition within the person exposed continues to worsen until (3) the condition is manifested. In cases in which the *triple-trigger theory* has been upheld, all insurers of occurrence policies in effect from the period of the first exposure, through exposure-in-residence, until sickness becomes manifest have been held contractually accountable.[3] The triple-trigger theory can involve a lot more years—and a lot more insurance policies—than either of the other exposure theories.

Stacking of Limits Right or wrong, the two exposure theories have required several insurers' occurrence policies to be "stacked" in response to a single injury. Also, the exposure theories have permitted the stacking of "per occurrence" limits within a single policy, in situations where a given injury is considered the result of several occurrences. Thus, the exposure theories, applied to occurrence policies without aggregate limits, have in some cases resulted in the payment of considerably more claims dollars than the insurers had anticipated. Also, the decades-long delay in determining actual losses attributable to a given policy year creates enormous uncertainty for insurers attempting to establish proper rates for upcoming policy years.

As one measure to prevent payout of policy limits many times for a given year, both the new occurrence form and the claims-made forms are subject to across-the-board aggregate limits affecting all policy coverages. Once an aggregate limit is used up in one or more claims during the policy period, coverage ends. The claims-made CGL goes even further in addressing this problem. The claims-made policy is designed so that only one claims-made policy will apply in some situations where coverage might otherwise overlap. And, since the time of the *claim* is the criterion, the issues surrounding when an injury begins and ends are much less relevant with the claims-made form than with an occurrence form.

It has been suggested that the occurrence form is suitable for insureds with no long-tail exposure, while the claims-made form is the more logical choice for insuring long-tail exposures. Insurers are not likely to use the occurrence form when there is a clearly identifiable long-tail exposure, because the occurrence form may provide coverage for claims that are presented many years after the policy expires.

However, the 1986 occurrence form, unlike its predecessor, would at least restrict the total dollar amount payable because all coverages are affected by its aggregate limits. The problem with this suggestion is that long-tail claims cannot always be foreseen—it has been said that virtually all entities can be confronted with the long-tail exposures. The basic concept of the occurrence approach to coverage is straightforward and requires little elaboration. Complicating factors are derived from the ways in which the courts have applied the policy language in determining when coverage is triggered. The claims-made form, however, requires detailed examination and careful analysis.

UNIQUE FEATURES OF THE CLAIMS-MADE FORM

Special or unique features of the claims-made form are the (1) trigger, (2) retroactive date options, (3) extended reporting periods ("tails"), and (4) so-called "laser beam" endorsement options.

Claims-Made Trigger

The following provisions are found in the insuring agreement of the claims-made policy:

> 1. a. ....This insurance does not apply to "bodily injury" or "property damage" which occurred before the Retroactive Date, if any, shown in the Declarations or which occurs after the policy period
> . . .
> b. This insurance applies to "bodily injury" or "property damage" only if a claim for damages because of the "bodily injury" or "property damage" is first made against any insured during the policy period.
> (1) A claim by a person or organization seeking damages will be deemed to have been made when notice of such claim is received and recorded by any insured or by us, whichever comes first.

Provision 1.a. of the insuring agreement sets the outside parameters of the claims-made form. The *bodily injury or property damage must occur*

(1) *after the retroactive date*, if one is applicable, and
(2) *prior to the expiration* of that policy.

Ramifications of the retroactive date are discussed later in this chapter. For the moment, it is important to know that if a retroactive date is entered on the declarations of the claims-made policy, no claims for bodily injury or property damage that occurred before that retroactive date are intended be covered by that claims-made policy.

Provision b. of the insuring agreement explains that the claims-made trigger applies only to Coverage A, and only if claim is first made during the policy period (and after the retroactive date specified, if any). *The first presentation of a claim triggers the policy.* Generally, if the claim is made after the policy period, the policy is not considered to be triggered. There are some exceptions to this general rule because of the "extended reporting periods" or "tail coverages," explained in detail later. (Briefly, when "tail" coverage applies, the period for reporting any claim involving bodily injury or property damage is extended after the claims-made policy's expiration through the period of the applicable extended reporting period or "tail.")

How the claims-made policy is triggered is explained in provision b.(1). The notice of claim must be *received and recorded* by any insured or the insurer; whichever occurs first triggers coverage. As explained later, it is the obligation of the insured to notify the insurance company of an "occurrence" that may result in a claim. However, the claims-made form specifically states that notice of an "occurrence" is not notice of a claim. There may be a delay between the occurrence or event that results in bodily injury or property damage and the time when actual claim or suit is filed. Insureds therefore may be required to notify the insurer twice:

1. as soon as practicable following the occurrence, and
2. again when the insured receives notice of the claim.

This requirement is not new or unique to the claims-made CGL; it has long been a part of general liability and umbrella policy provisions.

The phrase *received and recorded* is not defined. It could encompass a written or oral notice. The policy conditions, nonetheless, do require some *written* specifics of the claim as soon as it is practicable for the insured to provide them. The required specifics are also spelled out in the policy condition dealing with the insured's duties in the event of occurrence, claim, or suit.

Provision b.(1). also attempts to make clear that if several successive claims-made CGLs are involved and if claim was first made for bodily injury to the same person or property damage to the same person or organization in an earlier policy year, all damages stemming from that one claim are subject to the coverage and limits of the policy that was in force at the time when notice was first received and recorded by the insured or insurer.

Retroactive Date

When a claims-made policy is issued, a date may be entered in the space on the declarations page provided for designating the retroactive date. No claims for damages will be covered by the claims-made policy if the "bodily injury" or "property damage" alleged in that claim occurred *before* the retroactive date, if any, shown in the declarations. As a rule, triggering the claims-made form, as noted earlier, does not depend on time of injury; however, the retroactive date presents one exception to that rule.

One of three possible retroactive date approaches may be selected—the retroactive date may be (1) the same as the inception date or (2) a specified earlier date, or (3) there may be no retroactive date at all.

Same As Inception Date   Under the first option, the retroactive date is the same as the inception date of the claims-made policy. The effect here is to preclude any coverage for a claim made following the inception date of the policy if the claim involves any bodily injury or property damage that occurred prior to the inception (and retroactive date) of the claims-made policy.

In most cases, the retroactive date is initially set when an insured's occurrence policy is renewed with a claims-made policy and the retroactive date of the first claims-made policy that follows an occurrence policy will be the same as the inception date of that claims-made policy. Assume, then that a claim is made during the period of the first claims-made policy following an occurrence policy, because of injuries in an occurrence that happened before that policy period. The claim is not intended to be covered by the claims-made policy; however, the insured would probably have coverage under one (or more) of its earlier occurrence policies.

The concept of using a retroactive date to eliminate coverage for past occurrences is not unique to the CGL, nor is it new. Occurrence policies have an implied retroactive date which is always the same as the inception date—occurrence policies do not cover claims arising from occurrences that took place before policy inception. Some claims-made policies, such as those providing professional liability coverage, have long included retroactive dates. However, some specialty policies provide coverage without retroactive date restrictions, provided the insured will warrant that he or she is unaware of any circumstances that may give rise to an eventual claim.

Specified Earlier Date   The first claims-made policy written for any given insured will likely be subject to the retroactive date option noted above, i.e. it will be the same as the inception date of the policy. The second option is useful to maintain continuity of coverage when this first claims-made policy is renewed.

Suppose that an insured's first claims-made policy is written with an inception date of January 1987 and renewed in January 1988. When the policy is renewed in January 1988, the retroactive date on the renewal policy should again be January *1987*. Otherwise, there will be a gap in coverage. For example, if a bodily injury were to be sustained during the 1987 policy period but claim were not made against the insured until the 1988 policy period, and the 1988 policy has a January 1988 retro date, neither policy would apply. The original claims-made policy would not apply because claim was made after the expiration of the policy. The renewal policy also would not apply because the claim made during its policy period involved a bodily injury that occurred prior to its retroactive date.

When the renewal claims-made policy's retroactive date is the same as the expiring policy's retroactive date, there should be continuity of coverage. For example, if claim is made during the 1988 policy year because of a bodily injury that occurred during the 1987 policy year, and the 1988 policy has a January 1987 retro date, the 1988 claims-made policy applies.

The use of a specified earlier retroactive date can avoid a potential gap that might otherwise be created when the claims-made policy is renewed with the same insurer or rewritten by a different insurer.

No Retroactive Date If the retroactive date provision of the claims-made policy is designated with the word *open,* or *none* (or if no date is specified), then no retroactive date applies. The claims-made insurer will respond to any claim made during the policy period regardless of when the bodily injury or property damage may have happened. Because of the "other insurance" provision of the claims-made form, however, if any such claim is also covered by an occurrence form issued earlier, the occurrence form would apply as primary insurance. The claims-made form will apply only if excess limits are needed.

Rule Limiting Advancement of Retro Date

To prevent insurers from routinely advancing retroactive dates with each renewal, an ISO rule imposes certain restrictions. Once the retroactive date of a claims-made policy has been established, it can be advanced (i.e., moved to a later date) only with the consent of the first named insured *and:*

- if there is a change of insurance companies,
- if there is a substantial change in the insured's operations which results in an increased exposure to loss, or
- if the insured fails to provide the insurer with information the insured knows or should know concerning the nature of the risk.

Whatever the reason the retroactive date may be advanced, the insured has some protection against potential gaps in the policy's provisions dealing with extended reporting periods, or "tails."

Extended Reporting Periods ("Tails")

To summarize the discussion up to this point, to trigger the claims-made policy:

1. notice of a claim must be received and recorded during the policy period, and
2. must allege bodily injury or property damage that took place after the policy's retroactive date, if any.

Based on what has been discussed to this point, if the claim is made after policy expiration, the claims-made form is not triggered and no coverage applies—even if the claim involves bodily injury or property damage that occurred after the policy's retroactive date. To maintain continuity of coverage, protecting against a situation where the injury or damage occurs after the retroactive date but claim is not made until after the policy's expiration, it is necessary that the claims-made policy include an extended reporting period (ERP), commonly referred to as a "tail."

While there are variations of extended reporting periods, the underlying function of all "tails" is the same. When activated, the tail extends coverage of the claims-made policy to claims (1) first made *after* the expiration of the policy (2) for bodily injury or property damage that occurred *before* termination of the policy but after its retroactive date. The effect of such tail coverage is to extend the time within which a claim can be eligible for coverage. Section V of the claims-made form describes the "tails" and the situations in which they apply.

When "Tail" Coverage Becomes Necessary The extended reporting periods are designed to close, or at least reduce, certain gaps that are inherent to the use of a claims-made form. Thus, tail coverage may be necessary

1. when the claims-made CGL is renewed or rewritten subject to an advanced retroactive date,
2. when the claims-made policy is replaced with an occurrence form,
3. when the claims-made policy is cancelled or not renewed for any reason (e.g. when someone goes out of business or retires), or
4. when the claims-made policy is subject to a "laser beam" endorsement.

Exhibit 6-1
Coverage Gap When Retro Date is Advanced if There Were No "Tail"
Coverage

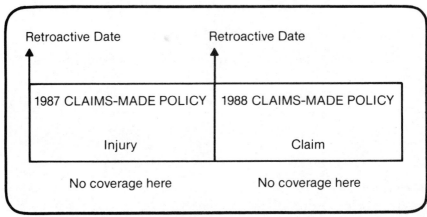

An Advanced Retroactive Date. As explained earlier, a claims-made policy that is renewed or rewritten with a later retroactive date than the policy it replaces (i.e., the date is advanced) creates a gap in coverage. Exhibit 6-1 illustrates the impact of a later retroactive date on claims-made coverage. Say, for example, the first claims-made policy written January 1, 1987 was subject to a retroactive date specified in the policy declarations as also being January 1, 1987. When the policy was renewed the following year, the retroactive date of the new claims-made policy was designated as January 1, 1988. Assume that a third party sustained bodily injury allegedly caused by the insured during the 1987 policy period and the first time the insured hears about the claim is during the 1988 policy period.

The 1987 claims-made policy would not respond because it expired before the claim was received. The 1988 policy would not respond, either, because the claim alleges a bodily injury that was sustained before the retroactive date of the 1988 claims-made policy.

Tail coverage is intended to address this problem by extending the time during which claims must be received and recorded. While the specifics of tail coverages are explained later, it is important at this point to note what the tail (extended reporting period) coverage would do, in general. The effect is that any claim first made during an extended reporting period ("tail") for bodily injury or property damage that occurred *before* the end of the policy and *after* the retroactive date will be considered to have been made on the last day of the expired claims-made policy.

To place this in perspective, assume that the 1987 claims-made

Exhibit 6-2
"Tail" Coverage Plugs Coverage Gap When Retro Date is Advanced

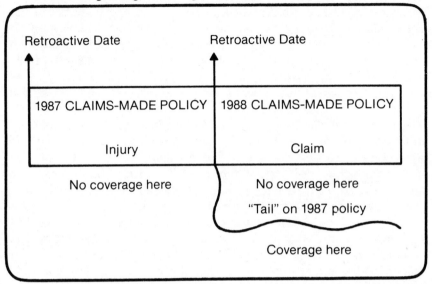

form discussed in the preceding example was amended with tail coverage. As Exhibit 6-2 shows, the claim that is received and recorded by the insured during the subsequent policy year (1988) would be covered under the 1987 policy year because the claim involved a bodily injury that occurred during the 1987 claims-made policy period and *after* the 1987 policy's retroactive date. The amount of additional time allowed for receiving and recording claims depends on which kind of extended reporting period ("tail") is applicable, as discussed later.[4] However, for the moment, *it should be clearly understood that an extended reporting period ("tail") merely extends the time to report or make claims; it does not extend the period during which covered occurrences may take place.* Thus, no coverage would apply under that policy if bodily injury or property damage occurs after the expiration of the claims-made policy, even if it occurs during an extended reporting period.

Occurrence Form Replacement. A coverage gap is automatically created whenever a claims-made form is replaced with an occurrence form. Part of the gap is caused by the occurrence form's trigger. This trigger provision, which appears in that form's insuring agreement, states that *this insurance applies only to "bodily injury" or "property damage" that occurs during the policy period.* In a sense, the occurrence form is also subject to a retroactive date (although that phrase is not used). But, unlike the retroactive date of the claims-made form, the occurrence form's retroactive date is always the same as the inception date. In any event, the occurrence form precludes any coverage for claims alleging bodily injury or property damage that happened *before* the inception date of the policy.[5] This aspect of occurrence coverage creates a gap, when replacing a claims-made form with an occurrence form, because of the trigger provisions of the claims-made form.

For purposes of illustration, assume that a claims-made policy was first written on January 1, 1987 and subject to the same January 1, 1987 retroactive date. The following year, the claims-made form is replaced with an occurrence form. Assume that a third party sustained bodily injury during the 1987 policy year but the insured's first notice of such claim is not made until 1988. *Without* "tail" coverage, the insured here would be confronted with a gap in protection as shown in Exhibit 6-3. The claims-made policy would not be triggered—even though the bodily injury occurred during the claims-made period and after its retroactive date—because the claim was not made until after the policy had expired. The occurrence form likewise does not apply because the alleged bodily injury did not happen during that form's coverage period. This gap would not exist if the expired claims-made policy has an appropriate extended reporting period. If tail coverage applies, the claim reported in the subsequent policy year is brought back into the expired claims-made policy's period.

Claims-made Policy Cancelled or Nonrenewed. Extended reporting periods can be important any time a claims-made policy is canceled or nonrenewed, unless a replacement policy provides complete continuity of coverage (e.g. by retaining the same retroactive date as the canceled policy).

The problem is compounded when an insured is unable to obtain a suitable replacement policy in time to avoid a period during which no policy is in force. Insureds must also understand the ramifications of *both* CGL forms if insurance is permanently canceled or nonrenewed because insureds go out of business. Neither the occurrence nor claims-made forms provides unlimited protection in such cases.

This point deserves emphasis. Claims-made coverage would not apply if claims are brought after the policy expires, and occurrence coverage may not apply either. Suppose an insured who has an *occurrence* policy decides to go out of business at the end of the 1990 policy year. If any claim is made against the insured after the expiration and nonrenewal of that occurrence policy, coverage will hinge on the timing of injury. To trigger the occurrence form, the bodily injury or property damage must have taken place before the expiration of that policy. Under no circumstances will the insured have

Exhibit 6-3
"Tail" Coverage Plugs Coverage Gap When Claims Made Policy is
Replaced With Occurence Policy

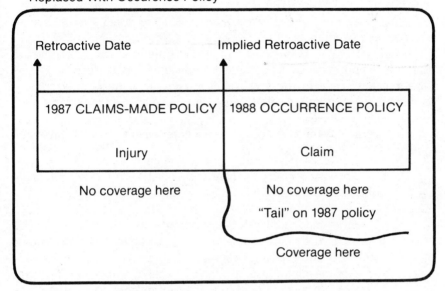

any protection if the bodily injury or property damage were to occur
after the occurrence form expires. This can be a problem for a
manufacturer's product or a contractor's "work" that continues to be
used long after it is sold or completed.

Suppose, instead, that a claims-made policy was in force at the time
the insured decided to go out of business. Two conditions must be met,
if a claim made against the insured after the expiration of the claims-
made policy is to be covered:

1. The claim involves bodily injury or property damage that
   occurred *before* the expiration of the claims-made form but
   after the retroactive date, and
2. The expired claims-made policy includes applicable "tail" coverage.

The same gap that affects the occurrence form also exists under
the claims-made policy. Thus, if a claim is made against the insured
after expiration of the claims-made form—even if it is made during an
extended reporting period—the last claims-made form is triggered only
if the alleged bodily injury or property damage happened *before*
expiration of the claims-made form. If the bodily injury or property
damage were to be sustained by a third party after the policy's
expiration (even if it is during a tail period), no coverage would apply.

Thus, a dormant manufacturer of a product that has a long useful life may need to continue to purchase insurance for an indefinite period under a claims-made form, as well.

The Laser Beam Endorsement. The so-called "laser beam" endorsement—officially titled *Exclusion of Specific Accident(s), Product(s), Work or Location(s)*—is an underwriting tool that is designed to limit the application of Coverage A and policy limits. The nickname "laser beam" reflects the fact that the endorsements cleanly cut out coverage for certain specific things while leaving coverage for everything else untouched.

Insurers may choose to use the endorsement to a claims-made policy when

1. an occurrence policy is being replaced with the claims-made policy and the retroactive date specifies some earlier date or is open,
2. the claims-made policy is being renewed and the insurer desires to prevent the renewal policy limits from applying to any known incident of the expiring policy's period, or
3. the expiring claims-made policy is already subject to a "laser beam" endorsement and the insurer desires to continue the endorsement's application with the renewal policy.

To understand how the "laser beam" endorsement applies and its relationship to the extended reporting periods, assume the following scenario. A business has been covered by the CGL claims-made form from 1987 to 1991. Beginning with 1992, the business entity changes insurance companies. During its underwriting analysis, the insurer finds that one problem product, produced in the past, continues to cause accidents that generate claims. Except for that discontinued problem product produced by the insured, the exposure meets underwriting criteria and would qualify for a claims-made policy that continued the 1987 retroactive date. (With a 1987 retroactive date, the new claims-made policy's Coverage A will apply to any claims made during the 1992 policy period, if the bodily injury or property damage occurred at any time from 1987 to the present.) However, the insurer will continue the earlier retroactive date in this case *only* if it can exclude claims arising from the problem product. The new claims-made policy can be amended with a laser beam endorsement which specifically describes the product in question and excludes coverage for claims arising from it. As noted, the real name of the so-called "laser beam endorsement" is "Exclusion of Specific Accident(s), Product(s), Work, or Location(s)." As the name implies, the endorsement can be configured so as to carve out and exclude coverage for many types of problem exposures. However, the present example will continue to use the illustration of a problem product.

The effect of that laser beam endorsement, as shown in Figure 6-4, is to preclude any coverage under the new claims-made policy for claims of bodily injury or property damage involving that excluded product. In order to obtain future coverage for claims arising out of the problem product, the insured will have to purchase an extended reporting period from the prior insurer. The extended reporting period ("tail") added to the expiring claims-made policy, will cover any claims made after the expiration of the 1991 claims-made policy, so long as the bodily injury or property damage took place prior to the 1991 policy's expiration. Any bodily injury or property damage from the excluded product that takes place after the expiration date of the 1991 claims-made policy (and during the claims-made form to which the laser beam endorsement is attached) is not intended to be covered.

Unless the next claims-made policy, for the period 1993 to 1994, also is modified with the same "laser beam" endorsement, the later policy could cover any claim of bodily injury or property damage stemming from the product which was excluded during the earlier policy period.

As is also important to note, for reasons explained more fully later in this chapter, no coverage will apply during the 1992 claims-made policy period for bodily injury or property damage that occurs during that policy period when caused by the problem product exposure which is specifically excluded. Also, there is no easy way to maintain continuous coverage for future occurrences on an exposure that has become uninsurable. A specialty insurer may be willing to provide such coverage, depending on the circumstances.

An alternative to the "laser beam" endorsement would be to make the 1992 claims-made policy subject to a 1992 retroactive date. The effect of this alternative would be to preclude all claims made during the 1992 policy period if they involve bodily injury or property damage that took place prior to the retroactive date. This approach is clearly more restrictive than the "laser beam" endorsement that only excludes (a) specified exposure(s). To overcome any coverage gaps, it would again be advisable for the insured to have an extended reporting period ("tail") from the insurer that provided the 1991 policy.

The "laser beam" endorsement also could conceivably be used to prevent a renewal claims-made policy's limits from applying to a claim that would otherwise be subject to payment under the earlier policy. For example, assume a claims-made policy during the 1987 policy year has a $500,000 per occurrence limit and a $500,000 aggregate limit for Coverage A. At policy renewal the insured is aware of a recent occurrence that is likely to give rise to a substantial claim sometime in

Exhibit 6-4
"Tail" Coverage Plugs Coverage Gap, in Part, When Renewal Policy Has
"Laser Beam" Endorsement

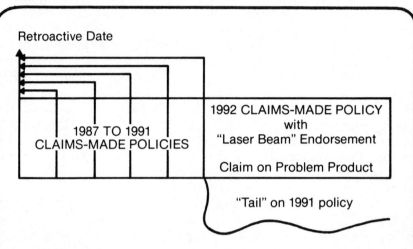

Retroactive Date

1987 TO 1991
CLAIMS-MADE POLICIES

1992 CLAIMS-MADE POLICY
with
"Laser Beam" Endorsement

Claim on Problem Product

"Tail" on 1991 policy

1. The 1992 claims-made policy was renewed with the 1987 retroactive date.

2. The 1992 claims-made policy is subject to the laser beam endorsement excluding any claim made during the 1992 period because of bodily injury or property damage involving the problem product that occurred at any time—i.e., during the 1987 to 1991 policy periods, as well as during 1992.

3. Tail coverage on the 1991 claims-made policy is necessary because any claim for bodily injury or property damage involving the excluded product will not be covered by the 1992 policy, in light of the laser beam endorsement. The tail extends the reporting period of the 1991 policy so that if claim is made for injury or property damage because of the excluded product after the 1991 claims-made policy expires, it will be brought back to that policy period.

4. No coverage applies to claims made during 1992 for occurrences during 1992 involving the problem product.

the future. The insured therefore requests that the renewal claims-made policy be written subject to $1 million per occurrence and aggregate limits. To prevent the application of the higher $1 million limits to this known occurrence, if claim should indeed be made during the renewal claims-made period, the insurer could amend the renewal with a "laser beam" endorsement specifically excluding any claims because of that occurrence during the earlier policy period. When this happens, the expiring policy will be subject to an automatic extended reporting period, as explained later, providing continuity of coverage, but subject to the $500,000 limits of the expired policy.

It is a condition of both CGL forms that the insurer be notified as soon as practicable of any "occurrence" that may result in a claim. If the insured should fail to notify the insurer of any occurrence that might eventually lead to a claim in order to avoid a "laser beam" endorsement, coverage of the entire policy could be in jeopardy.

Kinds of "Tail" Coverage

The ISO commercial general liability claims-made form offers three kinds of tail coverage:

1. a "sixty-day tail," also referred to as an automatic mini-tail;
2. a "five-year tail," also referred to as an automatic midi-tail or a limited tail; and
3. an "unlimited tail."

Together, the first two "tails"—which automatically come with the policy—are referred to in the policy as a "Basic Extended Reporting Period"; this can be abbreviated BERP, an acronym best left unpronounced. The "unlimited tail" is not automatically included in the policy, but the option to buy the "unlimited tail" is always included. Thus, "unlimited tail" coverage is not automatically provided by the basic policy. The "unlimited tail" is referred to in the policy as a "Supplemental Extended Reporting Period," which can be inoffensively be abbreviated and pronounced SERP. These three 'tails" are illustrated in Exhibit 6-5.

"Sixty-Day Tail" Provided without extra cost, the "sixty-day tail" extends by sixty days the period during which claims can be received and recorded. Any claim made during that sixty-day period after the policy expires must allege bodily injury or property damage that occurred (1) before the expiration of the claims-made form and (2) after the retroactive date. The "sixty-day tail's" function is to cover claims made during that short period, stemming from occurrences that were unknown before the policy expired and therefore not reported during the policy period. (An insured who desires a longer reporting period can purchase the "unlimited tail" discussed later.) This "sixty-day tail" is also useful when the insured experiences difficulty in obtaining replacement coverage, or while the insured decides whether to purchase "unlimited tail" coverage.

To avoid any gap, it is necessary for the insured to obtain a

Exhibit 6-5
Extended Reporting Periods

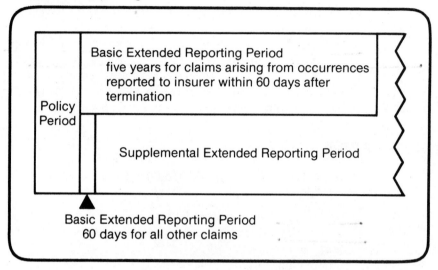

Basic Extended Reporting Period
five years for claims arising from occurrences
reported to insurer within 60 days after
termination

Policy
Period

Supplemental Extended Reporting Period

Basic Extended Reporting Period
60 days for all other claims

replacement policy whose retroactive date is the same as the expiration date of the last policy, rather than the expiration date of the "sixty-day tail" period. If the inception of the replacement policy were to coincide with the expiration of the sixty-day tail, there would be no coverage for occurrences during that sixty-day period.

For example, assume that a claims-made policy is written effective January 1, 1987, and this also is the retroactive date. During the policy period a third party is injured, but claim is not made during the policy period. The claim instead is received and recorded by the insured during the "sixty-day tail." The expiring policy should apply to this claim since it was reported during the "sixty-day tail" period. (See Exhibit 6-6.) Going one step farther, assume that the replacement policy's retroactive date is January 1, 1988, as illustrated in Exhibit 6-7. If claim is made during that same 60-day period, the "sixty-day tail" would still apply. Although there is a replacement policy, it does not apply because the occurrence took place prior to the replacement policy's retroactive date. Now assume that the replacement claims-made policy is not made effective until the end of the expiring claims-made policy's mini-tail or March 1, 1988. (See Exhibit 6-8). The insured in this case would be confronted with a gap in protection for any claim made during the "sixty-day tail" period and involving bodily injury or property damage that occurred after the expiration of the first policy and during the sixty-day period. This gap also would apply if the claim alleging such bodily injury or property damage during the "sixty-day tail" period

Exhibit 6-6
"Sixty-Day Tail" Provides Coverage for Claim Reported Within Sixty-Days of Policy Expiration When There is no Renewal or Replacement Policy

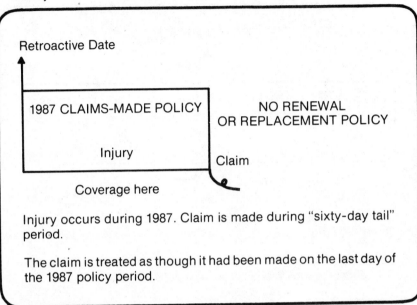

Retroactive Date

1987 CLAIMS-MADE POLICY

NO RENEWAL OR REPLACEMENT POLICY

Injury

Claim

Coverage here

Injury occurs during 1987. Claim is made during "sixty-day tail" period.

The claim is treated as though it had been made on the last day of the 1987 policy period.

were not to be made until after the renewal policy takes effects. Recall that the renewal policy also will not apply because the bodily injury or property damage during the "sixty-day tail" period was prior to the renewal policy's retroactive date. To avoid this problem, the replacement claims-made policy's inception date must coincide with either the preceding claims-made policy's expiration date or with some earlier retroactive date.

Other Insurance. The "sixty-day tail" is intended to be contingent insurance—it is not activated under circumstances when a claim is covered by other insurance (or would have been except for the exhaustion of another policy's limits). Thus, as mentioned in note 3 of Exhibit 6-7, if (1) other tail coverage becomes effective immediately upon expiration of the policy, or (2) the replacement policy's retroactive date is the same as the retroactive date of the expired policy, the "sixty-day tail" is not needed and it does not apply—not even as excess.

To summarize, the sixty-day BERP, or mini-tail, simply extends the reporting period of an expiring claims-made policy for sixty days. It is automatically provided without additional cost. However, the mini-tail does not extend the policy period, does not grant additional coverage, and does not provide additional limits. Also,

Exhibit 6-7
"Sixty-Day Tail" Provides Coverage for Claim Reported Within Sixty-Days of Expiration When Renewal or Replacement Policy Does Not Cover

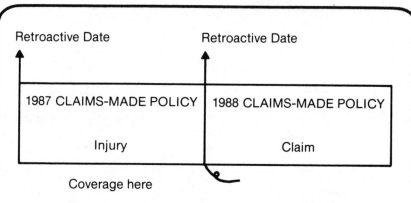

Injury occurs during 1987. Claim is made during the first sixty days of the 1988 policy period.

1. Coverage under the 1988 policy is precluded because the occurrence took place before that policy's retroactive date.

2. The claim is treated as though it had been made on the last day of the 1987 policy period.

3. If, instead, the 1988 policy had retained the 1987 retro date, the 1988 policy would provide coverage.

the "sixty-day tail" only applies in the absence of any other insurance. In other words, it does not apply as excess protection if replacement coverage applies to the claim or would apply but for exhaustion of the policy limits. The "sixty-day tail" is strictly a contingent form of insurance (it applies only if nothing else applies).

"Five-year Tail" This aspect of the BERP is designed to cover claims

1. reported during the five-year period following expiration of the claims-made policy, and
2. stemming from occurrences reported to the insurer no later than sixty days after the end of the policy period.

Exhibit 6-8
"Sixty-Day Tail" Does Not Provide Coverage for Occurrence During Sixty-Day Period

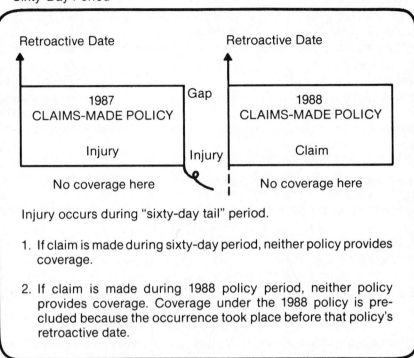

Injury occurs during "sixty-day tail" period.

1. If claim is made during sixty-day period, neither policy provides coverage.

2. If claim is made during 1988 policy period, neither policy provides coverage. Coverage under the 1988 policy is precluded because the occurrence took place before that policy's retroactive date.

This limited tail is automatically provided without additional direct cost; there is presumably some allowance for the coverage in the rate structure.

As noted several times, one of the explicit duties of the insured in the event of an occurrence, claim, or suit (under both CGL forms) is to notify the insurer as soon as practicable of an occurrence that may result in a claim. In the majority of cases, a claim will follow closely on the heels of an occurrence. But, in some cases there is a long delay between the occurrence and eventual claim or suit. And, the fact that notice of an "occurrence" is not considered to be notice of a claim under the claims-made form means that the insured may be obligated to notify the insurer twice—once when the insured becomes aware of an "occurrence" and again when notice is served of the resulting claim.

In light of the above, suppose that an insured notifies the insurer of two serious premises accidents involving business customers during the 1988 claims-made policy year. By the date of policy expiration, neither of the two occurrences has yet resulted in a claim against the insured. Nonetheless, at renewal the insurer decides that, to keep the renewal policy from covering any claims stemming from those occurrences, it is going to make the renewal policy subject to a "laser beam endorsement" specifically excluding those two accidents. When this happens, there is need for tail coverage on the expired policy, since any claims resulting from those two reported occurrences will be excluded under the renewal policy. The claims-made policy fills this need, to a degree, by automatically providing an extended reporting period of five years, beginning with the end of the policy period, for any claims resulting from those occurrences reported to the insurer (1) from the period following the expiring policy's retroactive date (2) provided they are not reported later than 60 days after the end of the policy period.

This "five-year tail" coverage also can be activated if the insurer advances the renewal policy's retroactive date or cancels or nonrenews the policy following the reporting of occurrences that have not as yet resulted in claims. This "five-year tail," therefore, is important any time there is a potential gap in the continuity of coverage stemming from the reporting of an "occurrence" that does not result in a claim by the expiration of the claims-made policy. Thus, if the replacement policy were to be made subject to an earlier retroactive date, thus encompassing the time when those accidents took place, this automatic five-year tail would not add anything. *Like the "sixty-day tail," the "five-year tail" also does not extend the policy period, does not grant additional coverage, and does not provide additional limits. Also, only bodily injury and property damage occurring between the retroactive date and the policy expiration date are covered.*

Remember that the automatic "five-year tail" applies only to occurrences (1) reported to the insurer (2) that have not culminated in claims by policy end and (3) only when there is no continuity of coverage. Otherwise, it has no effect (see Exhibit 6-9).

Depending on how the replacement policy is written, there may also be a gap in coverage for occurrences during the expired policy period. If the replacement policy retains the earlier retroactive date of the expired policy and a "laser beam" endorsement is used to exclude only the specific accidents that were reported, there should be no gap in coverage because of the "five-year tail" (although the possibility exists that the remaining aggregate limits are insufficient to cover any eventual claim during that automatic tail period). (See Exhibit 6-10.) If the replacement policy is made subject to a later retroactive date, additional tail coverage is necessary to cover the incurred-but-not-reported type of occurrences of the earlier policy period. (See Exhibit 6-11.) What would be required in both of these instances is the "unlimited" or supplemental tail discussed shortly.

Exhibit 6-9
"Five-Year Tail" Has No Effect When Coverage is Continuous

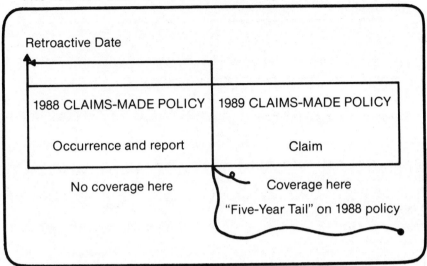

Other Insurance. The automatic "five-year tail" is activated if there is not other insurance applicable if and when a claim ultimately is made during the next five-year period. As with the "sixty-day tail," the expired policy limits apply also to claims within the "five-year tail." This could present a problem if the per occurrence limit is too low to cover the claim or the aggregate limit has been reduced by the payment of other claims.

If the occurrences reported during the earlier policy year do not result in claims by the end of the automatic-five year period, the "unlimited tail," discussed next, is designed to pick up where the limited tail leaves off—provided the supplemental tail is purchased within sixty-days of the expiration of the claims-made policy to which the automatic five-year tail applies. (See Exhibit 6-12.)

To summarize, the "five-year tail" is available without direct additional charge. It extends for five years the reporting period of the expired claims-made policy for claims stemming from occurrences reported to the insurer no later than sixty days after the end of the policy period. This limited tail coverage may be activated when the policy is cancelled or not renewed or the replacement policy is subject to a "laser beam" endorsement or later retroactive date or is replaced with an occurrence policy. Coverage of previously reported claims during that automatic five-year tail are contingent on availability of remaining aggregate limits. If the unlimited or supple-

Exhibit 6-10
"Five-Year Tail" Picks Up Coverage Excluded by "Laser Beam Endorsement"

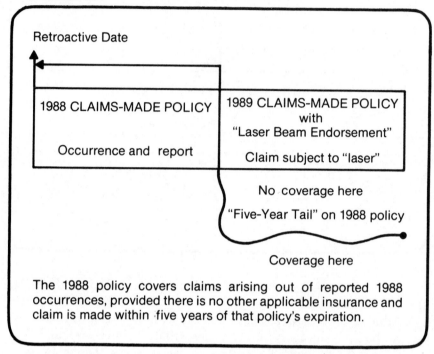

Retroactive Date

1988 CLAIMS-MADE POLICY	1989 CLAIMS-MADE POLICY with "Laser Beam Endorsement"
Occurrence and report	Claim subject to "laser"

No coverage here

"Five-Year Tail" on 1988 policy

Coverage here

The 1988 policy covers claims arising out of reported 1988 occurrences, provided there is no other applicable insurance and claim is made within five years of that policy's expiration.

mental tail also is purchased at the time the five-year tail takes effect, the five-year tail will not respond as excess insurance.

"Unlimited Tail" Unlike the other "tails," the "unlimited tail" is not automatically provided, but the insured has the right to purchase it as an option. The effect of this optional tail is to extend the "sixty-day tail" indefinitely. The "unlimited tail" may be required:

- When the claims-made policy is canceled or not renewed by the insured or insurer for any reason, including nonpayment of premium.
- When the claims-made policy is replaced with an occurrence policy.
- When an expiring claims-made policy is (1) renewed or replaced with a claims-made policy subject to a later retroactive date or to a "laser beam" endorsement, and (2) coverage is desired for claims (a) reported after the expiration of the first claims-made policy (b) stemming from occurrences that were unknown to the

Exhibit 6-11
Neither "Sixty-Day Tail" Nor "Five-Year Tail" Handles IBNR Claims
When Retro Date is Advanced

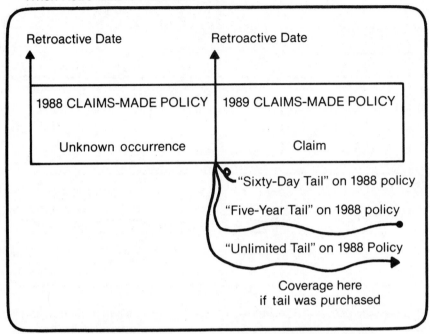

insured and therefore not reported before the expiration of the
first policy.

● When the claims-made policy is renewed or replaced with (A) a
claims-made policy subject to a later retroactive date or (B) a
"laser beam" endorsement, and coverage is desired for claims
reported (1) after the expiration of the automatic five-year tail
(2) stemming from occurrences that were reported (a) during
the policy period to which the "five-year" tail applies (b) but no
later than sixty days after that policy's expiration.

● When the claims-made policy is neither renewed nor replaced
and the insured desires protection in the event claim is made
after the expiration of the "sixty-day tail" because of bodily
injury or property damage that happened after the expired
policy's retroactive date but not later than the expiration date
of the policy. (No protection would be available for claims if the
bodily injury or property damage occurred during or after the
"sixty-day tail" period.)

Section V—Extended Reporting Periods of the claims-made form

Exhibit 6-12
For Known, Reported Losses, "Unlimited Tail" Takes Over Where
"Five-Year Tail" Leaves Off

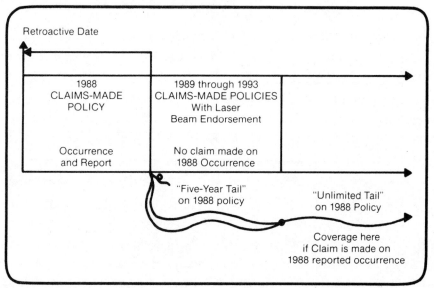

explains the procedure to follow if the unlimited or supplemental tail is desired. The first named insured must (1) make a written request for the supplemental extended reporting period within sixty days of the policy's expiration and (2) pay promptly the additional premium when due. Unless the additional premium is paid when due, the "unlimited tail" does not take effect. Once the premium is paid, it is fully earned, and the "unlimited tail" coverage can never be cancelled—it will continue to apply so long as there are sufficient limits to cover future claims.

The cost of the "unlimited tail" is capped at a *maximum* of 200 percent of the expiring policy's annual premium for the coverage part to which the "unlimited tail" coverage endorsement is attached. This means that when a CGL is written as part of a commercial package policy, the supplemental tail cost is limited to 200 percent of the premium for the commercial general liability coverage part and any applicable endorsements; other lines, such as commercial property, crime and inland marine, have no bearing on the CGL tail premiums.

The 200 percent is intended to place a ceiling on the tail premium. To prevent insurers from simply using the 200 percent in every instance when the unlimited tail coverage is purchased (in which case it would be not only a ceiling, but also a floor), advisory tail rating factors are made available to insurers. Since they are *advisory*, they do not necessarily have to be used. However, it is suggested that when the tail premium cost is determined, insurers should take into account:

1. the exposures insured;
2. previous types and amounts of insurance;
3. limits available under the coverage part for future payment of claims or suits; and
4. other related factors.

Of special note, the "unlimited tail," unlike the "sixty-day tail" and "five-year tail," is available only for an additional cost; it also provides a new set of aggregate limits equal to 100 percent of the expired policy's *original* aggregate limits. The *remaining* aggregate limits of the expiring policy continue to apply to the BERP, i.e. the sixty-day mini-tail and limited or automatic five-year tail. Most claims from reported occurrences will likely be made before the expiration of the five-year period of the automatic tail. However, should the automatic tail expire without any claims being charged against it, such claims that might have been covered except for the expiration of that tail will then be subject to the unimpaired aggregate limits of the "unlimited tail."

Other Insurance. The "unlimited tail" could apply as excess insurance, in some circumstances, unlike the other two tail coverages. This could happen when a claim is covered by both the "tail" and another subsequent policy. To compensate for those possible circumstances, the supplemental extended reporting period endorsement providing the "unlimited tail," which modifies the "other insurance" condition of the claims-made form to which it is attached, prescribes the method of loss allocation. The "unlimited tail" applies as excess over any other valid and collectible insurance available to the insured, whether on a primary, excess, contingent or other basis, when the other policy's period begins or continues after the "unlimited tail" coverage endorsement takes effect.

For example, assume that a claims-made policy is issued on January 1, 1988, which is also its retroactive date. After a one-year policy period, the policy is not renewed by the insurer and it appears that it will be difficult to find another insurer willing to handle the account. Even though there are no unsettled claims related to known or reported occurrences, the insured purchases the "unlimited tail" coverage. The insured later finds an insurer that will provide a replacement claims-made policy during 1989 subject to a retroactive date coinciding with the inception of the insured's first claims-made policy in 1988. During the 1989 policy period, a claim is made because of bodily injury sustained by a third party in an occurrence that took place during the 1988 policy period. The *1989* claims-made form is triggered

Exhibit 6-13

"Unlimited Tail" Provides Excess Coverage When Other Coverage Applies

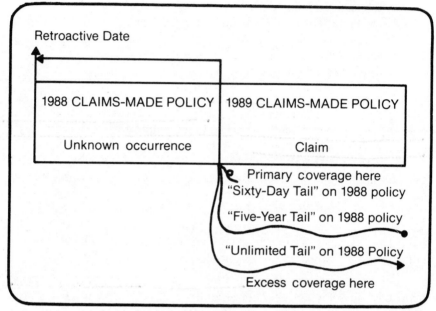

and applies to this claim because (1) the bodily injury occurred after that policy's retroactive date and (2) claim is now being made during the current policy period. The "unlimited tail" coverage also applies because (1) the bodily injury took place after the retroactive date and before the expiration of the first claims-made policy to which the unlimited tail endorsement, applies and (2) the claim was made during the extended reporting period of the "unlimited tail" coverage. There is overlapping insurance, however, so the "unlimited tail" coverage will apply as excess protection. (See Exhibit 6-13.)

In summary, the "unlimited tail" or supplemental extended reporting period of the claims-made form is designed to extend the "sixty-day tail" indefinitely. Its primary function is to cover claims involving bodily injury and property damage stemming from occurrences that were unknown and unreported to the insurer, if the bodily injury or property damage occurred after the policy's retroactive date but before its expiration date and the claim is not received and recorded by the insured or insurer until any time after the expiration of the policy's "sixty-day tail." A secondary function of the "unlimited tail" is to pick up if necessary where the automatic "five-year tail" leaves off.

The right to buy "unlimited tail" coverage is an integral provision of the claims-made policy. The supplemental extended reporting period is available whether the insured or insurer cancels or nonrenews the policy for any reason, including nonpayment of premium. It is also available when an insurer replaces the policy with one with a later retroactive date or renews or replaces the claims-made policy with an occurrence policy. (Furthermore, when an insurer adds a "laser beam endorsement" to its renewal policy, it must provide "sixty-day" and "five-year tails" and offer "unlimited tail" coverage on the expiring policy for the exposures specifically excluded under the new policy by that endorsement.) The "unlimited tail," unlike the other two tail coverages, is subject to an additional cost which in no event can exceed 200 percent of the expiring policy's annual CGL coverage part premium. The additional premium is considered to be fully earned when paid, and the unlimited tail can never be cancelled. In the event this tail coverage overlaps with a later claims-made form, the policy to which the tail coverage is attached will apply only as excess. The "unlimited tail," like the sixty-day and five-year tails, does *not* extend the policy period and does *not* extend the policy coverage. However, the unlimited tail, unlike the other tails, does provide a new set of limits.

USE OF CLAIMS-MADE FORM

As has been noted earlier, the major reason for developing the claims-made form was to eliminate deficiencies of the occurrence form in its handling of long-tail exposures. With the claims-made policy, one and only one claims-made policy is intended to apply to a claim—the policy that is in force when the claim is first received and recorded. (An exception may occur under circumstances where a supplemental tail on an expired policy overlaps with a subsequent claims-made policy, as noted above.) This is unlike occurrence policies whose limits have been stacked, because several policies have been deemed to apply to the same claim. Also, the claims-made policy is designed so that the loss experience attributable to any given policy is more readily determinable despite long-tail exposures, thereby making it possible for insurers to price insurance in a way that is more responsive to actual experience. Just how the mechanics of the claims-made policy vary from those of the occurrence form might best be understood with an illustration.

Illustration

Assume that Alpha Manufacturing Company had been covered continuously since 1975 under CGL policies written on an occurrence basis. At renewal on January 1, 1988 the insurer is willing to write only a claims-made policy with $500,000 aggregate limits, with a retroactive date the same as the inception date of that first claims-made form. One year later, in 1989, the policy is renewed on a claims-made basis without change of retroactive date. During this policy year of 1989, Alpha Manufacturing is confronted with a large product liability claim, because of an occurrence during the 1988 policy period that results in the payment of a $250,000 bodily injury liability judgment. As a result of this claim, Alpha Manufacturing Company's remaining products/completed operations aggregate limit is $250,000. Later in 1989 Alpha reports an "occurrence" to the insurance company dealing with a new product line the manufacturer has just introduced. By year end 1989, no claims have been made against Alpha Manufacturing because of that occurrence. As a safety measure against a possible large claim against it because of that reported 1989 occurrence, Alpha Manufacturing makes known to its insurer that it would like to increase its primary limits to $1 million when the 1990 renewal policy takes effect. Consider Alpha's reasoning here: If the insurance company renews the claims-made policy in 1990 and retains the 1988 retroactive date. Alpha Manufacturing Company will not have to worry about the reduced aggregate limit of the 1989 policy year because, once that policy expires, it is the next policy that covers any claim that might be made stemming from the occurrence reported during the preceding year. And, if the insurer honors the request of the insured to increase the per occurrence and aggregate limits on renewal, Alpha Manufacturing will now have access to $1 million limits, if claim is made during 1990, as opposed to $250,000, if the claim were to be subject to the expiring policy's eroded aggregate limit.

Insurance Company Options The insurance company is not required to honor the insured's request; also, the insurer has other options to protect its interests. Thus, the insurer can do the following:

1. nonrenew the policy,
2. make the 1990 claims-made policy subject to the "laser beam" endorsement, or
3. make the 1990 claims-made policy subject to a later retroactive date, i.e., move it from 1988 to 1990 (but this may be done only under certain circumstances that may not apply here).

If the insurer chooses to nonrenew the policy, it will still be obligated to pay up to $250,000 for claims made within the expiring policy's "five-year tail" period. Moreover, the insured will have the option of purchasing "unlimited tail" coverage with $500,000 aggregate limits that would apply if claim is made, say, six years after the nonrenewal.

Exhibit 6-14
Illustration

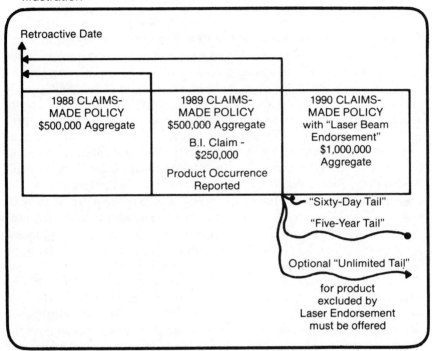

If the insurer elects the second option and makes the 1990 claims-made policy subject to a "laser beam endorsement" excluding the problem product, the effect of the new claims-made policy would be to preclude coverage in two important areas. (See Exhibit 6-14.) The first area would be to exclude any coverage of Alpha Manufacturing Company during 1990 because of any claim arising out of the occurrence excluded by the "laser beam" endorsement. When this "laser" endorsement is used, the retroactive date of the 1990 policy could remain as originally set in 1988. This also means that any claim made during 1990 because of an *unknown* occurrence involving bodily injury or property damage any time after the 1988 retroactive date would be covered under the 1990 claims-made policy. The second area would be to exclude any coverage during 1990 because of any other claim made during that period alleging bodily injury or property damage that happened during that same 1990 policy period as a result of the *product* that is specifically excluded by the "laser" endorsement. The impact of this move is explained below.

If the insurer were able to elect the third option and make the 1990 claims-made policy the subject of a later retroactive date, no claim during the 1990 policy period would be covered by the policy if it deals with bodily injury or property damage that occurred before the 1990 retroactive date.

Effect on Coverage   Any of the foregoing recourses, as exercised by the insurer, creates a situation that must be understood by the insured. Whether the retroactive date is advanced to the year 1990 or the laser endorsement is used instead, the 1989 expiring claims-made policy is subject to an *automatic* "five-year tail" that will apply only to claims arising out of the occurrence that was reported to the insurer during the 1988 claims-made policy year. When the "laser beam" endorsement is attached by an insurer to its renewal policy, the insurer *is required* to attach an "Extended Reporting Period for Specific Accident(s), Products, Work or Location (1) Endorsement" to the expiring policy. This endorsement amends the expiring policy to provide sixty-day and five-year basic extended reporting periods for the specified exposure, and also gives the insured the right to purchase a supplemental extended reporting period ("unlimited tail" coverage) applicable only to the exposure excluded by the renewal policy.

Recall that the automatic tail does not increase the limits of the policy to which it applies. In this case, any claim made after the expiration of the 1989 claims-made policy involving the occurrence reported during that year would be subject to coverage but only to the extent of the aggregate limit that remains. In this illustration, the insured would have protection only to the extent of the remaining $250,000 aggregate limit. However, the supplemental extended reporting period, if purchased would provide $500,000 aggregate limits applicable to other unknown occurrences from that specific product during 1988 or 1989.

When the retroactive date is advanced but no "laser beam" exclusion is used, there is still another potential problem that requires the attention of the insured. Also not covered under the policy for the year 1990, as illustrated in Exhibit 6-15, are claims for bodily injury or property damage that took place prior to the 1990 retroactive date from an occurrence that was unknown to the insured before the expiration of the 1989 policy period and therefore not reported to the insurer. If there had been such an occurrence, the claim made during 1990 would not be covered because of the policy's retroactive date.

To close this gap, the insured should request the "unlimited tail" immediately or some time within the "sixty-day tail" period following the expiration of the 1989 claims-made policy. Such request of the insured must be in writing. Once this tail is purchased, the reporting period of the insured's expired 1989 claims-made policy is extended indefinitely for *any* claims for bodily injury or property damage that

Exhibit 6-15
Illustration Continued

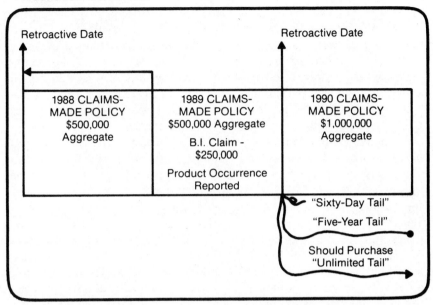

took place before the 1989 claims-made policy expired. In addition, the "unlimited tail" also provides a new set of aggregate limits corresponding in amount to the limits that applied to the expired policy to which the unlimited tail coverage endorsement is attached. However, this new set of aggregate limits applies only to claims stemming from occurrences that happened since 1/1/88 and during the preceding policy-year and which were unknown to the insured and therefore unreported. The new aggregate limits cannot be used to pay for claims involving occurrences that were reported during an earlier period if the claim is made during the "sixty-day tail" period or during the automatic "five-year tail" period that follows it.

Another Potential Gap The "laser beam" endorsement could also be used to exclude all future claims involving the new product of Alpha Manufacturing Company. The insurer, in other words, may be willing to retain the earlier retroactive date of 1988 but only on the condition that the 1989 and subsequent policies be subject to the "laser" endorsement specifically excluding the product that has produced costly claims in the past.

This is not a novel situation. Insurers often exclude coverage for specific exposures that are considered undesirable or uninsurable. However, it should be noted that no automatic tail coverages are activated when a "laser beam" endorsement is used to exclude coverage for future claims. The only time the insured obtains the automatic "five-year tail" is when an occurrence has been reported during an expiring policy period which does not result in a claim by expiration of the policy, and only when the insurer takes a course of action that eliminates continuity of coverage. When the "laser beam" endorsement is used to preclude covering any claims during the *subsequent* policy period produced by that particular product specifically described in the laser endorsement, no automatic "five-year tail" applies, since no occurrence has been reported.

One way Alpha Manufacturing Company could protect itself would be to purchase the "unlimited tail" coverage in the event a claim is made during a subsequent policy period because of an occurrence during 1989 of which Alpha Manufacturing was unaware. But suppose the product in question causes bodily injury and a resulting claim in 1990. The "unlimited tail" coverage of the expired 1989 claims-made policy will not apply, since its purpose is to extend the reporting period of the 1989 policy, not to extend the period of coverage. In this case, Alpha Manufacturing Company would be without protection. Unless it obtains other products liability insurance specifically for the exposure excluded by the laser endorsement, Alpha Manufacturing Company would retain future losses.

Many other situations could be used to illustrate the mechanics of the claims-made policy. However, the preceding discussion should provide a basic understanding of the claims-made policy and its retroactive date, tail coverages, and laser endorsements, that provides a foundation for analyzing specific situations that may develop.

COVERAGE B TRIGGER

Up to this point, the discussion of the claims-made policy and its special features has dealt solely with Coverage A. Coverage B, which encompasses personal injury and advertising injury liability coverages, is subject to an entirely different trigger. The trigger of Coverage B under both the occurrence and claims-made forms is "personal injury" or "advertising injury" caused by an *offense committed during the policy period* in the "coverage territory."

The coverage trigger is not that a *claim is made* involving personal injury or advertising injury. If an executive of Alpha Manufacturing Company were to say something untrue about someone else during 1988 CGL policy period, and a resulting suit for slander were to follow during that same year, there would be no question as to which policy provides coverage, since only one policy is involved. But if the offense were committed in 1987 and the personal injury claim is not made until 1988, the 1987 policy would be triggered. It is not always easy to ascertain when an offense has been committed. This can be an especially troublesome problem with regard to malicious prosecution cases, because the courts are divided as to the time when the offense of this kind of personal injury is considered to have been committed.[6]

Example

Assume that Alpha Manufacturing Company had the equivalent of Coverage B during the 1987 policy year when its commercial general liability insurance was first written on a claims-made basis. In 1988 the claims-made policy was renewed and the 1987 retroactive date was retained. (See Exhibit 6-16.) During 1988, suit is filed against Alpha Manufacturing Company which alleges both bodily injury and personal injury because of something one of the corporation's executives did during 1987. The current 1988 claims-made policy would apply to the bodily injury action because the Coverage A trigger is a claim first made during the policy period because of bodily injury that occurred after the retroactive date (1987) and before expiration of the policy (1988). The action concerning personal injury, on the other hand, would not be covered by the current 1988 claims-made policy because the Coverage B trigger is controlled by the time of the offense and *not* at the time when claim is made against the insured. In some situations like this, two policies could be affected by an action that claims damages because of Coverages A and B, just as has been the case when the commercial general liability insurance was available solely on an occurrence basis. What could further complicate matters, as noted later, is the fact that Coverages A, B, and C are all subject to the same aggregate limit which, if reduced or exhausted during the policy period, can impair the future protection of the insured.

COVERAGE C TRIGGER

Medical payments coverage, Coverage C of the CGL forms, is triggered by an *accident that takes place* in the "coverage territory." The word *accident* is not defined in the policy but is commonly construed to be an event which is both (1) accidental or unforeseen *and* (2) sudden or definite in time or place. Use of the word *accident* in lieu of *occurrence* is more restrictive, but probably addresses more easily ascertainable events, particularly in light of the kinds of exposures intended to be covered by medical payments.

In any event, Coverage C is subject to a trigger that differs from

Exhibit 6-16
Coverage A and Coverage B Have Different Triggers

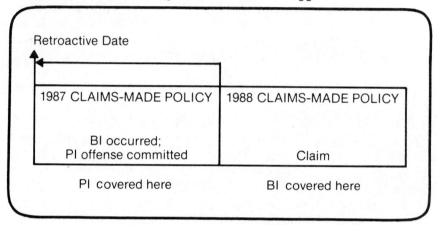

those of Coverages A and B. Coverage C does *not* depend on when bodily injury occurs or when claim is made. What triggers medical payments coverage is the *time of accident*.

POLICY LIMITS

The limits of insurance provision is the same in both CGL forms. The preamble provisions of the CGL policy dealing with limits of insurance state, in effect, that regardless of the number of insureds, the number of claims or suits brought against the insured, or the number of persons or organizations making claims or bringing suits, the insurer's liability is subject to the limits stated in the policy declarations. The applicable limit is not increased if more than one claimant, insured, or claim is involved.

The "per occurrence" limit applies whether the CGL policy is written on an occurrence or claims-made basis, since Coverage A of both forms is contingent on the happening of an "occurrence," as defined in the forms.

Basic Limits

The basic per occurrence and annual aggregate limits of insurance for all coverages are divided into two general groups, as illustrated in Exhibit 6-17. The first group encompasses Coverage A, other than the products-completed operations hazard; Coverages B and C; and fire legal liability. Coverages A and B are subject to a basic (i.e., minimum)

Exhibit 6-17
Illustration of the Basic CGL Limits of Liability Provision*

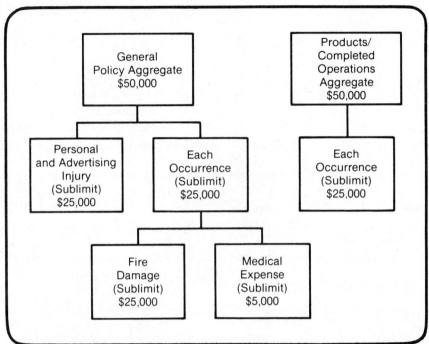

* Adapted from Jack P. Gibson, CPCU CLU, ARM, *Contracting Guide to the 1986 Commercial General Liability Program*, pp. 20-22, copyright 1985, *RTC* Communications.

per occurrence limit of $25,000. Coverage B likewise carries a $25,000 per person or organization minimum limit. Coverage C is subject not only to a $5,000 per person limit, but also to the Coverage A per occurrence limit. Finally, fire legal liability has a $25,000 limit for each fire and is also subject to the Coverage A occurrence limit.

All of the foregoing coverages also are subject to a general aggregate limit of $50,000. This general aggregate limit is the most the insurer is obligated to pay in any one annual period for any combination of losses covered under Coverages A, B, and C, other than damages within the products-completed operations hazard.

The second general coverage group, which is subject to a separate per occurrence and aggregate limit, is bodily injury or property damage within the products-completed operations hazard. Products-completed operations losses are also subject to a per occurrence limit (the minimum limit is $25,000) and an aggregate limit (minimum $50,000). There is no tie between the general policy aggregate and the products/completed operations aggregate; either could be reduced or exhausted without any impact on the other.

Minimum limits were mentioned in the above paragraphs. Actual policy limits can be—and usually are—increased well above these minimums.

Applying Policy Limits

Any combination of Coverage A, B, or C losses can exhaust the policy limits and leave the insured without further protection. Assume, for example, that a business entity purchases a CGL policy subject to basic limits for all coverages. During the policy year, the insured has the misfortune of committing a libelous act and also of being responsible for a fire legal liability loss. The libel claim is settled out of court for $30,000 in damages and the fire legal liability claim is settled for $12,000. Since the insured purchased its CGL policy subject to basic limits, it would retain $5,000 of the libel damages because the personal injury liability coverage sublimit at basic limits is $25,000. The entire fire legal liability limit, on the other hand, is payable because the sublimit of that coverage is $25,000.

The insurer's total payment for both claims is within the $50,000 general aggregate limit, which also governs the remaining protection available to the insured. The general aggregate limit was $50,000 at policy inception; and $37,000 has been paid against the aggregate, so only $13,000 remains for the rest of the policy period. If that amount were to be paid because of an occurrence involving Coverage A, the insured would be without further protection under its CGL policy except for products-completed operations claims (except, as noted below, when an insured purchases the unlimited or supplemental tail coverage and acquires a new set of aggregate limits).

If the insured had also been confronted with a suit seeking damages because of a products or completed operations loss, the payment of damages for such a suit would reduce the separate aggregate limit that pertains solely to products and completed operations coverages.

Applying Limits Under "Tail" Coverages

Section V of the claims-made form, dealing with extended reporting periods, explains how the limits of insurance provision of the CGL policy applies in relation to the tail coverages. This section addresses the matter of the "sixty-day tail," "five-year tail," and the "unlimited tail." The "five-year tail" is analyzed first.

"Five-Year Tail"   As noted earlier, a basic extended reporting period of five years is automatically provided for claims that arise from any "occurrence" reported to the insurer not later than sixty days after the end of the policy period. This tail is necessary only if some gap in coverage develops *after* the reporting of such an occurrence. Such a gap could be created with the claims-made form's cancellation or nonrenewal, with a replacement policy subject to a later retroactive date, conversion to an occurrence policy, or a "laser beam" endorsement specially targeted toward that reported occurrence. If none of the foregoing apply, there should be no gap and therefore no function served by the "five-year tail."

When the "five-year tail" is implemented, it does not apply to claims that are covered under any subsequent insurance that the insured purchases, or that would be covered but for the exhaustion of the insurance limits. Also, the "five-year tail" does not reinstate or increase the limits of coverage.

For example, assume that during the period January 1, 1988 to 1989, an "occurrence" is reported to the insurer of the claims-made form written subject to a $500,000 combined single limit and aggregate (see Exhibit 6-18). The policy is replaced by another insurer's policy subject to the earlier retroactive date of January 1, 1988, but also subject to "laser beam" endorsement CG 2702 specifically excluding coverage during the 1989 claims-made policy year because of the occurrence reported during the preceding year. As a result of the issuance of the "laser" endorsement, the insurer of the 1988 claims-made policy must pay claims made during a "five-year tail" period for that occurrence. Since no claim stemming from that occurrence will be honored if made during the 1989 claims-made policy year, the "five-year tail" provides primary coverage.

If claim were to be made during the 1989 policy period because of the "occurrence" subject to the "laser beam" endorsement, coverage would be subject to the 1988 claims-made policy and remaining aggregate limits. If the 1988 general aggregate limit of $500,000 had been reduced to $200,000 by the payment of any claim or suit, the claim made during the five-year tail would be covered only to the extent of the remaining aggregate limits.

Suppose, now, that no claim was made during 1989 because of the occurrence reported during the earlier policy year. Suppose, as depicted in Exhibit 6-19, when the 1989 claims-made policy expires, it is renewed subject to the earlier retroactive date of January 1, 1988 and is not made subject to the "laser beam" endorsement. (This means that the "five-year tail" that applied one year earlier is automatically eliminated.) If claim is made during the 1990 policy period because of the occurrence reported during the 1988 policy period, it would be subject

Exhibit 6-18
Limits and "Tails" Illustration A

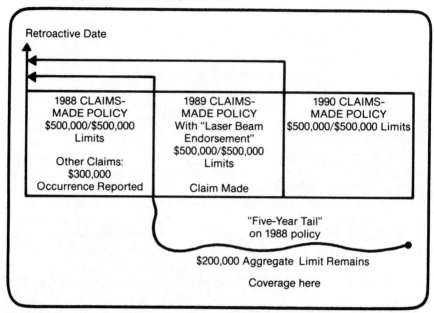

to coverage under the 1990 claims-made policy and its remaining aggregate limits. If the aggregate limits of the 1990 policy are insufficient to cover the payment of damages, the insured will have to retain the loss or look to other sources for protection (such as an umbrella or excess policy); it cannot look to the "five-year tail" of the 1988 policy.

"Sixty-Day Tail" The so-called mini-tail, as noted earlier, is designed to reduce the chances of any gap in coverage for the short period of sixty days. Like the "five-year tail," it is also provided without specific charge and is not applicable if any subsequent insurance applies or would have but for the exhaustion of insurance limits. The only difference between the "sixty-day tail" and the "five-year tail" is that the "sixty-day tail" applies only to claims or suits stemming from occurrences of which the insured had no knowledge. Thus, if a claim or suit is (1) made during the "sixty-day tail" period, (2) because of an occurrence involving bodily injury or property damage that took place before the claims-made policy expired but after that policy's retroactive date, the claims-made policy to which the "sixty-day tail" applies is available to respond (subject to any remaining limits of insurance). But if a subsequent policy applies to the claim or suit, the "sixty-day tail" does not apply at all—not even on an excess basis.

Exhibit 6-19
Limits and "Tails" Illustration B

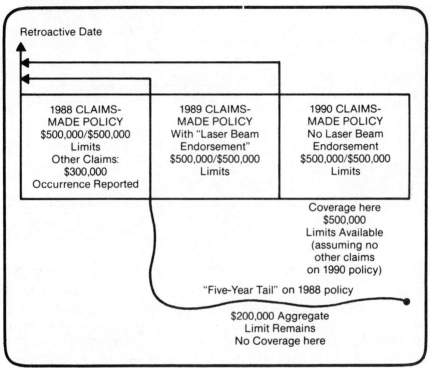

"Unlimited Tail" The *only* circumstance under which the aggregate limits can be replenished is when the insured elects to *purchase* the "unlimited tail" coverage (supplemental extended reporting period). "Unlimited tail" coverage will require paying an additional premium of no more than 200 percent of the expiring policy's annual premium for general liability coverages. The cost could be less. The "unlimited tail" is available whenever the insured or insurer cancels the claims-made policy for any reason, or when the following claims-made policy is made subject to a later retroactive date or "laser beam" endorsement. If this "unlimited tail" coverage is purchased, the new aggregate limits will be the same as the limits that *originally* applied to the expiring policy *and* apply only to future claims involving past occurrences that were unknown to the insured (or occurrences that were reported within sixty days after expiration, but for which no claim was made until the sixth or later year following). The privilege of obtaining an additional set of limits is limited to the coverage of the claims-made form only.

For example, suppose a claims-made policy for the policy year

Exhibit 6-20
Limits and "Tails" Illustration C

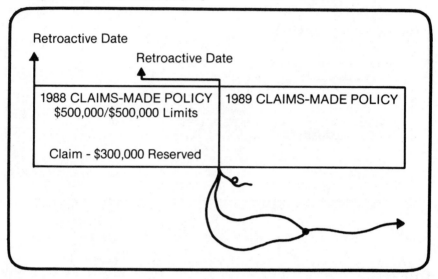

beginning January 1, 1988 is subject to a $500,000 combined single limit per occurrence and aggregate. (See Exhibit 6-20.) Early in the policy year, the insured is sued because of an alleged injury stemming from its product. After a reserve has been set at $300,000, the insurer decides to cancel the insured's policy. The insured obtains replacement coverage, but the new claims-made policy is subject to a later retroactive date, i.e., July 1, 1988. (That date was selected because it is later than the date of the major claim.) Since the insured's policy was already triggered by the suit, the "five-year tail" coverage is irrelevant, because such tail only applies to an occurrence that is reported to the insurer and does *not* culminate in a claim by policy expiration.

What the insured can do is to request, in writing and before expiration of the "sixty-day tail," the purchase of the "unlimited tail." When purchased, separate aggregate limits equal to the dollar amount shown in the declarations in effect at the end of the policy period will apply (a $500,000 aggregate limit in this illustration—even if the aggregate policy limits had been reduced by the payment of claims). This supplemental tail period begins (1) sixty days after the end of the policy period and applies to all claims other than those involving any occurrences previously reported to the insurer, and (2) five years after the end of the policy period (i.e., after the expiration of the "five-year tail" period). It also applies to claims arising out of any "occurrence" reported to the insured no later than sixty days after the policy period. Note that, if the aggregate limits of the claims-made policy to which "five-year tail" applies are exhausted by the payment of other claims, the separate aggregate limits on the "unlimited tail" do not provide reliable protection. No limits remain to cover a claim from the reported occurrence if claim is made during the "five-year tail" period. But if no claim were to be made against the insured during the five-year limited tail period, the insured will then have the new aggregate limits of the "unlimited tail" for protection after the "five-year tail" period—assuming the insured had elected to purchase the unlimited tail coverage.

CLAIMS-MADE VERSUS OCCURRENCE PREMIUMS

Claims-made CGL coverage premiums should be less than those for occurrence coverage. This reflects the average shorter time between policy inception and claim date, limited to a maximum of five years unless the insured requests and pays extra for the supplemental extended reporting period, versus the unlimited "tail" automatically provided, in effect, by all occurrence policies. During the first four years of claims-made coverage, an additional discount applies to claims-made policies because some claims will be ·covered by prior occurrence policies. In any case, occurrences prior to the retroactive date are not covered. This discount decreases each year, because more claims will be covered as the claims-made policy matures if the retroactive date is not advanced. Also, policies with no retroactive date or one earlier than the inception date of the claims-made policy will cost more than those with a later date, to reflect the extra coverage being provided for prior occurrences.

Two points are noteworthy here:

1. The policyholder who changes from occurrence coverage to claims-made coverage may think he or she is continuing equivalent coverage at a discount—particularly during the initial years of claims-made coverage when the additional discounts apply. In fact, the reduced premium does not reflect a bargain, but the fact that fewer claims are covered and there is no automatic unlimited "tail." The apparent savings may quickly vanish at any point when "unlimited tail" coverage must be purchased for an additional premium.
2. Advancing the retroactive date reduces the premium that an insurer may charge, according to rating manual rules. This gives the insurer an incentive for *not* advancing the retroactive date when a policy is renewed or replaced.

INSURED'S RIGHT TO OBTAIN
CLAIM AND "OCCURRENCE" INFORMATION

Claims-made insurance can make necessary a variety of decisions by insureds. In addition to the ubiquitous question whether to continue coverage with the same insurer, claims-made insurance raises additional issues relating to:

- advancement or nonadvancement of retroactive dates, with related premium adjustments;
- the potential impact of "laser beam" endorsements;
- the existence of reported occurrences that could give rise to a claim;
- the existence of reported and recorded claims that are not yet settled;
- the adequacy or inadequacy of "automatic tail" coverage of the basic extended reporting period;
- the possible need to buy "unlimited tail" coverage under a supplemental extended reporting period—a need that must be weighed against a potentially high premium; and
- the extent to which aggregate limits are or are not impaired by occurrences or claims.

Many, if not all of these issues can best be resolved when the insured has current information on reported occurrences and on paid and reserved claims.

To assure that policyholder has access to current information, the claims-made CGL contains a provision titled "Your Right to Claim and Occurrence Information." If the insurer elects to cancel or nonrenew the CGL, it is obligated to provide such information no later than thirty days before the policy terminates. In other circumstances, the information must be provided if the first named insured requests it in writing within sixty days after the end of the policy period. The information must then be provided within forty-five days of the time the request is received. Since a considerable amount of judgment is used in setting loss reserves, the CGL contains a strong disclaimer stating that the reserves should not be regarded as ultimate settlement values and noting that the insurer makes no representations or warranties about the information, although it does exercise reasonable care in gathering the information for its own business purposes.

FARM LIABILITY COVERAGE

The farmowners program of the Insurance Services Office was developed some years ago to handle the special insurance needs of farmers and ranchers whose exposures to loss simultaneously involve business and personal premises and activities. To treat these exposures, the current farm coverages correspond to both (1) the personal coverages of the homeowners policies and (2) the commercial coverages of appropriate business entities. Although a variety of farm property, farm liability, and other farm coverages are available, the discussion in this text deals solely with the farm liability coverages of the ISO.

The farm liability coverage form is designed to be used as a module together with other forms. The farm liability coverage can be combined with other documents to form a monoline policy, or can be combined with other coverage parts to form a commercial package policy. In any case, it is necessary that the monoline or package policy include the common policy conditions. And, if the farm liability coverage part is combined with some other ISO commercial insurance coverage part, it also is necessary to add a common policy declarations page.

The farm liability (FL) coverage form tracks very closely with the 1986 *occurrence* form commercial general liability policy provisions. Discussion here will focus on the FL's distinctive features.

Farm Liability Coverage Overview

The farm liability form closely resembles the occurrence-basis commercial general liability (CGL) policy used for other businesses. However, the coverages bear different letter labels. When the farm property coverage form was developed to replace the farmowners-ranchowners forms, the lettering system of those older forms was retained. Thus, the farm *property* coverage form includes Coverages A through G, and the farm *liability* coverage form is "stuck" with Coverages H, I, and J.

The FL coverage form is divided into four sections:

Section I—Coverages;
Section II—Limits of Insurance;
Section III—Definitions; and
Section IV—Conditions.

Section I—Coverages is further subdivided into three parts:

Coverage H—Bodily Injury and Property Damage Liability;
Coverage I—Personal and Advertising Injury Liability; and

Coverage J—Medical Payments.

The FL policy is available solely on an occurrence form basis:

- The trigger of bodily injury and property damage (Coverage H) is the time of such injury or damage.
- The trigger of personal and advertising injury liability (Coverage I) is the offense during the policy period,
- The trigger of medical payments (Coverage J) is an accident during the policy period.

Like the current CGL forms of the ISO, the FL policy also includes fire legal liability coverage subject to a separate sublimit of $50,000. Unlike the CGL forms, the FL policy adds coverage against statutorily imposed vicarious parental liability subject to a separate limit of $10,000, and coverage for damage to property of others subject to a maximum of $500 per occurrence. The FL is subject to a general aggregate limit that affects all Coverages H, I, and J, as well as fire legal liability and statutorily imposed vicarious parental liability.

Insured Location

While the FL coverage is said to be worldwide in territorial scope, it is subject to a definition of "insured location," intended to restrict coverage to the business of farming and ranching and to clarify the extent to which the policy will apply to liability from nonbusiness pursuits.

The term "insured location" is defined in the FL policy as:

a. The farm premises (including grounds and private approaches) and "residence premises" shown in the declarations;

b. That part of other premises, or of other structures and grounds, that is used by you as a residence and shown in the Declarations, or acquired by you during the policy period for your use as a residence;

c. Premises used by you in conjunction with the premises included in a. or b. above;

d. Any part of premises not owned by any "insured" but where an "insured' is temporarily residing;

e. Vacant land owned by or rented to an "insured," other than farm land;

f. Land owned by or rented to any "insured" on which a farm structure or farm family dwelling is being constructed as a residence for an "insured;"

g. Individual or family cemetery plots or burial vaults of an "insured;"

h. Any part of premises occasionally rented to any "insured" for other than "business" purposes; and

i. Any farm premises (including grounds and private approaches) that you or your spouse acquire during the term of this policy.

Who Are Insureds

Individuals and organizations that are automatically "insureds" under the FL policy correspond closely to those of the CGL, with two additions. Under the farmowners policy, "insured" also includes any person or organization legally responsible for animals or watercraft owned by an "insured" (other than employees), but only to the extent that (1) this insurance applies to an "occurrence" involving such animals or watercraft; (2) the person's or organization's custody or use of animals or watercraft does not involve "business" (e.g., a veterinarian would not be considered an insured); and (3) such person or organization who meets the criteria of (1) and (2) above also has custody or use of the animals or watercraft with the owner's permission.

Also included as an "insured" under the FL is any person using a vehicle on the "insured location" with the named insured's consent, provided the vehicle is not subject to an exclusion.

Other Policy Definitions

Many definitions of the FL are identical to those in the CGL forms:

- "advertising injury,"
- "bodily injury,"
- "coverage territory,"
- "impaired property,"
- "insured contract,"
- "loading or unloading,"
- "mobile equipment,"
- "occurrence,"
- "personal injury,"
- "property damage,"
- "suit,"
- "your product" and "your work."

Definitions of the FL policy not found in the CGL forms are as follows:

- "Business" includes trade, profession, occupation, but does not include "farming."
- "Farm employee" means any "insured's" employee whose duties are principally in connection with the maintenance or use of the "insured location" as a farm. These duties include the maintenance or use of the "insured's" farm equipment. But "farm employee" does not mean a "residence employee" or any employee while engaged in the "insured's" farm business.

- "Farming" includes the operation of roadside stands maintained solely for the sale of farm products produced principally by you.
- "Motor vehicle" means:
  (1) A motorized land vehicle and trailer or semi-trailer designed for travel on public roads and subject to motor vehicle registration, including any attached machinery or equipment. But not considered to be a "motor vehicle" is a motorized land vehicle in dead storage on an "insureds location." But a boat, camp, home or utility trailer is considered to be a "motor vehicle" only while being towed by or carried by a motorized land vehicle described above.
  (2) A trailer or semi-trailer designed for travel on public roads and subject to motor vehicle registration, and includes any attached machinery or equipment. A boat, camp, home or utility trailer is a "motor vehicle" only while being towed by or carried on a vehicle included in a. above.
  (3) A motorized golf cart, snowmobile, or other motorized land vehicle owned by an "insured" and designed for recreational use off public roads, while off an "insured location." However, a motorized golf cart is not considered to be a "motor vehicle" while used for golfing purposes.
  (4) Any vehicle, including attached machinery or equipment, while being towed by or carried on a vehicle as included above.

  But "motor vehicle" does not mean "mobile equipment." "Mobile equipment" is defined in the same way as with the CGL forms. The reason for separating motor vehicles from mobile equipment is to give mobile equipment automatic liability protection under the FL and other general liability policies, and to require all other exposures to be separately covered under auto and recreational vehicle policies.
- "Residence employee" means an "insured's" employee who performs duties in connection with the maintenance or use of the "residence premises," including household or domestic services, or who performs duties elsewhere of a similar nature not in connection with the "business" of any "insured."
- "Residence premises" means the named insured's principal residence. If also includes the grounds and structures appurtenant to it if the named insured owns the residence premises. However, not included as a residence premises is any part or parts of a building or structure that is used for "business," other than the farming business, of course.

Coverage H Exclusions

The insurer must pay the sums that the insured becomes legally obligated to pay as damages because of bodily injury or property damage that *occurs during the policy period* and is not otherwise excluded.

Many of the CGL exclusions are also found in the FL. These exclusions are:

- intentional injury exclusion,
- contractual liability exclusion,
- pollution exclusion,
- exclusion of damage to the named insured's product,
- impaired property exclusion, and
- sistership liability (recall) exclusion.

The remaining exclusions of the FL either differ in some way from those exclusions of the CGL forms or are unique to the FL. Each of these unique exclusions is discussed briefly below.

Pollution Exclusion—Aircraft Agricultural operations sometimes employ crop-dusters for aerial application of fungicides or insecticides. There are special hazards associated with crop-dusting, so coverage is excluded in the FL for bodily injury or property damage caused by or resulting from any substance released or discharged from an aircraft. For purposes of this exclusion, "aircraft" is defined to mean "any device designed or used for flight. However, it does not mean model or hobby aircraft. This exclusion is directed primarily to the exposures created by drift of chemicals during, as well as following, aerial application.

Aircraft and Motor Vehicle Exclusion The farm liability coverage form does not apply to bodily injury or property damage arising out of the ownership, maintenance, use, or entrustment to others of any aircraft or "motor vehicle"; thus far, it resembles the CGL forms. However, the FL form goes further and also precludes coverage for motorized bicycles or tricycles.

However, specifically excepted from this exclusion—and therefore covered if not otherwise excluded—is liability of the insured because of bodily injury or property damage arising out of:

- An aircraft that causes injury or damage to a "residence employee" who is not operating or maintaining such aircraft.
- The parking of a "motor vehicle" or motorized bicycle or tricycle on premises owned or rented to the named insured so long as such vehicle is not owned, rented or loaned to the "insured."

- A "motor vehicle" not subject to motor vehicle registration because it is used *exclusively* on the "insured location; it is in dead storage; or its exclusive use is as a device to aid the handicapped (e.g. a motorized wheelchair).
- A licensed recreational "motor vehicle" owned by the insured, provided the occurrence takes place either on the "insured location," or the bodily injury or property damage is caused by a golf cart of the insured being used for golfing.
- Operation of any cherry picker or similar device mounted on an automobile or truck chassis, or air compressors, pumps, generators and other equipment as itemized under paragraph f. (3) of the "mobile equipment" definition.

Vicarious liability stemming from the entrustment of a "motor vehicle" is specifically excluded by the FL, like most other nonauto policies. The FL excludes statutorily imposed vicarious parental liability for the actions of a child or minor using an aircraft, "motor vehicle," motorized bicycle or tricycle.

Watercraft Exclusion No insured has protection under the FL for bodily injury or property damage that arises out of the ownership, maintenance, operation, entrustment, use, loading or unloading of any watercraft (1) with inboard or inboard-outdrive motor power owned or rented to an insured, (2) that is a sailing vessel with or without auxiliary power, twenty-six or more feet in length, which is owned or rented to the insured, or (3) powered by one or more outboard motors that total over twenty-five horsepower—any of which are owned by the insured, may have been acquired before the beginning of the policy period and, hence, are not described in the policy declarations or the insured failed to inform the insurer in writing within forty-five days of any such acquisition. A similar exclusion is found in homeowners policies.

The above exclusion does not apply when the bodily injury or property damage, because of an occurrence, takes place on the "insured location"; is sustained by a residence employee in the course of his or her employment by the insured, involves watercraft that is stored; or, for any statutorily imposed vicarious parental liability for the actions of a child or minor while using a watercraft.

Mobile Equipment All *general* liability policies, including the farmowners, exclude liability stemming from the transportation of mobile equipment by a motor vehicle that is owned, operated, rented or loaned to any insured. This exposure is covered under the auto liability insurance of the vehicle's owner. The FL policy exclusions also eliminate coverage for any mobile equipment used in any prearranged racing activity or contest, as well as liability arising from the use of any livestock or other animals in riding or showing events. Such activities can be insured under special events forms.

Business Pursuits Exclusion The only business operations that are intended to be covered by the FL coverage form are the business of farming and the rental of land. Liability of the insured from any other business is not intended to be covered. However, there are many instances where the activities of a farmer could be interpreted as borderline between business and nonbusiness. While it is sometimes difficult to make a clear distinction, the intent of the policy drafters was to cover liability of the insured for an activity that is incident to a non-business pursuit.

Custom Farming Exclusion Any farming operation performed by the insured for others under any contract or agreement for a charge is referred to as *custom farming.* Liability arising the insured's performance of, or failure to perform, extensive custom farming operations for others for a charge is not covered. If a significant custom farming exposure arises, it can be covered subject to the addition of another policy form and an additional charge. Since many farmowners do some custom farming from time to time, the FL does provide protection for limited custom farming activity so long as the named insured's receipts during the twelve months immediately preceding the date of the occurrence did not exceed $2,000. *Incidental custom farming* activities therefore are covered.

Rental Property The FL policy does not cover bodily injury or property damage liability stemming from:

- The rental or holding for rental of any residence owned by the insured. The only exceptions are cases of occupancy of *intended* occupancy (a) by persons using the such residence *exclusively* as living quarters on an occasional basis, (b) of a part of the residence by no more than two roomers or boarders, or (c) of a part of the residence as an office, school, studio, or private garage.
- The rental or holding for rental of any part of the premises which are not residences.
- An act or omission in connection with any location owned, rented or controlled by the insured which is not an "insured location," as defined in the policy. The only exception is an occurrence of bodily injury or property damage sustained by a residence employee arising out of and during the course of his or her employment.

Some of the foregoing business activities excluded in the basic farm liability coverage form can be covered by endorsement.

Transmitted Diseases No insured will be protected under the FL for liability or alleged liability because of bodily injury or property damage arising out of the transmission of a communicable disease. This is a relatively new exclusion to many liability policies, particularly personal liability forms. It was prompted by the court-ordered payment of damages under a homeowners policy in at least one case involving the transmission of herpes between two people.

Employers Liability Exclusion Both the farmowners and other commercial liability policies exclude claims or suits involving bodily injury sustained by an employee of the insured, but employers liability insurance is intended for this kind of an exposure. Farmowners may also hire residence employees, however, and the FL does provide a certain amount of coverage against liability of the insured because of injury sustained by such residence employees. The extent of coverage, in fact, corresponds closely to the personal liability coverage of homeowners policies.

Thus, although coverage for injury to other employees is excluded, the farmowners policy provides coverage against any claim or suit stemming from a residence employee's bodily injury arising out of and during the course of his or her employment for which the insured may be legally liable. By definition, a "residence employee" is anyone employed by any insured to perform duties in connection with the maintenance or use of the "residence premises" including household or domestic services, or duties of a similar nature elsewhere except for a business of the insured.

Building Construction Exclusion Construction operations are covered, if the building or structure is:

1. a farm building or farm structure intended for the use and occupancy of an insured *and*
2. located on the "insured premises."

When both conditions are met, the policy will cover liability for bodily injury of persons who are *not* insureds, or bodily injury of residence employees of an insured when injury arises out of and during the course of employment. Bodily injury liability arising from any other construction operations would not be covered.

Cross Insured Exclusion To reduce the chances of collusion-type false claims, and to preserve the third-party nature of its coverage, the farmowners policy specifically excludes any claims or suits that could involve bodily injury sustained by the named insured or any "insured" under this policy.

General Property Damage Exclusion The farmowners liability policy excludes liability for property damage to:

1. *Property you own.* Some part of this exposure may be insured under Section I (property coverage) of the farmowners policy. Other forms of property insurance may be required.
2. *Property you rent or occupy.* This exposure is also insured under Section I of the farmowners policy (and it may be insured under other forms of property insurance). One exception is so-called fire legal liability coverage, which is automatically included in the farmowners policy when loss stems from fire or explosion subject to a $50,000 per occurrence limit and general aggregate.
3. *Premises you sell, give away, or abandon, if the "property damage" arises out of any part of those premises.* This is the so-called "alienated premises" exclusion. It is designed to preclude coverage for liability because of damage to premises after it was sold or otherwise relinquished by the insured. By exception, there is coverage for damage to property or destruction of the alienated premises.
4. *Property loaned to you.* A degree of protection is available under Section I of the farmowners policy, but it may be desirable to purchase other insurance.
5. *Personal property in your care, custody, or control.* The exposure may require additional insurance depending on the situation.

Farmowners Policy Conditions

For the most part, the conditions of the farm liability coverage form are identical to the CGL form conditions.

Endorsements

A variety of endorsements are available for attachment to the farmowners policy. From the standpoint of liability exposures, endorsements are available to modify the policy with: limited farm pollution liability coverage; personal liability coverage (which would be the equivalent of farmers comprehensive personal liability insurance); custom farming operations; coverage for additional watercraft of the kind excluded by the basic policy provisions; and additional residences rented to others.

Chapter Notes

1. Most long-tail cases have dealt with bodily injury. However, property damage also has become the subject of these types of cases in recent years. One notable one is *California Union Insurance Co. v. Landmark Insurance Company, 143 Cal. Rptr. 461, (1983)* where it was held that insurer "on the risk" at the time swimming pool leakage that caused damage began, and the insurer "on the risk" at the time the swimming pool was found to be the cause of property damage due to water leakage into the ground were jointly and severally liable for the full amount of damages.
2. See, for example, *Insurance Company of North America v. Forty-Eight Insulations, 633 F.2d 1212, cert. denied, 455 U.S. 1109.*
3. See, for example, *Keene Corp. v. Insurance Company of North American, 667 F.2d 1034, (1980).*
4. The insured at least receives the benefit of the basic extended reporting period for sixty days.
5. The effect of the occurrence form's retroactive date has not fared well in those cases where time of bodily injury or property damage is difficult to pinpoint and instead extends over a period of years as, for example, in continuous exposure (triple trigger) cases. In these events, more than one insurer of an occurrence form can be held accountable.
6. One school of thought holds that it is when there has been a favorable termination of the malicious action; the divergent view holds that it is at the commencement of the malicious action.

CHAPTER 7

Other Liability Exposures and Their Treatment

This chapter deals with a variety of liability exposures and coverages that are generally beyond the scope of, or excluded or limited by, the CGL. The first topic is environmental impairment (pollution) liability, an exposure of dramatic significance for which CGL coverage is severely limited. The second major topic is directors and officers (D&O) liability. A related topic, condominium association directors and officers liability, is examined next. The ubiquitous nature of employee benefits programs creates yet another set of special exposures, which can be treated with employee benefits liability insurance and/or fiduciary responsibility insurance—topics also addressed in this chapter. Municipalities and other governmental entities also have some unique or unusual exposures that will be discussed. Finally, on a somewhat different track, is the specialized area of railroad protective liability. For each of these varied topics, the presentation begins with a discussion of the exposures, continues with a description of applicable insurance coverages, and concludes with a brief overview of relevant noninsurance techniques.

Most of the insurance coverages described in this chapter are available only on nonstandardized policies. This means that there may be considerable variation from one policy to another of the same type. Where insurance is described in this chapter, the approach therefore tends to generalize, since specifics in any individual situation depend heavily on the wording of the particular policy in question.

ENVIRONMENTAL IMPAIRMENT LIABILITY (EIL)

The pollution exposure presents a major problem for the insurance industry. Past pollution occurrences have cost the government, insurers, and private industry millions of dollars. This section addresses liability exposures inherent in environmental protection problems. Topics discussed include federal and state regulations affecting the EIL exposure, insurance coverages available under various forms, and noninsurance methods to control the exposure.

History of Pollution Liability Insurance

The role of insurance coverage to protect against liability for damage to the environment is controversial. The ecology movement in the 1970s caused insurance leaders to reexamine gradual pollution coverage. Today, insurers require industries engaged in polluting activities to take extra precautions aimed at protecting the environment.[1]

Recent History of Pollution Liability Insurance The ecology movement of the 1970's caused insurance leaders to reexamine the issue of liability coverage for pollution that occurs gradually. In 1970, the comprehensive general liability policy was amended with the addition of the pollution exclusion. The exclusion read:

> to bodily injury or property damage arising out of the discharge, dispersal, release or escape of smoke, vapors, soot, fumes, acids, alkalis, toxic chemicals, liquids or gases, waste materials or other irritants, contaminants or pollutants into or upon land, the atmosphere or any water course or body of water; but this exclusion does not apply if such discharge, dispersal, release or escape is sudden and accidental.

New York was the first jurisdiction to pass legislation prohibiting insurance companies from insuring against pollution. This 1971 law was based on the rationale expressed by Governor Nelson A. Rockefeller:

> New York State has adopted stringent standards to prohibit despoiling our environment through the discharge of noxious substances into the water and air. As strict as these laws are, however, their effectiveness would be substantially reduced if polluters were able to insure themselves against having to pay the fines and other liabilities that may be imposed upon them for polluting.
>
> Many insurance companies have voluntarily initiated action to protect the environment by refusing to insure against liability arising out of environmental pollution.
>
> The bill will help to assure that corporate polluters bear the full burden of their own actions spoiling the environment, and will preclude any policy offering this type of insurance protection.[2]

Opposition to Governor Rockefeller's statement and legislation was quite vocal. The New York State Department of Commerce stated that, although a polluter may be able to shift the cost of the first act of pollution onto the insurer, insurance companies would thereafter be able to shift the costs of future occurrences back to the polluter by adjusting the premium. Essentially, the cost of cleaning of the environment would rest with polluters, not insurers.

Also the New York Commerce Department proclaimed that innocent business organizations would be unable to obtain insurance against lawful discharge activities. This would put honest businessmen into the same category as those who do not abide by the law.

A memorandum submitted by the Long Island Lighting Company in opposition to the legislation added one telling argument to those made by the Commerce Department. The memo stated that the bill would be detrimental to the public interest because it could leave those suffering from bodily or property damage unprotected if the polluter should become financially insolvent.

Federal Regulations

Reacting to public pressure, Congress enacted many federal laws attacking the pollution problem. Federal regulations, state laws, and the decisions of our courts impose strict standards of care upon industry. The penalties for noncompliance are stiff.

Coverage Requirements Attitudes regarding businesses insuring themselves against the consequences of pollution accidents changed in 1976 when Congress enacted the Resource Conservation and Recovery Act (RCRA). This legislation prompted the Environmental Protection Agency (EPA) to develop a nationwide hazardous waste management system.

RCRA also required the EPA to establish financial responsibility requirements for owners and operators of hazardous waste treatment, storage, and disposal facilities. These regulations created by the EPA, pursuant to its statutory authorization, require surface impoundments, landfills, and landfill treatment facilities to carry gradual and "sudden and accidental" pollution insurance.[3]

The New York law prohibiting insurance companies from insuring against pollution damages was repealed in 1982. The Love Canal pollution problems and the identification of toxic dump sites in New York and other states forced the New York lawmakers to shift focus from punishing polluters to protecting victims and attempting to guarantee a source of funds to pay for damages.

The EPA, as of June 1983, had referred thirty-seven hazardous waste cases to the Department of Justice for prosecution. At the state level, the first two criminal indictments for improper waste disposal were rendered by grand juries in Texas and New Hampshire.[4]

Court Interpretations of Earlier Pollution Exclusions

Although general liability policies of the 1970s and 1980s provided a considerable degree of coverage for pollution claims, the extent of coverage was open to some debate. In particular, the scope and meaning of the pollution exclusion was disputed frequently in the courts. The exclusion's intent was to eliminate claims arising out of gradually occurring impairments that might presumably be recognized and halted. This means the insurance company intended to respond for *sudden* discharges resulting in bodily injury or property damage neither expected nor intended by the insured.

However, some courts interpreted the exclusion so as to provide coverage for even *gradual* occurrences that are unexpected from the policyholder's viewpoint. In these cases, court interpretations were not in accord with the intent of the policy drafters. For example, in *Lansco v. Department of Environmental Protection*[5] the courts held the words "sudden and accidental" were to be understood by their common usage and dictionary meanings. It was decided that the CGL pollution exclusion did not apply in this case where vandals opened oil tank valves and polluted the Hackensack River.

In 1978, New York courts took a strong position on the interpretation of the pollution exclusion. In *Farm Family Mutual Insurance Company v. Bagley*[6] the judge stated that, though an act was intended, the results were not. Thus the act is considered sudden and accidental. This opinion allowed insurance coverage for unintended consequences of intentional acts.

Other courts followed New York's lead and ruled against insurance companies, finding coverage for insureds under the comprehensive general liability form. A 1983 Washington case continued this theory by holding that a leak of gasoline from a tank over an extended period of time was "sudden and accidental." The act was neither intended nor expected by the insured; consequently, the pollution exclusion did not preclude coverage.[7]

Such court decisions caused insurance companies much concern. Specific endorsements to clarify the pollution exclusion were subsequently added to comprehensive general liability contracts. Since the courts found coverage for many pollution claims despite exclusionary language in the policies, many underwriters simply refused to consider applicants having pollution exposures.

Not all pollution exposures involve the current use of pollutants. The EPA has identified many hazardous wastes of the past that pose future pollution sources unless and until they are cleaned up. For example, some businesses have purchased property from petroleum companies after gasoline stations were closed. In some cases, the underground gasoline tanks have not been drained, cleaned, or removed. Businesses such as banks, florists, and camera stores located in former auto service stations may be exposed to a contamination liability problem from leaking tanks. The financial consequences of a pollution clean up can be catastrophic. If one multiplies EPA estimates of the costs to clean up a single site times the number of EPA sites, the resulting figure exceeds the assets of the entire insurance industry.

Revised Pollution Exclusion To combat unfavorable court interpretations of the comprehensive general liability pollution exclusion, the Insurance Services Office (ISO) developed a new pollution exclusion. The exclusion was filed countrywide by endorsement to all general liability policies issued prior to the 1986 implementation of the commercial general liability policy. The revised exclusion is automatically included in the comprehensive general liability policies issued after January 1, 1986.

Pollution Coverage under the Commercial General Liability Policy

The commercial general liability (CGL) policy excludes coverage for all bodily injury and property damage arising from on-premises liability discharges and certain off-premises discharges. Products and completed operations hazards are not excluded. All governmentally directed "clean-up" costs, whether from on-premises discharges or off-premises (including products or completed operations) are not covered. This exclusion—and the few exposures that are covered by exception to the exclusion—will be examined later.

Common-Law and Statutory Liabilities

Firms that generate toxic and hazardous wastes or use hazardous materials in production may become subject to liability under the common law. For example, companies are subject to tort liability under the theories of negligence, strict liability, or such intentional interference torts as trespass and nuisance.

In addition to common-law exposures, a number of statutes and regulations relate specifically to the protection of the environment. Several such statutes are described under the following headings. Many of them contain provisions for civil and criminal penalties.

River and Harbor Act[8] This 1899 act prohibits the obstruction of various waters of the United States by the building of structures;

unless the work has been recommended by the Chief of Engineers and authorized by the Secretary of the Army. It also prohibits the discharge or deposit of any refuse matter of any kind or description (other than that flowing from streets and sewers and passing therefrom in a liquid state) into any navigable water or any tributary of navigable water of the United States.

Every person or corporation that violates the provisions of the act is guilty of a misdemeanor. On conviction, the violator is liable to punishment by (1) a fine of not less than $500 nor more than $2,500, (2) imprisonment for not less than thirty days nor more than one year, or (3) both fine and imprisonment at the discretion of the court. One-half of any fine is to be paid to any person or persons giving information that leads to conviction.

The requirements of this act could have restricted any and all discharges from factories into waterways during most of its many years of existence, but it was formerly interpreted to apply only when a discharge would impede navigation. In recent years, however, environmental considerations have prompted the government to use the authority of the statute to force corporations to cease water-polluting activities.[9]

Oil Pollution Act[10]   The Oil Pollution Act was enacted on August 30, 1961 and amended in 1973. It prohibits the discharge of oil or oily mixtures from a tanker or ship, unless such discharge is for the purpose of securing the safety of a ship, preventing damage to a ship or cargo, or saving a life at sea. Section 1005 provides both criminal and civil penalties for violations, as follows:

> ... (a) any person who willfully discharges oil or oily mixture from a ship in violation of this chapter or the regulations thereunder shall be fined not more than $10,000 for each violation or imprisoned for not more than one year, or both; (b) ... in addition to any other penalty prescribed by law any person who willfully or negligently discharges oil or oily mixture from a ship in violation of this chapter or any regulations thereunder shall be liable to a civil penalty of not more than $10,000 and any person who otherwise violates this chapter or any regulation thereunder shall be liable to a civil penalty of not more than $5,000 for each violation.

Pollution Control Act[11]   The Federal Water Pollution Control Act stipulates that any pollution (of interstate or navigable waters in or adjacent to any state or states) that endangers the health or welfare of any person shall be subject to abatement as provided within the statute. It encourages local action in the abatement of water pollution, seeks to identify sources of such pollution, and encourages local solutions to pollution problems. Any person who violates either the act, any permit, condition, or limitation implementing any section thereof, or any order issued by the administrator, shall be subject to a civil penalty not to exceed $10,000 per day of such violation.

In *U.S. v. Detrex Chemical Industries, Inc.*[12] the court held that under the aforementioned section, the maximum civil penalty for violation of a permit is $10,000 per day, regardless of the number of violations occurring on that date. It also held that an Environmental Protection Agency Order that required the holder of a permit to comply with terms of the permit before a specified date did not preclude the assessment of civil penalties for violations occurring before that date. In *U.S. v. Phelps-Dodge Corp.*,[13] the court stated that while the administrator must act upon any violations, he has alternative methods of acting (that is, either by civil or criminal proceedings), and he is not required to proceed first to effect a correction by civil means before instituting criminal proceedings.

The Federal Water Pollution Act Amendments of 1972 provide that any person who willfully and negligently violates its provisions is guilty of a crime and punishable by a fine of up to $50,000 per day of violation (or up to two years' imprisonment for second offenses). The statute specifically states that "for the purposes of the" ... (criminal prosecution subsection) ... "persons shall mean, where appropriate, any responsible corporate officers." Section 309(c)2 makes it a crime, punishable by not more than a $10,000 fine, imprisonment for not more than six years, or both, for "any person who knowingly falsifies information required under the Act" or who "knowingly renders inaccurate" any monitoring equipment which is required to be maintained. It is also important to note that the "anti-discrimination clause" of the 1972 amendments protects employees against discharge or discrimination that results from their initiating or participating in proceedings under the act.[14]

Clean Air Act[15] Under the Clean Air Act, the administrator, upon receiving information of a violation, is given authority to proceed to abate the violation. If the violation is of a federally set emission limitation, such as a hazardous emission standard or a standard of performance, the administrator has the authority to proceed directly and immediately. At his or her discretion, he or she may issue an administrative abatement order, seek criminal prosecution (in the case of a knowing violation), or obtain injunctive relief directly in a federal district court.

The sanctions that accompany the act provide that for first violations the court may impose maximum fines of up to $25,000 per day or imprisonment for not more than one year. These sanctions escalate to up to $50,000 per day or imprisonment for not more than two years in the case of subsequent violations. However, since the sanctions are expressed in terms of maximum penalties, the court has wide latitude in applying them.[16]

In order to preserve enforcement proceedings undertaken pursuant to earlier law and to assure a procedure for abatement of international air pollution, the 1970 amendments continue the authority of the abatement conference in the international abatement procedures. The act provides that no order or judgment under an abatement procedure shall relieve any person of any obligation to comply with any requirement of any implementation plan or other standard required under the 1970 amendments.[17]

National Environmental Policy Act[18] The National Environmental Policy Act requires that federal agencies file an "Environmental Impact Statement" on all projects that will have a significant impact on the environment. Generally speaking, the guidelines require the preparation of an impact statement at an early stage in the decision-making process. The draft should be prepared and available prior to any public hearings, to insure that other federal, state, and local agencies with relevant expertise, as well as the public, can comment on the draft statement prior to the making of even a tentative decision or recommendation. The chief function of the National Environmental Policy Act is administrative in nature. It does not define civil or criminal penalties.

Water Quality Improvement Act.[19] This act initially provided that the President should determine those discharges that were deemed harmful for the purposes of the act. Upon the occurrence of a harmful discharge, the person in charge of the vessel or facility that made the discharge had to notify the appropriate agency. If the discharge was not then appropriately cleaned up by the discharger, the federal government could remove the oil or arrange for its removal. The discharger would then reimburse the government for any removal costs it incurred, up to a specified dollar limit, unless the discharger could show, as a defense, that the discharge was solely due to an act of God, an act of war, negligence of the government, an act or omission of a third party, or a combination of these causes. Vessels of over 300 gross tons had to maintain evidence of financial responsibility, through insurance or other means, to cover a cleanup liability of up to the lesser of $100 per gross ton or $14 million. Onshore and offshore facilities were liable to a limit of $8 million per occurrence. The statutory liability limits did not apply where the government was able to prove "willful negligence or willful misconduct in the privity and knowledge of the owner." A third party who caused the discharge was held to the same limits. When an owner or operator acted to clean up the discharge, the removal costs from the government could be recovered if one of the aforementioned defenses to a liability suit could be proven to exist. Authority was also given to establish procedures to be used in containing, dispersing, or removing oil.[20]

The 1972 amendments to the Federal Water Pollution Control Act added a major change to the provision of the Water Quality Improvement Act of 1970. Hazardous substances were folded into the structure of the oil section on a par with oil.

Under the old act, the civil penalty was imposed only if the discharge was a "knowing one." Since controversy arose over the Coast Guard's implementation of the knowledge requirements, Congress deleted them from the section when making the 1972 amendments. Congress also reduced the maximum possible penalty to $5,000 (from $10,000). Discharges of almost any quantity of oil or hazardous substance are subject to a penalty of up to $5,000.[21]

CERCLA With the passage of the Comprehensive Environmental Response, Compensation and Liability Act of 1980 (CERCLA), the potential liability faced by companies dealing with hazardous materials increased. CERCLA established a "Superfund" for the clean up of actual or imminent impairment from hazardous substances.

Violators of the 1980 Act are strictly liable for all government response costs, as well as for injury to, or destruction, or loss of natural resources. The potential liability can be as high as $50 million, and liability cannot be transferred.

Essentially, the statute is designed to achieve one key objective:

to facilitate the prompt cleanup of hazardous dump sites by providing a means of financing both governmental and private responses and by placing the ultimate financial burden upon those responsible for the danger.[22]

CERCLA also created a very broad definition of liability that delineates (1) who is potentially liable, (2) the acceptable defenses, and (3) what costs must be borne by the polluter. Those potentially liable are:

1. the owner or operator of the facility from which the release took place,
2. the owner or operator of the facility at the time of disposal of the toxic substance,
3. any person or organization that arranged for the disposal, treatment, or transportation of the substance, and
4. any person or organization that accepted the substance for transport.

The defenses of the person or organization are limited to the following:

1. an act of God,
2. an act of war, or
3. an act or omission by a third party who is not in a contractual relationship with the defendant, if the defendant exercised due care with respect to the foreseeable acts or omissions of this third party.

The costs for which the polluter can be held liable include:

1. governmental costs for responding to the threat;
2. private person expense incurred "by any other person" consistent with the national contingency plan; and
3. damage to natural resources.

CERCLA allows claims to be brought only by the federal government. Third-party actions are not allowed under the act, but they can be tried separately under common law. In other words, a polluter can be held liable to the federal government, under the statute, *in addition to* its common-law liability to any other person or entity that claims damages from the pollution occurrence.

RCRA The Resource Conservation and Recovery Act (RCRA) of 1976 allows the federal government to order a cessation of such activities as the handling, storage, treatment, transportation, or disposal activities that are presenting an imminent and substantial danger to the public's health or environment.

Actions have been brought against owners of hazardous inactive disposal facilities based on RCRA. Defendants have argued that RCRA should be applied only prospectively, not applied against practices that expired before it was enacted, but the jury is still out on this issue. The trend appears to be toward using RCRA for current and prospective actions, while using CERCLA to establish retroactive liability.

RCRA defines hazardous waste as anything that has one or more of these characteristics:

- Corrosivity
- Reactivity
- Toxicity
- Ignitability

These characteristics are found in numerous materials. For instance, three hazardous wastes specifically mentioned in the Federal Register are coal, paper, and glue.

SEC Regulations In 1973, the Securities and Exchange Commission (SEC) adopted amendments to its registration and reporting requirements. The amendments require corporations to report activities or litigation regarding environmental impairment.

The disclosures must include capital expenditures for the remainder of the fiscal year and predictions for all future fiscal years. Owners are required to report the effect on the corporation's expected earnings, plus the impact on the company's competitive position. All occurrences where the potential EPA fines are in excess of $100,000 must be declared. A further requirement is that litigation against the company must be explained in detail.[24]

Mergers and Acquisitions Pollution problems can have a serious impact on merger and acquisition decisions. Organizations considering the acquisition of another company, a merger, or even the purchase or financing of real estate are wise to investigate the impact of environmental impairment liability exposures. In the absence of a prior environmental assessment, the new owner could unwittingly assume the obligations for substantial third-party liability.

One such potential liability is for the clean-up costs associated with an environmental impairment claim. Three hypothetical loss possibilities illustrate this exposure:

- A bank might be required to pay substantial clean-up costs if an abandoned fuel tank leaks oil on property taken over by the bank after the owner defaulted on the mortgage.
- A pharmaceutical company might acquire land from a chemical company and subsequently spend millions of dollars to decontaminate the property. The pharmaceutical company might not have known that the property contained buried drums of hazardous wastes.
- A chemical company might be liable for groundwater clean up if arsenic, buried by the previous owners, contaminates the adjacent town's drinking water.

Remembering the old adage, "An ounce of prevention is worth a pound of cure," some corporations retain the services of independent environmental survey companies to obtain a complete environmental impairment liability research study before purchasing or merging. In view of the potential exposures and the costs to remedy environmental hazards, this can be money well spend.[25]

The CGL Pollution Exclusion

The commercial general liability policy excludes coverage for all pollution liability losses except various exposures arising out of the "products-completed operations hazard." An endorsement to the CGL also excepts heat, smoke, or fumes from a hostile fire.[26] The exclusion reads as follows:

> This insurance does not apply to:
>
> f. (1) "Bodily injury" or "property damage" arising out of the actual, alleged or threatened discharge, dispersal, release or escape of pollutants:
>
> (a) At or from premises you own, rent or occupy;
>
> (b) At or from any site or location used by or for you or others for the handling, storage, disposal, processing or treatment of waste;
>
> (c) Which are at any time transported, handled, stored, treated, disposed of, or processed as waste by or for you or any person or organization for whom you may be legally responsible; or
>
> (d) At or from any site or location on which you or any contractors or subcontractors working directly or indirectly on your behalf are performing operations:
>
> (i) if the pollutants are brought on or to the site or location in connection with such operations; or
>
> (i) if the operations are to test for, monitor, clean up, remove contain, treat, detoxify or neutralize the pollutants.
>
> (2) Any loss, cost, or expense arising out of any governmental direction or request that you test for, monitor, clean up, remove, contain, treat, detoxify or neutralize pollutants.
>
> Pollutants means any solid, liquid, gaseous or thermal irritant or contaminant, including smoke, vapor, soot, fumes, acids, alkalis, chemicals and waste. Waste includes materials to be recycled, reconditioned, or reclaimed.

The endorsement excepting fire-related pollution amends the exclusion as follows:

> Subparagraphs (a) and (d)(i) of paragraph (1) of this exclusion do not apply to "bodily injury" or "property damage" caused by heat, smoke or fumes from a hostile fire. As used in this exclusion, a hostile fire means one which becomes uncontrollable or breaks out from where it was intended to be.

"Pollutants" is defined in the exclusion. The wording of the definition is so broad as to encompass almost any type of pollution imaginable, with the possible exception of noise pollution, light pollution, or nuclear radiation.

Paragraph (1) of this exclusion applies only to bodily injury and property damage liability; paragraph (2) deals with cleanup costs. The absence of any limiting reference to "sudden," "accidental," "gradual," or "intentional" losses means that, regardless of the event's suddenness or the insured's lack of intent, coverage is excluded.

Paragraph (1)(a) deals with pollution *at or from* premises owned, rented, or occupied by the insured. Because of this exclusion, there would be no coverage for the *owner* of an underground storage tank that leaks, whether or not the contamination or pollution damage is limited to the insured's premises.

Paragraph (1)(b) excludes coverage for firms in the waste disposal business, as well as for other firms whose waste is disposed of in landfills or other facilities.

While (1)(a) and (1)(b) deal with pollution at or from the insured's premises or an off-premises waste-handling facility, paragraph (1)(c) excludes coverage for pollutants in transit. For example, no coverage would apply in a situation where the insured's toxic wastes are spilled in an auto accident while en route to a disposal facility.

Paragraph (1)(d) deals with other sites, away from the insured's premises, that are not excluded by (1)(a) and (1)(b). The first part of the exclusion would, for example, preclude pollution liability coverage for a contractor who is applying weed-killer to lawns or fields. The second part would preclude coverage for a firm in the business of monitoring or correcting pollution problems.

Paragraph (1)(d) is significant, in part, because of what it does *not* exclude.

- The present tense "are performing operations" makes it clear that this exclusion does *not* apply to liability arising out of products or completed operations. Thus, an insured would be covered for pollution liability claims in the following cases:
  (1) The insured's chemical products are sold to a manufacturer and escape while being used in the manufacturer's operations.
  (2) The insured installs a tank on someone else's premises and the tank leaks, resulting in the release of pollutants. (This example presumes that the tank was not installed on a waste disposal or treatment site.)[27]
- The first part of the exclusion deals with "pollutants brought on or to the site or location in connection with such operations." This exclusion would not eliminate coverage for a situation where the insured, working at an off-premises jobsite, ruptures an oil pipeline by accidentally ramming it with a bulldozer.[28]

Paragraph (2) of the exclusion deals with government-required monitoring and cleanup costs. This exclusion is not linked to paragraph (1) in any way, making it clear that such cleanup costs are not covered under any circumstances—even in situations where the bodily injury and property damage liability is not excluded by paragraph (1).

When the CGL was introduced, concern was raised that a literal interpretation "might preclude coverage for liability not ordinarily considered pollution, namely bodily injury or property damage caused by smoke from a hostile fire.[29] The endorsement cited earlier states that *the pollution exclusion* does not apply to property damage caused by heat, smoke, or fumes from a hostile fire on the insured's premises or job location. Depending on the circumstances, other exclusions or limitations may, of course, apply.

Environmental Impairment Liability Coverages

Coverage against pollution losses is sometimes available in environmental impairment liability (EIL) policies offered through surplus lines insurers and the Pollution Liability Insurance Association companies. The *Pollution Liability Insurance Association* (PLIA) is an organization formed by a number of insurers to provide reinsurance for hazardous waste and pollution coverage written by member companies.

PLIA uses a pollution liability form, developed by ISO, which covers sudden and accidental, as well as gradual, discharges. When the pollution policy is written, a total pollution exclusion should be added to the buyer's CGL to prevent duplicate coverage.

Policy Coverages Several environment impairment liability forms exist. The typical policy describes pollutants as emissions, discharges, dispersals, disposals, releases, escape or seepages of smoke, vapors, soot, fumes, acids, alkalis, toxic chemicals, liquids or gases, waste materials, irritants, and contaminants that spoil the land, atmosphere or water. Some policies extend the description to include damaging odors, noises, vibrations, light, electricity, radiation, or changes in temperature and other sensory phenomena. The broad term "sensory phenomena" has numerous interpretations. This is to the policyholder's advantage. For example, one interpretation includes coverage for foliage damage caused by a municipality's incandescent street light as within the meaning of sensory phenomena.

Pollution liability coverage is invariably provided on a claims-made basis. Prior acts coverage may sometimes be obtained, usually on a site by site basis. Limits usually range from $1 million to $5 million, depending on the entity, its inherent hazards and the reinsurance agreements underwriters have negotiated.

There is a deductible applicable to each claim, usually at least $5,000, with many policyholders selecting a $100,000 level. In some instances, the policyholder pays all of the legal, investigative and court costs involved in the defense of a claim for less than the deductible amount (or, in larger claims, the portion attributable to the deductible amount).

Environmental impairment liability policies pay for damages in the nature of bodily injury or direct property damage, and sometimes the loss from an impairment or diminution of an environmental right. An EIL policy generally reimburses the insured for expenses to remove or clean up substances away from the premises that caused environmental impairment. Defense costs may be covered within or in addition to the limits of liability.

Policy Exclusions Since each environmental impairment liability policy is unique, some exclusions may not appear in all contracts. Also, some exclusions may be deleted from a pre-printed form for an additional premium.

The exclusions usually preclude coverage for injury to the insured's employees and noncompliance with statutes or regulations. Claims for expenses such as neutralizing a waste disposal site or dumping toxic or radioactive substances into international waters are not covered. Another area where financial remuneration is not granted is for claims arising from the ownership or use (by or for the insured) of oil and gas platforms and deep water ports.

Also typically excluded are environmental impairment claims that may result from:

- contractual liability agreements,
- operation of autos, ships or aircraft,
- operation of airports,
- products and completed operations,
- sudden and accidental occurrences (in some policies), or
- damage to property in the insured's care, custody and control.

Obtaining EIL Policies Environmental impairment liability insurance markets are limited. Naturally, when the exposure is great, underwriters require detailed information. Many insuring organizations require financial reports as part of the application. Another essential application element is an independent engineering report detailing activities and exposures that could result in a major pollution event. This engineering report generally must include the following information:

1. A complete list of raw materials, finished products, and hazardous substances used in the manufacturing process, currently or previously produced, identified by chemical abstract service registration name and number.
2. A description of seasonal projects, special runs, and continuous operations.
3. A flow chart outlining entry of the materials into the manufacturing process, waste collection and disposal operations.
4. A description of pollution citations and indications of pending violations or investigations by federal or state authorities.

5. The details on waste materials, including the names, daily or weekly weight of the items, in-house collection processes and remote disposal details.
6. A complete description of all incineration.
7. The complete details regarding emergency release methods.
8. Any contingency or emergency plans.
9. A complete description of surrounding topography, neighborhoods, slopes, water table levels, streams, creeks, rivers or other bodies of water in the vicinity.
10. The soil type, if an underground disposal site is used.

(A lot of this information is useful for other risk management purposes, as well.)

Underwriters will review all reports and, if acceptable, offer the insured a maximum policy limit, a deductible (or retention level), and advice as to what exclusions may be deleted for additional premiums. The cost of the environmental impairment liability survey and report compilation must be borne by the insured. Underwriters accept reports only from engineering firms they approve.

Other Environmental Impairment Coverages

The CGL and the environmental impairment liability policy are only two of the insurance policies that offer some protection for claims arising out of pollution occurrences. Other contracts are the (1) fire insurance policy, (2) boiler and machinery contract, (3) auto liability form and the (4) protection and indemnity marine policy. In light of the generally reduced availability of general liability coverage for pollution, an increasing number of claims is being made against these other policies. In response, insurers are restricting pollution coverage on some of these other forms.

Property Insurance Policy   The standard property insurance policies, either specified causes of loss or special ("all-risks"), provide remuneration for some forms of pollution contamination of the insured's property. In other words, coverage for first-party claims, arising out of an otherwise insured peril (such as the smoke peril) and causing pollution damage would be honored by the fire insurance company.

As the "sudden and accidental" exception to the pollution exclusion was deleted from many general liability policies (use of the exclusion began in early 1985), ISO discovered the property insurance claims were beginning to be made in situations that previously would have been handled as liability claims.

Specifically, the Debris Removal clause in the property forms is being used as the basis of asking property insurers to respond to environmental clean-up costs. A key case is *Lexington Insurance Co. v. Ryder Systems* (234 S.E. 2d 839), a Georgia Court of Appeals decision which extended the Debris Removal clause to cover the cost of removing oil-soaked ground from around a leaking oil storage tank, in spite of the fact that the policy arguably did not cover the value of the land.[30]

In response to this claim and others, ISO filed changes to its commercial property insurance policies in April, 1986, with a proposed effective date of May 1, 1986. The major changes:

- revise the debris removal clause, principally by introducing a cap of 25 percent of the direct loss on the amount of the debris removal loss;
- introduce a new additional coverage for clean up and removal of pollutants from land or water at the described premises, subject to a $10,000 annual aggregate limit; and
- replace the pollution exclusion in the special ("all-risks") form with a new exclusion that limits covered pollution losses to those caused by the so-called "specific causes of loss."[31]

Boiler and Machinery Policies The standard boiler and machinery insurance contract includes coverage for pollution to the policyholder's property if the contamination or pollution is caused by an accident to a covered object. There is a specific coverage for the pollution exposures with a stated coverage limit (typically $5,000). For certain businesses, this limit may be too low. However, it is sometimes possible to increase the limit. For example, in industry, many boilers are lined with asbestos. Businesses with this equipment need a higher limit to guarantee remuneration for clean-up costs that are potentially higher because of the asbestos.

Auto Policies Transporters of hazardous wastes or materials, such as a private or common carriers, are subject to the Motor Carrier Act of 1980.[32] This legislation mandates that trucking operators must file proof of pollution liability insurance, such as:

Type of Carriage	Commodity Transported	Limits
1. For-hire	Nonhazardous property	$1,000,000
2. For-hire and Private	Hazardous substances	$5,000,000
3. For-hire and Private	Oil & hazardous waste	$1,000,000

Standard auto policies can be endorsed to include environmental impairment liability arising out of the transportation of hazardous materials. There is no additional premium charge for this endorsement, unless underwriters believe that the exposure is of a catastrophic nature.

The auto policy is endorsed with the Motor Carrier Act Endorsement, MCS-90. This endorsement includes coverages for accidents that may occur when the policyholder transports hazardous materials. The MCS-90 also meets the requirements of the Hazardous Materials Transportation Act.

Protection and Indemnity The protection and indemnity (P&I) contract, an ocean marine form, provides third-party legal liability coverage for ocean marine exposures. Vessel owners may, for example, be liable for pollution damages if they are involved in a ship collision with another vessel that is carrying hazardous materials. However, many P&I insurers exclude coverage for pollution losses, leaving shipowners to insure these coverages through the Water Quality Insurance Syndicate.

As noted earlier, the Oil Pollution Act prohibits the discharge of oil or oily mixtures from a tanker or other vessel. The exceptions are when discharge is to secure the safety of a ship, prevent damage to a vessel or cargo, or save a life at sea. Criminal and civil penalties exist for violations, including a fine up to $10,000 and a one year prison sentence.

Vessel owners and operators are liable for the costs of removal, remedial actions, and damages to natural resources. For vessels carrying hazardous substances as cargo, the minimum requirements are $300 per gross ton or $5 million, whichever is greater. Also the law mandates a $300 per gross ton limit or $500,000, whichever is greater for other vessels. Vessel owners are liable for all additional damages resulting from a pollution occurrence.

Noninsurance Techniques

Obviously, environmental impairment losses can be costly. One small oil leak may result in millions of dollars being spent for a remedy. The problem is magnified by unknown hazards arising from underground fuel storage tanks or closed gasoline stations; uncontrolled land fill operations; and transportation of hazardous materials across highways and bridges, and through tunnels. Another pollution problem is acid rain, which has caused unforeseen damage to the environment. Still another example occurred when a sulfuric cloud destroyed a building's electrical system.

The risk management process takes into consideration five alternatives for handling loss exposures. The five strategies are (1) retention,

(2) avoidance, (3) loss control, (4) transfer by contract or (5) transfer by insurance. Transference by insurance has been the major subject of this section. The other techniques will be the focus of the remainder.

Retention　Many large and financially capable organizations are able to retain all or a major part of the EIL exposure. They pay for pollution liability damages, up to set levels, out of their operating revenues. In cases where independent analysis reflects a major problem, environmental impairment liability insurance will be impossible to purchase. Such uninsurable entities may not be able to survive a pollution claim.

Avoidance　One way to avoid the pollution problem is for a business to perform only operations that do not result in the use of production of known hazardous wastes. Even then, it may be learned that some material that was considered innocuous has a deleterious effect when released into the environment.

Loss Control　The most realistic option for many companies is to find acceptable ways to handle potential pollution problems. Numerous examples exist.

For instance, a business can hire an independent environmental risk assessment company to evaluate its on-site exposures and recommend corrective measures. These inspections may take from six to eight weeks. The final report usually addresses potential and actual environmental pollution concerns, new training and site maintenance procedures required to control or prevent problems, and additional operations needed to comply with regulatory legislation.

The report can be used when applying for insurance. (Underwriters normally require the report 60 days before issuing coverage). If the prospective policyholder makes the recommended corrections, an environmental impairment liability policy may be issued.

A word of caution is in order for a firm that fails to make corrections recommended by independent experts. In a lawsuit, expert opinions as to what the firm should have done, including those in written environmental assessment reports, can be admitted as evidence and applied as the standard of care reasonably to be expected from the firm.

Other methods of loss control are to alter the production process or replace a hazardous chemical with a nonhazardous substitute. In some plants, chemical engineers can study manufacturing operations and suggest nonhazardous replacements for certain pollution-causing materials.

Unnecessary or abandoned storage tanks can be drained and removed or filled with sand. Metal storage tanks can be replaced with plastic models that do not rust, but this is not a perfect solution to the problem as plastic tanks may crack or otherwise lose their integrity. Also, on-site facilities can be installed to neutralize production wastes.

It might also be possible to modify operations or install safety equipment. Air scrubbers, vacuum control of air movement, and other air pollution-control devices might help. Safety measures such as sprinkler systems, halon fire suppression units, heat detectors, and temperature alarms give prompt warnings and responses to an occurrence that might otherwise result in a polluting fire or chemical reaction.

The institution of an emergency response team consisting of trained company personnel may reduce losses in case of an occurrence. The team must be "on call" and ready to react to chemical spills, vehicle accidents, fires, and natural disasters, such as hurricanes, tornados, floods, or earthquakes. The emergency response team must have knowledge of all chemicals used in the manufacturing process. Disaster plans should be tested annually. Local authorities and rescue units also can provide assistance.

Further, companies must devise and enforce specific rules to reduce loss potential. Procedures for protecting the property and public from injury should be written and reviewed annually. Examples of rules include: (1) the number of visitors must be kept to a maximum of "x" persons; (2) only authorized employees are allowed near the production process; (3) everyone must wear proper protective clothing when working near the processing line; and, (4) all contaminated clothing must be destroyed properly.

Protective clothing, alarm signals and evacuation procedures reduce personnel injuries. Eye washes, showers, and other first aid measures lessen bodily injuries caused by pollutants. Full-time occupational health nurses can offer wellness promotion programs such as stress management, first aid, health education, cardio-pulmonary resuscitation (CPR) training, and physical assessments.

Pre-employment physical exams and annual medical check-ups will spot or eliminate potential problems. For example, a physically or emotionally impaired worker should not be given the job of handling toxic materials. A compulsively neat person may be assigned clean up duties.

Noninsurance Transfer Another way to handle exposures is to transfer them. For instance, a firm can shift the production process so that it deals only with partially or fully finished goods. The exposures associated with the handling of hazardous raw materials can thus be transferred to another firm.

DIRECTORS AND OFFICERS LIABILITY

Business firms may take the form of proprietorships, partnerships, joint ventures, or corporations. Each type of entity has a distinctive organizational structure with liability exposure implications, as noted in Chapter 1. For example, a sole proprietor retains profits and responsibilities for legal liabilities. Partners usually share duties, profits, losses, and liabilities.

Corporations are owned by stockholders and operated by boards of directors. The board of directors appoints personnel to oversee daily operations. Power to conduct business affairs, such as the purchase of insurance or the institution of loss control procedures, is delegated to the management team. Stockholders share profits in direct proportion to their stock ownership. Their liability is limited to the loss of invested money.

The management of a corporation includes the board of directors, executive officers, and higher-ranking employees. Outside business or social leaders may serve as directors, officers, or members of an advisory board. These individuals bring a variety of backgrounds, political viewpoints, and skills to guide the company's activities.

Corporate officers and directors may be sued for the breach of corporate duties. Further, directors or officers who are the object of a claim or suit can receive much undesirable publicity.

Loss Exposures

In general, directors and officers must manage the business in compliance with the law and the corporate structure. Seven major responsibilities of corporate directors are:

1. establish the basic objectives and broad policies of the corporation;
2. elect the corporate officers, advise them, approve their actions and audit their performance;
3. safeguard and approve changes in the corporation's assets;
4. approve important financial matters, and see that proper annual and interim reports are given to stockholders;
5. delegate special powers to others to sign contracts, open bank accounts, sign checks, issue stock, make loans, and conduct any activities that may require board approval;
6. maintain, revise, and enforce the corporate charter and by-laws; and

7. perpetuate a sound board through regular elections and the filling of interim vacancies.

In addition to performing these functions, directors and officers occupy a position of trust for shareholders, the board of directors, and the general public. Thus, directors and officers are said to have "fiduciary duties"—that is, they have legal obligations to others by virtue of the positions they hold. These include (but are not limited to) the following duties.

- *The Duty of Care.* Directors and officers have the general duty to exercise reasonable care in the performance of their corporate functions. Here, "reasonable care" is the degree of care that a prudent director or officer would ordinarily exercise in similar circumstances.

  In applying the general duty to exercise reasonable care, courts have held that directors and officers are not guarantors of the profitability of the enterprise. Nor are directors required to have special business skills. Even so, according to the so-called "business judgment rule," the decisions of both directors and officers must be within the range of disagreement normally to be expected among *prudent* directors and officers.

  Both officers and directors also have a duty to keep themselves informed of the facts and other matters that are required to make prudent decisions of the type each must make. At a minimum, directors have a duty to attend board meetings and meetings of the committees on which they serve. They cannot successfully plead ignorance of what was going on in the corporation because they did not attend such meetings. Directors may reasonably rely upon reports and financial statements prepared by persons believed to be competent and trustworthy, including officers, employees, or outside advisors of the corporation (such as public accountants and attorneys), but directors cannot safely rely on unsupported declarations or opinions of managerial employees.
- *The Duty of Loyalty to the Corporation.* Directors and officers have the general duty of undivided loyalty to the corporation they serve. Accordingly, an officer or a director cannot secretly seize for himself or herself a business opportunity that properly belongs to the corporation. For the same reason, an officer or a director cannot own or operate a business that competes with the corporation. In fact, a director normally cannot even enter into a contract to provide goods or services to the corporation, unless the contract terms are approved by a vote of the Board

or the shareholders and/or the terms are fair and reasonable to
the corporation in relation to the alternatives.

● *The Duty of Loyalty to the Stockholders.* Since officers and
directors obtain their positions by the vote or consent of the
stockholders, they also owe a duty of loyalty to the stockholders. Under the common law and the Securities and Exchange
Act of 1934, no person—including an officer or a director—is
allowed to use "insider information" to buy or sell stock of the
corporation, whether the information was obtained directly or
from others. Persons who do so can be sued for damages by the
stockholders.

Under the aforementioned Act, if an officer, director, or
owner of at least 10 percent of the outstanding stock makes a
profit (within a six-month period) by dealing in shares of the
corporation, the profit may be taken by the corporation—
whether or not such a person actually had "insider information." If the person used material inside information that was
not disclosed, the party who bought or sold the stock to the
insider may also have an action for damages.

The duty of reasonable care and the business judgment
rule are also applied to situations involving abuse of minority
stockholders. Under circumstances beyond the scope of this
summary, a minority stockholder may have a valid cause of
action against the directors and/or officers of the corporation in
which it holds a minority interest.

● *The Duty of Disclosure.* Officers and directors have the general
duty to disclose material facts to all persons who have a right to
know such facts and would not otherwise be able to obtain
them. Examples include the duty of officers to disclose facts
that are material to directors; the duty of officers to disclose
facts material to various regulatory bodies; the duty of
directors to disclose potential conflicts of interest; the duty of
officers and directors to disclose facts material to creditors or
potential creditors; and the duty of officers and directors to
make public disclosures of facts that are material to stockholders, bondholders, and potential investors in the securities of the
corporation. Many such disclosure requirements are contained
in the Securities and Exchange Act of 1934 and in SEC
regulations, but similar or identical requirements may also be
found in court decisions and state statutes and regulations.

● *Duties Under ERISA.* The Employee Retirement Income
Security Act of 1974 (ERISA) will be discussed later. Here, it
should be noted that the Act is applicable to most employee
benefit plans, and it imposes statutory duties on all persons who

may be deemed "fiduciaries" within a very broad definition of the concept. Generally, an officer or a director (or anyone else) who exercises discretionary control in the management of a benefit plan or its assets, or who gives investment advice, is a fiduciary with prescribed statutory duties and liabilities. The duties include the duty to act solely in the interest of plan participants, the duty to exercise the care and skill that a prudent person would exercise in like circumstances, the duty to observe sound and safe investment practices, and a variety of other duties.

Any fiduciary who breaches such a duty may be held *personally liable* for any resulting loss to the plan. The violator may also be subject to other penalties stipulated in ERISA.

An officer or a director may be held individually liable for the breach of *any* common-law or statutory duty that is imposed on officers and/or directors. However, other than the illustrations above, no further attempt will be made to summarize the scores of statutory duties that might apply individually to officers and directors. The discussion will instead focus on the common-law duties imposed on officers and directors as a matter of tort law.

As an entity, a corporation may be held vicariously liable for the tortious conduct of an employee or some other agent. As an individual, an officer or director is not vicariously liable for the *unauthorized* tortious conduct of an employee or another agent. Yet, officers and directors may be (1) individually liable for their own torts or (2) jointly and severally liable for the tortious acts or omissions of another agent of the corporation, if they either authorize or participate in the tortious conduct. All officers and directors of a corporation are legal agents of the corporation, and there are many situations when one of them will act in concert with or with the authorization of another. There are likewise many situations when one officer or director will act alone. In either case, the officer or director may be held *personally* liable to the injured party.

Tort actions against officers and directors may be based on negligence or intentional interference torts. The actions may take the form of (1) derivative suits by stockholders or (2) nonderivative suits by outsiders.

Derivative Suits   A *derivative suit* is a suit brought by one or more stockholders on behalf of the corporation. Any damages recovered in a derivative suit go directly to the corporation, not to the plaintiff-stockholder(s)—though successful plaintiffs are often awarded the expenses of suit, including reasonable attorney's fees.

The defendants in derivative suits are usually directors and/or officers of the corporation. But derivative suits may also be brought by stockholder against outsiders, such as public accountants whose negligence in auditing the book of account may have damaged the corporation.

To be successful in a *negligence* action against officers and directors, it is often necessary for the plaintiff-stockholders to establish that the defendants' conduct was outside the permissible boundaries of the business judgment rule mentioned earlier. Essentially, this rule prevails in the absence of fraud, breach of trust, or the commission of an ultra vires act. (*Ultra vires* means beyond the scope of the powers of the corporation, as defined by its charter or act of incorporation.) The *business judgment rule* dictates that the conduct of directors is *not* negligence when the alleged acts or omissions were discretionary, performed in good faith, and within the outside boundaries of prudent business conduct.

The decision of the Foremost Dairies suit, a San Francisco court case, was a major departure from the business judgment rule. A Foremost Dairies subsidiary guaranteed a loan to one of its suppliers. In exchange for the guarantee, certain benefits (such as a new source of raw materials) were afforded the corporation. When the supplier went bankrupt, the $2.5 million loan was uncollectible. The bank, acting on the indemnity guarantee by Foremost Dairies subsidiary, asked the parent firm to pay off the loan. The company refused and the bank sued. A California court directed the directors and officers to pay $200,000 of the loss themselves. The dairy paid $1,750,000. The remaining $550,000 was absorbed by the bank.[33]

None of the directors profited from the original transaction. No one was guilty of fraud, mismanagement, abuse, or wasting of the dairy's assets. Their only apparent vice was their alleged ignorance of a California statute prohibiting a nonbanking firm or noninsurance company from acting as a surety.

This case highlights the need to monitor carefully all corporate activities. One small incorrect decision can result in thousands of dollars being paid to defend a lawsuit or pay a judgment.

Nonderivative Suits Nonderivative suits against corporate officers and directors may be initiated by competitors, creditors, governmental units, or other persons outside the corporation. The outside party must show that an injury or injustice resulted from tortious acts or omissions of officers and/or directors. Examples are claims for violations of legislative statutes; failure to fulfill legal duties; and intentional, unfair, or harmful conduct.

For instance, a borrower took legal action against a bank's board and a senior vice-president. The bank had sold the plaintiff's equipment (held as collateral) to satisfy a defaulted loan.

The borrower alleged fraud, violation of the Uniform Commercial Code, interference with contractual relationships, interference with business relations, and conversion. The borrower contended that the bank sold the equipment below its fair market value, and the borrower sought the $215,000 difference.

Directors and officers may be held liable for acts of misfeasance, nonfeasance, or malfeasance. *Misfeasance* is defined as the performance of an act in an improper manner. *Nonfeasance* is failure to perform an act one has the duty to perform. *Malfeasance* is an illegal action. Courts will hold individuals liable for breach of duty if misfeasance, malfeasance, or nonfeasance is the proximate cause of the loss.

Stockholders who suffer injuries may also bring nonderivative suits.[34] These claims name specific directors or officers and the corporate entity as co-defendants. If the stockholder wins the case, other stockholders may bring derivative suits to recover the judgments from the directors or officers individually.

An example is when a person makes an unwise corporation stock purchase under the encouragement or faulty advice of the corporation's director or officer. The stockholder can sue the director or officer individually for damages. On the other hand, if a financial loss is inflicted upon a corporation in its entirety, all stockholders may bring actions against the directors and officers as a derivative action.

Damages

When there is a violation of the duties owed by the corporate officer or director, the types and amount of damages to which the injured party is entitled are dependent upon the nature of the action brought and whether the violation is of statutory origin or based in common law. To illustrate, in an action against directors of a corporation to recover damages for fraud and deceit in the sale of stock, the plaintiff is entitled to recover an amount equal to the difference between the actual value of the stock at the time of purchase and the value the stock would have had if the false representations had been true, less any dividends the plaintiff has received. In private civil actions brought pursuant to the Securities and Exchange Act and the rules and regulations promulgated thereunder, recovery is limited to actual damages sustained and the recovery of punitive damages is precluded.

Remote and speculative damages generally may not be recovered, but corporate officers may be held liable for profits lost by management.[35] In some circumstances, punitive damages may be allowed by the court for the fraudulent breach of a fiduciary duty.[36]

In the area of federal law, the courts may invoke a wide variety of legal devices to redress wrongs committed by corporate officials. These may include injunctions, rescission, accounting and restitution, an award of compensatory but probably not punitive damages, attorney fees and, in some instances, litigation expenses.

Indemnification of Corporate Officers and Directors

When a director or officer was a defendant in a law suit, there has been considerable debate over the director's or officer's right to be indemnified by the corporation for costs incurred in the suit. This debate obviously has a bearing on the subject of directors' and officers' liability insurance. Of particular importance is the question whether (1) individual directors or officers, or (2) the corporate entity will ultimately bear the burden of any loss. In any situation this question is answered by the effect of applicable statutes and by any indemnification agreements the corporation might have made with directors and officers. However, the numerous situations, statutes, and indemnification agreements make this a difficult subject to describe in general terms.

Legal Background At common law, a corporate officer or director who had been unsuccessful in the defense of derivative suit had no right to indemnification from the corporation. It was reasoned that a wrongdoing insider cannot justifiably be reimbursed by the very party that his or her misconduct had harmed. Although this rationale would seem inappropriate when the insider was successful in defense of a derivative suit, early cases denied indemnification in such situations, because the expenditure of corporate funds would not produce a benefit to the corporation and thus would be *ultra vires*

As a result of the confusion surrounding the right to corporate indemnification—especially in the context of a stockholders' derivative suit—the legislative bodies of various states have enacted statutes granting the right to indemnification in certain situations. Some of the statutes permit indemnification; others require it; and still others make court approval or a court order a necessary prerequisite. Some of the indemnification statutes are "exclusive" in that they authorize indemnification only to the extent provided by the statute. Other statutes declare that statutory indemnification will not be considered exclusive of any of the rights to which the officer or director may be entitled under any bylaw, agreement, vote of stockholders or disinterested directors, or otherwise.

Indemnification Agreements In most states, as a prerequisite to indemnification, the corporation must have adopted some form of contractual provision that sets guidelines for reimbursement, since the statutes are merely permissive. This provision, whether incorporated in the bylaws, a corporate resolution, or other written agreement, such as an employment contract, can obligate the corporation to indemnify the corporate official as long as the standard of conduct that must be followed is in harmony with the statute.

The basic difference among corporate indemnification agreements is the standard of conduct that must be maintained by the insider in order to obtain indemnification. Some agreements deny indemnification to the insider who has been adjudged liable for negligence or misconduct, while others deny indemnification only when the official's action constituted gross negligence or willful misconduct.

In certain situations an officer or director has the right to obtain indemnification from the corporation pursuant to the principles of agency law and independent of any corporate or statutory obligation to indemnify. For instance, an agent, whether an officer or director, is entitled to reimbursement for legal liability arising out of his or her principal's acts, but not for liability arising out of his or her own wrongful conduct. An agent is also entitled to be indemnified against loss and liability for acts he or she commits at the principal's direction when such acts are not manifestly known by the agent to be wrong.

Directors and Officers Liability Insurance

The directors and officers legal liability insurance policy, popularly referred to as the D&O, is a two part contract.

- The first part provides coverage for the individual directors and officers (D&O Liability). It provides protection for the directors' and officers' personal liability when they are not indemnified by the corporation.
- The second part insures the corporation (Company Reimbursement). This section repays the corporation if it has paid money to directors and officers for personal expenses associated with a claim.

Each policy section contains an insuring agreement, definitions, extensions of coverage, exclusions, and specific terms and conditions. Claims will be paid under either section of the contract.

Directors and Officers Liability Coverage

This first section of the D&O policy provides coverage for the individual liability of executives who are not indemnified by the corporation for their legal or judgment expenses. The coverage will respond only when the entity's bylaws or charter prohibits the company from reimbursing the individuals.

Insuring Agreement A D&O liability insuring agreement may be long and complex. Each insurance company's form reflects individual wording. No two insurers' D&O policies are identical. One insuring agreement reads:

> **INSURING CLAUSE**
>
> In consideration of the payment of the premium and subject to the terms, conditions, definitions, exclusions and limitations hereinafter provided Underwriters agree (A) to pay to or on behalf of the DIRECTORS and OFFICERS of the COMPANY LOSS arising from any claim or claims made against the DIRECTORS and OFFICERS, jointly or severally, during the Policy Period (as set forth in Section 2 of the attached Schedule) by reason of any WRONGFUL ACT done or attempted or allegedly done or attempted by the DIRECTORS and OFFICERS during or at any time prior to the Policy Period. . .[37]

The insuring agreement covers any person who was, is, or will be a director or officer. This means a person can leave the corporation and still be covered by the policy. An example is a board member retiring and subsequently being named in a legal action.

The policy provides protection for "joint or several" claims. In other words, coverage will be given to an individual director or officer or a group of directors and/or officers. The policy limits are not increased if two or more people are included in the action.

The total policy limits are also the annual aggregate limits. This is the most one can collect for claims filed during the policy year. The limits are not automatically restored to their original level after a claim is paid.

The D&O form is a "claims-made" policy. Coverage begins only if the claim is first made against the insured during the policy period. If the claim is received before the policy period begins or after the policy expires, there is no coverage.

Some forms mandate that both the occurrence and the original claim must occur during the policy term. This can create a dangerous coverage situation, for example, when an officer receives a complaint in a tort action. The original complaint is treated as a first notice. The complaint must be reported to the insurer for future coverage to apply. When the insured changes insurance companies, it must inform the previous D&O insurer of this complaint before the policy expires. If this is not done, the new D&O insurer will deny coverage as the original claim occurred during the previous D&O policy's term. The past D&O carrier will deny the claim as that policy was not renewed.

Each insurance company defines wrongful acts differently. The definition is the key element of the D&O policy. This definition from one form reads:

> "Wrongful Act" shall mean any actual or alleged error or misstatement or misleading statement or act or omission or neglect or breech of duty by a Directors and Officers in the discharge of their duties, individually or collectively, or any matter claimed against them solely by reason of their being Directors or Officers of the Company.[38]

The definition is very broad, given the phrase "any matter claimed against them solely by reason of their being Directors or Officers of the Company."

Only directors and officers are included in the insuring agreement, but the coverage also protects the individual's heirs, estates, legal representatives, and insolvent, bankrupt, or incompetent executives.

Directors and officers of subsidiary companies acquired or created during the policy term are automatically covered. The parent organization must give written notice to the underwriters "as soon as practicable" and pay any additional premium. Upon renewal, the new subsidiaries must be declared on the renewal application to continue coverage. If the parent entity fails to notify the insurance company of the new subsidiaries, there is no protection.

Definitions The D&O liability section includes specific definitions. There are usually between four and six terms defined. Some of the major meanings paraphrased from a typical policy are:

- *Director or Officer:* Any duly elected or appointed Company director or officer named in Item 1 of the Declarations. Coverage will apply automatically to newly elected Directors and newly appointed Officers after the policy date, subject to (1) written notice of changes to the insurer with thirty (30) days after each anniversary date, or the termination date, and (2) payment of an additional required premium.
- *Policy Year:* The period of one year following the effective date and hour of the policy or anniversary thereof—or, if the time between the effective date or anniversary and the termination of the policy is less than one year, such lesser period.

- *Loss:* The amount that the Directors and Officers are legally obligated to pay for claims made for Wrongful Acts. The loss shall include, but not be limited to damages, judgments, settlements, cost of investigation (excluding salaries of Company officers or employees) and defense of legal actions, claims or proceedings, plus cost of attachment or similar bonds. Further, the loss shall not include fines or penalties imposed by law for matters uninsurable under the law pursuant to which this policy shall be construed.
- *Wrongful Act:* Any breach of duty, neglect, error, misstatement, misleading statement, omission or other act done or wrongfully attempted by the Directors or Officers. (See policy language quoted earlier).
- *Subsidiary Company:* A Company under the auspices of the named insured; the named insured owns more than 50% of the voting stock.

Exclusions The rationale behind exclusions of the D&O policy are based on three factors.

1. Some excluded acts or omissions are considered uninsurable.
2. Some coverages excluded here may be obtained from another insurance policy, such as the commercial general liability or the business auto coverage form.
3. Previous D&O policies may provide coverage. (This occurs when the claim was reported to the previous D&O carrier. The claim may be covered by the previous D&O carrier if it is filed during that policy's extended discovery period.)

Typical exclusions may preclude coverage for:

1. libel or slander;
2. personal profit or advantages to which directors or officers were not legally entitled;
3. dishonest acts;
4. failure to effect and maintain insurance coverages;
5. bodily injury, sickness, disease or death of any person;
6. damage to or destruction of tangible property, including loss of use or the loss of use of other tangible property that has not been physically damaged or physically damaged or destroyed; and
7. all pollution events, sudden, accidental or otherwise.

Additional exclusions may apply to legal actions existing at policy inception. The responsibility for these claims belongs to the previous D&O insurer or to the insured. The standard nuclear energy exclusion is attached to all D&O policies. This excludes coverage from claims arising out of hazardous policies of nuclear materials. If the insured has this exposure, coverage is available from nuclear liability insurance pools.

Violations of fiduciary responsibilities arising out of the Employee Retirement Income Security Act of 1974 (ERISA) are the subject of another exclusion. Coverage may be acquired through the purchase of a Fiduciary Responsibility Liability policy discussed later in this chapter.

Payments, commissions, gratuities, benefits, or favors to domestic or foreign governmental officials, agents, representatives, employees, family members, or their employers (also referred to as "bribes") are excluded. These illegal payments are defined in the Securities and Exchange Act of 1934.

Retention Provisions Directors and officers legal liability coverages have an unusual condition concerning payment of claims. Usually, under other types of liability insurance, a *deductible* can be selected by the policyholder. The insurance company provides legal services, pays defense costs and investigation fees, and negotiates with the claimant. The insured only pays a portion of the settlement or judgment based on the deductible level.

D&O insurance does not operate in this usual fashion. The D&O policyholder selects a retention level in place of a deductible. This retention level applies to both defense costs and settlements or judgments. This means the insured is responsible for the investigation charges, attorneys' fees, court costs and other expenses involved with the claim. Above the retention level, the insurer will be liable for 95 percent (or some other stated percentage) of the cost of claims exceeding the stated retention. The policyholder will pay the entire retention, plus 5 percent of all claim expenses and judgments exceeding the retention. Therefore, if the corporation selected a $100,000 retention, it is responsible for this amount, plus 5 percent of judgments and expenses over $100,000, up to the first $1 million.

The specific policy terminology as reflected in one D&O form reads:

> The insurer shall be liable to pay 95% of loss in excess of the amount of the retention shown under Item D (the monetary retention level) of the Declarations up to the limit of liability as shown under Item C (policy limits) of the Declarations, it being warranted that the remaining 5% of each and every loss shall be carried by the Company or the Directors and Officers at their own risk and uninsured.[39]

Underwriters may remove the 5 percent retention, by endorsement, for an additional premium. The insurance company will then pay 100 percent of the claim in excess of the retention.

The policyholder may select a split retention option with two retentions applicable to each claim. The first retention applies to each defendant. The second retention applies to the total claim. An example of this option is a $5,000 retention for each involved director or officer, up to a $25,000 per total claim. The policyholder assumes no more than $25,000, plus an additional 5 percent, no matter how many persons are involved.

Discovery Clause As mentioned earlier, D&O policies are written on a "claims-made" basis. If the policy should be cancelled or nonrenewed, all coverages for the policy term would terminate, but a policyholder has the option of purchasing a coverage extension.

The terminating company might not permit this extension if they think a "wrongful act" claim will surface during the extended discovery period.

A typical clause reads:

> If the Insurer shall cancel or refuse to renew this policy the Company shall have the right, upon payment of the additional premium of 25% of the three-year premium hereunder, to an extension of the cover granted by this policy in respect of any claim or claims which may be made against the Directors or Officers during the period of twelve calendar months after the date of such cancellation or non-renewal but only in respect of any Wrongful Act committed before the date of such cancellation or non-renewal.[40]

This clause extends the policy discovery period for twelve months at a cost of 25 percent of the three year premium. It is available at the *insured's* option when the *insurer* cancels or nonrenews the policy. This tail provision is clearly much more limiting than the provisions of the CGL, and it demonstrates the need to carefully examine the "tail" provisions of any claims-made policy.

Company Reimbursement

The second part of the D&O contract, company reimbursement, indemnifies the corporation for money paid to individual directors and officers when the directors or officers are sued for wrongful acts and incur personal expenses in legal defenses, settlements, or judgments. As noted, the corporation will reimburse each director and officer for personal expenses, if required, by corporate bylaws and permitted by state law.

In the D&O liability provisions, the first section of the contract, payment is provided for the individual claims for which the corporation does not authorize reimbursement in its charter. In contrast, under company reimbursement coverages, the insurance company pays the corporation to provide remuneration for expenses paid to the executives based on the corporation's bylaws and charter. The corporation's practice of indemnifying directors and officers must be stated clearly by the corporation prior to a claim.

The two coverages of the D&O policy are mutually exclusive. One coverage or the other in the D&O policy will respond to a covered loss.

The D&O policy's company reimbursement section has definitions, exclusions, terms and conditions similar to the D&O liability coverage provisions, but the insuring agreement and definition of a loss are different. Where the D&O liability portion *pays claims on behalf of the corporation's directors and officers*, the Company reimbursement section *indemnifies the corporation for all expenses paid to the officers and directors.*

> The company reimbursement insuring agreement in one form states: To pay on behalf of the Company, in accordance with the terms and conditions of the policy, all Loss arising from any claims or claims made during the policy period against the Directors and Officers, individually or collectively, by reason of a Wrongful Act for which the Company may be required or permitted by law to indemnify such Directors and Officers.[41]

The key terms are "... for which the company may be required or permitted by law to indemnify such Directors and Officers." Simply put, this says that the corporation's bylaws or charter can allow permission to reimburse the individuals. The clause also excludes payments for *punitive* damages, fines or penalties that are uninsurable under the law.

The retention level and the additional 5% assumption applies to company reimbursement coverages. The individual or corporation will be responsible for all costs associated with the claim and resulting judgments.

Once the initial retention total amount is reached, the insurance company is responsible for 95 percent of all costs and expenses when the form contains such a provision. This also includes settlements and judgments. The 5 percent additional retention over and above the initial retention limit is the responsibility of the policyholder.

Noninsurance Techniques

Legal actions generate expenses for the corporation's defense, including legal assistance. They have a negative impact on earnings, and also require management time defending an action.

A related problem is the organization's need to convince qualified individuals to serve as directors. People are reluctant to assume that role if it could cause them to incur substantial uninsured and un-reimbursed liabilities. These individuals must be assured that the company has policies and procedures for individual and corporate legal protection.

Noninsurance techniques available to corporate entities can be organized under five risk management options. The four options below can be employed in addition to a fifth strategy, which is insurance.

Retention Total retention of any exposure with high potential loss severity is dangerous because of the potential of catastrophic loss. Retention is usually appropriate for the D&O exposure only when the insurance coverages are not available or the cost is prohibitive. This is likely to be the case for small, closely-held corporations.

The corporation uses partial retention when purchasing D&O coverages subject to a retentional level. A $100,000 retention level is the usual. Large organizations will increase this amount to $1 million. This gives the entity protection from larger claims while it retains smaller losses.

Avoidance A corporation cannot totally avoid "wrongful act" exposures. An individual can avoid the exposure by declining a board membership or an officer's position. When this occurs, that person need not be concerned with the corporation's D&O program. The exposure has been totally avoided.

Loss Control Corporations can prevent or reduce the number of wrongful acts by obtaining and following the advice of competent legal counsel. Full disclosures to the board of board members' and officers' personal finances are a must. Strict voluntary adherence to a meaningful code of ethics will reduce loss probability. Open, clear, and concise communications among officers and directors is an important ingredient to reducing losses. Effective communications also creates an environment for strong management. Clear understanding of the antitrust acts and knowledge of the corporation's charter and bylaws, by all officers and directors, can also reduce the likelihood of loss. This includes Securities and Exchange Commission laws and local statutes. A final method is to avoid making controversial decisions without allowing employees and stockholders to vote.

Noninsurance Transfer One method is to transfer the D&O exposure to another through a contractual arrangement. In a sense, this is done by officers and directors who are parties to indemnity agreements with their corporations. Corporations would rarely (if ever) be able to transfer their indemnification exposure, except by buying insurance.

CONDOMINIUM ASSOCIATION
DIRECTORS AND OFFICERS LIABILITY

Condominium living continues to grow in popularity, especially in the South and West. In addition, many office buildings are offering the condominium concept to private-sector companies. In lieu of paying rent or purchasing an expensive building, small companies are purchasing condominium offices.

Condominiums come in many sizes, shapes, colors, and styles. They may be high-rise buildings, mid-rise structures, garden type apartments, rows of townhouses, or clusters of detached homes. Commercial condos also fit similar descriptions.

Many older apartment and office buildings are being converted into condominiums. This allows the building owners to sell what was otherwise rental property and generate cash to invest elsewhere. Though tenants of buildings being converted to condos often do not have a choice in the matter, a tenant who can handle the down payment is offered many of the advantages of ownership, without the necessity of moving, and is freed of such ownership responsibilities as lawn care, building maintenance, and refuse disposal.

Condominium Ownership

Condominium ownership refers to an estate or legal interest in real property that consists of (1) the ownership of a separately defined area, called a "unit," plus (2) a tenancy in common interest in the areas that serve the owners of all units. The first element, the unit, is similar to an apartment or an office, but technically the unit is a "box of air." The second or common element consists of the land, the building, hallways, storage rooms, parking lots, and other areas that serve two or more unit owners. Each unit owner has a specified percentage interest in the common areas. The two elements combine to form an overall property interest, called an "estate," that can be sold, mortgaged, inherited, or otherwise treated like individually-owned real property.

State laws pertaining to condominiums are not uniform; nor are the legal instruments that create the condominium and define the relationships between the unit owners and the association or entity that serves as the operating organization on behalf of the unit owners. A brief review of the advantages of condominium ownership helps to stress the need for a formal organization that can manage the common areas.

Condominium Advantages

The appeal of residential condominium ownership reaches all ages and socio-economic levels. Many properties are located near golf courses, shopping centers, beaches, lakes, recreational areas, airports, marinas, and other attractive locations. The condo unit owner can deduct property taxes for federal income tax purposes. Some jurisdictions also allow a homestead exemption on state income taxes.

The condo owner accumulates equity in the property, both on an individual basis and for the entire complex. Building maintenance and repairs are handled by the condo maintenance personnel or by independent contractors hired to provide the services. There is no yard work, painting, pruning, or swimming pool maintenance for the unit owner. Property and liability insurance relating to common areas is a responsibility normally undertaken by the condominium association's board.

Many condominiums provide recreational facilities or activities for their owners. Also, security is provided for the safety of tenants and guests. The condominium concept allows the owners most of the privileges of ownership without many of the usual responsibilities.

Condominium Management

Owners of condominium units assume joint responsibility for maintaining the commonly owned areas. For this purpose, a condominium owners' association is established. The owners elect a board of directors from among themselves. The directors govern the building; raise and collect monies; arrange for special assessments; hire, supervise and fire personnel; and maintain security. They also handle problems and complaints. Committees may provide additional services, such as welcoming new members, arranging social functions, publishing a newsletter, making announcements, or presiding over business matters. The business matters include the purchase of insurance, building repairs and maintenance, election of board members, interior decorating of the common areas, and the purchase of adjacent property for added security or future construction projects.

A set of regulations must be created to outline the rules, restrictions, and privileges for the residents, as well as remedies for rule infractions. Other items concern planting vegetables, owning pets, minimum ages of residents, use of the swimming pool or other recreational facilities, and parking vehicles. For example, a condominium may prohibit residences under the age of sixteen, assign one auto parking space per unit, or forbid the renting or resale of the unit to others.

The condominium's board governs the financial activities of the association. Claims for the mismanagement of the condominium association's activities can be brought by any owner. For example, an upset unit owner who wants a special Christmas party at a local social club can bring suit if the function is held at another location, claiming the party's costs were too high. Another owner can claim the monthly assessment is unfair based on a real or imagined dispute with the association.

Condominium Loss Exposures

The condominium board of governors must operate and maintain the condominium's property in a businesslike and prudent manner. Problems handled by the board members of the condominium association include many items, some of which are beyond the control of the board. These include the sale of a unit to an undesirable person; the parking of an old, inoperative auto in the parking lot by a unit owner; improper building repair that cause additional building damages; and the increase in maintenance costs due to inflation.

Individuals can sue for any alleged wrongdoings, such as improperly maintaining the common areas, budgeting improperties, or establishing and maintaining adequate monetary reserves for the repair and maintenance of the building. Also, suits can arise from failure to repair heating and air conditioning systems, elevators, swimming pools, health club facilities, common area furniture and fixtures, glass breakage, and other damage to the property.

The board also faces legal actions for the failure to properly audit and account for association monies. A claim can be made alleging the mismanagement of the association, or alleged faulty decision making practices.

Condominium association directors and officers have many of the same problems as their counterparts of corporate boards. Both can be held liable for wrongful acts or omissions. Suits may occur when condominium members or outsiders believe the board made an improper decision. The condominium association board and its officers must follow many of the same general standards of conduct as corporate officers and directors. Any deviation from these standards can result in legal action.

For example, assume a condominium association board is sued for failure to replace a twenty-year-old roof. Water leaked into four units, causing $23,000 damages. Previously, the unit owners had filed complaints about small roof leaks, but no action had been taken. A year after their complaints, when a heavy rain caused water to seep into the units, the angry tenants brought legal action.

In *Plaza Del Prado Condominium Association, Inc. v. Richman*,[42] the validity of a board's action in a rule or architectural control decision was questioned. The board sought the removal of porch railings that the unit owner had constructed and which differed in color and material from the other units' railings. The court held that the board had the authority to control and remove architectural elements such as railings.

Condominium officers and directors are volunteers, but they still have legal duties to unit owners and to third parties. Moreover, a condo director's present or past occupation can be taken into consideration in a tort lawsuit. For instance, an accountant serving as a condominium association director or officer must use knowledge and experience when handling the association's budget. Or, an insurance agent must act in a professional manner when assisting the board with the purchase of the association's insurance policies. Similarly, an attorney should advise fellow board members of proper legal methods and the consequences of failing to follow them.

Attracting Condominium Board Members

Many condominium associations consist of retired persons, single people, widows, the handicapped, and others seeking a private living environment without the day-to-day responsibilities associated with individual building ownership.

Some of these people are not aware of the problems associated with the operation of condominium property. Others at least realize that condominium directors are vulnerable to tort lawsuits. For this reason, knowledgeable persons often refuse to serve on the association's board of directors or to hold officers' position unless they are properly insured. To attract such persons and be able to benefit from their skills, experiences, and judgments, the condominium association should purchase a condominium board of governors legal liability policy, also known as condominium directors and officers legal liability (D&O), or Condominium Association D&O.

Condominium D&O Insurance

Most condominium board of governors legal liability policies are similar to most corporate directors and officers legal liability contracts (though neither is completely standardized). Both provide coverage on a claims-made basis. Each is a two-part contract, providing indemnification and individual liability coverages. The contracts include their separate insuring agreements, definitions, extensions of coverage, exclusions, and specific terms and conditions.

The typical policies are likewise similar in that they mandate a specific retention per each loss, and they may require a 5 percent participation by the insured. A retroactive date is noted in the claims-made form. The coverage limits are the same for the standard D&O policy and the condominium D&O contract. There is a "per loss" limit, subject to an annual aggregate for all paid claims occurring during the policy's term.

The condominium association D&O policy begins with an insuring agreement. One such agreement states:

> The Company shall pay on behalf of the insured:
> A. any loss caused by a Wrongful Act of the Board of Governors, individually or collectively, while serving in their capacity as such, which the Insured may be required or obligated to pay as indemnities to them; and
> B. any loss caused by a Wrongful Act of the Board of Governors, individually or collectively, while serving in their capacity as such for which they personally are legally obligated to pay for any claims made or lawsuits brought against the Insured during the policy period arising from any Wrongful Act occurring during the policy period. Written notice of any such lawsuit must be given to the Company during the policy period.[43]

As previously noted, the first coverage provides protection for the condominium as an entity, while the second clause provides coverage for the individual officers and directors. The insuring agreement sections also are known as the company reimbursement and directors and officers liability clauses.

The remaining sections of most condominium D&O contracts are similar to most corporate D&O policies. One notable difference in some condominium forms can be found in the definition of a wrongful act, which includes, in addition to negligent acts or omissions, such intentional interference torts as:

1. false arrest, detention or imprisonment, or malicious prosecution;
2. publication or utterance of a libel or slander or of other defamatory or disparaging material, or a publication or utterance in violation of an individual's right of privacy; and
3. wrongful entry or eviction, or other invasion of the right of private occupancy.

These same torts may be found in other policies in their definitions of "personal injury" offenses. Since these are among the exposures commonly faced by condominium directors and association, some condominium D&O forms include personal injury coverages automatically. This may produce a double coverage situation for the policyholder. When this occurs, the "other insurance" clause of each policy must be reviewed to determine which contract(s) will provide coverage.

Exclusions The basic exclusions found in corporate D&O policies are also included within the typical condominium D&O form. In addition, a few exclusions in condominium D&O policies are worded to accommodate the unique nature of a condo association. Examples of losses commonly excluded are:

- financial gain based upon or attributable to the insured gaining any personal profit or advantage to which he or she was not legally entitled,
- judgments or settlements against the insured based on a determination that the acts of fraud or dishonesty were committed by the insured, and
- failure to maintain and effect insurance on behalf of the condominium association.

These exclusions apply to the acts or omissions of board members. The condominium association board consists of unit owners who are in very powerful positions. They could easily abuse this position of trust.

Noninsurance Techniques

The same noninsurance techniques available to handle corporate directors and officers liability exposures also may be available to handle condominium exposures. However, the condominium association may have a particularly difficult time dealing with exposures associated with the property rights of others.

Retention As noted previously, the association elects directors from its membership. The majority of members, including the majority of directors, seldom have insurance and risk management expertise. The aggressive use of the retention technique is rare.

Nonetheless, the association must retain part of each loss due to the mandatory retention feature of the condominium D&O policy. A $1,000 retention is usual, though some insurance companies reduce this amount to $250 or $500. The 5 percent participation feature is also a form of retention, if it is not removed from the policy.

Avoidance This is not a viable method for the association. The unit owners must create the board, as stated in its bylaws. A unit owner does have the option of refusing to serve as an officer or director.

Loss Control The association and the directors can reduce the likelihood of wrongful acts and omissions by obtaining and following competent legal advice. A management firm also could be employed to manage the property and answer to the board. But the latter option diminishes the extent to which the owners are allowed to govern themselves, and it does not relieve the directors of their legal duties.

Noninsurance Transfer Many of the association's activities can be transferred by contract to others. Outside security services can be hired; independent contractors can be retained to handle the building and grounds maintenance and repairs. A Certified Public Accounting firm can handle the association's financial records and give guidance concerning its management. Legal services can be obtained.

There is a growing business of condominium management companies hired to handle all of the decisions normally made by a board, thus leaving only one major decision for the board to make: selection of a management company.

It should be stressed that the use of these noninsurance transfer methods does not eliminate the need for D&O coverages. The board can be held liable for its omissions or commissions, even if an outside firm has been secured.

Another form of transfer takes place when condominium association members are assessed in order to pay a D&O claim. If a condominium association experiences a retained loss, it might have to levy an assessment against association members. Owners of residential condominium units might have protection for such assessments under the loss assessment coverage of a homeowners policy. The 1984 edition ISO homeowners policies, for example, provide $1,000 of coverage when an association of residential property owners makes an assessment against an insured arising from a claim against the association based on the association's liability due to the act of an association director, officer, or trustee.

EMPLOYEE BENEFITS LIABILITY

The liability exposures associated with employee benefit plans are faced by literally thousands upon thousands of individuals and businesses, including: almost all private employers of common-law employees; those employees of commercial entities who are directly involved in employee benefit management, such as benefit managers, personnel managers, labor relations specialists, in-house legal advisors, tax specialists, and financial managers; and various legal agents and subcontractors of employers, such as insurance agents, benefit consultants, outside legal advisors, public accountants, consulting actuaries, investment advisors, benefit plan administrators, trust officers, labor union leaders, insurers, and others who are involved in the design, installation, financing, and administration of specific employee benefit plans or overall employee benefit programs.

To facilitate a better appreciation of employee benefit exposures and the corresponding insurance coverage available, it is helpful to begin with overviews of (1) the general nature and scope of modern employee benefits and (2) the complexity of the legal environment in which such benefits are necessarily provided.

Nature and Scope of Modern Employee Benefits

Virtually all employers now provide at least some noncash benefits as a part of the total compensation of their full-time employees. These noncash employee benefits are no longer "fringes." In the aggregate, corporate employers now spend more each year for employee benefits than they pay in total annual dividends to stockholders. And the benefit contributions of individual employers range from one-fourth to over two-thirds of the amounts they pay in cash wages.

Through privately sponsored retirement and medical expense insurance plans are by far the most costly employee benefits, the overall benefit programs of most employers also include: group life insurance, group nonoccupational disability income insurance, and group dental expense insurance; paid time off for vacation, national holidays, funerals, jury duty, and military reserve duty; educational assistance plans; and moving and travel expense allowances. Many employers provide additional employee benefits, such as profit-sharing plans, stock ownership plans, personal financial counseling, child-care assistance, wellness programs, prepaid legal expense plans, employee discounts on the purchase of employer goods or services, club memberships, annual physical examinations, alcohol and drug abuse assistance, Christmas or performance bonuses, recreational facilities for employees and their families, employer-owned or leased autos, and collectively merchandised auto and homeowners insurance plans.

Nearly all employers also view the OASDHI program (popularly called "social security") and workers compensation insurance as employer-financed benefits for employees and their families, since employers pay half of the OASDHI payroll taxes and all of the workers compensation insurance premiums (or benefits, to the extent that compensation obligations are retained). The same can generally be said of the unemployment compensation system. While employers frequently are able to charge high enough prices for their goods or services to recoup all or a portion their contributions to compulsory public programs, most of the costs of such public programs are borne initially by employers.

Increasingly, privately sponsored employee benefit plans are provided on a "noncontributory" basis under which (1) no employee contributions are required and (2) the costs of the plans are paid entirely by employer contributions and the investment earnings thereon (the latter are especially important in the funding of private retirement plans). But many private benefit plans continue to be provided on a "contributory" basis, especially the benefits available to spouses and dependents of employees. Under a contributory financing arrangement, the employee may either reject the benefit or voluntarily elect to accept the benefit and authorize the necessary payroll deductions.

Even under traditional benefit programs, employees always have some choices to make. Under contributory plans, they must decide whether to participate in the plans or cover their spouses and dependent children. Under both contributory and noncontributory plans, employees must make decisions concerning such matters as naming of beneficiaries and the selection of settlement options under life insurance plans, the selection of annuity options under retirement plans, and whether to convert group insurance to individual insurance when the employees terminate employment or their spouses or dependent children cease to be eligible for the plans because of divorce, age, marriage, termination of dependency status, or the death of the eligible employees.

The range of employee choices has expanded significantly, in recent years, for the employees of employers that have adopted so-called "cafeteria," "flexible benefit," or "flexible compensation" programs. The specific features of such programs vary from one program to another, but they all have one noteworthy thing in common. They increase the number of choices that must be made by eligible employees.

Under traditional benefit programs—and even more so under modern flexible compensation programs—the available choices constitute a burden on employees. Some of the decisions to be made are inherently complex. Incorrect decisions can have enormous financial consequences for employees and/or their survivors. Understandably, many who are faced with such decisions will turn to others for advice. Therein lies one important source of liability exposures. Benefit managers, insurance agents, attorneys, trust officers, and others who give such advice have long been exposed to tort liability as a result (and the employers of advisors may be held vicariously liable, under the usual circumstances).

However, advising employees is not the only source of employee benefit liability. Federal and state statutes now prescribe a large number of duties, and they are owed by almost all persons who become involved (in a managerial, decision-making, or discretionary capacity) in performing such employee benefit functions as the investment of plan funds, plan administration, disclosure and communication of benefits to employees, plan design, and compliance with numerous other statutory obligations.

Legal Environment of Employee Benefits

The legal environment in which employee benefit programs are established and operated is complicated by the fact that various aspects of benefit programs are governed by dozens of different statutes and regulations. Not infrequently, there are overlaps and conflicts among the applicable federal and state statutes, federal and state regulations, and the functions and rulings of the corresponding regulatory agencies, as well as the courts.

For example, there are fifty state insurance statutes and the promulgated regulations of each state insurance department. There are securities laws, banking laws, licensing laws, and general consumer protection laws, all of which have some applicability to benefit plans. Pursuant to the Civil Rights Act of 1964, the Equal Employment Opportunities Commission (EEOC) was created and charged with the responsibility of promulgating anti-discrimination guidelines for employee benefit plans. These guidelines have the force of law, unless and until they are overturned by the courts or an act of Congress. Some Supreme Court decisions have upheld or clarified the EEOC rules. Others have not.

Perhaps the two most important federal statutes governing employee benefits are the Employee Retirement Income Security Act of 1974 (ERISA) and the Internal Revenue Code of 1954 (IRC), both of which Congress has altered frequently and significantly since their original enactment. Furthermore, the ERISA and the IRC overlap with one another, and the federal agencies with some jurisdiction over employee benefit plans now include the Internal Revenue Service, the U.S. Department of Labor, the EEOC, the SEC, and several others.

The primary purpose of this listing is to underscore how easy it is for benefit planners to breach a statutory duty. These statutory duties combine with the common law of torts to form the rather awesome dimensions of modern employee benefit liability exposures. Though no attempt will be made to identify all of the relevant statutory and common-law duties, a sense of the common-law duties can be conveyed by reference to one landmark court case. A sense of the statutory duties can be conveyed by providing an overview of ERISA.

Landmark Case In the landmark case of *Gediman v. Anheuser Busch*[44], an employer was held liable to an employee's estate for providing incorrect pension information. The employee had a vested interest in Anheuser Busch's pension plan with a present value of $78,356 in 1956.

For health reasons, Gediman took an early retirement. His written request was to take his pension benefits in cash or in the form of an annuity. An Anheuser Busch employee advised Gediman to defer his retirement benefits until 1958, two years later, so they would increase to $84,582. This option was selected.

In 1957, Gediman died. Anheuser Busch offered a $32,000 death benefit in place of the retirement funds. Gediman's executor refused the offer and sued for the $78,356 retirement benefits. The executor claimed Anheuser Busch was vicariously liable for the incorrect advice given to Gediman, which caused Gediman to lose his vested monies in the Anheuser Busch plan. In addition it was the Anheuser Busch that had the responsibility to Gediman to give him proper guidance concerning his specific situation. Gediman's health problems were known by Anheuser Busch, and the advice to defer the retirement benefits was to Anheuser Busch's advantage, not Gediman's. The courts ordered Anheuser Busch to pay Gediman's estate $78,356, plus interest from 1956.

This judgment was one of the first to put employers on notice of their benefit-related duties to employees. There have since been a number of similar court decisions. Incorrect information or negligent advice to employees can be the basis of a liability action against the employer.

Long before the Busch decision, it had already become quite clear that persons whom the courts regard as "professionals" can be held liable for torts they commit in rendering professional services to employer-sponsors, eligible employees, and other beneficiaries of employee benefit plans. Such torts can include intentional interference torts, as well as negligence, and they can even result in liability for punitive damages (under the circumstances prescribed in a particular jurisdiction). In negligence actions, most courts today are also willing to impose professional-level standards of reasonable care on practitioners in a number of occupations regularly involved in employee benefit plans. And all courts now recognize that corporate officers and directors may be held liable for tortious conduct that adversely affects benefit plans and/or individual plan participants or other plan beneficiaries.

Beyond employers, corporate officers and directors, and outsiders who render professional services per se, other individuals may now be held personally liable for the breach of legal duties prescribed in the various statutes that may be applied to employee benefit plans. Of these, the ERISA duties are probably the most important. They are certainly among the most complex.

ERISA The single most far-reaching body of employee benefit law consists of the Employee Retirement Income Security Act of 1974, the subsequent Congressional amendments to the Act, the countless regulatory rules promulgated to implement the Act (and each of its amendments), and a host of court decisions in which the statutory provisions and regulations have been interpreted and applied in specific factual situations. Generally speaking, this body of law applies to almost everyone involved in the employee benefit plans of *private* employers that are engaged in interstate commerce or otherwise subject to federal minimum wage law. Federal, state, and local governmental bodies are specifically exempted from the ERISA law. Religious organizations are exempt from some of the provisions of the law.

Despite the word "retirement" in the official title of the Act, many important provisions of ERISA apply to almost every imaginable kind of employee benefit plan. This is an especially valid generalization with respect to "qualified" benefit plans—that is, plans that meet all the conditions necessary to qualify for favorable treatment under federal tax laws.

The specific rules prescribed under ERISA law pertain to such matters as disclosure of plan information, minimum funding requirements, the pension rights of terminating employees, restrictions on the investment of plan funds, who must be covered under the plans, communication of plan features to employees, required plan documents, the deductibility of employer contributions, the taxation of plan benefits, and a host of other matters related to the design and financial security of plans and the legal rights of plan participants and beneficiaries.

Violators of ERISA law are subject to such penalties as fines and loss of favorable tax status. However, of particular importance to this discussion are the duties and liabilities imposed on plan fiduciaries.

The Act defines the term "fiduciary" broadly enough to include practically anyone whose role in employee benefits involves discretionary control or judgment in the design, administration, funding, or management of a benefit plan (or in the management of its assets). Each fiduciary has the specific duties that are prescribed with respect to the particular function the fiduciary is performing. All fiduciaries are under a general duty to act solely in the interest of plan participants, to abide by the relevant dictates of plan documents, and to avoid doing things that are expressly prohibited by the Act.

In the observance of specific or general duties under the Act, fiduciaries are held to a standard of care that has been called a "federal prudent person rule." Like others, a fiduciary is expected to exercise reasonable care under the circumstances; however, "reasonable" care for a fiduciary is that degree of care and skill which would have been exercised by a prudent person to discharge the stipulated fiduciary duties. This is a relatively high standard of care. The statutory duties are already quite numerous, and they are frequently amended by Congress and the federal regulators. Yet, as one who holds a position of trust, a fiduciary must at least make a good-faith effort to comply with all the applicable duties.

If a fiduciary breaches a statutory duty and the breach causes loss to a benefit plan, *the fiduciary is personally liable to the plan for the full amount of the loss.* Additionally, the guilty fiduciary might also be subject to a fine and an action for money damages brought by an aggrieved plan participant. A fiduciary may even be liable for the breach of a duty by a second fiduciary, if the first fiduciary knowingly participates in the breach, conceals it, or makes no attempt to correct it.

As mentioned several times before, any employer—including the employer of a fiduciary—may be held vicariously liable for (1) torts committed by its employees in the scope of their employment and (2) torts committed by its other agents in the scope of the agency relationship. This liability is joint and several. The plaintiff may recover damages from either or both of the defendants. Theoretically, the vicariously liable employer might be able to recover its share of the damage payments in a negligence action against the agent. As a practical matter, the better alternative is for the employer to purchase liability insurance that covers the employer, as an entity, and all employees who may be involved in employee benefit functions, especially those who may be deemed fiduciaries under ERISA.

Employee Benefits Liability Insurance

Employee benefits liability insurance may be added by endorsement to the commercial general liability policy. A separate employee benefits liability policy is also available to provide the coverages. Since the various forms and policies in use are not uniform, each form must be reviewed to determine the scope of its coverage.

All forms are designed to protect the insureds against claims alleging improper advice or other errors or omissions in the administration of the named insured's employee benefit plans. One endorsement reads:

> The company will pay on behalf of the insured all sums which the insured shall become legally obligated to pay as damages because of injury to the rights or interests of employees or their beneficiaries in employee benefits programs caused by any improper advice, error or omission in the administration of such programs by persons authorized by the insured, and the company shall have the right and duty to defend any suit against the insured seeking damages on account of such injury, even if any of the allegations of the suit are groundless, false or fraudulent, and may make such investigation and settlement of any claim or suit as it deems expedient, but the company shall not

be obligated to pay any claim or judgment or to defend any suit after the applicable limit of the company's liability has been exhausted by payment of judgments or settlements.[45]

Coverage is provided for employer-sponsored employee benefit plans, including the usual kinds of group insurance and retirement plans. Also covered automatically are public programs requiring employer financing, such as workers' compensation insurance and the unemployment compensation and OASDHI programs. Underwriters may request a description of all employer-sponsored plans when reviewing a submission.

Employee benefits liability insurance usually provides coverage for the liability exposures involved in the performance of four basic functions:

1. giving counsel to employees on existing or future benefits,
2. interpreting employee benefits,
3. processing employees' personal records, and
4. enrolling, terminating, adding, and removing employees for benefits.

In performing these basic function, a fiduciary and the fiduciary's employer may be held jointly and severally liable for the breach of *any* duty recognized by statute or by common law. Furthermore, the employer and fiduciaries hired by the employer are under a statutory duty to *"communicate"* the benefits and options to all eligible employees. They cannot avoid liability simply by refusing to become involved at all in the interpretation of plan provisions. They can (and should) recommend to employees that they consult their legal advisors to resolve questions for which the answers are not readily apparent.

One coverage limitation is not found in the exclusions per se; namely, that coverage applies to the employee only if that employee performing the function is authorized to do so by the employer. Any employee receiving advice, information, or service from an *un*authorized person could still bring action against the employer, but employee benefits liability insurance does not protect that unauthorized person. For example, suppose a personnel department file clerk tells an employee that the employee's spouse is covered under the employer's major medical expense plan. In reliance on this information, the employee does not purchase individual insurance on the spouse or authorize payroll deductions to cover the spouse on the contributory group plan of the employer. The employee is later informed that the spouse is not, in fact, covered under the group plan, *after* the spouse is hospitalized for the injuries suffered in a serious boating accident. If the employee then sues the employer and the file clerk, it might be argued that the file clerk was neither trained nor authorized to counsel employees. If so, the employee benefits liability coverage would not protect the file clerk.

Employee benefits liability insurance forms contain several exclusions. The exclusions in one insurer's policy are:

1. dishonest, fraudulent, criminal, or malicious acts;
2. bodily injury to, sickness, disease, or death, of any person; property damage including loss of use;
3. claims for failure to provide benefits because they are not properly funded by any insurer or the insurer fails to honor its policy;
4. claims based upon the insured's failure to comply with any law concerning workers compensation, unemployment insurance, social security, or disability benefits; and
5. claims based upon the failure of stock to perform as represented by an insured; advice given by an insured to an employee to participate or not to participate in stock subscription plans; and the investment or non-investment of funds.[46]

The insurance company will not respond, under this particular form, merely because there is a lack of financial gain from stock, compensation, investment, or savings plans. An example would be when executives invest plan funds in speculative stock and lose all the money. Fiduciary liability insurance, discussed later, is intended to address exposures of this type.

Coverage is excluded in other circumstances as well. For instance, the insurer will not pay in situations where employers are unable to provide benefits outlined in employee contracts. Even if the inability to honor promised benefits results from oversight, miscalculation, or a difference of opinion as to what compensation is due, there is no coverage. This situation would arise if the company guarantees the employees a 25 percent return on invested money and the actual interest is only 5 percent. The 20 percent difference is not covered by the employee benefits liability policy.

Employee benefits liability coverages do not fulfill ERISA *fidelity bond* requirements. The employer's fidelity bond may be endorsed to provide the coverage, or a separate bond may be purchased. The employee benefits liability form covers only losses arising out of advice, error, or similar act or omission that is to the detriment of the employee and/or the plan. Dishonesty losses can be covered by an appropriate fidelity bond.

Policy limits are provided on a per claim and aggregate basis. This gives the policyholder the same limits format as provided by the commercial general liability policy to which employee benefits liability coverages are often added by endorsement. After the aggregate limits are paid by the insurance company, no coverage remains for future claims. Umbrella or excess policies will sometimes provide coverage, subject to their self-insured retention.

FIDUCIARY RESPONSIBILITY INSURANCE

Fiduciary responsibility liability and pension and welfare legal liability insurance apply to specified wrongful acts arising out of employer-employee benefit programs. Several insurers have been the leading writers of this form.

This separate policy covers many of the same exposures covered by the employees benefits liability form. However, the fiduciary responsibility policy gives the insured broader coverage.

The fiduciary responsibility policy insures administrators, trustees, and other fiduciaries for their individual liability while handling the covered employee benefit programs. The coverage intent is focused on the Employee Retirement Income Security Act of 1974 (ERISA). To be covered, the plans must be named in the application or within the policy. All administrators and trustees must be named in the application.

An employer is asked to appoint one person to be responsible for claim notices to the insurance company. This person is generally named in the policy. There is a $1,000 deductible, which may be increased. Deductibles can be increased to $100,000. Employers may accept the higher retention levels to reduce the premium.

Coverage is provided for *breach of any fiduciary duty*. The typical policy's definition includes, as a breach of duty, any neglect, error, misstatement, misleading statement, omission, or act wrongfully attempted. Each policy has somewhat different insuring agreements, definitions, terms, conditions, and exclusions.

When an employer decides to purchase insurance for its fiduciaries, it must make sure the policy does not contain a recourse provision. The *recourse provision* allows the insurance company to subrogate against individual fiduciaries who breach their duties.

An example would be a company officer investing the pension fund in a speculative venture. Should the money be lost or the investment yield lower than originally believed, the employees can bring a claim for misuse of the fund monies. The fiduciary responsibility insurance policy applies to such a claim.

If the fiduciary responsibility policy contains a recourse provision, the insurance company can go after the corporate officer to collect the funds. The insurance company must prove that the individual breached the duty owed to the employee. This is allowed only when pension plan funds are used to purchase the coverage on behalf of the pension program. When the employer or sponsor of the benefit plan, buys the policy, the recourse provision is not desirable. With the recourse provision removed, the entire claim is the responsibility of the insurance company. There are no subrogation rights given to the insurance company, which stops any recovery from the officer or employer, individually. This is to the employer's and employee's advantage. In essence, the removal of the recourse provision makes the insurer fully responsible for any loss without the right to try to recover from either the insured or an insured's employee.

Noninsurance Techniques

Noninsurance alternatives available to companies are varied.

Retention   The company can retain 100 percent of any employee benefit loss. A separate fund might be created to provide the money to handle the legal costs and pay judgments or settlements.

An example is where a small company with few employees creates a pension program. Since there are only a few employees involved in the program, the employer may decide to retain the loss exposure. The purchase of employee benefits legal liability insurance may not be cost effective.

Avoidance   To avoid the improper administration of employee benefit programs, companies may refuse to offer benefits to new employees. Additionally, present benefit packages for the current workforce can be terminated.

Loss Control   One loss prevention measure is the implementation of strict company employee benefit practices. Strong internal controls, coupled with written procedures, will reduce the possibility of claims.

Included in these programs are written communications to employees on an annual basis with an explanation of benefits, termination procedures, coverage options, and account finances. Easy-to-read annual reports, distributed to every employee, will help clarify benefits, thus helping to prevent possible legal actions.

An internal system of checks and balances for monies handled must be implemented. Outside accounting services, used to audit the benefit program's financial condition, will reduce the chance of embezzlement or improper investments.

Transfer by Contract   Employers may elect to enter into contractual arrangements with outside firms for the provision of employee benefits. The independent contractor is then responsible for all program activities, including enrollments, terminations, written materials, eligibility requirements, claims handling procedures, investments, and accounting activities.

This places some exposures onto another firm, but does not transfer all of the employer's exposures. The employer still will have liabilities under ERISA. Many banks, financial institutions, and life insurance companies provide employee benefit administration services.

MUNICIPAL LIABILITY

Governmental bodies have a number of liability exposures that are quite similar to those of private-sector organizations. The major difference lies in the doctrine of sovereign immunity.

As explained in Chapter 1 in greater detail, governmental bodies were once able to invoke sovereign immunity as a complete defense against nearly all third-party liability claims. This is no longer true at the federal level. At the state and local level, sovereign immunity has been eroded by court decisions and legislative fiat, but is still alive and well in many jurisdictions. In some situations, absolute or qualified immunity is also available to public officials.

Cities, towns, counties, parishes, and public authorities have been involved in many legal actions, as have public officials. The courts have upheld the sovereign immunity defense in some cases and declined it in others. Many liability exposures remain.

Illustrative Exposures

Various legal actions have been brought against municipal entities and public officials. They include:

1. discrimination in employment, including hiring, promotion, and termination, and the design of employee benefits;
2. antitrust;
3. negligence in hiring, training, and supervision of police officers;
4. negligent building inspection or failure to inspect;
5. discrimination in the allocation of municipal services;
6. acts pursuant to a statute subsequently declared unconstitutional;
7. disputes arising from zoning, zoning changes, and the issuance or refusal to issue building permits;
8. actions taken in accordance with a state law that are in conflict with federal law; and,

9. enforcement of the so-called "headshop" acts.[47] "Headshop" acts concern retail outlets for drug paraphernalia. Many jurisdictions have outlawed such establishments.

School boards and board members also have many liability exposures. These include:

1. failure to promote students;
2. expulsion or suspension of students;
3. violation of students' civil rights;
4. the failure to desegregate or integrate schools, activities or athletic programs;
5. sex education classes;
6. sex education in non-related classes;
7. improper selection of textbooks and other reading assignments;
8. failure to grant tenure to teachers or to observe tenure rights;
9. budgeting or tax irregularities;
10. dress code enforcement;
11. claims of ineffective or lax administration practices;
12. lung disease from asbestos fibers;
13. child molestation by employees or third parties; and
14. negligence in removing asbestos or other carcinogens.

Items 13 and 14 are bodily injury and property damage liability situations that are covered by CGL policies. However, the board may have a claim against it that does not involve prior physical damage to tangible property, due to its policies regarding such matters as internal investigations or not removing asbestos in certain areas of school buildings. Although the CGL will cover the bodily injury and property damage liability claims, only the school board legal liability (SBLL) policy applies to these other kinds of claims, if only for defense purposes.

School divisions can obtain teacher's liability and corporal punishment liability coverages as an endorsement to their CGL. Protection from the above fourteen specific exposures, and others, can be provided by the school board legal liability policy.

Municipal entities may engage in commercial ventures such as selling water, operating sewage treatment facilities, or sponsoring athletic teams, athletic complexes, wharf and marina activities, garbage and trash pickup, landfill operations, nursing homes, hospitals, airports, gas and utility companies, transit authorities and housing authorities. Some municipalities also allow their police and sheriff deputies to work part-time for local department stores, schools, and colleges, while wearing their uniforms. In at least one state there is no coverage under the law enforcement legal liability policy unless the municipal entity passes a resolution allowing specific moonlighting services. If this is done the governmental entity must be paid for the services, not the individual policeman or sheriff deputy.

The exposures are complicated when board members are replaced through elections or retirement. Existing board members may be hostile to the new members. The political makeup can be changed, placing the old majority into a minority position. The philosophy of the new governing body can change previous actions. In some cases, the new board will vote to overturn the actions of the previous board, causing political problems and reactions of the community.

In addition, the municipality's executives may be charged with malfeasance, nonfeasance, and misfeasance arising out of their actions or omissions. Conflicts of interest charges also may be brought against any board member or executive.

Public Officials Liability Insurance

The public officials liability insurance (POL) policy provides coverage for various wrongful acts or omissions of municipal entities and their public officials. This contract is similar to the directors and officers liability coverages for corporations. The POL policy includes coverages for exposures usual for a municipal body, while the D&O contract provides coverage for a private organization.

The POL contract is a claims-made policy, with the same concept as the commercial general liability claims-made form. The POL is issued based on the representations in the application. Statements in the application may be included in the policy as warranties. If so, a breach of a material warranty can be used by the insurer as grounds for rescinding the policy or denying liability under the policy.

An example is when a municipality operates a hospital. If the application does not declare the hospital, the POL will not provide coverage for the medical facility's operations. The POL application is a very important document. It should be completed as accurately as possible.

Insuring Agreements The insuring agreements as reflected in one insurer's policy read:

(A) The Company will pay on behalf of the Insureds all Loss which the Insureds shall be legally obligated to pay for any civil claim or claims first made against them because of a Wrongful Act, provided that the claim is first made during the policy period and written notice of said claims is received by the Company during the policy period.

(B) The Company will reimburse the Public Entity for all Loss for which the Public Entity shall be required by law to indemnify the insureds for any civil claim or claims first made against them because of a Wrongful Act, provided the claim is first made during the policy period and written notice of said claims is received by the Company during the policy period.

(C) The Company will pay on behalf of the Public Entity all loss which the Public Entity shall be legally obligated to pay for any civil claim or claims first made against it because of a Wrongful Act, provided that the claim is first made during the policy period and written notice of said claim is received by the Company during the policy period.[48]

The insuring agreements and definitions of the POL policies are not standardized, and may vary substantially from one policy to the next. The definition of "the insured" can include the public entity named in the declarations and all persons who now are, have been or will be elected or appointed officials of the governing body. In addition, employees and volunteers may be included. Boards, commissions, and other units operating within the entity's total operating budget may be covered.

Wrongful Act A "wrongful act" can consist of any error, misstatement, act, omission, or breach of a duty. Misfeasance, nonfeasance, malfeasance, and the violation of federal or state civil rights laws can be included. The definition of a wrongful act may be very broad. Coverage usually applies only for acts committed within an insured individual's scope of authority.

Exclusions Every POL contract has its exclusions. Below is a list of exclusions paraphrased from various POL contracts. Not covered are claims based on:

1. an insured enjoying profit or advantage to which the insured was not legally entitled;
2. a fraudulent dishonest act;
3. bodily injury, sickness, mental anguish, disease or death of any person, or damage to or destruction of any tangible property, including the loss of use;
4. false arrest, slander, defamation of character, invasion of privacy, wrongful eviction, assault or battery, strikes, riots or civil commotions;
5. inverse condemnation and/or adverse possession;
6. a breach of a fiduciary duty;
7. a willful violation of any statute, ordinance, or regulation, when committed by or with the knowledge of consent of any insured person;
8. pollution exposures, including sudden and accidental occurrences; and
9. professional liability claims against attorneys, medical personnel, architects, engineers, or accountants.

Limits The POL contract has a per loss and annual aggregate limit. Many insurers offer a standard per loss limit of $1 million. The annual aggregate is also $1 million. Until recently, when a cost and availability crisis emerged, smaller municipalities were able to obtain limits of $5 million or more. The larger populated areas, such as New York, Dallas, San Francisco, and New Orleans, were generally able to obtain higher limits only if they were willing to accept a deductible or self-insured retention of at least $1 million. If and when previous market conditions return, each POL submission will once again be considered on its own merits, and underwriters will offer coverage limits and retention options tailored to each local government's desires.

An underlying POL limit of $1 million is often necessary for umbrella liability insurers to include the public officials legal liability exposures within their excess or umbrella contracts. When primary POL underwriters are restricted by reinsurance treaties, a $1 million limit may not be available. In turn, other underwriters may not be interested in providing excess or umbrella liability coverage, leaving the municipal entity with only their primary $1 million coverage policy to provide protection.

Deductibles A deductible applies to each claim. The deductibles usually begin at $1,000, with some municipal entities increasing this level to $5,000 or $10,000. The larger cities and counties (or parishes) may accept a self-insured retention (SIR) in place of the deductible. When this occurs, the SIR may be as high as $1 million per occurrence. The retention option is identical to that of the directors and officers legal liability policy, except it may not include an additional retention of 5 percent over the selected retention level. This means the municipal entity is only responsibily for the first $100,000 of any claim. The additional 5 percent for all expenses and judgments over $100,000 is borne by the insurance company. Since each POL placement is on an individual basis, the actual deductible/SIR is open to negotiation between the underwriter and governmental body.

School Board Legal Liability (SBLL)

School board legal liability contracts provide coverage similar to the directors and officers legal liability and public officials legal liability policies. The form covers wrongful acts of the school board members, such as those previously described.

The SBLL policy is designed to protect the entity and its employees from lawsuits claiming wrongful acts or omissions. In the past, school officials were rarely sued. This is certainly not true today.

The SBLL coverage should be purchased in addition to CGL

coverage. The CGL will cover claims for bodily injury, property damage, personal injury, teachers' liability, and corporal punishment liability. The SBLL will cover various other kinds of claims.

Insuring Agreement The insuring agreements of SBLL policies usually designate the "wrongful acts" that will be covered. The insuring agreement of one policy reads:

> This agreement protects against losses and expenses that occur when claims or suits are brought against you or any protected person for a wrongful act based on:
> * an error or omission,
> * negligence,
> * breach of duty, and
> * misstatement or misleading statement.
>
> All such acts or omissions will be referred to as wrongful acts in this agreement.
>
> This protection applies even if a claim is groundless, fraudulent or brought solely because a person holds or held a position on the board of education or is protected under the "Optional employee protection" section.[49]

The purpose of the SBLL policy is to protect the individual board member or employee from personal financial loss based on a covered kind of wrongful act.

Wrongful Act The phrase wrongful act is defined very broadly in most policies. The wording is similar to that of the POL contract definition. To paraphrase, a wrongful act means any actual or alleged error, misstatement, misleading statement, act, omission, neglect or breach of duty by the insureds, during the discharge of their duties, individually or collectively. This wording includes any claims arising out of the school board's action.

Exclusions Each SBLL policy has its own exclusions; no two forms are identical. The following kinds of claims are excluded by one policy:

1. bodily injury, property damage and personal injury liability;
2. pollution, both gradual and sudden and/or accidental;
3. failure to procure proper insurance;
4. back pay, if it is part of a judgment or settlement;
5. any activities assumed under a contractual relationship;
6. pension plans and other fiduciary responsibility exposures; and
7. failure to integrate or desegregate the student enrollment or extracurricular activities, or the altering of attendance boundaries or other standards for the purpose of avoiding the integration or desegregation of student enrollment.

Limits   Insurers generally offer $1 million limits on a per claim and aggregate basis. Higher limits may be available, depending on the exposures. Larger school divisions might not be able to obtain the higher limits. Some underwriters believe that the higher the student enrollment, the greater the chances of legal actions.

Deductibles   The SBLL has a self-insured retention (SIR) provision. It is identical to that of the public officials legal liability form. The SBLL policyholder is responsible for claims costs and judgment or settlement expenses up to the SIR. The minimum SIR is $1,000. Boards of larger school districts may have to accept an SIR of $10,000 or more. The SIR applies to every loss. There is no aggregate SIR applicable to this form.

Noninsurance

Public entities and school boards are unfortunate because few noninsurance measures are applicable.

Retention   Because POL and SBLL exposures are of a catastrophic nature, total retention is not wise, though mandatory deductibles or retentions require partial retention. When the entity cannot "afford" or obtain any insurance coverage, a special fund could be established for legal defense, court awards and settlements.

Municipalities have a source of funding not available to most other organizations. If necessary, a municipality could raise taxes to fund a retention program or to pay a judgment that is not insured. For example, by increasing the personal property taxes on cars, boats, and other taxable property, money is raised to satisfy judgments or defense costs. Of course, this technique is not politically popular and it can give rise to additional lawsuits. Thus a funded retention program may be a better alternative than ad-hoc tax increases.

Many public servants will not serve on a board if there is no POL or SBLL insurance coverage in force. Difficult decisions may have to be avoided if the board's action could result in legal repercussions. One example is a school board that will not take a stand on allowing girls to play on the school's tackle football team. The board can defer the decision to the state board of education and transfer many of the problems associated with this problem. A local government body can refuse to become involved in an argument among builders concerning who will receive permission to construct a hotel complex within their jurisdiction. In this case, the board could refrain from making any comments and allow all parties concerned to reach a settlement among themselves.

Loss Control The exposure can be controlled by formulating policies and procedures to decrease the chance of loss. Legal counsel should be consulted regularly. Even when the legal counsel's advice is proper, citizen influence may sway the board not to follow the advice of counsel. When this occurs, lawsuits are more likely.

Public entities must follow EEOC regulations, among other statutes and regulations. Knowing and observing the applicable law—and seeking official interpretations, when necessary—can help reduce the number of discrimination claims. Municipal and school entities face most of the same discrimination problems as the private sector. In addition, school divisions may have to provide busing to desegregate their student enrollment. Special classes may have to be provided for gifted, talented, exceptional, and handicapped children.

Formal written codes of ethics and disciplinary procedures can be created. These are to define ethical conduct for public officials and employees. Carefully articulated standards, effectively communicated and enforced, can help to avoid conflict-of-interest charges, favoritism toward vendors, or other such claims.

Insurance agents serving on boards are among those who may have a conflict of interest, especially if they provide some or all of the entity's insurance coverages. To prevent problems, the board is best advised to allow others to bid on the insurance portfolio periodically; the agent should refrain from voting on the bid awards.

LAW ENFORCEMENT LEGAL LIABILITY

Municipal entities employ law enforcement personnel such as police and sheriff departments, animal wardens, arson investigators, parole officers, undercover and vice squad personnel. These individuals can create dangerous loss exposures, as well as face them, in the performance of their jobs. Law enforcement is complicated by court decisions mandating that law enforcement personnel follow a pre-scribed set of rules regarding the apprehension and prosecution of suspected criminals (such as "reading their rights").

The power to use physical restraint and firearms increases the chances of loss. Many law enforcement personnel are subject to life-threatening situations. Defending themselves can cause legal actions if damages result. In addition, the public expects law enforcement officers to have knowledge of first aid, medical and psychological procedures, firefighting experience, and tremendous patience.

Law enforcement officers are under much stress, as evidenced by high divorce and suicide rates (for anyone who needs proof). They constantly see life's negative side, including the crimes and accidents involving autos, boats, airplanes, and firearms. Police officers are viewed by some with fear or suspicion. Naturally, this creates tension.

The Exposures

Law enforcement liability can arise from various actions and situations, at headquarters or in the field. Illustrations of some of these actions include:

1. excessive use of physical force, including assault and battery and cruel and unusual treatment of prisoners,[50]
2. illegal search and seizure, and
3. coercion to obtain confessions.

Prisoners initiate a wide variety of complaints, such as (1) lack of or improper medical care, (2) failure to maintain sanitary conditions, (3) placement of inmates in cells with other inmates with known violent propensities, (4) overlooking physical abuse or forced sexual activities of prisoners, (5) allowing a "kangaroo court" by inmates, (6) cruel and unusual punishment, and (7) overcrowding.[51]

The public body or corporation can be held vicariously liable for the acts of law enforcement personnel. One landmark case, *Monell v. Department of Social Services*,[52] applied the doctrine of vicarious liability. The court ruled that supervisors can be held liable for the acts or omissions of their employees. Further, in 1979, the courts followed this same line of reasoning in *McClelland v. Facteau*,[53] holding that public entity administrators can be held liable for the acts or omissions of their law enforcement personnel.

The major exposures for which vicarious liability may be imposed include:

1. negligent hiring practices,
2. failure to properly direct law enforcement employees,
3. failure to properly train law enforcement employees,
4. negligent supervision by superiors,
5. negligent assignment of duties,
6. negligent retention of an officer,
7. negligent entrustment of a weapon to an off duty employee, and
8. allowing law enforcement officers to wear their uniforms while providing security services for others ("moonlighting").

These exposures are usually not intended to be covered by the CGL, and underwriters will often exclude coverage for these exposures by means of manuscript endorsements. Such exclusions leave gaps in the policyholder's liability insurance program. To provide the necessary law enforcement liability insurance, the public body or private employer must purchase a law enforcement legal liability (LEL) policy.

Law Enforcement Legal Liability Insurance

The LEL contract is similar to the CGL; however, it includes special coverages designed for law enforcement activities. One insuring agreement states:

> The company will pay on behalf of the insured all sums which the insured shall become legally obligated to pay as damages because of wrongful acts which result in:
> A. Personal Injury
> B. Bodily Injury
> C. Property Damages
>
> caused by an occurrence and arising out of the performance of the insured's duties to provide law enforcement and/or other departmentally approved activities as declared in the application, or arising out of the ownership, maintenance or use of the premises designated in the declarations, and all operations necessary and incidental thereto.[54]

The intent is to provide third-party legal liability insurance for the approved activities of the law enforcement agency. This insuring agreement is broad enough to include coverage for false arrest, wrongful detention, malicious prosecution, libel, slander, defamation of character, wrongful entry or eviction, Federal Civil Rights (Section 1983) claims, the violation of the rights of others, improper first aid, and approved "moonlighting" activities.

"Moonlighting" activities include a uniformed officer being employed by a private firm for security. Moonlighting occurs mostly during holiday seasons, although some private firms hire local sheriff's deputies and police officers for weekends or special events. The problem is, the officer may be wearing the official uniform of the governmental body. This raises two issues that must be resolved. First, does the employer have proper personal injury liability coverages and, second, does the local government's law enforcement liability policy cover moonlighting activities?

In addition, does the private business want its CGL aggregate limits impaired due to the actions of a law enforcement officer? There is also the question of whether the officer is an employee or an independent contractor. Most municipalities have passed ordinances allowing their law enforcement personnel to accept part-time jobs. However, if the municipality has not approved these moonlighting activities, will the law enforcement legal liability policy respond on either the municipal entity's or individual officer's behalf? These and similar questions can be resolved only on the basis of facts and insurance coverages applicable in any given case. Occurrences within the premises are covered. This means claims arising out of jail fires, prisoner-to-prisoner assaults, and damages to the property of others in the care, custody, or control of the entity are insured by the LEL policy.

The definition of personal injury in the LEL policy is broader than that of the CGL. In the LEL, the term includes assault and battery, discrimination, false or improper service of process, humiliation or mental distress, violation of civil or property rights, and malicious prosecution.

A wrongful act is defined as any actual or alleged act, error, omission, neglect, or breach of duty by an insured. Coverage includes violation of civil rights, such as withholding favorable evidence, and prejudicial treatment against minority groups.

Police Dogs Injuries caused by police dogs are covered. The canines are trained to sniff for drugs, explosives, and other contraband. Further, they are used in crowd control and they are present in train stations, bus terminals and airports in New York, Philadelphia, and other large metropolitan areas in an effort to prevent robberies, assaults, and other criminal acts.

Products and Completed Operations Products and completed operations coverages are also included in the form. Coverage is designed for the penal institution's food preparations and the sale of old equipment. Usually, the LEL policy will not name products liability as an insured hazard. However, there is no products liability exclusion in the contract. If the preprinted form reflects a products liability exclusion, it usually may be removed at the policyholder's request.

Exclusions LEL contracts have as many as twelve exclusions. Typically excluded are claims covered by other policies, such as workers compensation, and ownership, maintenance, operation, use, leading or unloading of any automobile, watercraft or aircraft, either owned, leased, rented or used by the law enforcement agency.

Coverage is also precluded for acts arising out of the law enforcement entity's policies and procedures, which are covered under a public officials legal liability policy; criminal acts, real property care, custody or control coverages; nuclear exposures and hazards; and injunctive relief law suits. Coverage for some of these exposures is provided by the CGL and POL forms.

Uninsurable exposures include criminal acts and injunctive relief lawsuits that force the public authority or law enforcement agency to provide a special service or facility, or to refrain from an activity. An example is when the county jail inmates bring suit to get basketball courts installed at the penal facility. The LEL policy does not cover this type of suit.

The remaining exclusions are designed for law enforcement activities. The policy excludes bodily injuries, property damage, and personal injuries sustained by any full-time, part-time, auxiliary or voluntary law enforcement officer. Contractual liability is not covered, except under mutual law enforcement assistance agreements; the police activities of any other political body or individuals not employed by the named insured; and any actions where there is other coverage available.

Care, Custody, and Control Liability The LEL provides property damage liability insurance with respect to the personal property of others while in the care, custody, or control of the law enforcement agency. Included within this protection is prisoners' clothing, jewelry, money, and other items, plus evidence held for use in a trial. Some LEL contracts do not cover the loss of confiscated drugs or currency.

In addition, the storage of autos, as defined within the business auto coverage form, is usually excluded from the LEL contract. The law enforcement department must purchase a policy for this exposure. The garagekeepers coverage will cover for any direct damages to the vehicles in the possession of the police.

Other possessions, including boats, airplanes, real property such as buildings, land, mobile equipment, and other special categories of property may be excluded.

Premises Liability Coverage A public body's commercial general liability (CGL) policy may be endorsed to exclude law enforcement activities. Likewise, some insurers will not provide premises liability coverage for penal institutions in a CGL. The LEL policy provides excess premises liability insurance, over the CGL contract.

Obtaining LEL Coverage LEL insurers are concerned about the number of law enforcement employees, their training, and the physical plant exposures. The LEL application is detailed, and may become a part of the LEL contract, serving as a warranty. In addition to the number of law enforcement personnel, underwriters generally want a complete record of:

- dogs, or other animals used by the department;
- claims history for three years, including the amounts paid or reserved;
- written policies, including medical treatment procedures, sick call;
- inmate discipline, grievance procedures, access to legal services and materials;
- recreation provided to all inmates;

● intake screening, strip searches;
● correctional officers training procedures;
● name of public body to be included for vicarious liability;
● authorized moonlighting activities; and
● the details surrounding the policies and procedures manual.

With this information, the underwriter will decide if the applicant is acceptable for insurance purposes. The premium will be based on a number of factors, including the number of persons and dogs, limits requested, deductible selected, and the type of jurisdiction, such as a state, city, town, county or small authority. A $1,000 deductible is usual for smaller counties and towns, with the larger populated communities having to accept up to a $1 million retention.

Noninsurance Techniques

Public bodies and private organizations may implement any of the noninsurance techniques regarding the law enforcement liability exposures.

Retention Many larger municipal entities retain all law enforcement liability exposures because of either unavailability or high premiums. In addition, the deductible or self-insured retention features of the LEL contract make partial retentions mandatory. Deductibles and/or retentions range from $1,000 to $1 million. The deductibles will not be waived by the insurance companies.

Avoidance Complete avoidance is usually impossible for public bodies. However, specific exposures can be avoided by measures such as limiting the use of police motor vehicles and substituting foot patrols, or forgoing the use of canines.

Loss Control Detailed paperwork reflecting all actions can reduce lawsuits. A policy manual, with well-written procedures and rules, is necessary. Competent training and testing of officers on a regular basis is another part of a sound loss control program. In-service programs on legal issues are essential. The creation of a complaint review committee to give officers and jail inmates proper channels of redress can resolve many problems. The retention of legal counsel specializing in civil rights and law enforcement liability cases in helpful.

Also, in some areas, money has been appropriated for a wellness benefit. Law enforcement officers may join a health facility. It is believed that exercise helps to reduce the stress created by career duties.

Noninsurance Transfer This is accomplished when a small public body, such as a town, borough, township or authority, obtains its law enforcement services from a larger community. For example, a town can obtain sheriff's protection from the county or state, or a public authority will be protected by a city's police department under a contractual agreement.

Within the private sector, businesses can contract for local police services, including night watchmen protection, security services during holiday seasons, and assistance when transporting large cash deposits to a bank. The provider of the services is generally liable for the activities of the law enforcement officers.

RAILROAD PROTECTIVE LIABILITY

Railroads are located in every state. Tracks cross roads, bridges, highways, and the property of others. They are adjacent to docks, wharves, airports, and the train terminals. Tracks can be found within stockyards, chemical plants, manufacturing facilities, petroleum companies, and other hazardous businesses. Railroad representatives must be certain the tracks are safe for their equipment and will not cause damage to the property of others.

In addition to the value of rolling stock, the transported cargo can consist of highly valued items. The aggregate loss exposure for each train and its cargo can easily be in the millions. Railroad companies need to repair and maintain tracks and equipment, to prevent loss. Even when an accident is not the responsibility of the railroad company, the railroad may have to absorb a large portion of the loss. The railroad's reputation and goodwill can be reduced with each accident. Safety and loss prevention are major concerns of railroads.

Since tracks are situated throughout the country, it is necessary to allow landowners and public authorities to complete construction work over, under, on or adjacent to railroad property. This work includes road construction, storm, and sewer pipe installation, television, telephone and electric cable burial, bridge construction, tree removal and building erection activities. These endeavors are usually completed by independent contractors, hired by the landowner or public body.

Railroads are concerned about such work and its method of completion. The finished product must have the railroad's approval before trains will be allowed to use that portion of the tracks. Faulty or improper work may cause an accident. To provide for the safety of passengers, the public, shippers, and rolling stock, the railroads demand strict adherence to proper construction techniques. Railroad inspectors visit each job site to confirm the work is completed properly and the job site is safe for the contractor's employees and the public.

Contractors are required to hold the railroads harmless for claims arising out of work on the railroads right-of-way, whether it be on, over, below, or adjacent to the tracks. Even if the contractor is not at fault liability loss payment thus becomes the contractor's responsibility.

The railroad company will demand insurance protection from the contractor for activities arising out of the work performed. The coverage is *for the benefit of the railroad only.* The insurance must be in force before any operations can begin. The premium is paid by the contractor or a public body.

Insurance to meet the railroad's demand for liability protection arising out of the contractor's work is known as railroad protective liability insurance (RRPL).

Railroad Protective Liability Insurance Policy

The railroad protective liability policy was developed to provide the coverage demanded by railroad companies (and not provided in the CGL). This is an unusual contract, providing both first party and third party liability coverages.

The policy names only the railroad company as the "named insured." Coverage applies to the railroad company only. There are two insuring agreements: (1) bodily injury liability and property damage liability and (2) physical damage to property. The ISO insuring agreements can be paraphrased as follows:

Coverage A:
We will pay those sums that the insured becomes legally obligated to pay because of bodily injury (including damages claimed for care, loss of services, or death) or property damage (including loss of use of tangible property that is not physically injured). This insurance applies only to bodily injury or property damage that occurs during the policy period and arises out of acts or omissions at the job location that relate to the work described in the Declarations.

Coverage B:
We will pay for physical damage to property to which this insurance applies. The physical damage to property must occur during the policy period and must arise out of acts or omissions at the job location that relate to the work described in the declarations. The property sustaining the physical damage must be owned by you, leased to you, or entrusted to you under a trust agreement.

A contractor's commercial general liability underwriter will normally provide the railroad protective liability insurance. The premium is based on each $100 of the total contract or equipment rental costs. An advance premium is required and the policy is subject to an audit and premium adjustment. The form is an occurrence policy.

Underwriters desire to know the type of work, its cost, the number of passenger and freight trains traveling over the tracks, and the frequency of the tracks' use. Details regarding the contractor's work experience may be requested. The contractor, landowner, and public authority are named on the declarations page. The job site location and a description of the work is included. The policy gives the entity paying the premium the right to receive return premiums. This stops the railroad, as the named insured, from claiming the premium credit.

Limits begin at $1 million, and can be increased for additional premium at the railroad's request. A straight excess liability policy can to be purchased to meet the railroad's liability requirement for excess limits.

Exclusions The liability portion of the RRPL has seven exclusions. There are two major coverage restrictions. First, there is no coverage if the acts or omissions of the insured are the proximate cause of the injury or damage. This removes coverage for most acts of the railroad that could result in a liability claim.

The second major exclusion applies when notification has been given to the railroad that the work was completed or accepted by the landowner or public body. This exclusion has the intent of covering operations in progress but canceling the policy once the work is completed and accepted. Coverage is be provided for occurrences arising out of the removal of tools, uninstalled equipment, and abandoned or unused materials.

The remaining exclusions include an intentional injury exclusion, a contractual liability exclusion, a pollution exclusion, and an exclusion for damage to property owned, leased, or entrusted to the insured. The last exclusion eliminates any duplications between Coverage A and Coverage B.

Exclusions under Coverage B preclude coverage for physical damage occurring after the work is completed or put to its intended use, losses caused solely by acts of an insured (with some exceptions), a nuclear exclusion, and a pollution exclusion.

Noninsurance Techniques

Railroad protective liability is actually a tool for implementing the railroad company's transfer of risk to the contractor. Contractors must accept the railroad's hold harmless agreement for operations on, above, below, or in the vicinity of the railroad's property. This transfer is accomplished by the railroad via the contractual agreement. The contractor then transfers the risk to the insurance company by purchasing the railroad protective liability insurance policy.

Retention   The contractor may totally retain the exposures. This is possible only for large, solvent contractors and is seldom, if ever, advisable. The railroads may not allow the contractor to go uninsured. If they do, a bond or letter of credit would be given to the railroad to satisfy the construction contract's requirements. The railroad protective liability policy's premium is usually affordable, making this option unattractive.

Avoidance   A contractor can refuse to perform operations adjacent to railroad property. This will eliminate the need for the railroad protective liability insurance.

Loss Control   Loss control measures can be implemented at the work site to reduce the chance of loss. Safety professionals and mechanical engineers can provide assistance. Security personnel can be retained to provide watchman services. The railroad will send inspectors to the workplace to monitor the work's progress and make safety suggestions. The purchase of railroad protective liability insurance may be mandatory in these instances.

Noninsurance Transfer   A public authority will hire a contractor to do the work. The agreement holds the public body harmless for claims arising out of the work. The contractor may hire a subcontractor to perform the services. When this occurs, the contractor will require the subcontractor to provide the railroad protective liability policy. The subcontractor will hold the contractor and the railroad harmless. The railroad protective liability policy protects the railroad. The contractual transfer is between the public authority and the general contractor or subcontractor.

Chapter Notes

1. E. R. Anderson and A. C. Moskowitz, "How Much Does the CGL Pollution Exclusion Really Exclude?" *Risk Management*, Vol. 31, no. 4 (1984), pp. 28-36.
2. Anderson and Moskowitz.
3. Anderson and Moskowitz.
4. E. C. Beck, "Hazardous Waste Disposal: Most Firms Urgently Need to Review Loss-Control Programs," Business Insurance (June 20, 1983), pp. 17-18.
5. Lansco v. Department of Environmental Protection, 350 A. 2d. 520, New Jersey, 1975.
6. Farm Family Mutual Insurance Company v. Bagley, 409 NY 2d. 2394, 1978.
7. United Pacific Insurance Company v. Van's Westlake Union, Inc., 664 P. 2d 126 (Washington Ct., App. 1983).
8. Act of March 3, 1899, C. 425, Sec. 16, 32 Stat. 1151.
9. Ralph C. Nash, Jr., and Susan Linden, "Federal Procurement and the Environment," *Federal Environmental Law*, Environmental Law Institute (St. Paul, MN: West Publishing Co., 1974), p. 488.
10. Public Law 93-119, 87 Stat. 424.
11. Public Law 87-88, 75 Stat. 204.
12. 393 F. Supp. 735 (D.C. Ohio 1975).
13. 311 F. Supp. 1181 (D.C. Ariz. 1975).
14. "Criminal Responsibility of Corporate Officials for Pollution of the Environment," *Albany Law Review*, Vol. 37, 1972-1973, p. 84.
15. 42 USC, Sec. 1857 et seq.
16. Thomas Jorling, "The Federal Law of Air Pollution Control," *Federal Environmental Law*, Environmental Law Institute (St. Paul, MN: West Publishing Co., 1974), p. 1108.
17. Jorling, p. 1072.
18. Public Law 91-190, 83 Stat., 852, 42 United States Code, Sec. 4321 et seq.
19. Public Law 91-224, 84 Stat. 91.
20. Charles F. Lettow, "The Control of Marine Pollution," *Federal Environmental Law*, Environmental Law Institute (St. Paul, MN: West Publishing Co., 1974), pp. 606-607.
21. Lettow, p. 612.
22. H. E. Beal, "The Coming Trend in Lawsuits: Courts Are Turning to Strict Liability in Hazardous Waste Trials," *Business Insurance* (November 28, 1983), pp. 41-42.
23. L. M. Miller and M. J. Murphy, *CPCU Seminar: Environmental Impairment Liability Insurance.* Seminar conducted in Washington, DC by Risk Science International, October 3, 1984.
24. Miller and Murphy.
25. Miller and Murphy.

26. This endorsement was filed in May 1986 for use on all policies written on or after June 1, 1986, according to ISO Circular GL-86-140, May 15, 1986, copyright ISO 1986.
27. *Workbook—Policy Forms and Endorsements; Policywriting Rules.* Copyright Insurance Services Office, Inc., 1985, pp. 33-35.
28. *Workbook.*
29. *Explanatory Memorandum.* Attached to ISO Circular GL-86-140, Copyright Insurance Services Office, Inc., 1986.
30. ISO Circular CF-86-36 and attachments, April 15, 1986.
31. ISO Circular CF-86-36.
32. Federal Register, 49 CFR, Part 172.10.
33. T. F. Sheehan, *The Liabilities of Directors and Officers: With Practical Solutions for Their Discharge*, 3rd ed. (Bartlett, IL: Directors Press, 1978), p. 8.
34. R. A. Hersbarger and M. L. Cross, "Nature and Major Provisions of Directors and Officers Liability Insurance," *CPCU Journal* 32(1), (1979), pp. 37-43.
35. Goodwin v. Milwaukee Lithographing Co., 171 Wis. 351, 177 N.W. 618 (1920).
36. Jacobson v. Yaschik, 249 S.C. 577, 155 S.E. 2d 601 (1967).
37. Lloyd's of London Directors and Officers Liability Policy designated Lydando No. 1.
38. Seaboard Surety Company. (No year given). *Directors and Officers Liability and Company Reimbursement Policy Form 515D* New York, NY.
39. Seaboard Surety Company.
40. Seaboard Surety Company.
41. Seaboard Surety Company.
42. Plaza Del Prado Condominium Association, Inc. v. Richman, 345 So. 2d 851 Fla. 1977.
43. Great American Insurance Companies. (1980, Jan.) *Condominium Board of Governors Legal Liability Coverage Endorsement Form F 14-69-2-B* Cincinnati, Ohio.
44. Gediman v. Anheuser Busch, 193 Fed Supp. 72, 1961.
45. Liberty Mutual Insurance Company (1984) Notice of transportation insurance requirements and schedule of limits. Boston, MA.
46. St. Paul Fire and Marine Insurance Company. *St. Paul Fire and Marine Insurance Company Employee Benefit Liability Form 17372* St. Paul, MN.
47. H. J. Moskowitz and V. R. Fontana. Defending Suits Against Public Officials, *Insurance Counsel Journal* (October, 1982), pp. 490-507.
48. National Union Fire Insurance Company of Pittsburgh, Pennsylvania.
49. St. Paul Fire and Marine Insurance Company. (May, 1983) *St. Paul Fire and Marine Insurance Company Employee Benefit Liability Form 42038 TLD* St. Paul, MN.
50. R. Vogt, Sources of Police Professional Liability Suits, Preventive Measures

428—Commercial Liability Risk Management and Insurance

and Defense Techniques, *Governmental Risk Management Reports*, 4, (12), (March 1983), pp. 1-4.

51. R. Vogt.
52. Monell v. Department of Social Services, 436 US 6 58, (1978).
53. McClelland v. Facteau, 610 F 2nd. 693, New Mexico, 1979.
54. National Casualty Company. (July, 1982). *Comprehensive Law Enforcement Liability Policy Form PL-0001000 [PL D 1].* Scottsdale, Arizona.

Index

A

Abnormally dangerous
instrumentalities, *55*
Absolute privilege, *32*
Accepted work doctrine, *80*
abandonment of, *82*
departures from, *81*
Accident, *210, 305*
Accident Facts, 149, 156
*Accident Prevention Manual for
Industrial Operations:
Administration and
Programs, 173*
Accident theory: causes and effects,
159
Act, wrongful, *386*
Act or omission, *41*
Action, breach-of-contract, *24*
Action at law, *24*
Actions, legal, *24*
Activities, *253*
Actual malice, *30*
Adhesion, contracts of, *13*
doctrine of, *202*
Administrative act, *52*
Adult business invitees, *69*
Adult licensees, *67*
Adult trespassers, *66*
Advanced retroactive date, *312*
Advertising injury, *295*
Advertising and sales literature,
182

Agency, *18*
Agency relationships, *18*
Agent, *18*
Aggregate limits, *226*
Agreement, waiver, *12*
Agreements, indemnification, *384*
Agreements required by
municipalities, *260*
Aircraft, autos, and watercraft
exclusion, *269*
Aircraft and motor vehicle
exclusion, FL, *351*
Alienated premises exclusion, *284*
Alteration or modification of
product by plaintiff or third
party, *104*
American National Standards
Institute data, *155*
Analysis of legal, economic, and
social environment, *142*
Animals, wild and domestic, *56*
Annual Survey of Occupational
Injuries and Diseases, *150*
ANSI data, *155*
Arrest, false, *35*
Assault, *33*
Assault and battery, defenses to,
34
Assembled insurance policy, *203*
Association, *17*
Assumption of risk, *47, 101*
Atmospheric conditions, *173*
Attractive nuisance doctrine, *72*

M

N